Merit, Aesthetic and Ethical

MARCIA MUELDER EATON

UNIVERSITY PRESS

2001

OXFORD
UNIVERSITY PRESS

Oxford   New York
Athens   Auckland   Bangkok   Bogotá   Buenos Aires   Calcutta
Cape Town   Chennai   Dar es Salaam   Delhi   Florence   Hong Kong   Istanbul
Karachi   Kuala Lumpur   Madrid   Melbourne   Mexico City   Mumbai
Nairobi   Paris   São Paulo   Shanghai   Singapore   Taipei   Tokyo   Toronto   Warsaw

and associated companies in
Berlin   Ibadan

Published by Oxford University Press, Inc.
198 Madison Avenue, New York, New York 10016

Oxford is a registered trademark of Oxford University Press.

Library of Congress Cataloging-in-Publication Data
Eaton, Marcia Muelder, 1938–
    Merit, aesthetic and ethical / by Marcia Muelder Eaton.
        p.   cm.
    Includes index.
    ISBN 0-19-514024-9
    1. Aesthetics.   2. Ethics.   3. Art—Moral and ethical aspects.   I. Title.

BN39.E265 2000
1119.85—dc21   00-028555

9 8 7 6 5 4 3 2 1

Printed in the United States of America
on acid-free paper

Preface

Many people believe that looking good and being good are distinct and that, more generally, aesthetic and ethical merit are fundamentally separate kinds or classes of value. In this book, I discuss a kind of merit in which being good and appearing (looking, sounding, tasting) good are integrated.

In the introduction to the letters that constitute his *Aesthetic Education of Man*, Friedrich Schiller thanked his Danish patron, Prince Friedrich Christian, Duke of Schleswig-Holstein-Augustenburg for allowing him to have "the appearance of merit where I am in fact only yielding to inclination." It is surprising that he bowed to popular usage, for Schiller, like me, envisioned an education that would harmoniously unite aesthetics, ethics, science, and politics. What I seek is a merit whose appearance can reside at the surface only because it has deep roots.

I believe strongly that the nature and value of art cannot be understood in isolation from a wide range of human endeavors and institutions. I have argued for this from several directions in other books and papers. This earlier work constitutes pieces of a puzzle that I try to put together here into a more coherent pattern. This has required some new links and the reshaping of already existing parts. Thus, while some material has been published before, it has undergone significant revision. I do not claim to have the full picture yet, but I hope that I do now have a better sense of contours that make salient the ways in which aesthetics and ethics come together.

My basic argument is this: a correct view of the nature of aesthetic experience implies a particular theory of the nature of aesthetic properties. This characterization suggests that aesthetic concerns can be as serious and important as ethical concerns. Furthermore, it is at least consistent with and may even require the integration of aesthetics and ethics. Once one recognizes this integration, there are important consequences for other areas, especially educational, environmental, and community policy. Each of these points is taken up in a separate part of the book, but since mine is an integral, contextual theory, there will be lots of looking back and forth.

Unlike Schiller, I have not had a patron per se. But I have been blessed with resources and associates who supported me as I have yielded to my inclination: a desire to try to make sense not just of what others have had to say on this topic but of what I myself have said in a variety of contexts over the past two decades. The University of Minnesota granted me a sabbatical leave for 1998–99 and provided me with research travel funds that enabled me to have sustained reflective time in the Netherlands. Rob van Gerwen from the University of Utrecht was an especially helpful listener and commentator. Ronald Moore of the University of Washington has provided ongoing encouragement, as well as lengthy reading lists. In the summer of 1999, Tanya Rodriquez served very ably as my research assistant. She read the entire manuscript, provided insightful examples, identified some mistakes, and helped me to clarify many points. James Harold, a graduate student at the University of Minnesota, has also been a resourceful sounding board. I have been blessed as well with many years of support from my husband, Joe, who at once challenges me to fly high and reminds me when it is time to return to earth.

Permissions to reprint materials have been obtained from the following:

Henry Holt and Company, LLC, Robert Frost, "Spring Pools"

Harvard University Press, Emily Dickinson, "If I Could Tell How Glad I Was"

Island Press, Marcia Muelder Eaton, "The Beauty That Requires Health"

Journal of Aesthetics and Art Criticism, "The Intrinsic-Non-Supervenient Nature of Aesthetic Properties"

Journal of Aesthetics and Art Criticism, "Aesthetics: The Mother of Ethics?"

Journal of Aesthetics and Art Criticism, "Fact and Fiction in the Appreciation of Nature"

Philip Alperson, editor, *Diversity and Community: A Critical Reader,* New York and Oxford: Blackwell Publishers, 2000, "The Role of Art in Sustaining Communities"

Kluwer Academic Publishers, *Philosophical Studies,* Volume 37, 1992, "Integrating Moral and Aesthetic Value"

Johns Hopkins University Press, *Philosophy and Literature,* Fall, 1985, "Anthony Powell and the Aesthetic Life"

The American Philosophical Quarterly, "Laughing at the Death of Little Nell"

Oxford University Press, *The British Journal of Aesthetics,* "The Social Construction of Aesthetic Response," "Where's the Spear? The Nature of Aesthetic Relevance," "Intention, Supervenience, and Aesthetic Realism."

Contents

PART I

Aesthetic Experience and Aesthetic Properties

The *real* understanding of art and hence *real* aesthetic experience, according to formalist theorists, depend exclusively on properties that human beings can perceive directly, at least those human beings of suitable sensitivity. In genuine or pure aesthetic experience, they insist, everything depends on what is presented, nothing on how or why. The chapters of this book constitute an attempt to refute this position. Instead, I insist that aesthetic experiences can be (and, I believe, usually are) tied to the context in which they occur—to aspects of the history of an object or event, to its cultural setting, to the interests, beliefs, and attitudes of the persons who have them. Mine is an inclusive rather than exclusive view of the aesthetic.

For a variety of reasons, formalists ignore the roles that artworks play in the life of a community and, conversely, ignore the ways in which communities determine the very nature of what counts as artistic or aesthetic experiences that exist within them. I begin this section with a discussion of ways in which the aesthetic is socially constructed. Once one recognizes this, one sees that what is aesthetically relevant (the topic of chapter 2) goes well beyond immediately manifest formal properties residing in what are taken to be aesthetic objects and events.

In chapter 3, I propose characterizations of aesthetic properties and experiences that build on a broad contextual view of the role of art in human experience. In this chapter, I deal centrally with the question of whether aesthetic properties are supervenient; this technical issue will be of interest primarily to philosophers of art (and to only some of them). But the definitions I provide do constitute a foundation for a view of aesthetic justification presented in chapter 4: aesthetic properties are intrinsically located in objects and events viewed by persons who share a culture and hence share ways of perceiving and reflecting that permit rational debate about and justification for aesthetic judgments.

What and Why Is Art?

ARTISTIC activity can be understood and appreciated only when we recognize and acknowledge what and why people have engaged in it for as long as we have reason to believe that there were any people doing anything at all. From making things to looking at things, individuals and groups may not always have used terms translatable without loss to 'art' or 'aesthetic', but when from our own temporal and cultural viewpoint, we describe what people did and do, these terms come forth as readily as 'harvest' or 'parent', 'prayer' or 'battle'. I am not interested here in arguing that art should be such and such or that when people engage in aesthetic activity they should do it in special ways. Rather, I insist, we must consider what people in fact do and have done when they dress up and dance, climb a hill for a better view, listen to a story, make sounds that blend with sounds others are making, or point to an image in clouds or acrylic. No matter how often or long people are told that aesthetic activity is isolated from science or morality or religion or politics, we keep using aesthetic objects and events for all of these ends. People always and everywhere have and, unless human nature undergoes a radical transformation, will continue to make love, commemorate those we admire, instruct, insult, amuse, and try to make sense of the world by using aesthetic objects and events. Despite some theorists' insistence that the aesthetic is separate from the rest of our lives and that its importance derives from this separation, human experience contradicts them.

My theory of the aesthetic derives from a very inclusive view of art. I provided a detailed exposition of my theory of art in *Art and Nonart: Reflections on an Orange Crate and a Moose Call*, and very recently updated it in "A Sustainable Definition of 'Art'."[1] Here I need only provide a brief sketch, for I am less concerned in this volume with defining 'art' than I am with discussing aesthetic experience, what such experience demands of a theory of aesthetic properties, and how aesthetic values are related to other human values, particularly ethical values.

A work of art is an artifact that is treated in aesthetically relevant ways, at least when it is being considered as a work of art, not as a doorstop or an alarm. Things are art when they are treated in such a way that someone who is fluent in a culture directs attention to an artifact's intrinsic properties that are considered worthy of attention (perception and/or reflection) within that culture. Furthermore, the person who attends to the artifact and has what he or she would describe as an aesthetic experience[2] realizes that the experience is caused, at least in large part, because he or she is attending to intrinsic properties of the artifact considered worthy of attention in his or her community. The key concepts here are *artifact, treated, aesthetically relevant, fluent in a culture, attention, intrinsic properties, worthy of attention, community.* Because they are key, they will appear again and again throughout this volume; none can be easily or very succinctly defined. However, by way of introduction I shall say a bit about each one here.

a. *Artifacts.* Works of art are, I believe, artifacts, because they are *works* of art. I understand 'work' in this phrase loosely—so loosely, of course, that *work* can even be understood as *play.* What matters is that people do something with something—act intentionally and produce movements or images or sounds via some medium. What is created can be long-lived or short-lived, simple or complex, intense or superficial, and so forth. My inclusive view of art allows artifactuality to extend from sticks stuck in the sand to huge architectural complexes, nursery rhymes to epics, "Ring 'round the Rosy" to *Swan Lake,* and so on. An artifact, as I understand it, can be either an object or an event.

b. *Treatment.* For artifacts to achieve the status of art, however, they must be treated in special ways within communities. My use of this concept shows how deeply my theory has been influenced by institutional theories of art. In and of themselves, objects and events, however they are created, cannot be art. Others must respond appropriately. (I shall explain later what I believe this entails.) Different communities devise and develop different ways of treating artifacts so that the kind of attention required (aesthetic attention—about which much will be said later) is forthcoming. Again I understand this term very broadly. Treatment can include building special venues for the display of artifacts or simply calling to a friend to come have a look.

c. *Aesthetically relevant.* This is the topic of chapter 4. I use the term to refer to what we think matters when we are engaged in aesthetic activity. Is it aesthetically relevant to consider what an object is made of or who is performing an event or what it is about? No secrets will be given away prematurely by announcing here that I also construe this notion very inclusively.

d. *Cultural fluency.* In every culture and subculture, traditions develop that lead to a sharing of attitudes about worthwhile activities. Some, of course, are aesthetic. Although human history exhibits commonalities with regard to what is pleasing or otherwise valuable about objects and events, it also exhibits unique practices. To fully understand a community's aesthetic practices and values, it is essential that one understand a great deal generally about that community. Typically this means that one must "speak the language"—but linguistic fluency is not enough. One must also know a great deal about a culture's religion, politics, family structures, physical environment, and other matters.

e. *Attention.* A central thesis of my view of the aesthetic is that one cannot have aesthetic experiences unless one is paying attention to an object or event. This utterly obvious point accounts, I believe, for whatever appeal formalist theories of art may have. I interpret 'attention' to include both perception and reflection—not simply seeing or hearing (though sometimes aesthetic activity may stop with this) but also thinking about what one perceives. As I shall explain, it is also essential that one be aware of the fact that one is paying attention if one is to describe oneself as having an aesthetic experience.

f. *Intrinsic properties.* The object of one's attention in aesthetic experiences is aesthetic properties. I shall define these in detail later. Basically these are properties to which one must directly attend, properties "in" an object, properties that cannot be experienced without direct attention. Not all of the intrinsic properties of an object or event are aesthetic. Which ones are depends on the traditions of a community.

g. *Worthy of attention.* Since the aesthetic is one kind of value, aesthetic attention must be repaid. Thus whatever property kinds are traditionally identified by a culture as aesthetic will be generally regarded as repaying attention, usually sustained perception and reflection. I say "property kinds" because, after all, negative aesthetic experiences are possible. Colors may generally be considered worthy of attention, but that does not preclude some instances of colors that are dull or unpleasant.

h. *Community.* I use the terms 'culture', 'subculture', and 'community' interchangeably to refer to groups of individuals who are aware of a connection to others in the group and are expected to take some responsibility for one another. They can be big and small, long-lived and short-lived, healthy and unhealthy. They share what Ludwig Wittgenstein called "forms of life," practices and institutions that emphasize their connections and responsibilities.

All of these terms will recur and, I hope, will be much clearer by the end of the book. For now, it is enough to notice that when people dress up and dance or listen to a story or do any of the ordinary and extraordinary things that people do when they describe themselves or others as being engaged in artistic activity, they interact with an artifact, consciously paying attention to intrinsic properties of that artifact that their culture has identified as worthy of perception and reflection. I don't just move; at least sometimes, I move aware of the fact that my movements exhibit properties of the sort that others fluent in my culture know repay attention. Something as simple as noticing that I am not very graceful is aesthetic noticing. When others begin treating my action in ways that draw attention to those of its intrinsic properties considered worthy of perception and reflection in our community, my movement becomes art. That is, when I or others respond to an object or event aesthetically, it is, for however short a time, art.

Aesthetic response is a basic element of humanity.[3] There are probably biological reasons for this. Some evolutionist theorists believe that aesthetic preferences for certain landscapes (such as savannahs or those with running water) developed from and contributed to survival advantages. Nonetheless, there is also a social determinant to the way in which persons react aesthetically to objects or events. This is one of the elements of my contextualism, my turn away from formalism or universalism—away, that is, from theories insisting that the only things aesthetically significant are formal properties responded to directly or without reliance on external information such as artist biography or historical setting. It is also a result of growing awareness of claims of cultural diversity and the attendant recognition that the artworks and art-critical practices of a Eurocentric elite do not exhaust human aesthetic enterprises.

One way of understanding the influence of social factors in aesthetic response is by considering how social construction theories of emotion apply to such response,[4] for although, strictly speaking, aesthetic responses are not simply emotions, they do involve emotions, and there is much that is similar between emotional and aesthetic response. The main tenet of SC (as I shall refer to social constructionism and constructionists) is that emotions cannot be reduced to physiological or psychological states of individuals. As Errol Bedford puts it, "Emotion concepts . . . are not purely psychological: they presuppose concepts of social relationships and institutions, and concepts belonging to systems of judgment, moral, aesthetic, and legal. In using emotion words we are able, therefore, to relate behavior to the complex background in which it is enacted, and so to make human action intelligible."[5] SC does not deny that inner physiological or psychological states are part of emotion. It rather insists that additional components figure, such as experience, displayed behavior, cognitive interpretations, and moral assessment.[6] This is particularly obvious, SCs argue, when one considers emotions such as grief and remorse, or shame and disappointment, where the distinctions between them are not made solely on the basis of inner feeling but in addition on the basis of situations in which the agents find themselves. It would be impossible to distinguish grief from disappointment merely by a physical examination—of one's pulse, muscle tension, tears, and so on—for these alone will not establish the difference. Instead, one looks for the necessary evidence in the context—at whether a loved one has recently died or a lottery ticket has not paid off. Emotion is an open or, as James R. Averill describes it, 'polythetic' concept, where there is no list of necessary and sufficient conditions for the occurrence of an emotion, but instead some combination or subset of physiological changes, subjective experience, and expressive reactions that are "institutionalized" interpretations and responses to particular classes of situations.[7] Understanding emotions requires not just a study of individual bodies or minds, but of language, moral systems, social functions, rituals, and other sociological and anthropological phenomena—including art and aesthetic activity.

To see how SC relates to aesthetic response, we must look at the details of SC theory. Different theorists, of course, emphasize different points or aspects. Nonetheless, there are three common claims that one can describe and try to apply to aesthetic response and experience.

- Emotions are learned.
- Emotions are culture-bound.
- Emotions are socially prescribed and proscribed.

I shall discuss each of these points separately and then turn to a discussion of the extent to which each is true of aesthetic response and thus exposes points that must be covered in any adequate theory of the aesthetic.

Emotions Are Learned

According to SC, emotions depend on one's ability to make appropriate judgments. As knowledge and capacity increase, emotional responses develop and change. How one feels depends to a great extent on how one learns what one is expected to feel. One reads, like David Copperfield, "as if for life," and learns what one's culture expects and admires emotionally as well as—indeed, concomitantly with—

behaviorally and morally. "Having by this time cried as much as I possibly could, I began to think it was no use crying any more, especially as neither Roderick Random, nor that captain in the Royal British Navy had ever cried, that I could remember."[8] David does not just learn to hold back tears, he learns to be and feel brave by imitating the heroes of children's fiction popular in his community. (In chapter 10, I shall discuss specifically how fictions teach moral lessons.)

There is a significant developmental component to emotion: what one feels as a child one does not necessarily feel as an adult in similar situations. One learns appropriate attitudes, the logic and rules for expressing emotions, and the language used to describe, prescribe, and proscribe them. We even learn what bodily states are appropriate and permissible. In some cultures, women, but not men, can faint or beat their breasts from grief; little boys, but not grown men, are allowed occasionally to beat their fists and feet on the floor in anger.

The sources for emotional learning are numerous, but here I will be, of course, interested in how aesthetic objects and events, particularly artworks, provide moral lessons. As Ronald de Sousa has written, "We are made familiar with the vocabulary of emotion by association with paradigm scenarios. These are drawn first from our daily life as children and later reinforced by the stories, art, and culture to which we are exposed. . . . Paradigm scenarios involve two aspects: first, a situation type providing the characteristic *objects* of the specific emotion type . . . and second, a set of characteristic or 'normal' *responses* to the situation, where normality is first a biological matter and then very quickly becomes a cultural one."[9] I would add that artworks also teach us what to approve and disapprove of emotionally.

As individuals mature, they internalize more and more complex logical and strategic directions for what they should do. Much of the work done on the logic of emotion concerns what philosophers of language refer to as its intensionality: there must be an object of an emotion—something or someone that one loves, fears, takes joy in. To a great extent, learning the appropriate object enables one to differentiate emotions, to distinguish sorrow from remorse, or disappointment from shame, for example, People do not just feel grief; they feel grief about something, such as the death of a loved one. I am not just "in love"; I am in love with someone. Lust is not generic; it has a particular object. One learns which objects determine that this is annoyance, that indignation. Learning what emotion one feels, thus, is not only a matter of introspection but also coming to understand the context—the objects, our and others' relation to it and to us.

One of the most convincing elements of SC is the claim that language plays a crucial role in emotion. Having or not having "a word for it" often determines whether an individual will have or not have a particular feeling. Thus, one must learn the language of a community before one can have or understand specific emotions.

Emotions Are Culture Bound

Since language is crucial to emotion, and since language is culture-bound, it is not surprising that SC views emotion as culture-specific. Emotions develop and are shaped by a community's beliefs and values. Like philosophers of language such as Hilary Putnam, who argue that meaning is not just "in the head" but world-dependent, SC believes that two individuals can be particle-for-particle identical and yet have different emotions in different cultures. Emotions are internalized community values; one hates what one's culture hates and grieves at what one's culture considers deep loss.

Strong versions of SC maintain that all emotions are culture-dependent—that is, there are no *natural* emotions. Weaker versions allow for some natural, un-learned emotions but insist that most are cultural products. If all people feel fear when they are chased by a large animal or when their shelter catches fire, not all people fear the hill folk or certain cloud formations. What counts as a "delinquent" emotion will vary from culture to culture and even between subcultures. Age, gender, class—all serve to determine what someone feels in certain circumstances. All are relevant to norms that operate locally and that must be internalized if one is to be considered emotionally "normal."

A great deal of fascinating research has been done on emotions across cultures and times. Rom Harre and Robert Findlay-Jones have discussed *accidie,* an emotion often referred to in medieval Europe but no longer commonly referred to in the West.[10] Accidie was a feeling of guilt that those leading often tedious, lonely religious (e.g., monastic) lives experienced, not because they failed to do their duty but because they failed to do it with proper fervor. One prayed, but one's heart wasn't in it, and one felt accidie. (It is surprising that this term has not experienced a comeback in academic institutions plagued by endless meetings!) Work such as Paul Heelas's on emotions across cultures shows that even basic emotions such as fear and anger show little cross-cultural constancy.[11] The Javanese of Ponorogo, for example, use liver-talk instead of heart-talk to describe their emotional responses. (One wonders if their livers are in their mouths when they are startled!)

In general, the way in which cultures make sense of their world influences the emotions felt and vice versa. For example, when 'self' is defined socially, there are enormous differences in how emotions are constructed and described from cultures in which 'self' is defined individually. It will determine, for instance, whether one person or an entire clan appropriately feels anger at an insult or whether an action honors just me or my whole family. The way emotions are understood presupposes a whole view of the human and of human action. What one considers oneself responsible for is a crucial part of a community's emotional scheme. Guilt and a sense of responsibility are conceptually and logically linked to what a society views as obligatory.

It must be added that believing that emotions (and aesthetic response, as we shall see later) are socially constructed in being culturally determined does not imply anything about the specific course of the determination. As Richard Eldridge writes, "We are what we are only through our languages and cultures, and their pasts. . . . But nothing follows from this about the ultimate determinants of language, culture, and history."[12] In particular, Eldridge thinks, Marxism or Freudianism and a whole range of other "isms" do not follow. I agree; the specifics of methods and causes of cultural construction remains an open question.

Emotions Are Socially Prescribed and Proscribed

Cultures have histories at least in part because their interests, purposes, and needs change. As these change, so do emotions. SC takes this as evidence that emotions play a role in serving the functions of society; in other words, emotions have a social function.

It follows that there should be socially prescriptive and proscriptive aspects to emotion, and this is exactly what one finds. Emotions function to promote desirable behaviors and attitudes and to regulate undesirable ones. Persons learn to feel certain emotions, or to control them appropriately. One learns to hate what one's community views negatively, to feel anger against transgressors, and guilt when one transgresses oneself. One learns to feel affection for those who need and deserve protection and pity when they suffer. These obviously serve social interests, not just the goal of individual survival. The "rules" one must learn are cultural creations that serve to internalize social strategies for promulgating mores. "I'm ashamed of you" expresses not only the speaker's emotion but also a direction to the hearer that he or she should also feel shame. Sorrow too openly demonstrated or disappointment too long indulged brings criticism. "Cheer up" or, as in American slang, "Deal with it!"

Such demands or requests or advice would not make sense if emotion were not thought to be, to some extent at least, within one's control and valorized by a community. Of course, the methods a community has for prescribing and proscribing emotions can be very subtle. David Copperfield succeeds for a time in modeling himself after Roderick Random but has a relapse. He asks a coachman to give him back the handkerchief they had set on a horse's back to dry. The driver suggests that it is probably best left where it is. Davy's agreement is a step on the road to emotional maturity, at least as conceived by Victorian culture.

One of the basic tenets of SC is that the use of emotion words is heavily dependent upon the moral order of a community, for example, on rights and duties. Feeling jealous, for instance, depends upon believing that you have certain rights with respect to another person. Accidie will be felt only in communities that, for some reason, value tedious activity that should be dutifully and enthusiastically performed.

The social functions of emotions are furthered not only by proscriptive language ("Stop feeling sorry for yourself!") but also by justificatory language. Emotions from fear to surprise to love can be described as 'unjustified'. Such language would be meaningless, or at least vacuous, if emotions were, like breathing or retching, purely physiological. It requires shared analysis of context, such as mutual understanding that a situation is dangerous. "You *ought* not to be afraid of snails." "You *ought* not to love such a scoundrel." "You *ought* not to have been surprised at the salesman's tactics." "You *ought* to be proud of yourself." All of these 'oughts', according to SC, prove that there is a social element to emotion.

So, to what extent are these assertions true of aesthetic response? We must remind ourselves that there is no single aesthetic response, let alone a single aesthetic emotion. However, there are several emotions picked out by English terms (and terms in other languages, of course) that refer to mental events that are something like emotions and that frequent discussions of aesthetic experience: 'uplifted', 'sentimental', 'amused', 'suspenseful', 'bored', 'moved', 'exhilarated', and 'entranced', for example. Though we do not feel "pangs" of these the ways we feel pangs of fear or regret, there are even some bodily states associated with these responses. One's heart pounds as one reads a novel. One is overcome with a view and grabs one's chest. There are goosebumps, tears, or constrictions of the throat as one listens to a song. The hair on the back of one's neck stands up as one watches a film. One's ears hurt when the choir is off-key or the organ goes into too low a register. But none of these states—indeed, no bodily state—is a necessary component of aesthetic experience. Nor is any of them sufficient. All occur in other types of experiences, and none singly or in combination guarantees an aesthetic experience. Furthermore, I suspect that many aesthetic responses lack any noticeable physiological component. Analysis of a fugue or comparison and contrast of Chinese and Indian Buddha statues may be enjoyable aesthetic activities in the absence of any flutterings or palpitations.

Nonetheless, there does seem to be something loosely referred to by the term 'aesthetic response', and it is this complex I want to examine in the light of SC. I do not think that this response can be precisely defined. I shall, however, use the following characterization:

> An aesthetic response is a response to aesthetic properties of an object or event, that is, to intrinsic properties considered worthy of attention (perception or reflection) within a particular culture.

The fact that the properties responded to are considered worthy of attention does not necessarily imply that the response is "positive." Color, intonation, and rhyme may be characteristics that repay perception and reflection *in general*. However, some may be vibrant, pure, and intriguing, and others boring, flat, and trite. The response will correspondingly be positive or negative. Furthermore, positive aesthetic experiences often involve emotions generally identified as "negative"—fear or pity, for example. There has recently been a great deal of discussion of this phenomenon.[13] Here, all one need acknowledge is that the experiences one identifies as *aesthetic* are directed at certain properties of things and events and that one is conscious that one's response is causally connected to those properties. As I said previously, *worthiness of attention* is a matter of what communities consider worth drawing attention to in general. One's response to particular colors would be neither negative nor positive in the absence of any sustained attention whatsoever to color. As the definition stands, the question of SC is not begged, for it is consistent with the definition that all cultures pick out the same intrinsic properties for attention because there is a "natural" human response to specific intrinsic properties.

Before proceeding, I must provide a more detailed account of what I mean by 'aesthetic property' and, because I use the notion rather specially, 'intrinsic'. The first term I define as follows:

> A is an aesthetic property of O (an object or event) if and only if A is an
> intrinsic property of O and A is culturally identified as a property worthy
> of attention (i.e., of perception and reflection).

Being intrinsic means being "in" something. This "in-ness" has usually been understood metaphysically; properties intrinsic to objects or events have been taken
to be, in some way or other, part of an object's being or makeup. But I prefer an
epistemological interpretation of the concept. (I shall say much more about this in
later chapters.) Perception and attention are at the core of aesthetic experience and
are activities performed by viewers; thus, what matters most is that a person be cognitively engaged.[14] One or more of the five senses are engaged, but so are one or
more of what used to be called the "five wits": common wit, imagination, fantasy,
estimation, and memory. We look at things, or listen or touch or smell them; we
think about how the objects stimulate our responses to them both individual and
collectively. To this extent, we realize that the properties we are interested in are really "in" the objects. However, the particular properties to which individuals attend
when they have what they recognize as aesthetic experiences differ from culture to
culture and even within cultures as subcultures develop. Wine connoisseurs attend
closely to features of what they drink that nonconnoisseurs not only disregard but
also often fail to notice at all. Similar observations can be made about responses to
paintings or buildings or quilts—potentially to any object at all which has properties that some group has picked out as worthy of attention. What is perceived as
being "in" the wine depends at least as much and often more on the taster than on
the liquid; the features of a building actually take recognizable shape as different
observers organize parts into a variety of patterns and elements. Thus, I define 'intrinsic' as follows.

> F is an intrinsic property of O if and only if direct inspection of O is a
> necessary condition for verifying the claim that O is F.

F is an extrinsic property of O if and only if it is not intrinsic. That is, one can decide whether an object has an extrinsic property by means other than personal, direct perception and reflection. For example, one can know that a poem was written in Mali by consulting evidence other than that provided directly to one's
senses—indeed, it is hard to imagine how one would verify a claim that a poem
was written in Mali simply by reading it. But to know that a poem is written in
iambic pentameter, one must read or hear it for oneself. Perceptual and reflective
evidence is the only kind of evidence that will settle the issue. One must taste the
liquid to know if it has a slight vanilla flavor and look at a building to know if it is
neo-Gothic. The same is true of all aesthetic properties, for these are always intrinsic. One must perceive the work for oneself.

In earlier writings, I also claimed that direct inspection is a sufficient condition
for verifying a claim that O has the property F, as long as one knew the meaning of
'F'. I no longer insist on this. Although direct inspection is usually all one needs to
decide whether an object has a property or not, some aesthetic properties can be
attributed to objects only when augmented by some extrinsic information. If one

knows the meaning of 'tannic', then it is indeed enough to drink some wine to decide whether it has this property. (Assuming, of course, that one is in what David Hume described as a "sound state."[15] One cannot decide what properties a glass of wine has if one has a bad cold, for example.) But there are some aesthetic properties, such as. 'represents Trajan', that may require additional extrinsic information. Still, deciding whether something represents Trajan will necessitate direct inspection.

The intrinsic nature of aesthetic properties will be discussed in chapter 3, when I consider the nonsupervenient nature of aesthetic properties. But for now, we return to the question of whether aesthetic properties might be said to be socially constructed. To what extent do the three claims made about SC apply to aesthetic response? We shall consider each of the three points in turn.

Aesthetic Response Is Learned

If emotions depend on a capacity to judge and compare, this is equally true of aesthetic response. Even at the most naïve level, learning that a flower is pretty or a garbage dump ugly depends on contrasting these objects with other sorts of things not picked out for such assessments. Appreciating the clever ending of a Mozart sonata or the exuberance of a Shivah figure is possible only when sophisticated listening and looking skills have been developed. The aesthetic lives of children and mature adults differ just as their emotional lives do, with pronounced cognitive and behavioral variations. We do not expect senior citizens to swoon or scream at classical music concerts. Experienced readers of spy novels often fail to feel suspense at a particular tale when less sophisticated readers are on the edge of their seats as they read it.

We also respond according to learned aesthetic roles: performer, critic, audience member, artist, tourist, and the like. Such roles with their special logic and strategies must be learned. People learn to play the audience game, the critic game, and so on. One learns to express being uplifted differently from being bored (although there may be some behavioral overlaps, e.g., closed eyes) and learns how to distinguish the objects appropriate to them (e.g., boredom, not upliftedness, is appropriate for trite interpretations.) Training is at least as important as physiology.

One possible objection here is that one often hears such sentences as "There's no word for the way I feel" in what one identifies as an aesthetic discussion. Don't such utterances show that aesthetic responses are inner states that are independent of specific language communities?

Rather than undermining the centrality of language in determining aesthetic response, this objection actually supports it. Consider the sorts of occasions when such statements occur. They are never uttered in isolation. That is, in aesthetic as in nonaesthetic contexts, the speaker always goes on to describe (or has just done so) the context of the response. "I can't tell you how I felt *when my mother died.*" "*My experience upon first seeing* Guernica was simply indescribable." "*The sound of the saxophone* affects me as nothing else does—there's no word for it." In every case, identifying the object of the emotion does provide "a word for it" (typically a phrase) and hence picks out or individuates a specific feeling. Were the speaker to believe that the hearer really had no idea how the speaker felt, the utterance would be pointless. Even those responses that are alleged to be "indescribable" are at least partially described by referring to a particular object—the death of a parent or *Guernica*. The speaker assumes some shared understanding—understanding that springs from a shared community. "I just can't say how I felt at all—not even what I was feeling a response to" would make sense, I think, only if the speaker and hearers were members of radically different cultures—when even specification of the object or circumstances would leave the hearer without a clue.

Just as the linguistic determinedness of emotion is one of the most compelling arguments for SC theories of emotion, so, I believe, it is for aesthetic response. One is not born able to distinguish a fugue from a gigue, nor an early from a late Indian Buddha figure. Doing so depends on acquiring a very specialized vocabulary. Appreciating these things, and the differences between them, is also language-dependent, as is the particular response shaped by the words used to describe something. A guidebook tells us when to be uplifted or amused, deeply impressed or contemptuous. When one learns that the Weeping Angel in Amiens Cathedral is not mourning the death of those memorialized in the monument of which it is a part but expressing the dismay the sculptor is said to have felt because he believed he was underpaid, our responses changes. It is hard to imagine feeling sentimental where there is no word for this particular kind of self-indulgence. As recognition of the linguistic dependence of emotion leads directly to a recognition of its culture-boundedness, so, too, with aesthetic response.

Aesthetic Response Is Culture-Bound

If such remarks as "They have a word for it that we just don't have" apply in the case of emotion, so, too, they are often encountered in aesthetic discourse, and hence SC is strengthened in both domains. Having a word for it is a cultural phenomenon, and having certain kinds of responses is also a cultural phenomenon. Roger Scruton writes of music (and what he says is true of all art forms, I believe), "To aim to produce music is to aim to produce a musical response. And only in the context of a musical culture is such an aim coherent. It is custom, habit, the intertwining of music with everyday life, which generates the basic discriminations."[16] One person learns to be thrilled and exhilarated, another to be repulsed, even depressed, at the spectacle of boxing. Rap gives some people hope but causes others fear. A fugue enraptures one but bores or mystifies another.

I have said that aesthetic response is a response to intrinsic properties that a culture values for their capacity to engage and repay attention. Several combinations, therefore, are possible. Culture A picks out P, and most members enjoy it. Culture B does not pick out P—doesn't even have a word for it—so no one attends to it with either pleasure or displeasure. But members of B do pick out Q, and some subcultures of B delight in it while others do not. Culture C picks out P, and most members are displeased by it. Within Culture A, a few individuals fail to learn either to pick out or to respond to P. Some members of Culture P visit Culture A and learn to pick out and eventually to delight in P. Subcultures develop in B—Aophiles—and paradigms begin to shift.

To understand how an emotion-word differs across cultures or across time, one must obviously know a lot about these cultures. *Accidie* provided one clear example. This is true of aesthetic response as well. Eduardo Crespo points out that being sentimental is much more positive in Spanish culture than it has been in Anglo-American cultures.[17] (I will in chapter 9 discuss in detail the responses that fall under the term 'sentimental'.) Aesthetic response-talk, as well as emotion-talk, varies with language, and hence one must be fluent in a language and its culture to understand its nature within that culture. For people not fluent in Japanese language and culture, the term 'makoto', according to those who do have the requisite fluency, can at best only be glossed as "a sincere or genuine expression of an appropriate emotion."[18] For one thing, it is most often attributed to haiku, a genre with which most Westerners have at best a fleeting acquaintance. For another, it involves not just an indication of "real" feeling but requires knowing which emotions are appropriate to the particular kind of place being described and what constitutes the proper and improper uses of forms and techniques with respect to a particular magnitude of feeling. Clearly these will be socially determined. How should one feel about a lake in the sun as opposed to a lake in the fog? Which forms would be improper when describing a frog jumping into a foggy lake? Since there is no universally correct answer to these questions, there will be no universally appropriate aesthetic response.

Of course, one has an aesthetic analogue to the problem of whether any emotions are completely "natural"—that is, not socially constructed. There may be situations that stimulate aesthetic response cross-culturally. While admitting that responses to Bach are not universal, standing on a cliff on the Oregon coast, watching waves crash against the rocks hundreds of feet below, it is hard for me to believe that there is anyone who would not feel as I do—namely, the way I feel, which may be describable only as "the-way-you-feel-when-you-see-waves-crashing-against-a-cliff." Nonetheless, a typically American response to the view (saying, "Wow!" or shouting, "Hey, Joe, you gotta see this!" or hurrying on to the next viewpoint, etc.) will probably not be exactly the same as the response of a person from a subtler culture. "Oh, isn't it lovely" may be as excited as it gets. And there will be age, gender, and class variations within a single culture. Enthusiasm is not always obstreperous; it may or may not be accompanied by reaching for one's heart (or liver) or camera. These behaviors, varying as they do across cultures, will result in different teaching and learning methods and styles. Just which practices result in which aesthetic responses will, of course, themselves be largely socially constructed.

Aesthetic response, like emotion, has a history. Research is required for specific responses. As I have said, I do not claim that aesthetic response is possible *only* within socially constructed contexts; I do not know this, and I doubt that at this stage in the development of the cognitive sciences anyone does. But some aesthetic responses certainly are. The one whose history I know something about, which is the subject of chapter 9—sentimentality—certainly has changed over the years, and the changes tell one a great deal about how social constructionism applies to a particular aesthetic response. In its original eighteenth-century British use, it was positive, but within a generation it had become negative. In some periods, it was permissible for women, but not for men, to be sentimental. There is some indication that now, as it becomes permissible, even laudable, for men overtly to express their feelings, sentimentality is becoming more generally positive again. "Lacks a sentimental tug" was a derogatory remark recently made in a review of a play. We have seen convincing arguments within SC that emotion is a complex of which inner states are only a single component. So it is with aesthetic response: it, too, is a complex of behavior, attitude, belief, values, object, and physiology—all of which can and do change over time.

There is a further way in which aesthetic response is culture-bound, or at least culturally shaped, a way suggested by Paul Guyer in an article on Kant's aesthetics. Guyer wants to explain why Kant is unclear about whether universalizability of aesthetic judgment (Kant's view that when individuals feel aesthetic pleasure, they believe that everyone else will and ought to feel similarly) is a cause of pleasure or an observation about the nature of that pleasure. Guyer thinks it is because Kant was, in the decades preceding his more mature theories, convinced by a communicability theory of beauty, namely, the view that judgments of beauty arise only in society. He suggests that Kant did not think that a Robinson Crusoe would fail to take pleasure in the beauty of, say, the flower on his island, but only that "in the absence of society these objects would not take on any value *in addition* to their natural beauty, such as that of occasioning communication either with or about the individual. . . ."[19] Agreement with others may not be required to explain why an individual finds something beautiful, but "it may well be that the art of reflecting upon one's own pleasures and discriminating them, by conjectures about their origin, into pleasures in the agreeable, the good, and the beautiful is an art which has a point and can even be acquired only in a social setting."[20] That there are some pleasures that we describe as 'aesthetic' which derive at least in part from the recognition that others are sharing in our experiences cannot be denied, I think. Obviously, this demands deep fluency and entrenchment within a community; and such pleasures could be felt only in society and hence must be socially constructed.

Aesthetic Response Is Socially Prescribed And Proscribed

With respect to emotion, SC asserted that there is a history because cultural interests and purposes change. Emotions have social functions, and so are prescribed and proscribed correspondingly. Can the same be said of aesthetic response? This is, I think, the most controversial or at least the most difficult claim to articulate and to justify. But in many ways, it is also the most interesting and most important.

Two arguments, analogous to ones we met in SC, support the position that aesthetic response is socially prescribed. The first is that some aesthetic responses depend on a culture's moral order, and since the latter is obviously a matter of social prescription, so is the former. The second argument is that aesthetic responses are justified, and justification of responses makes sense only in a context of prescription. A nagging question remains, however. But first the arguments.

There are two important ways in which aesthetic response is connected to a culture's moral order. One must, first of all, know and understand a culture's moral system to appreciate much of its art. (I shall argue for this claim in several of the following chapters.) Novels such as *Middlemarch* or *Things Fall Apart* cannot be understood without a deep understanding of the moral values both explicit and implicit in them. A grasp of *accidie* may be required if one is to have access to a particular painting of a religious hermit such as St. Jerome. Examples such as these can be found in all of the arts. What one does not understand, one cannot fully respond to. Thus, aesthetic response to such objects is connected to a community's moral order.

In the second place, certain experiences themselves will not obtain in the absence of shared moral values. An emotion such as jealousy or pride depends on sophisticated internalization of a society's system of rights and responsibilities. There are equally vivid examples of such a connectedness in aesthetic experience. Sentimentality, for instance, has and requires both aesthetic and moral components. (See chapter 9.) Indulging sentimentality, like indulging grief, not only has moral parameters but also cannot be understood without attention to both moral properties, like self-deception, and aesthetic properties, like exaggerated gesture. There are, I suspect, other aesthetic responses and judgments in which this interplay is at the core: sincerity, cleverness, shallowness, offensiveness, and poignancy, for instance.

The fact that some emotions are justified and some unjustified proves, according to many social constructionists, that emotion is more than an involuntary inner feeling. "Your surprise was hardly justified" says more about beliefs that it does about physiology. Are there examples of justified and unjustified aesthetic responses? The constructionist Claire Arman-Jones writes, "[Assessment of emotions] as warranted depends not only upon judgments concerning the extension of the object (e.g. that there really is an x of which M is afraid) but also upon agreement over the agent's construal as being a plausible construal of the object (e.g. that x can be construed as menacing or dangerous)."[21] Is this also true of aesthetic response? Are there plausible and implausible construals of objects that make some aesthetic responses appropriate, others inappropriate? Or, if someone responds positively to an object—exclaims at its joyfulness, for instance—no matter how disgusting most members of his or her community find it, does it simply end there? If someone stands looking down on a garbage dump, feels goosebumps (positive ones), says, "Wow!" and grabs for her camera, and so on, do we, should we, can we meaningfully say, "Your aesthetic response is not justified"?

Barrie Falk, in a paper on the communicability of feeling, makes some observations that may help us answer these questions. Feelings of emotions such as pity, he says, are marked by resonance and salience. Resonance is "a certain current conative state"—one in which the agent is absorbed by certain features of an object or event; salience is a sense that "*this* . . . is what the world is like."[22] Suppose a scene is pitiful, and I, in fact, feel pity. Falk writes, "All that has been required of me is the ability to perceive pitifulness when it is there. And when, in such a situation, I do feel pity, the feeling will therefore be the proper one, no more in need of justification than my belief, in appropriate circumstances, that there is a daffodil before me. . . . If my feeling is right, my state will be a communicable one, its proper description transcending reference merely to events occurring within a discrete subject of sensory and affective states."[23] No *more* in need of justification—but in need, nonetheless. We suppose that both we and others (in our culture, though Falk is not explicit on the culture-specificity of what is communicable, as I would be) will be sensitive to what we are sensitive to. Our beliefs, says Falk, "bestow" resonance and salience.[24] Where such beliefs are shared, feelings can be communicated. This lies at the heart of the communicability of feelings via art, he argues.[25] The belief and the feeling that a daffodil or a painting of a daffodil is beautiful are part of the same phenomena; hence, where beliefs differ, the response will differ. Beliefs about and attitudes toward garbage dumps in Minnesota make it unlikely that someone there will have positive goosebumps while peering down on a garbage dump.

But are aesthetic responses socially prescribed and proscribed to the extent that one is justified in saying, "You ought not find garbage dumps beautiful?" Do aesthetic responses have a social function; if so, what is it? Do aesthetic responses "sustain and endorse cultural systems of belief and value,"[26] as many social constructionists believe emotions do? Do they help to regulate undesirable behavior and promote desired attitudes?

I do not believe that aesthetic response has a single function any more than art (or a specific emotion, for that matter) does. But that they have some social functions does appear to be the case. We teach art appreciation (part of which is surely aesthetic response) because we believe it enriches life, not just individuals' lives. Shared aesthetic experiences are often parts of rituals that bind communities. (I will discuss this in chapter 14.) Ellen Dissanayake has developed an almost Darwinian argument to support her claim that art is for survival. "The arts [are] a collection of describable activities (and responses to these activities) based on the proclivity to make special. What this behavior was 'for' in human evolution was to facilitate or sugarcoat socially important behavior, especially ceremonies, in which group values often of a sacred or spiritual nature, were expressed or transmitted."[27] Perhaps this is no longer so important in Eurocentric contemporary cultures where "art for art's sake" has created an elite artist class that seems often to pay little attention to the general population. But there are certainly communities where art continues to play a very important role in sustaining what its members regard as significant. The connoisseur culture from which many influential aestheticians have come in this century has underplayed the social nature of aesthetic response. But even among "us," there are aesthetic responses that depend on collective rather than simply individual experience: attending concerts and plays, singing in choirs, going to museums with groups or classes. Something is absent when one sits in a darkened movie theater and watches a film alone. Perhaps one of the failures of contemporary elitist art is that it divides the "ins" from the "outs."

The force of "You ought not to respond to that garbage dump with aesthetic delight" clearly depends on shared—that is, collective—values. Only a heartless bean counter such as Gradgrind would find most mid- and late-twentieth-century low-income housing developments beautiful. As technological societies come to have a better understanding of the causes of social deviance, more and more cities have given up plans that involve high-rise concrete structures that have come to be recognized as perfect environments for breeding and supporting criminal behavior. Many have actually been torn down. The idea that beautiful behavior and beautiful surroundings go together is gaining credence. "You ought to find the architecture in the Cabrini development in Chicago ugly" is by no means a meaningless statement. And it indicates that aesthetic response, like emotion, is tied to a culture's moral order and, like emotions, will be used to prescribe and proscribe the sort of life one has and leads.

I HAVE tried to show that claims made by SC about emotion are true of aesthetic response. The dependence on language and culture for a full understanding of the latter as well as the former is thus underscored. The contextualist turn away from formalism and universalism is to that extent justified. It is as difficult to specify what it is in the context that demands and deserves attention as it is to define 'social'. Aesthetic response, like the individual emotions prominent in so many of them, must be investigated as particulars. Case histories of accidie or sentimentality will disclose factors that shape them. It is unlikely that the same factors will always be present or will play equally determinant roles in all cases.

I have attempted to show not that aesthetic response is an emotion, but that, nevertheless, things that have been shown to be true of emotions with respect to the ways in which social and cultural features generate and shape them can also be said of aesthetic response. Recognizing this is a crucial first step in understanding the nature of the aesthetic and of aesthetic properties. If those human responses that we describe as "aesthetic" are not simply inner states caused by a closed set of properties intrinsic to object and events, but rather depend at least in part on the circumstances in which those states and properties are located, then the contextuality of what counts as an aesthetic property must be accounted for in any adequate theory of the aesthetic. And, as I have already said, no set of intrinsic properties can a priori be established as the one and only set of aesthetic properties.

I will argue in the next chapter that any intrinsic property can be an aesthetic property. It does not follow that every intrinsic property is an aesthetic property. Relativity to a culture does not imply that everything is aesthetic, any more than it implies that anything is a prime minister. Once the institutions and practices of a community are set, only some things will count as aesthetic, for not everything will be considered worthy (for whatever social reasons) of attention. Specifying which things matter aesthetically in communities, determining which things do, in fact, get constructed socially as repaying perception and reflection, requires broad and deep familiarity—what I call "fluency" in a culture. It demands, among other things, identifying what is relevant to aesthetic discussion and activity. It is to the question of aesthetic relevancy that we now turn.

TWO

Aesthetic Relevance

In THE first chapter I proposed a very inclusive view of art. Such a broad view of what counts as art is not unrelated, of course, to an equally broad view of what counts as "doing things with art." Anything people do, I believe, can be done using art. (One need only think of the elaborate commodes that bedecked royal residences!) An equally broad, and simple, answer to the question "Why do people use art?" is also called for: because art shapes and enriches all forms of human activity. This, I have also argued, is consistent with a view of aesthetic response or activity as "socially constructed." People learn how to use and respond to art, the uses and responses are culturally bound and determined, and because art plays many important roles that satisfy a community's needs, the uses of and responses to art are prescribed and proscribed.

The integral relation between art and the rest of human interests will be the main theme of this book. It does not follow that whenever anyone does anything, it counts as art. There are many things that do not satisfy one or more of the conditions I stipulate for 'work of art'. And the distinction between art and nonart is a very useful one. I am claiming only that anything can be given aesthetic attention and that anything, given the appropriate treatment within an appropriate cultural tradition, can become art. Similarly, not every way of responding to art is an aesthetic way, and not everything one says about an object or event is relevant to considering it aesthetically. One consequence of thinking of art and the aesthetic broadly—of putting no a priori limitations on what might count as art or artistic activity or purpose—is that what matters to aesthetic discussions, what is, as I put it, aesthetically relevant, also knows no a priori bounds. But there are bounds— that is, one can distinguish what is aesthetically relevant from that which is aesthetically irrelevant. However, my view of art and aesthetic experience is much more inclusive than the universalist, formalist theories that so influenced twentieth-century aesthetic theory.[1]

In his book *Poesis: Structure and Thought*, H. D. F. Kitto states that "if on looking at a pediment, we noticed that one warrior had no spear, we should not think of asking where he had dropped it, or whether he had forgotten it: we should at once ask ourselves why the sculptor had represented himself spearless."[2] Assuming that this is obvious, Kitto goes on to argue that discussion of dramatic or theatrical works should also dismiss questions that confuse art and life.

One might first ask, Who is the "we" that Kitto is talking about? Clearly, it is not the class of all those who visit and enjoy pediments wherever they are found (either in their original locations or in museums), for anyone who has visited these spots knows that questions such as "Where's his spear?" abound. Thus, the "we" must be rhetorical; it must refer to Kitto and his friends, or to Kitto and those who share his formalistic leanings—that is, those who believe that the only questions worth pursuing in connection with works of art are those that deal with properties such as line, color, shape, organizational structure, and the like. In other words, "we" must be people who have bought into theories of significant form or new criticism or some other school of formalistic criticism and aesthetic theory.

Thus Kitto's implication cannot be that people *do not* raise questions about missing spears (or other questions about life outside the work of the sort that he assumes are illegitimate) but rather that they *should not* raise them. The question "Where's the spear?" may be relevant but only if interpreted in very restricted ways. If it means "Where was the spear lost?" or "What could have made the warrior forget or lay down his spear?" it is not aesthetically relevant on such a view. If it means "What compositional function does a spearless warrior in this region of the artwork perform?" it is aesthetically relevant. According to this position, aesthetically relevant questions about artworks are about artistic activity and what it produces. Questions about "life," while interesting in their own right perhaps, should not intrude and distract viewers when they want to engage in aesthetic conversation. In this chapter, I shall examine this view and explain where I think it is right and where I think it goes wrong. In particular, I shall attempt to explain why Kitto's position and others like it, consistent as they are with theories which distinguish and separate aesthetic experiences and considerations from all others (from moral, religious, political, social, and scientific attention, for example), contribute to what I think is a shortsighted and stultifying concept of the value of artistic and aesthetic activity.

Let us begin by considering two examples of discussions about works of art where spears are, in fact, missing. The first is a real case, the *Artemision Zeus*, a sculpture in which a raised hand is empty. From the pose and general stance, one can conclude with some probability that when originally created the figure did hold something, but that the ravages of time or vandals have removed it. Some scholars have argued that it must have been a spear that the man held; others have favored a trident. Here the question is not so much "Where's the spear?" as "Was it a spear?" and questions of classification (Is it Zeus or Poseidon or perhaps just a human warrior?) predominate. One might also wonder whether the statue was meant to be a representation of someone who had just dropped or thrown a spear. In any case, I hope to show that each of these questions is a candidate for genuine aesthetic discussion.

The second is an imaginary example. Suppose we come across a relief of the sort Kitto describes. Suppose I look at it with a friend, who, in fact, says, "I wonder whether that warrior lost his spear, and if so, where and how? Do you think he may have simply left it behind in the tent? If so, what kind of warrior was he? Or what circumstances could have led to so foolish an act?" Again, I hope to show that raising such questions is not necessarily an indication that my friend has failed to have an aesthetic experience or has confused questions about art with questions about life. Indeed, I hope to show that often questions about art simply are questions about life, and vice versa.

One of my fundamental assumptions (or intuitions or dogmas or nonnegotiable demands, depending on how sympathetic readers are to my view) is that an adequate account of the nature of art must explain or at least not contradict explanations of why people have valued and continue to value art and to take it seriously. As I noted previously, I define a work of art as an artifact treated in such a way that people consciously delight in aesthetic properties of the artifact, where 'aesthetic property' is to be understood as follows.

> A is an aesthetic property of a work, W, in a culture, C, if and only if A is an intrinsic property of W and A is considered worthy of attention in C; that is, in C it is generally believed that attending to A (perceiving and/or reflecting upon A) will reward attention.

What counts as an aesthetic property will differ from culture to culture both at the macro level and at the micro level. Within the contemporary United States, there is a plurality of microcultures—rural, urban, black, Hispanic, white, Eastern, Midwestern, and many more. Even families and small groups of friends qualify as subcultures or minicommunities, and they often develop their own aesthetic traditions. That is, they come to value certain special sets of intrinsic properties, regarding them as a potential cause of delight when they are perceived or reflected upon. Cultures overlap and, of course, sometimes clash. But I believe it is possible to come to understand, appreciate, and enthusiastically seek out aesthetic traditions from cultures and subcultures other than those into which one is born. (This should, in fact, be one of the basic goals of education, and it is the topic of chapter 14.)

My definitions of 'work of art' and 'aesthetic', emphasizing as they do the role of attention and reflection, begin (but only just begin) to account for why people value art and take it seriously. There are both perceptive and cognitive rewards. Art repays perception and reflection; good art repays sustained perception and reflection. The "payment" can take various forms—from simple sensuous pleasures to interesting but trivial information, to feeling that one's life has been changed, to bonding with other members of a community. I shall return to this "payoff" later in this chapter and later in this book.

The definitions also begin to explain how an object can be a work of art in some times and some places, but not always and everywhere. Like being a mother or to the north, being a work of art is a relational concept. (I prefer 'relational' to 'relative' since the latter is too easily confused with 'subjective' or 'lacks a truth-value'.) It is a two-place predicate—two things must be named, or two blanks filled in for a meaningful statement to result:

> . . . is the mother of. . . .
> . . . is to the north of. . . .
> . . . is a work of art in. . . .

Propaganda can become art, and art can become propaganda, for example. Pornography can become art, and art can become pornography. An ashtray or highway can become a work of art; a work of art can become an ashtray and perhaps even a highway. At each stage in the history of an object, what matters is whether and which properties receive the focus. If a work is discussed primarily in terms of how it aroused a crowd, it is propaganda. If interest depends on how it fits into a nation's history, it is primarily a historic artifact. If it is discussed primarily in terms of aesthetic properties (e.g., in the West in terms of color or pitch or metrical arrangement), it is a work of art. The same photograph may be smut or art, depending on whether it is valued for its ability to sexually stimulate viewers (in which case one focuses primarily on things outside the picture) or for its ability to reward attention to treatment of light or focus (in which case genuine intrinsic properties sustain attention). Highways and ashtrays may straddle the line (which is rarely firm or clear in any case) between art and nonart. Paintings often straddle the line between artworks and commodities; marches can be analyzed rhythmically and psychologically.

A very simple, clear test for *aesthetic relevance* follows from my view of art:

> A statement (or pointing gesture) is aesthetically relevant if and only if it draws attention (perception, reflection) to an aesthetic property.

This way of understanding aesthetic relevance is very close to one suggested by Richard Wollheim in *Painting as an Art*. He argues that what matters aesthetically is what allows us to get at the meaning or content of a work. He writes, "Often careful, sensitive, and generally informed, scrutiny of the painting will extract from it the very information that is needed to understand it."[3] But the phrase 'generally informed' carries a great deal of weight. The viewer must have a great deal of what Wollheim calls "cognitive stock." Put simply, cognitive stock is the information that a viewer brings with himself or herself to the experience of a work. Wollheim intentionally refrains from restricting the kind of information a priori, for he thinks there is no way to characterize what may be necessary or relevant in advance. In the case of a van der Weyden, he explains, knowledge of conventions governing the representation of religious apparitions will help to preclude misinterpretation. Familiarity with Goethe's novel *Effective Affinities* will facilitate fuller understanding of Terborch's *L'Instruction Paternelle*. What is relevant, thus, will range from broad knowledge (information about widely shared cultural conventions, for instance) to minutiae (such as obscure references known to only a few members of a community).

Wollheim's notion of cognitive stock is closely related to what I am getting at by my reference to shared cultural traditions. Aesthetically relevant information will be "such that by drawing upon it a spectator is enabled to experience some part of the content of the picture while otherwise he would have been likely to overlook it."[4] Without shared traditions, as I would put it, a looker or listener will probably miss many, if not most, of the intrinsic properties that have the capacity to reward attention. Aesthetic relevance is determined by learning whether what is offered draws attention to the aesthetic properties, and, like Wollheim, I believe that any-thing is a candidate.

Peter Kivy argues for a similar point in his *Music Alone*, where he asserts that ap-preciation of music is always a cognitive activity, even in those cases in which the listener is not "learned" in music theory. "Our enjoyment of music alone is of cog-nitively perceived musical sound. We take musical pleasure . . . in how we perceive musical events to take place."[5] This is done at various levels of musical sophistica-tion, he claims. I think that what Kivy means is that we hear music as structured sound. One might just like hearing a particular noise—a lawn mower or eggbeater, for example. But musical enjoyment involves appreciating a sound as structured. One enjoys a pattern of notes that is repeated, or a trumpet coming in just here, not there. I believe that information helps us to cognize as well as to perceive. In music, it helps bring us to an awareness of the structure, and I agree with Kivy that this awareness is a necessary condition of our enjoyment. This observation can, I think, be generalized to the other arts.

Since people's attention can be affected by almost anything, nothing can be ruled out a priori. It is not the precise nature of the *information* brought to bear that matters; it is wholly a matter of the *experience* that the information brings about. If a viewer sees more of the expressive or representational content when given information of any sort whatsoever, Wollheim insists, then the information is relevant. I prefer to speak not just in terms of expressive or representational con-tent, but of intrinsic features generally. Whatever directs attention to intrinsic properties aesthetically valued is aesthetically relevant. It is, I think, as simple as that at the end of the day.

In twentieth-century Eurocentric culture, art criticism and art theory abound, of course, with objections to what has been called "fallacious" reference to artistic intentions, artist psychology, social causes, emotional affect, and the like. Even as firm a historicist as Hans-Georg Gadamer, when he comes to discussing the con-tribution of poetry to the search for truth,[6] insists that real poetry (as opposed to the sort of verses lovers write to communicate their sentiments[7]) is autonomous. Real poetry stands alone; we do not ask, for example, about the intentions of the author, Gadamer asserts. (Here we have the poetic analogy to Kitto's disdain for asking where the missing spear must be.) In everyday discourse, when we talk about a house, we usually mean for the hearer to get information about a specific house. But when authors talk about "a house," this is not the case, according to Gadamer. Each reader forms a different image, and in poetry this is appropriate. In ordinary discourse, it can be fatal.

However, Gadamer is correct at most about a limited number of poems (and by extension, about a limited number of artworks in general). There are, undoubtedly, wholly successful poems that do not generate any questions about intentions or other outside information. But even here, I suspect, Gadamer must rely not only on "pure" poems but also on "pure" readers. When a poet writes, "A house stood on the hill," it may be all right to picture a stone cottage on a rocky rise or a colo-nial manor house on a grassy knoll. It will probably not be all right to imagine a boat on a pond. Chances are that the rest of the poem will cause the mental image to go in one direction or the other—toward the cottage or the mansion, or even toward a decision that the poem is, after all, about a houseboat on the crest of a wave. Nor, I think, will it be possible to fully characterize pure readers without reference to something like Wollheim's notion of cognitive stock or mine of traditions. If we do not think of asking for information about intentions or missing spears, it may be because we have it already. The information we have, or feel a need for, is an integral part of our experience of works.

As Peter Kivy points out in a description of listening to music, people are capable of thinking about and attending to more than one thing at a time. We can hear four parts of fugues at once, as well as notice many different details of compositions. This may, of course, take years of training; but nothing prevents us in theory from hearing a cello and a harpsichord, or of hearing the harpsichord and thinking about Bach's life.

Theorists and critics have often worried that certain bits of information will cause us to act as if we are wearing distorting lenses when we approach artworks. As Charles Hope writes, "The study of iconography frequently makes art historians behave like second-hand car salesmen, optimistically twisting the facts to fit their case and suppressing inconvenient problems in a desperate attempt to display their favorite theory in the best possible light."[8] Such concern might lead one to put a restriction on the sorts of "facts" that could or should be brought into artistic discussion. But I think one should not try to take such action. I am not very worried about twisting the facts (though with Hope I believe it is all-too-often done) because for me the end is not *the* correct interpretation. Rather, it is drawing attention to intrinsic features, and obscure references or distorted psychological theories may serve to do this as well as more accessible or acceptable information. This is not to say that good interpretations (and I certainly do believe that some interpretations are better than others, even if there is usually no single correct one) do not more commonly serve as more efficient and effective pointers.

What we scrutinize when we confront works of art are an object's intrinsic features. I have used the acronym FRET to describe aesthetic attending.[9] We see and think about Formal, Representational, Expressive, and Technical properties. 'FRET-ing' is intended, of course, to play on the notion of fretting, not exactly an irritated or annoyed or peevish concern when it characterizes aesthetic experience, but concern, nonetheless. Aesthetic attention is marked by intense, single-minded, and highly focused perception and thought. Raising questions such as "Where's the spear?" may very well draw us to formal, expressive, and technical features as well as to representational ones. How did the artist achieve the absence felt by the missing spear? What colors or lines create the expression of the overwhelming fear that the warrior feels? How does a missing spear contribute to the overall frenzy or comedy that is communicated? Is the warrior without the spear at the center of the composition—or is the center filled with warriors who still have their weapons? If so, why? It is precisely because questions such as these can and do draw us into a work that I am not afraid of confusing art and life, as Kitto is.

But is reference to external information *necessary*? Even granting that such information may sometimes be relevant, may we not nonetheless do without it? Is it the case that for some work, W, there is some bit of information, p, such that knowledge of p is essential for appreciating (perceiving and reflecting upon) W?

No one doubts that when 'p' includes reference to intrinsic properties knowledge of at least some p's is necessary. One must know that a painting has certain colors, shapes, or lines, or that a poem has certain words or a particular rhythm, for instance. One must hear the pitches to appreciate a song, know that certain sequences are repeated to appreciate a fugue, and so on for all art forms. Complete or ideal appreciation would probably entail complete knowledge of a work's intrinsic properties. Appreciation begins, however, when some minimal set of these properties is attended to. There is a complex continuum between no appreciation and total appreciation, and it corresponds to a continuum from no knowledge about W's intrinsic properties to complete knowledge about them. Knowledge concerning nuances of coloration may not be required for some level of appreciation, but complete lack of knowledge about color will surely preclude the appreciation of a work's color. (Color-blind people may appreciate paintings—spatial relationships, linear structure, and so on—but theirs will fall short of total appreciation.)

It follows that when 'p' refers to extrinsic information about a work, that piece of information will be *necessary* just to the extent that it brings about knowledge concerning an intrinsic property.

Let

$$\text{`}p_e\text{'} = \text{an extrinsic fact about W}$$

$$\text{`}p_i\text{'} = \text{an intrinsic fact about W}$$

Then,

Knowing p_e is necessary for the aesthetic appreciation of W if and only if without knowing p_e knowing p_i is not possible, and knowing p_i is necessary for aesthetic appreciation of W.

Needless to say, there will be critical arguments about precisely which p_is are crucial, and hence about which p_es are necessary. Amassing evidence in support of a claim typically consists of bringing a whole group of facts together; in building a case, a single fact rarely suffices, and a fact of a particular sort can often be left out. This is true in art just as it is in science, law, politics, medicine, and other areas. One may not need to know the blood type of the accused to decide whether he or she is guilty. And knowing the accused's blood type will not be enough to establish his or her guilt. One may not have to know a composer's intention to perceive that a work is a fugue; and simply knowing that the composer intended to write a fugue is certainly not enough to make it one.

Two different sets of evidence (p_e1, p_e2, p_e3) and (p_e4, p_e5, p_e6) may both point to p_i1. Two observers of W will quite probably bring two different cognitive stocks with them to their experience of W. In some cases, these cognitive stocks will intersect. For example, to know that a musical composition is a fugue (a p_i), both observers will need to possess a rough traditional definition of 'fugue' (a p_e). For two observers to know that the work is in the Baroque style, it need not be the case that there be some particular p_e that they share. However, the following weak claim is true: for everyone who aesthetically appreciates W, there must be some p_e (again, not necessarily the same particular piece of external information) that he or she knows.

There is an interplay of p_i and p_e: the more one learns, the more sustained one's attention is. One sees that the spear is missing and looks for features in the work that might explain it. One then notices the look on the face of the spearless warrior and thinks about war. These thoughts bring one to notice the way in which the artist has portrayed hand-to-hand combat. One then thinks about modern technological warfare and then looks back at the ways these warriors have been grouped in a phalanx, thereby requiring as well as permitting the artist to use a triangular composition, and so on and so forth. The distraction that Kitto worries will wipe out aesthetic experience materializes only when one stops looking or listening to valued intrinsic properties. As long as information continues to bring one back to those properties, distraction is not a danger. Tanya Rodriquez reports that upon learning something about the structure of contemporary Chinese families, in particular the fact that couples are legally required to have no more than one child, she noticed things in an exhibit at the San Francisco Museum of Modern Art's 1999 exhibit "Inside Out: New Chinese Art" that would have remained invisible otherwise. This is a good example of the way in which socially constructed relationships in the world are reflected in art—but visible only to the fluent observer.[10]

Thus far I have been describing aesthetic relevance in terms of the ways in which information draws attention to aesthetic features of objects and events. In doing so, I have suggested an epistemological test. But my characterization of 'aesthetic' not only requires that attention be directed at certain intrinsic properties but also requires that these features be *valued* within a particular culture's traditions. As I have said, any adequate account of aesthetic relevance must account for or at least be consistent with an explanation of why certain things and not others are aesthetically valued within a community. It has become so clear to contemporary observers that sources of aesthetic delight are not universal that it is almost embarrassing to point it out once again. One weakness of theories of aesthetic value that try to narrow or reduce this source of value is that they cannot account for the fact that some people cherish and love minimalist art or Russian icons, rap or atonal music, for instance, while others fear and hate them. But for my purposes here, the most serious weakness of such theories is that they fail to provide for the multiplicity of reasons that real people actually give for their preferences. Arthur Danto writes, "The moment something is considered an artwork, it becomes subject to interpretation. . . ."[11] In becoming subject to interpretation, a work also becomes subject to the offering up of various sorts of scrutiny. Putting limits on the kind of interpretation or scrutiny permitted, I believe, amounts to putting limits on the sources of aesthetic value. But there is no reason to place such limits, and doing so can deprive art itself of its relevance to the human condition. No single sort of explanation prevails, whether it be formalistic, emotional, economic, political, or whatever. People say all sorts of things, from "It is skillfully unified by a minor second," to "It reminds me of visits to my grandmother," to "I just like war stories," to "You could probably get a lot of money for that." I see *no* reason to rule out any of these, as long as one is reasonably certain that the speaker is, in fact, focusing on intrinsic properties traditionally identified as worthy of attention within a particular culture.

It is worth noting here that a person A can believe that a person B from a culture to which A does not belong is aesthetically delighting in something, even when A does not delight in that thing. The fact that I hate the noise does not prevent me from believing that others may be delighting in intrinsic properties of what they perceive as structured sounds. It was often arrogance and snobbery, I think, that led formalists to believe that theirs was the only genuine aesthetic experience. Such attitudes defeat in advance the possibility of one's ever hearing culturally unfamiliar sounds as wonderful music and not as horrible noise, and thus defeat an important goal of education.

This is not to say that all artworks are equally valuable. Horrible noise does exist, I think, and some works are better than others. Great art rewards sustained attention.[12] The greater the art (or more valuable the aesthetic object), the more it repays sustained attention. Attention is sustained in a variety of ways; I have previously tried to indicate how complex and how idiosyncratic the paths may be. One need only consider the vast literature on masterpieces such as *Hamlet* to discover the diverse payoffs that individuals in quite different times and places have garnered from it. By allowing a bit of external information (a p_e) that draws an observer to aesthetic properties to count as aesthetically relevant, one allows for and rejoices in this diversity. Any restriction, such as the formalistic requirement that one stick to talk of formal properties, only limits the possible rewards of aesthetic attention.

What follows from this characterization is the by no means original view that great art withstands the test of time.[13] Recently, several authors have criticized this test precisely on the ground that it precludes the diversity that I am seeking to allow. One such objection is forcefully and clearly articulated by Barbara Herrnstein-Smith:

> What is commonly referred to as 'the test of time' . . . is not, as the figure implies, an impersonal and impartial mechanism; for the cultural institutions through which it operates (schools, libraries, theaters, museums, publishing and printing houses, editorial boards, prize-awarding commissions, state censors, and so forth) are, of course, all managed by *persons* (who, by definition, are those with cultural power and commonly other forms of power as well); and, since the texts that are selected and preserved by 'time' will always tend to be those which 'fit' (and, indeed, have often been *designed* to fit) *their* characteristic needs, interests, resources, and purposes, that test mechanism has its own built-in partialities. . . . Also, as is often remarked, since those with cultural power tend to be members of socially, economically, and politically established classes (or to serve them and identify their own interests with theirs), the

texts that survive will tend to be those that appear to reflect and reinforce establishment ideologies. However much canonical works may seem to 'question' secular van-
ities, such as wealth, social position, and political power, 'remind' their readers of
more elevated values and virtues, and oblige them to 'confront' such hard truths and
harsh realities as their own mortality and the hidden griefs of obscure people, they
would not be found to please long and well if they were seen *radically* to undercut establishment interest or *effectively* to subvert the ideologies that support them.[14]

I am in complete agreement with Herrnstein-Smith that institutions that are dominant tend to restrict the things that are candidates for the test of time. Dominant,
oppressive cultures too often narrow the focus in their attempt to maintain and increase their power. This is true at the macro or global level, where, for example,
whole nations prevent artistic expression on the part of certain oppressed genders,
races, or religions, and at the micro level, where, for example, factions within even
tiny university departments struggle to define and control the canon. But I am
more optimistic than Herrnstein-Smith is. In short, I believe that the human spirit
is expressed even when oppressed. Within nondominant cultures, people seem always to manage to produce artworks. In spite of being dismissed or denigrated as
"women's work," some women's creations that do not (or did not before now) make
it into dominant institutions (museums, concert halls, publishing houses, etc.) do
last—and to that extent they do withstand the test of time. For example, knitting
and sewing patterns and techniques are passed on, sometimes institutionally
(through published pattern books), sometimes by informal apprenticeships and
"circles," and sometimes via oral traditions within a subculture. Those of us who
knit should not share in the denigration of our artworks, even if books about them
are found more often in supermarkets than in research libraries. If pattern books
or quilting techniques are not considered genuinely aesthetic by our oppressors,
this does not mean that the most interesting techniques or most beautiful stitch-
ing sequences do not meet or have not met the test of time. The same is true of
recipes. To discount a recipe for a state fair-winning apple pie or a particular
method of canning beans or advice on how to throw a curveball, for that matter, is
to become as elitist as those who seek to maintain domination. Herrnstein-Smith
gives away too much, I believe. In cultures where individual products are not permanent—for example sand paintings or individual jazz performances—the traditions that produce and shape them also are such that they stand the test of time,
and specific cases are judged accordingly.

Remember that my definitions of 'work of art', 'aesthetic', and 'aesthetic relevance' all revolve on attention to and reflection on intrinsic properties traditionally valued. As I look at an illustration in *Vogue Knitting* and read, "Norah Gaughan
channels her talents into a pullover with a cabled yoke tapering to a funnel neck. . . .
The twisted stitch rib and braided cable yoke smoothly descend to see stitch diamond sleeves and body; Crystal Palace bulky wool has just the right thickness,"[15] I
have what I believe is a genuine, recognizable aesthetic experience. Many passages
describing food and baseball also work this way—call attention to intrinsic properties considered worthy of attention in subcultures' aesthetic traditions.

What is best within any culture tends to get passed on, and so it does, in fact, pass the test of time. (Of course, individual works are sometimes destroyed, but the traditions in which they are created endure.) Admittedly, my optimism rests to some extent on faith, but justification for it comes from those nondominant cultures with which I have some familiarity, for example, knitting circles. Here, notions of 'better' and 'best' are fully meaningful, and practitioners are able to make recommendations about what is likely to reward sustained attention. This is why asking members of cultures other than those into which one was born to "send us your best" makes sense. Members with adequate cognitive stock and experience will know what to send, for they know what has withstood, and probably will continue to withstand, the test of time. They know what p_es are relevant and hence are in a position to offer advice about what we should learn and attend to. This advice will be as various, of course, as the cultures themselves.

Once one acknowledges the breadth and depth of considerations relevant to aesthetic experience and assessment, one begins to understand the impact that art (and other aesthetic objects and events) has on human life. One begins to grasp why and how art *permeates* life, and hence why one errs not in "confusing" art and life. One realizes how mistaken it is to advocate the separation of art and life. This is the point of Rilke's poem "Archaic Torso of Apollo," as crystallized in the final sentence. The impact of great sculpture is so powerful, Rilke asserts, that in its presence one realizes that:

> . . . here there is no place
> that does not see you. You must change your life.[16]

Agreeing with Rilke, Gadamer insists that the symbolic and festive nature of art overwhelms us.[17] Art elevates us "into a transformed state of being," he says.[18]

To say that art changes our lives, can, of course, be terribly sentimental. Phrases such as Gadamer's "transformed state of being" seem to require too much. Works of art, even the great ones, worse luck, do not always (even often?) make people more sensitive morally or psychologically or more intellectually acute. I will have more to say about this later but for now will make some more modest claims for art that relate to the notion of aesthetic relevance.

In *Painting as an Art*, Wollheim quotes Proust's remark to the effect that his delight in Chardin involved going from Chardin to reflecting on domesticity and back again: "If, looking at a Chardin, you can say to yourself: this is intimate, this is congenial, this is full of life like a kitchen, then you will be able to say to yourself, walking around a kitchen, This is strange, this is grand, this is beautiful, like a Chardin."[19] Proust was not necessarily better or wiser for having seen a Chardin, but he did see kitchens differently. We all have similar stories to tell, I believe. I like umbrellas more since I came to admire the work of Maurice Prendergast. In one sense, this is a trivial claim. As I said in an earlier chapter, when one has an aesthetic experience, one's senses and wits are engaged. This engagement often leads to an application of what we see in artworks to what we see in the world, and vice versa. Sitting in a restaurant overlooking the plaza next to the cathedral in Cologne, I could not help perceiving the movements of people crossing the square, stopping to chat, pausing to look up at the magnificent building, retracing their steps, and so on in terms of a dance. I could imagine how a great choreographer might replicate it—how the skateboarders might be suggested, for instance. And I considered whether the music of Bach or jazz or rock would be more appropriate. Even a person with passing interest in dance could have shared in my speculations—for appreciation of dance changes the way one perceives and reflects on human movement generally.

Art does not always suddenly transform one into a Muslim or a democrat or a Marxist—though it may contribute to such transformations. It does make one experience kitchens and umbrellas and blonde hair and crowds and birches and Lincoln and the Danube differently. It also opens one to and makes one more enthusiastic about seeking what other cultures have to offer. These "trivial" changes are, of course, potentially profound.

Thoughts of missing spears stimulated by ancient friezes do, through complex perceptive and reflective experiences that mark aesthetic attention, lead to thoughts of the nature of war. This is precisely why one must resist the demand that we stop asking about the missing spear. It is only by "confusing" art and life that we recognize how and why each is relevant to the other and that either fulfills its promise.

The Nature of Aesthetic Properties

In the attempt to explain the nature of aesthetic properties, philosophers have used a variety of distinctions borrowed from metaphysics and epistemology, for example, primary-secondary, objective-subjective emergent-nonemergent, intrinsic-extrinsic, descriptive-evaluative, physical-mental, rational-irrational, relative-absolute, and supervenient-nonsupervenient.[1] It would be very unfair to accuse aestheticians of muddling or muddying these distinctions, for they were muddy and muddled long before aestheticians got their hands on them. But aestheticians have added to the confusion. I cannot hope to clear up all of the distinctions and explain how they apply or do not apply to relations of aesthetic and ethical value. But because I use 'intrinsic' and 'extrinsic' so centrally in my characterization of 'aesthetic', it behooves me to say more about it than I have. And because contemporary discussions of this distinction in aesthetics often connect this distinction to that between supervenience and nonsupervenience, I shall relate the intrinsic-extrinsic pair to this one. Briefly stated, I believe that aesthetic properties are real and intrinsic but that they are not supervenient.

It is crucial, I believe, to ask first what "work" aestheticians are trying to do when appeal is made to these distinctions. That is, what question is one trying to answer, or what problem is one trying to solve? In an ongoing debate between Robert Wicks and Nick Zangwill,[2] the latter points explicitly to the fact that different writers sometimes talk past each other in the discussion. Zangwill correctly, I think, identifies Wicks's discussion as "epistemological," since Wicks does write that "the goal of supervenience is to articulate law-like regularities . . . between naturalistic and non-naturalistic properties,"[3] whereas Zangwill asserts that he himself is interested in "metaphysical" questions.[4] Zangwill believes, "The prime motivation for deploying the notion of supervenience has always been to allow that the relation between two sorts of properties is one of dependence without laws."[5] Whereas Wicks, he thinks, wants to explain why supervenience is of no help in illuminating how one might make predictions about what aesthetic properties something has (Zangwill agrees with this), Zangwill is concerned with illuminating the nature of aesthetic properties.

I think there are at least five different though related questions that the notion of supervenience has been brought in to help answer:

1. What is the relation between *ascribing* aesthetic properties to something and ascribing nonaesthetic properties to that thing?

2. How are aesthetic properties *related* to nonaesthetic properties?
3. How are nonaesthetic properties used to *justify aesthetic judgments*?
4. How can one show that aesthetic properties are *real*?
5. How can judgments which seem so personal ("I love Ruth Rendell's mysteries") also play a *role in interpersonal critical discussions* ("Ruth Rendell is a great mystery writer")? In other words, why are we pulled both in the direction of interpreting critical remarks as personal, subjective statements and in the direction of interpreting them as public, objective statements?[6]

Let us begin to clarify the aesthetician's task (try to answer the question, "What do aestheticians want?") by first integrating the metaphysical and epistemological issues. Let us combine 1 through 5 in this way: "How can one prove or rationally justify that an object has an aesthetic property?" The property can be a very general one like beauty (Zangwill calls these "verdictives") or a very specific one like sentimentality (Zangwill calls these "substantives").[7] In general, if one believes that O has some property F, then one believes that both O and F are real in some sense (and of course there are many senses of this). And one also believes, if one is rational, that one has an obligation to prove or justify one's belief that O has F. Proof or justification consists of showing that a property or set of properties, F, is related in some way to some other property or set of properties—say, G—and that, therefore, one can say

If O has G, then O has F.

'Related' can be interpreted in several ways, and when an aesthetic theorist chooses a particular relationship, he or she is often drawn to one of the metaphysical or epistemological distinctions that I listed at the beginning of this chapter. The relation between F and G might be any of the following or combinations thereof. (And for some theorists, they overlap.)

1. Scientific reduction: F can be wholly explained (indeed eliminated) in terms of G.
2. Semantic or conceptual equivalence: F means the same as G.
3. Causation: F is caused by G.
4. Logical or mathematical necessity: F can be deduced from or is entailed by G.
5. Emergence: F emerges from G.
6. Supervenience: F supervenes on G.

Aestheticians have used all of these bases of proof or justification in the attempt to show that aesthetic attributions are amenable to justification. Some of them emphasize or reinforce a belief held by many theorists (not only aestheticians) that there is something special about the nature of aesthetic properties—that they differ in essential ways from "natural" or "scientific" properties. Similar differences are often felt with respect to ethical properties, and, indeed, in these respects aesthetic and ethical properties are often compared, even equated. Ethical and aesthetic attributions are not claims about the world per se, it is often alleged. There is a personal involvement implied by these attributions that is lacking, or at least not necessary, in nonaesthetic or nonethical attributions. Or, it is often claimed, distinctions that play a role in nonaesthetic attributions are not present in aesthetic attributions: something can appear square or healthy but not really be square or healthy, but there is no appearance-reality distinction in the aesthetic case, some have argued. If something appears or seems beautiful or balanced, it is—end of story. It will become clear later that I do not accept all of these reasons for claiming that there are nontrivial differences between aesthetic and nonaesthetic properties. But it is helpful to keep them in mind when one asks why certain relations from the list (those relating Fs and Gs) have been found more applicable than others in aesthetic theories.

Recently, one of the most influential of these relations (not just in aesthetics, but in many fields of philosophy, perhaps all of them) is *supervenience*. Discussions of it often include reference to other of the distinctions (e.g., to reduction or necessity). But my primary interest in examining whether supervenience is part of what it is for something to be or not to be intrinsic.

Varieties of Supervenience and Their Problems

Supervenience gained its first prominence in the field of ethics, and G. E. Moore is generally credited with its initial significant use: "If a given thing possesses any kind of intrinsic value in a certain degree, then not only must that same thing possess it, under all circumstance, in the same degree, but also anything *exactly like it*, must under all circumstances possess it in exactly the same degree."[8] In 1952, R. M. Hare explained the concept via the following example: "First, let us take that characteristic of 'good' which has been called its supervenience. Suppose that we say, 'St. Francis was a good man.' It is logically impossible to say this and to maintain at the same time that there might have been another man placed exactly in the same circumstances as St. Francis, and who behaved in exactly the same way, but who differed from St. Francis in this respect only, that he was not a good man."[9]

For both philosophers, supervenience flagged an important feature of value properties. One can imagine two women, identical in all respects except that one is a brunette, the other a blond; one cannot imagine that one of these women is a virtuous person and the other not, if their behavior is identical. Nor can one imagine two women alike in all respects except that one is beautiful and the other not. (What Moore and Hare, initially at least, failed to note, if not to notice, is that even in the evaluative case there is an important *if*, that is, if 'same' includes *according to the same moral theory*. I shall return to this point later when I discuss the problem of interpreting 'same' more generally.)

Hare has more recently written that while his own first use of 'supervenience' was in an attempt to distinguish evaluative and descriptive terms, he now thinks that it is not just a feature of evaluative concepts but "of the wider class of judgments which have to have, at least in some minimal sense, reasons or grounds or explanations."[10] Thus, he thinks, one can logically distinguish 'nice' from 'blue' or 'hexahedral'. 'Blue' and 'not blue' predicated of otherwise identical rooms are not self-contradictory. 'Hexahedral' and 'not hexahedral' predicated of otherwise identical rooms are self-contradictory if 'otherwise identical' includes shape. 'Nice' and 'not nice' are simply always self-contradictory if predicated of otherwise identical rooms. This shows that there is a special relation between evaluative properties and nonevaluative ones, at least for those who want to claim that evaluative properties must be explained by reference to nonevaluative properties.

Another philosopher who has discussed supervenience in the context of moral philosophy, specifically with regard to the issue of moral realism, is Simon Blackburn. Supervenience, he claims, is one property of moral truths that creates a problem for the moral realist, at least when conjoined with the problem of entailment. The problem of entailment is that there is no moral proposition whose truth is entailed by any proposition ascribing natural (nonmoral) properties to its subject.[11] Coupled with supervenience, nonentailment makes it the case that whereas one may believe that a particular state of affairs may not entail, say, goodness, one may at the same time believe that if that state of affairs continues to obtain, it will continue to be good. How can one rationally believe the second of these, while also believing the first? In other words how can one rationally be a moral realist? We shall return to this issue in a bit.

'Supervenience' has often been used, no matter what the branch of philosophy, when one feels at the end of one's philosophical rope. As Hare puts it, "When one has on one's hands a somewhat mysterious relation between two things, it is very natural to cast around and look for analogous mysterious relations between other things which might have the same explanation."[12] For example, it has been utilized in the mysterious field of metaphysics, with the work of Jaegwon Kim at the forefront. Kim argues that supervenience is generally a relation of "dependence or determination between two families of properties *without* property-to-property connections between the families."[13] (This way of putting it shows why it is so attractive to aesthetic realists who at the same time deny the existence of aesthetic laws.) Supervenience makes sense of our belief, for example, that very different sorts of properties are related in lawlike ways. "Ordinary physical properties seem no more nomologically commensurable with fundamental microphysical properties than are mental properties. But this fact appears to have no tendency to diminish our conviction that microphysics is the fundamental science, and the processes that occur at the micro-level, together with the laws operative there, wholly determine everything that happens in the world."[14] (I do not agree with Kim that microphysics determines what happens at every level in the world. Consider what we might call the "political level." The predicate 'is our leader', for example, does not seem connected to or determined by the microphysical level the way 'is boiling' or 'is spherical' or even 'wants to go to Nairobi' does. I shall argue that aesthetic attributions are like political attributions in this respect.)

Some philosophers have rejected a type-type identity between mental and physical properties (pains in the knee and particular physical states cannot be identified generally, for instance) but retain a belief in token-token identity (the pain in my knee now is identical with or reducible to the particular physical state I am in now).[15] Thus, supervenience might be construed as relating particular nonaesthetic states of affairs with particular aesthetic attributions. James C. Klagge suggests something like this in the moral realm in his attempt to solve the problem

Blackburn proposes for the moral realist. Klagge puts Blackburn's objection this way: "Since the natural properties of an object do not necessarily determine its moral properties, it is puzzling that their persistence should guarantee the duplication of moral properties."[16] An attitude theorist, Klagge thinks, can admit that belief depends on facts in the world (and hence be a realist) while also holding that attitudes toward those states depend on the way people respond to those states on particular occasions. Now the necessary supervenient connection (no change in G without a change in F, and vice versa) comes to this: "If a thing of a certain naturalistic description has certain moral properties, then it is impossible that it should have been different in some moral respect without being different in some naturalistic respect."[17] This form of supervenience is consistent with nonentailment. (But, I shall argue later, it does not make the aesthetic relationship any less mysterious, nor is one able to do the "work" we want to do any better with this sort of supervenience than without it.)

Our worry here, of course, is how supervenience can or cannot help us to understand aesthetic properties. Thus, we turn to three discussions of how this concept does or does not help us explicitly here.

Philip Pettit is particularly interested in "working" to establish aesthetic realism. He begins by making three observations about aesthetic attributions. First, he claims that they are not the same as pictorial attributions, for example, color descriptions.[18] Second, he asserts that aesthetic attributions are "relatively primitive," that is, "if a characterization applies to one work, then it applies to any which subject to rectification for colors, is observationally indistinguishable from that work; there is no possibility of an unobservable difference affecting how the works are respectively characterized."[19] (I am not sure what the phrase "subject to rectification for colors" implies here. Does Pettit believe that colors can vary without aesthetic properties changing? If so, I think he needs to provide some examples to show that this is so. On the face of it, one would think that color alterations would affect enormous changes. Perhaps I just don't understand 'rectification' here.) Third, aesthetic attributions, according to Pettit, supervene on pictorial characteristics. "The indiscernibility of any two works with respect to their pictorial characterizations entails their aesthetic indiscernibility; equivalently, there cannot be an aesthetic difference between two works unless there is also a pictorial one."[20] I shall later argue that this last claim is false or, at best, trivial and misleading.

Pettit goes on to show that there is a version of aesthetic realism consistent with these three observations. As on Blackburn's analysis, supervenience, coupled with nonentailment, creates a problem for the aesthetic realist. Pettit, assuming that aesthetic properties supervene on nonaesthetic ones, must fiddle around with *entailment*. His strategy involves showing how the apparent "quasi-assertive" nature of aesthetic statements (in Crispin Wright's sense, where evidence presented cannot fail to command agreement unless the statement is misunderstood) disappears when one fully understands the role of perception in aesthetic attributions.[21] But such tinkering would perhaps not be necessary if the machinery of supervenience were not considered a necessary tool for doing the work at hand.

Jerrold Levinson also assumes that aesthetic properties are supervenient. His goal is to explain the particular form that this supervenience takes, and he opts for this: "(AS): Two objects (e.g. artworks) that differ a*esthetically* necessarily differ *non-aesthetically*."[22] That is, there could not be two objects that were aesthetically different yet nonaesthetically identical; fixing the nonaesthetic properties of an object fixes its aesthetic properties. Levinson then posits three kinds of nonaesthetic properties as the bases upon which aesthetic ones supervene: perceivable, nonperceivable, and contextual. He couples supervenience with emergence (instead of reductionism or condition-governedness) to provide a foundation for proving or rationally justifying the attribution of the aesthetic properties that seem to him so ontologically different from the nonaesthetic ones that one refers to in these proofs and justifications.

Justification—getting from nonaesthetic to aesthetic properties in the absence of laws—is John Bender's main concern, and I shall discuss his work again in the next chapter when I deal with aesthetic justification itself. However, his work is also relevant here. He increases the number of observations from the three that Pettit suggests to six, describing them as "common fare for aestheticians."[23] They may be common fare (though many would not find them palatable, for example, Wicks), and this is one reason that aesthetics is so often muddled, I think. They deserve close scrutiny.

The first "commonplace" is that "artworks and other aesthetic objects have both descriptive, structural, perceivable properties, such as certain lines, colors, notes, sentences, chemical properties, etc., and aesthetic properties such as balance, unity, tranquility, poise, charm, coherence, energy, grandness of design, etc. Pretty clearly, when conceived as universals, aesthetic properties are not identical to non-aesthetic ones."[24] I do not accept this a priori distinction. As I suggested previously, color may be an aesthetic property. The line between 'design' and 'grandness of design' is fuzzy, I believe. The "etc." at the end of the lists of both aesthetic and nonaesthetic properties that Bender provides is typical, unfortunately, of aesthetic writing. The assumption is that all readers know how to go on and provide for themselves additional items in each list; but I, for one, do not.

Bender's next two claims do seem correct to me. The second "commonplace" is that two objects with different nonaesthetic properties can be described by the same aesthetic term. Both wine and music can be balanced, for example. The third states, "There are, at least in general, no logical equivalences between aesthetic and non-aesthetic predications."[25] The sixth claim is rather more troublesome. "The most common and *apparently* most forceful strategy for justifying aesthetic judgments . . . is to cite those non-aesthetic properties of the thing which one believes are responsible for or result in the work's having the property one has claimed for it."[26] While it is certainly the case that people often cite nonaesthetic properties when explaining why they have attributed an aesthetic property to an object or event, I am not sure that this is, in fact, the most *common* practice. I suspect that, just as often, other aesthetic properties are pointed out.

However, it is the fourth and fifth claims that Bender takes essentially as givens with which I most strongly disagree. The fourth is "Short of imagining vast and

general alterations in human sensibilities, in order to change the aesthetic properties of any work it is necessary to change at least some of the non-aesthetic properties of that work," and the fifth is "Necessarily, if two artworks were to have precisely the same physical and sensory properties, they would have to have the same
aesthetic properties."[27] It is because I deny both of these that I am dubious about
the prospect for supervenience's doing much aesthetic work, for Bender correctly
believes that together they provide an imprecise but nevertheless close statement
of aesthetic supervenience. If two or three of the central claims are false, supervenience topples.

As I argued in chapter 1, aesthetic attributions are culture-bound. Thus, I do
not have to believe that someone must differ "sensibly" from me to grant that he
or she may apply different, even contradictory aesthetic terms to the same object
or event. Even I myself may, staying sensibly the same, come to apply different or
contradictory terms to an object whose nonaesthetic properties are stable—if, for
example, I put myself into different cultural shoes. (I shall expand on this point
later.)

Using the notions of supervenience developed by Kim and Blackburn, Bender
goes on to develop what he thinks is a more precise statement of aesthetic supervenience—retaining what he takes as the core truths expressed in his six claims. He
includes in the set of base properties not only particular nonaesthetic properties
but also their complements, for it is not just the properties that something actually
possesses that matter. It is also properties that the object explicitly lacks. For example, says Bender, the aesthetic properties of Brancusi's *The Bird* do not depend
on just polished surface, tapering curves, and seamlessness. Its aesthetic quality also
depends on the fact that it has not been splashed with blood. Bender acknowledges
that such an interpretation of supervenience goes well beyond the properties usually or actually cited in justifying that *The Bird* is, say, elegant; one must limit oneself to the *relevant* absent properties, and he admits that it may be difficult to give
instructions for doing this. Bender believes, however, that supervenience is necessary for the objectivity of aesthetic attributions, and so he is willing to tinker with
it until he has a version of it that seems to work.

Zangwill, incidentally, is also something of a "tinkerer." Whereas Bender extends
the base set of nonaesthetic properties from classes of sensory and physical properties to those plus their relevant complements, Zangwill is also willing to admit
certain extrinsic properties. He makes this move in a response to Wicks, who
rightly, both Zangwill and I think, insists that in order to specify the base set of nonaesthetic categories, one must assign a work to the correct "interpretive category."[28]
One will have to know whether one is dealing with a fugue or a sonnet. Zangwill
introduces the notion of A^*—the total conjunctive set of aesthetic properties of an
object.[29] And this set is what supervenes on the set of sensory, physical, and relevant extrinsic properties. Since critics rarely if ever talk about a work's A^*, this
strikes me as the act of a man desperate to save supervenience; this is a job for
Occam's razor if ever there were one. I do not think that supervenience is required
for the jobs that Bender and Zangwill want to do; I hope to show that their goals
can be accomplished without tinkering with what is already a messy situation.

Put simply, supervenience does not help because the distinctions on which it depends do not hold up. It is important to remember that supervenience was brought in to explain, as Hare put it, a mysterious relation between what seemed to be two different kinds of properties. Philosophers who use it assume that they (and the rest of us) know how to distinguish the two kinds. Some philosophers think this can be done in terms of one or more of the distinctions listed at the beginning of this chapter; the primary-secondary and objective-subjective distinctions have been particularly popular. Both secondariness and subjectivity point to what is thought to be an ontological dependence on some properties of a sentient being. But, as John McDowell has pointed out, there is nothing about the phenomenal nature of our experiences that distinguishes objective from subjective or primary from secondary qualities.[30] Ultimately, these distinctions depend on "an absolute conception of the world"—"a mode of investigation that gives us the world itself, as that against which all mere representations of it are to be measured."[31] If supervenience can carry its load only after such an absolute conception is forthcoming, it will not be helpful anytime soon, I fear.

Like reductionism or emergence, where one kind of property can be defined in terms of or comes forth from another kind of property, supervenience presupposes the existence of (and usually the ontological priority of) some *base set* of properties. Blackburn, for example, defines supervenience in this way: "Necessarily if x is F and G* (a set of facts) underlies F then anything else in state G* is also F."[32] Here a "set of facts" "underlies." In other writers, the base consists of a set of "natural" or "structural" or "physical" or "descriptive" properties. Aestheticians have used all of these terms but usually simply refer to "nonaesthetic properties." Blackburn himself acknowledges a problem with supervenience. "Of course, G* can contain all kinds of relational truths about the subject, truth about other things, and so on. In fact, one of the difficulties about thinking at all of this properly is that it rapidly becomes unclear just what can be allowed in our conception of the totality of G* states."[33] Is the century in which an object is produced a member of G* or a member of the set of nonaesthetic properties? If so, the apparent supervenience of properties like being realistic, exciting, graceful, or even beautiful begins to come into question. This is at the heart of my own skepticism concerning the usefulness of supervenience, and I shall say more about it later.

Statements of supervenience that do not explicitly mention two ontologically different sets (these tend to be early, nonformal articulations) nonetheless typically provide a "test" that supposedly enables one to make a distinction between the base properties and those that supervene on that base. The test can be stated as follows.

> TEST: If one can imagine two objects or events identical in all respects
> except that one has a property F and the other does not have property F,
> then F is not supervenient; if one cannot imagine two objects or events
> identical in all respects except that one has property F and the other does
> not have property F, then F is supervenient.

This test invites one to play a kind of "Can you, Can't you" game. In the early days, philosophers such as Hare believed that "I can't" marked off evaluative (ethical and aesthetic) properties. Recently, as we have seen, writers have been forced to admit the "I can't" does not provide an identifying mark of the evaluative, but accounts for a variety of "mysterious" connections.

Let us play a simple version of the game. Imagine two coffee mugs exactly alike in all respects except one. Which properties can one do this with, and which can't one do this with? Initially, one might provide the following lists.

CAN	CAN'T
Owned by Queen Elizabeth II	Delicate
Yellow	Holds twelve ounces
Is holding coffee now	Is shaped like a duck

Writers who rely on supervenience to explain the "mysterious" relation that seems to exist between some properties assume that everyone's intuitions will match and that they will thus be able to play this game without hesitation or doubt. But I find myself very quickly in a quandary. Where would 'is cylindrical' go? On the one hand, it seems to be a *Can*, for one might at first think it possible to imagine two coffee mugs of the same capacity, color, material, and height, one cylindrical and the other cubical. But wait—if the mugs have the same capacity, then they must either have different heights or different base widths. So 'cylindrical' must be a *Can't*. The *Can*s on the list (owned by Queen Elizabeth II, etc.) do seem right to me, but some of the *Can't*s begin to trouble me. If delicacy is a microphysical property, then it seems to be a *Can't*, but if it is a visual property, I *can* easily imagine two mugs identical in all respects except that one is delicate according to Dick but not according to Jane. One even begins to wonder about some so-called physical or sensory properties. Suppose the mugs are made from lead-based ceramic materials. Given different constitutions and susceptibilities, as Dick and Jane drink out of the mugs identical in all respects, Dick might find his mug poisonous, and Jane might find hers nonpoisonous.

Being poisonous, of course, like being to the left of or shorter than, is a relative predicate (not in the sense of being noncognitive, but in the sense of requiring two names or descriptions to fill out the predicate). So are many aesthetic properties, and thus supervenience fails to help explain anything special about aesthetic proof or rational justification. (I say more about this in the next chapter.) Just as we saw that it is not clear what counts as G^*, it is not clear how one is to interpret "in all respects" in the test. Does it or does it not include what Blackburn calls "relational truths"? The intuition behind supervenience is that when all base properties remain stable, the supervening properties must remain stable. All aesthetic attributions must remain stable if the underlying nonaesthetic attributions remain stable. But if relational truths ("made in the sixteenth century" or "seen by Jane," for instance) are included in the base, the test for supervenience breaks down—and we are no longer in possession of a helpful conceptual tool. Two objects particle-for-particle identical with one another viewed by two persons particle-for-particle identical with one another (or one person particle-for-particle self-identical on different occasions) in two cultures particle-for-particle identical will undoubtedly be given the same aesthetic attribution. This tells us nothing special about *aesthetic* attributions. It certainly does not distinguish them from perceptual, mental, moral, scientific, religious, economic, or political attributions or tell us how proof or rational justification can be carried out in the aesthetic realm if we thought there was a special problem there (one that did not exist, for example, in the scientific realm).

After acknowledging the problem of properly specifying the members of G^* and F, Blackburn states that supervenience demands that there be no "mixed worlds."[34] There can be worlds where all G^*s are F and worlds where all G^*s are not-F. I claim that in the case of aesthetic attributions what we have is precisely a "mixed world." My argument is straightforward. Supervenience can provide a lawlike relation that allows for proof or rational justification of aesthetic attributions and/or explain the nature of the aesthetic only if there are no mixed worlds and if the base properties and supervening properties can be clearly distinguished. In the aesthetic realm, there are mixed worlds, and base and supervening properties cannot be clearly distinguished. Therefore, supervenience does not provide the lawlike relation we are after or explain the nature of the aesthetic.

Certainly, one must agree that if everything about an object or event, everything about the viewer, and everything about the context of viewing (community, language, viewing conditions, history, time of viewing, time of utterance, etc.) remains stable, then if the viewer says, "O is F," he or she contradicts himself or herself in saying "O is not-F." But, to repeat what I said earlier, this is true of all attributions. Aesthetics must restrict the base set. For example, Pettit, as we saw, identifies the base as *pictorial* properties. But surely this will not be enough for all aesthetic properties to fall on the *Can't* side (i.e., be supervenient). If the background of the viewer, the century of production, or community traditions (all nonpictorial properties) do not remain stable, then two objects identical in all pictorial properties *can*, in fact, be imagined to be both F and not-F. Indiscernibility with respect to pictorial properties does not entail aesthetic indiscernibility, unless, of course, 'pictorial' is so broadly construed as to no longer be useful (or even meaningful). Pettit claims that the sense in which two paintings must be the same (pictorially) though they are said to be different, say, because their makers' motives differed, is not an "aesthetically interesting" difference.[35] I think he dismisses motivation much too quickly and easily. Imagine two pictorially indiscernible paintings: one is said by its maker to be a portrait of Aunt Mabel but has been described by its critics as a hopeless failure; the other has been titled by its maker *Scream in Purple and Green* and has been described by critics as an exciting abstract expressionist study. Are the makers' motives really aesthetically uninteresting? I will come back to the special case of the relevance of intentions later. For now, an even simpler example should suffice to make my point. If Dick likes yellow and Jane hates yellow, one and the same yellow coffee mug may be described by one as "beautiful" and by the other as "ugly."

Writers who rely on supervenience assume that the base set is not aesthetic. Monroe Beardsley explicitly begins a discussion of supervenience with the words, "Assuming that we can identify a class of A-attributions."[36] Pictorial, descriptive, structural, perceivable—whatever the chosen set, these are assumed by him (and others) not to be aesthetic. What are ruled out are such things as color, shapes, sounds, and movements. Being yellow or being loud, for example, is not aesthetic on such a view. Short of begging the question "Why?" the friends of supervenience must have a test for putting yellow or loud in a set of nonaesthetic properties rather than in a set of aesthetic properties. But they fail to provide one. As I have said repeatedly, they simply appeal to readers' intuitions, intuitions that I, for one, do not always share. I cannot, for example, accept an a priori announcement that color is not an aesthetic property or that there is a firm line between aesthetic attributions of 'grandness of design' and nonaesthetic attributions of 'designed' itself. Victoria Ball, in a review of psychological literature on color through 1965 shows how varied the role of the attribution of color has been[37]—and one assumes it has not become any simpler since then. Sometimes colors themselves seem to be the focus of aesthetic attributions, with references as simple as to "that shade of blue." Other times associations are emphasized (the "green of springtime"), emotions are involved—("furious red"), or compositional analysis is referred to—("delicately balanced pastels"). Color attributions are thus used in a variety of contexts and do a variety of descriptive jobs. To dismiss out of hand color per se as nonaesthetic is a serious mistake.

Goran Hermeren has insightfully enumerated a long list of different sorts of aesthetic qualities and has described their various ranges of application. He points, for instance, to comments on color, indications of unity, analysis of facts with an end of classifying works into styles or schools, and psychological speculation. He is interested in showing that interpretation and description cannot be separated; what he shows additionally is how "mixed" is the world of aesthetic attribution.[38]

I have elsewhere shown how an apparently "base" physical-sensory property, loudness, is used aesthetically. One eleventh-century writer praised the fact that a group of instruments and performers created "a considerable uproar in the hall."[39] My son once said to me after attending a performance of a Mahler symphony, "Wasn't it wonderful? Just when you thought it couldn't get any louder, it did!" I see no a priori reason to decide that "How wonderfully loud" is any less aesthetic than "How wonderfully balanced." Contemporary video art uses speed as a way to capture the notice of persons whose attention span is decreasing. In his work depicting the meeting of Elizabeth and the Virgin Mary, the video artist Bill Viola uses slow motion to great effect. But the fact that it is very slow is obvious to everyone. Is being slow a base property or an aesthetic property? I believe the question itself shows that the distinction breaks down.

What this shows is that the particular properties that figure in aesthetic attribution are culture-bound—a finding consistent with what I argued in chapter 1. If loudness or yellowness or cylindricalness or being designed (all candidates for base properties) are properties of an object, if it is considered worthy of attention in a culture, if a viewer shares the traditions of that culture, and if the viewer assents to "That object is loud (yellow, etc.),"[40] then that viewer indeed seems to be appreciating the object aesthetically, at least to some degree. We need have no further recourse to some property distinguishable ontologically and supervening upon loudness (or yellowness, etc.). Aestheticians have failed to notice how mixed the world of aesthetic attributions is, I believe, because they have concentrated on complex properties like being balanced or lilting or unified, and have failed to notice how often aesthetic enjoyment is a matter of attending to simple, "base" features of objects and events.

Norman Chase Gillespie comes at the impossibility of distinguishing ontologically different property sets (in a way required for supervenience to make sense) from another direction, but ultimately the point he makes is much the same as mine. "Suppose two paintings differ physically only in some minor way. Would that difference be a *nonaesthetic* difference? Only, I think, if that difference makes no aesthetic difference at all. But if the physical difference makes an aesthetic difference, it will satisfy the set of aesthetic predicates. So if there is a physical aspect of a painting that is aesthetically relevant, it will satisfy both physical and aesthetic predicates and thereby be *both* a physical and an aesthetic property of a painting."[41] Something can be both a physical property and an aesthetic (or moral) property, even if these are not reductionally equivalent. At most, there is a token-token, not a type-type identity. And if something can be both physical and aesthetic, there is no way of distinguishing the base from the supervenient.

Artistic Intentions as a Test Case

One particularly common, if controversial, sort of information that is often thought relevant to aesthetic discussion is that concerning artistic intentions. Intentions, I think, provide a good test case for the helpfulness of supervenience. Intentions are often cited when individuals attempt to describe or justify interpretations and evaluations of artworks. Does this make them part of the "base" set on which aesthetic properties are supposed to supervene? Uncovering difficulties that arise as one attempts to answer this question sheds further doubt on whether supervenience can do any of the work that aestheticians hope to do.

According to the definitions of 'art' and 'aesthetic' that I laid out in earlier chapters, when one has an aesthetic experience of an artwork, one's attention is directed at the intrinsic properties of the object or event. The problem of "locating" artworks is notoriously difficult. Which thing *is* Beethoven's *Fifth Symphony*, or Shakespeare's *Hamlet*? However one answers such questions, I insist that whenever one claims to be having an aesthetic experience, one must be able to point to intrinsic properties, and at least for the duration of the experience, those intrinsic properties must be fixed. This explains partly, I think, why friends of supervenience give so much weight to what they call "base properties." There must be some set of properties to which one attends which accounts for the experience that one has.

For now, let us consider texts that serve as the focus of aesthetic experiences. The following must be true, according to my theory.

- One attends to intrinsic properties of the text, where the text is identified in terms of some set of intrinsic properties.
- One takes pleasure or displeasure in the intrinsic properties.
- One realizes that one's pleasure or displeasure is caused by the intrinsic properties to which one attends.

Texts are, of course, made up of words in a certain order; therefore, when one attends aesthetically to texts, one must attend to those words in that order. The attribution of some aesthetic properties, for example, of 'joyous rhythm' will be possible just by attending to the words. But often just knowing what the words are is not enough. Literary interpretation consists in assigning meaning to the words, and this often entails construing the words as one speech act rather than another, as a request rather than a command, for instance. Often this cannot be done simply by considering the words; one must also attend to contextual facts or features, perhaps to the intention of a poet. The meaning of the term that picks out the property F to which one attends—'joyous' or 'warns', for example—will determine the kind of attention to the text that is required and will determine whether supplemental information is required. Extrinsic information will be relevant to deciding what intrinsic properties a work actually has. As we saw in chapter 2, paying attention to intrinsic properties is not precluded by, and indeed sometimes necessitates, attention to extrinsic properties.

Suppose we wonder whether a line of poetry has a particular intrinsic property. I claimed in chapter 2 that properties are intrinsic just in case one can verify that something has that property only by directly inspecting that thing. Obviously, we must look at or, in this case, read the work. Consider Robert Frost's poem "Spring Pools," in which the protagonist describes the pools of water that one finds alongside trees in early spring before the water has been sucked up by the roots to produce foliage.[42]

> These pools that, though in forests, still reflect
> The total sky almost without defect,
> And like the flowers beside them, chill and shiver,
> Will like the flowers beside them soon be gone.
> And yet not out by any brook or river,
> But up by roots to bring dark foliage on.
>
> The trees that have it in their pent-up buds
> To darken nature and be summer woods—
> Let them think twice before they use their powers
> To blot out and drink up and sweep away
> These flowery waters and these watery flowers
> From snow that melted only yesterday.

"Let them think twice," the poet writes, before they suck up the water, for this will only speed the processes and hurry the passage of seasons. Now, someone might ask, do these words constitute a request, of God or Mother Nature, perhaps, to slow down so that we, or maybe the trees, can better enjoy the moment? Or is it a warning to the trees to slow down because they are only hurrying on to their own death? Is the protagonist warning himself or reminding himself to slow down—to get his priorities straight? Is being a warning or a request an *intrinsic* property of the poem? I assert that it is, for one must inspect the poem directly in order to decide whether we have a request or a warning. Questions may remain after one has inspected the poem carefully. One can, nonetheless, determine that an object has aesthetic property F *or* G, for example, decide that the poetic line in question is a warning *or* a request. (And one can rule out other interpretations; the line is not a question or command or invitation.) Both warning and request are compatible with the words, so one can say it is either or, perhaps, even both. Knowing that Frost intended it to be a warning does not in itself make the words a warning. One cannot make words mean or do something just by willing it. But knowledge about Frost's intention does constitute one piece of evidence.

Suppose I read the words "Let them think twice" as a request of Mother Nature that, perhaps, displays self-protective irony of the sort Frost often uses.[43] I later somehow find out that Frost intended the words to be a warning. Then, attending to the intrinsic properties of this line and to the rest of the poem, I see that being a warning is also compatible with the words that I initially construed as a request. I may even come to see it as more compatible. Knowledge of the poet's intentions will lead to a particular interpretation that, in turn, directs my attention to other intrinsic properties of the words of the line in question and of the words of the poem of which this line is a subset. Authorial intentions do not *settle* the intrinsic properties, but they certainly constitute evidence that supplements direct attention to word sequence. As in conversations and other linguistic encounters, attributing the intrinsic property of being one kind of speech act rather than another requires direct attention to what is said, but also to where, why, and how it is said. In short, it requires attention to conventions governing linguistic interpretation. These conventions differ from one community to another. One can imagine a subculture in which it makes no sense at all for the words "Let them [trees] think twice" to constitute anything except a request.

Theorists who interpret 'intrinsic' metaphysically by using supervenience chafe at the claim that intrinsic properties are not settled forever—that a thing or event can (intrinsically) have one property for one viewer or community but not for another. But as I have shown previously, an epistemological interpretation of 'intrinsic'—one that does not require use of supervenience at all—results in its being perfectly reasonable to believe that different aesthetic properties are compatible with the same set of intrinsic properties. My position makes being an intrinsic or extrinsic property relative to beliefs, various sources of evidence, and community practices; a word sequence can constitute a warning in one community, but not in another. 'Is a warning' is nonetheless intrinsic and is thus a candidate for becoming an aesthetic property, should a community come to regard it as worthy of attention.

FOUR

Aesthetic Justification

ONE OF the central questions in aesthetics is whether aesthetic descriptions and evaluations can be rationally justified. A number of people, both inside and outside of philosophy, believe that aesthetic remarks are "subjective" in the sense that they are simply reports of individual preferences. But if this were true, there would be no more point to saying that a work of art is good or bad than there would be to saying that one does or does not like liver. Immanuel Kant is justifiably famous for his attempt to reconcile two conflicting intuitions: aesthetic statements, on the one hand, are expressions of the individual pleasure or pain a person feels with respect to something, and on the other hand these statements imply something about how others will react to the same objects. Indeed, he argued, though aesthetic judgments are statements about individual pleasure, they are also universal, for when one says, for instance, "That rose is beautiful," one implies that everyone ought to find it so.[1]

Kant's proposed solution is clever, but by no means universally accepted. So theorists look elsewhere for an explanation of why we engage in commenting about our aesthetic experiences and believe that we are obligated to give our reasons for judgments about the objects that give rise to them. When I remark that I do not like liver, it is not likely that I will be asked to state my reasons. If asked "Why don't you like liver," there seems little left to say except "I just don't like it, that's all." We might try to give an explanation—"Whenever liver was served in my home as a child, my brother always threw a fit"—but we do not claim to be saying anything about liver per se, or to be giving others reason to share our opinion. Aesthetic comments are not like this. We do expect ourselves and others to justify these claims. "Why do you think that movie is good" or "What's sentimental about that song?" does call for more than "It just is, that's all." Furthermore, we expect that reasons given for aesthetic judgments will be general—not just explanations of my own preferences, but reasons for others to share my opinion.

As I said at the beginning of the last chapter, one kind of "work" that aestheticians try to do is explaining how judgments which seem so personal also play a role in interpersonal critical language games. To do this work, aestheticians often turn to supervenience, for they believe that we justify aesthetic judgments by pointing to nonaesthetic properties. One current philosopher who is at the center of the circle of the friends of supervenience is John Bender. He has argued that justification without supervenience is nothing short of impossible. I have argued that the distinction between aesthetic and nonaesthetic properties collapses and that supervenience is meaningless and useless. How then, short of going down Kant's path, can I explain how aesthetic justification—that is, giving reasons for our aesthetic descriptions and evaluations—is possible?

Obviously, since 'intrinsic' is so central to my definition of 'art' and hence of 'aesthetic' and since it is to intrinsic properties that one points to explain why one describes one's experience as 'aesthetic' at all, justification will turn on explaining how reference to the intrinsic properties of an object or event justifies any descriptions or evaluations that one makes concerning it. Let me restate the relevant definitions here.

> A work of art is an artifact that is treated in aesthetically relevant ways, that is, treated in such a way that someone who is fluent in a culture is led to direct attention to intrinsic properties of the artifact that are considered worthy of attention (perception and/or reflection) within that culture; furthermore, the person who attends to the artifact and has what he or she would describe as an aesthetic experience is aware of the fact that it is the intrinsic properties of the artifact that are the cause of that experience.

> A is an aesthetic property of a work, W, in a culture, C, if and only if A is an intrinsic property of W and A is considered worthy of attention in C; that is, in C it is generally believed that attending to A (perceiving and/or reflecting upon A) will reward attention.

> A is an aesthetic property of O (an object or event) if and only if A is an intrinsic property of O and A is culturally identified as a property worthy of attention (i.e., of perception and reflection).

My test for being an intrinsic property is simple: do you have to look, listen, taste, smell, or feel for yourself to know if an object has a property or not? If so, it is intrinsic. Examples of intrinsic versus extrinsic will help.

INTRINSIC	EXTRINSIC
Is yellow	Was painted with paint bought in Mexico
Looks Indian	Was made in India
Is in seventeenth-century Baroque style	Was written in 1616
Expresses the frenzy of war	Was composed during World War I
Tastes bitter	Cost $330
Looks cheap	Hangs over Lincoln's bed in Springfield
Is loud	Was first performed in London
Is a warning	Was intended by Frost as a warning
Is frenzied	Caused a riot
Is complex	Was written by Henry James
Feels smooth	Was made using 3M #150 sandpaper
Smells beautiful	Is a rare orchid

Even readers who admit that my definition provides a crude distinction—will work to distinguish the extrinsic 'was made in India' (which can be shown to satisfy an object without direct inspection, for example, via archival research) from the intrinsic 'looks Indian' (which can be affirmed or denied by oneself only by looking, and then only if one is familiar enough with Indian art or culture to know what this predicate means, of course)—may still object that it disqualifies clear aesthetic properties. I admitted in the last chapter that there might be some question about 'represents Aunt Mabel', for example. Can someone tell just by looking at a painting whether this is true of it? Certainly, one must rely on some extrinsic information to know that something represents Aunt Mabel; one can't know just by looking unless one also knows who Aunt Mabel is, what she looks like, what the artist intended, how the painting is being used by Uncle Milton, and/or what constitutes portraiture in the community in which it was created. No single bit of evidence from this list may be enough; all of it may require supplementation. But what matters is that direct inspection is necessary, not that it is sufficient.

Another possible objection is this: surely artists and composers do not have to look or listen—they know that terms apply to their work before there is a physical embodiment to be perceived. Couldn't Beethoven make true aesthetic attributions about how his music sounded even after he went deaf? Here I think we nonartists must be generous, but something like a "mind's eye" or "mind's ear" will be required to explain what goes on. When I asked the British composer John Casken if he uses a piano to compose, he said, "I do now, because I no longer trust my ear."[2] "But surely," I responded, "you mean you no longer trust your brain—if you didn't trust your ear, a piano wouldn't help." After some discussion, he agreed it was his "mind's ear" he no longer trusted. I am willing to allow such an apparatus in my notions of 'direct inspection' or 'perceive for oneself'.

In earlier chapters, I argued that simply attending to intrinsic properties is rarely enough. I do not insist that one attend only to intrinsic properties—that one must not think about Aunt Mabel or the life of Beethoven or the sort of sandpaper that must have been used or the horrors of war. It does not follow from the necessity of direct inspection that one's experience must be restricted to attention to intrinsic properties. Sometimes one *must* consider certain kinds of extrinsic information in order to make aesthetic attributions whose focus is intrinsic properties. Martha Nussbaum gives the following insightful description of a scene in Henry James's *The Golden Bowl* between Maggie and Adam Verver: "What makes their embrace a wonderful achievement of love and mutual altruism is not the bare fact that it is an embrace; it is the precise tonality and quality of that embrace: that it is hard and long, expressive of deep passion on his side, yielding acceptance of that love on hers; yet dignified and austere, refusing the easy yielding to tears that might have cheapened it."[3] It is not just attention to intrinsic properties that makes it possible for Nussbaum to thus describe the scene. She is sensitive to the tonality of James's writing, but she also must think about relations between fathers and daughters, the responsibilities of love, and different ways and occasions of embracing. The intertwining of focus on intrinsic properties with extrinsic information is, I believe, one of the reasons that artworks have such a profound role in our lives. As I suggested before, we go back and forth between the work and the world. Scrutiny for oneself is necessary; but it is not sufficient, and it is by no means exclusive.

Two identical objects, as we have seen, may admit of different attributions. Suppose one object has been painted by a human being, the other produced by a snake moving through paint on a canvas. Both may be said to be "beautiful," but only the painting by a person can be said to be "well-executed." (Whether snake or ape or elephant productions are well executed will depend on how one's community agrees to define 'execute' and views snakes, apes, and elephants.) Both attributions demand attention to intrinsic properties, but attributing 'well-executed' demands a realization that someone had reasons for putting the paint where it is. One appreciates not just the paint but how it got where it is, where *how* is not just a matter of skill at manipulating the medium but also a matter of fitting the artifact into a context of freedom and responsibility; one perceives the object as a product of choice. One cannot appreciate something as a choice merely by looking, though one must, of course, look.

So how does all of this relate to the task of justification? I agree with Hare, who wrote, in the context of discussing the realist-antirealist dispute in ethics, that the bottom line is not settling an ontological dispute.[4] "What should concern us, rather, is how we should rationally determine, or satisfy ourselves, whether an act is right or wrong."[5] And, I would add, whether an object does or does not have the aesthetic property it is claimed to have. So how can my epistemological, nonsupervenient account of aesthetic properties lend itself to rational justification? Short of applying aesthetic laws, which if they exist have not yet come to light, how can we show whether something is beautiful or ugly, a warning or a request, moving or boring, looks Indian or does not?

Observation of the aesthetic activity of attributing properties to an object or event, combined with a proper understanding of 'intrinsic', shows us why and how people engage, if not in proof (which would, I think, require laws), then certainly in judgments for which one can provide rational justification. What goes on in such circumstances? People stand or sit in the presence of what they consider an aesthetic object or event. Sometimes they talk, and, I claim, when their remarks report on intrinsic properties of the object or event deemed worthy of attention within their community (and people can simultaneously belong to several communities), they are making aesthetic attributions. As discussion proceeds, the experiences of the participants often change. They see more, and what they see they see more clearly or deeply.

In chapter 2, I argued for the following definition of 'aesthetic relevance':

> A statement (or pointing gesture) is aesthetically relevant if and only if it draws attention (perception, reflection) to an aesthetic property.

Often (I believe even usually when one is fortunate enough to engage in aesthetic discussion with insightful attenders), aesthetically relevant remarks bring one to perceive and reflect in ways one would never have realized on one's own. Roger Scruton has made a remark about musical discussion that I believe applies to all the arts and to aesthetic discussion generally (to discussions about sunsets and storms as well as sambas and sonnets): "Although there is a sense in which we always know how things appear to us, the study of an appearance is appropriate when the concepts which inform it are not fully within the perceiver's grasp. I may see something as a snake, but have an imperfect grasp of snakehood: here there is something I could learn, which would change the appearance of what I see. Musical criticism has just such a 'change of appearance' as its goal."[6] One comes to perceive something that might have been missed or misunderstood or misconstrued.

What is crucial for understanding aesthetic justification is the realization that one's aesthetic attributions are grounded in intrinsic properties of an object or event. Suppose I stand in the presence of a yellow car. I have an idea of a yellow car. The idea, of course, is not yellow. But I realize that the idea I now have would not be of a yellow car unless I were in the presence of a car that is yellow. One might, probably will, of course, have other ideas; I may have an idea of this car in green or purple. The part of the experience that I want to emphasize is the realization that some of the ideas that I have now I have had in all likelihood because I am in the presence of and perceiving a yellow car.

In aesthetic experience, by analogy, one is in the presence of a painting of a yellow car. As in the case of seeing a car, there is no limit to what one can think about. One can have an idea of a painting of a yellow car and/or an idea of a yellow car and/or an idea of a painting of a green car and/or an idea of yellow sky and/or an idea of yellowness and/or an idea of driving a car and/or an idea of how paint is applied to a canvas and/or—the list is endless. The only restriction is that if one has an aesthetic experience of the painting, one must be conscious that one's experience is grounded in attention to intrinsic properties of the painting.[7]

In making an aesthetic attribution, one is conscious that the attribution is tied to and/or directed at intrinsic properties of an object or event. Rational justification amounts to providing adequate evidence; rational justification of aesthetic attributions amounts, then, to bringing someone to grant that evidence has been provided for that attribution. In aesthetics, this amounts to bringing someone to perceive for oneself once one understands the meaning of the terms used in the attribution.

Aesthetic objects and experiences of them are, of course, usually very complex. One may enjoy something simply because it is yellow and express that delight with a straightforward "Isn't it yellow!" But typically, more is involved. There is not simply a correspondence between an intrinsic property—a yellow patch, for instance—and an experience of something yellow; there are correspondences between the ways many intrinsic properties are related and the ideas thereby generated. A vermilion triangle next to a mauve oval above a magenta square, all arched by a cerise curve, gives rise to all of these ideas plus, perhaps, many more: ideas of sunsets or of Aunt Mabel's quilt or of studies of color compositions or—the list, as I have said before, is endless. Charles Altieri reminds us of what Wittgenstein said about this: "The color of the visual impression corresponds to the color of the object (this blotting paper looks pink to me, and is pink)—the shape of the visual impression to the shape of the object . . .—but what I perceive in the dawning of an aspect is not a property of the object, but an internal relation between it and other objects."[8] Then Altieri comments that "certain musical figures come to play significant roles in an entire piece, or understood in this context the entire piece takes on extraordinary resonant historical or thematic connections to other works. And yet the proliferation of connections can remain anchored in a specific and shareable picture."[9] Aesthetic experiences and hence attributions of aesthetic predicates to objects and events will, as I have said, vary tremendously from community to community. But since they must be anchored in intrinsic properties, it is always conceivable that within a community they will be rationally justifiable.

Rational justification of "O is A" consists in a speaker's bringing a hearer to agree that O is A, based on the listener's recognition that the speaker has provided good evidence for the statement. Agreement is possible because evidence is forthcoming, where the evidence consists of pointing to intrinsic properties via statements that members of the same community understand. There is no limit on what one can say as long as one realizes that the goal is getting the hearer to tie the statement to intrinsic properties—and thereby to focus on that property. One's own anchor then becomes (possibly) the anchor for another observer.

One points to intrinsic properties to justify aesthetic attribution because aesthetic attributions always grow out of and refer back to intrinsic properties. "The painting is unified." "Why do you say that?" "Well, just look at the way the cerise curve pulls together the vermilion triangle and the mauve oval supported by that magenta square." One does not make such comments because one believes that unity can be reduced to, equated with, emerges from, supervenes on, or is always caused by that set of properties, but because those color areas can be experienced as unified, and within a particular community may even be likely to be experienced as unified.

A drawing cannot be reduced to marks on a page. But given a full enough description of the marks and with adequate knowledge of the viewer and the viewer's culture, one can predict fairly well what sort of experience the viewer will have. I give you a piece of graph paper with numbered squares and a code for filling in colors (as people who do counted cross-stitch embroidery are given) and, Nelson Goodman notwithstanding,[10] you can produce a picture of a cow. Someone who knows a Holstein from a Jersey may even see a picture of the former. Someone who knows almost nothing of farm animals may recognize only that it is an animal of some kind. Via the same method, we can also produce a duck-rabbit figure. The duck-rabbit figure reminds us that supervenience does not help to explain aesthetic properties, because one and the same figure might occasion very different aesthetic responses. Suppose Jane is an intelligent adult with normal vision and lives in a duck-loving community where not only are there lots of real ducks but also lots of duck paintings, ceramic ducks, duck-shaped teapots, and the like. It is hard to believe that when she looks at a duck-rabbit figure she will fail to see a duck. But she may be utterly sick of ducks and so respond with boredom and describe what she sees as trite and sentimental. Her brother Dick, on the other hand, responds with glee and insists that this is an original, subtle drawing. Their older brother, Joe, having just discovered abstract expression, may insist that the picture is anxious. A visiting cousin from a community that has neither ducks nor rabbits and does have taboos against representing either may be puzzled—see only some marks on the paper. There are no guarantees that anything any of these folks say will produce agreement in the others. But it is certain that agreement will be forthcoming only if they point to and get others to see the intrinsic properties, and see them in similar ways.

We point to intrinsic properties, supplemented by extrinsic information, to justify a complex aesthetic remark, just as we point to the shape of an eye because we believe it may help someone to recognize a type of duck or Aunt Mabel. My definition of 'intrinsic' does not require that intrinsic properties exist prior to or independent of a viewer. Just as a viewer with a different visual mechanism may see green where I see red, so Jane may see as clumsy what Dick sees as graceful. Being red or graceful or looking like Aunt Mabel is anchored to epistemologically intrinsic properties, but there is no need to posit ontologically different classes of properties either to explain the aesthetic or to explain aesthetic justification. Sometimes an experience may be such that one immediately sees the duck or Aunt Mabel or gracefulness or beauty. Or a viewer may need help; one may need a great deal of additional pointing to other intrinsic properties or to extrinsic properties before these aspects "dawn" on one. One may even have to learn a whole different language (and the associated different forms of life) before one sees that a picture is beautiful or a portrait of Brother Sabi. "They all look (or sound or taste) alike"—until one knows more about them, whether 'they' refers to pictures of people of a different culture or avant-garde musical compositions or Russian icons or burgundies. We have to become deeply fluent in a culture before justification of aesthetic attributions can take place. We need sustained exposure and attention. However, if sustained perception and reflection bring us to see those intrinsic properties referred to by aesthetic terms, then aesthetic discussants do often reach the kind of agreement required for justification to make sense at all. An epistemological interpretation of 'intrinsic' enables one to do away with unnecessary, muddled metaphysical concepts that rest on nonexistent distinctions between different classes of properties and still account for rational, evidence-providing justification for a mixed bag of aesthetic remarks.

John Bender writes that "the justificatory process involves citing the work's properties and the relations among those properties that one thinks *cause* one to respond in such a way as to believe that the aesthetic concept F applies to the work."[11] I agree completely. As I have said previously, in aesthetic experiences one is conscious that the one's response is caused by intrinsic properties of the work. Where Bender and I disagree is that he believes that only by relying on supervenience can one account for those properties in such a way that one can save aesthetic realism and hence rational aesthetic justification. Bender worries, "If Eaton is ultimately correct in her injunction that we wean ourselves of supervenience, is there any hope for a view of aesthetic judgments and aesthetic justification more rigorous than subjectivism?"[12] I believe there are sources for such rationally supporting aesthetic judgments that exist without reliance on supervenience.

The topic of realism is so large as to be beyond the scope of this discussion, but a word must be said about what I think aesthetic realism amounts to, and ways in which it differs from scientific and moral realism. Both are relevant to an understanding of the nature of aesthetic justification. Scientific realists believe that there are states of the world, and hence facts about the world and statements describing those states, that are true independent of whether anyone believes them. Water is composed of certain chemicals, boils and freezes at particular temperatures, is needed to sustain organic life, and so on. These things are true regardless of whether people know or have evidence for them; indeed, states of the world are what they are regardless of whether there are any people at all. Theorists have described moral realism analogously. There are moral truths or facts, and these truths or facts are independent of the evidence for them.[13] Slavery is wrong, whether or not anyone believes or has evidence for this fact.

An analogous interpretation of aesthetic realism would require that there be aesthetic facts or truths independent of the evidence for them. Such a strong interpretation has few adherents, for the very meaning of aesthetic terms carries a subjective element; that is, aesthetic terms refer at least in part to the subject judging. (In my definition, being 'worthy of attention' and understanding 'intrinsic' epistemologically account for this element.) Even people who accept that water boils at a certain temperature or that slavery is wrong whether anyone believes it or not resist a view that insists that something—a rose, for instance—is beautiful whether anyone believes it or not. (There have been exceptions, of course. Plato did have a strong interpretation of aesthetic realism.) Most people are reluctant to insist that the works of Shakespeare would be valuable even if no one ever has believed or will ever believe that they are valuable. Something's having aesthetic value requires that someone have a valuable experience. Furthermore, that person must be caused by something to have some degree of satisfaction, and this degree of satisfaction is so closely integrated with the belief that something is aesthetically valuable that claims about possession of aesthetic value that are completely independent of belief or evidence are unacceptable. (This is by no means to claim that aesthetic statements are wholly reducible to statements about inner states of individuals.)

Thus, I take aesthetic realism to consist of the following. At least some aesthetic judgments of the form "Object O has property A" are true, and there are ways of adjudicating disputes about whether O is A. It is not the case that whatever anybody says about the aesthetic properties possessed or not possessed by O is as "good" in the sense of being as justifiable as whatever anybody else says. Radical relativism of this sort is false. Beauty may *in part* be in the eye of the beholder; that is, 'beauty' refers in part to the experience of some subjects. But beauty is not *simply* in the eye of the beholder. Evidence for the truth of aesthetic judgments requires more than reports of individual pleasures or pains.

Both Bender and I are realists of the weaker sort. That is, we believe that it is true or false that a movement is graceful, a painting allegorical, a symphony unified, or a poem a warning. Thus, we both demand that there be evidence relevant to determining the truth-value of such judgments. But truth or falsity is possible only if there is some way to ground an aesthetic judgment such as "*Mozart's G-Minor Symphony* is unified" in properties that are really in the object—in such things as the repetition of certain chords or patterns of rhythm or tonal intervals. Most aesthetic realists, including both Bender and myself, do not believe that there are *laws* that connect aesthetic judgments to nonaesthetic judgments. There are no true lawlike generalizations of the sort that stipulate that, for example, any symphony with a repetition of minor seconds will be unified. But if aesthetic realism is to stand, there must be some way of anchoring aesthetic judgments in properties of the objects or events they refer to. Bender is convinced that the only viable connection is supervenience: a property F supervenes on B if and only if as long as B remains stable, O will either be A or not-A. As long as what he calls the base properties (B) remain the same, the symphony will either be unified or not unified.

I do not think that supervenience does the trick. In chapter 3, I have stated my reasons for dismissing it. We cannot adequately characterize the set of base properties; there is no clear way to distinguish between aesthetic properties and the nonaesthetic properties on which they are supposed to supervene. Even if we could identify the set of base properties, it is possible for two things to be exactly alike with respect to base properties and for it still to be the case that one is A and the other not-A, for having an aesthetic property is a matter of being located within a community.

Someone like me who rejects supervenience but nonetheless wants to be an aesthetic realist must, Bender believes, accept the burden of showing how justification of an aesthetic judgment is possible. He thinks this cannot be done, but I have argued that it can. What goes on in the activity of justification—whether one justifies that it is raining or that women need not have regular mammograms until after they are fifty or that Hitler was evil or that Mozart's *G-Minor Symphony* is unified via minor seconds—is that reasons are given for making these claims; these reasons consist of providing grounds for belief for other members of one's community. And when members of a community share standards of evidence, rational justification is possible—in aesthetics as well as in science or ethics.

Bender implicitly believes that rational people will consider something evidence for something else only if they see a metaphysical connection; this is why he is wedded to supervenience. In the course of criticizing Alan Goldman for insisting that one must consider the role played by the tastes or values of a critic in arriving at an aesthetic judgment, he writes:

> [A] relativized supervenience is . . . no supervenience at all. Supervenience is a metaphysical and alethic dependency relation asserting that changes in supervenient properties arise only with changes in relevant base properties. The constraint we are left with after relativization is nothing more than the rather trivial, and epistemic, constraint of consistency upon rational judgments. It amounts to saying that from identical sets of features used as a basis for evaluation, and from the evaluative standards, the same evaluative conclusion rationally follows. Notice that this is true irrespective of what metaphysical relations, supervenience or otherwise, might connect the grounding properties and the inferred property.[14]

Bender suggests that trying to justify a claim in the absence of supervenience is to engage in nonsense. But justification is a matter of providing evidence and demonstrating rational consistency—of insisting that evidence in one case will be evidence in another. Justification is not genuine only in those cases where we believe that properties are metaphysically "in" something. When Tony Blair became prime minister in Great Britain, he did not undergo a metaphysical transformation; nonetheless, one can give evidence for his having attained that office. From where I now sit, the university's Student Union is to the north. The very same building can also be to the south, west, or east of other sitters. Or all around them, on every side.

I go beyond Goldman's inclusion of tastes and values of individuals to include standards and practices of communities. One kind of evidence that "our" community (the community of realists seeking rational explanations within certain, mainly Eurocentric, traditions) takes seriously is artistic intentions, something I considered as a kind of case study in the last chapter. We have seen that both warnings and requests are compatible with identical poetic words. What counts as evidence for one rather than the other will include the word sequence but also public conventions covering what distinguishes a request from a warning, the intentions of the poet, one's understanding of cultural norms of behavior, and similar factors—none of which it is unreasonable to consider.[15] Indeed, it seems unreasonable not to consider them. The fact that various interpretations are compatible with a single set of words does not mean that justifying the decision to choose one interpretation over another is impossible. What it does show is that justification does not require supervenience.

When one participates in an aesthetic discussion with others who expect to give and receive reasons for their judgments, one acknowledges that one's own aesthetic experience is anchored in intrinsic properties of objects and events that are regarded as worthy of attention—properties that one must perceive for oneself but that one also believes are perceivable by others. Any remark that draws attention to and gives insight into intrinsic properties of artworks acts both as pointer and justifier. The fact that different sets of intrinsic properties may be picked out in different cultures to support different descriptions and evaluations does not undermine aesthetic realism. Within the conventions of a particular community, a word sequence may really be a warning, and a sound sequence may really be unified by the repetition of minor seconds. Justification, I have tried to show, simply consists in pointing to epistemologically intrinsic properties in a context of rules, conventions, values, and tastes that operate within cultures. Relativity to cultural practices undermines supervenience; it does not result in the sort of relativity that undermines aesthetic justification and realism.

PART II

Taking the Aesthetic Seriously

In part I, I argued that aesthetic properties are intrinsic to objects and events. To this extent, formalist theories get it right: to have an aesthetic experience, it is necessary that one attend directly to objects and events and perceive and reflect upon their properties. But formalists go much further than this. They insist that aesthetic experiences preclude any other kind of attention or reflection. In particular, they typically single out moral considerations as incompatible with aesthetic attention. As Richard Posner puts it, "The moral content and consequences of literature are irrelevant to its value as literature."[1] Extending this claim to all of the arts, he describes moral content as "almost sheer distraction."[2] In part III, I shall show that since moral properties are sometimes, at least, inseparable from aesthetic properties of an artwork, it cannot be irrelevant, let alone distracting, to attend and reflect upon the moral when one experiences it. The necessity of attending to intrinsic properties of objects and events does not preclude connecting one's attention to other real-life concerns—to interests in truth and goodness especially. Indeed, grounding aesthetic properties as I have in cultural traditions and recognizing the extent to which aesthetic response is socially constructed require that one give due attention to ways in which our aesthetic values are connected to other life values.

In this part, I shall first say more about what I call "the separatist mistake," the mistake of insisting that aesthetic experiences preclude or are isolated from other kinds of experiences. I shall claim that the correct approach is one that recognizes that aesthetic experiences (constituted as they are by responses to aesthetic properties) are special, that they can be distinguished from nonaesthetic experiences (responses to nonaesthetic properties), but that they are not always separated or separable from them. "Different but inseparable" is the motto of the first chapter of this part.

Before turning in part III to a positive account of ways in which moral and aesthetic values are integrated, I want to advocate that the aesthetic be taken more seriously than it often has. Too often, the aesthetic is considered a "frill"—the last thing to be attended to after the more "serious" moral, economic, political, medical, and other matters have been tended to. Separatists often become separatists not because they demean the aesthetic but because they want to give it equal time, as it were. They have thought that by creating a special niche for the aesthetic, they can elevate it to the position it deserves. But, in fact, their insistence upon the "purity" of the aesthetic—its divorce from other concerns and values—has given comfort to those who devalue artistic and aesthetic pursuits.

I argue that separatism is a mistake, but that their motivation—trying to give the aesthetic its due—is admirable. In this part, I will introduce a nonseparatist account of the importance and seriousness of the aesthetic.

FIVE

The Separatist Mistake

A DEEP mistake has colored value theory.[1] The mistake is believing in the general separability of the aesthetic and the moral. This mistake extends to insisting that the aesthetic is separated from all other human ends and activities—the scientific, political, religious, economic, and so on. I am concerned with the aesthetic and the ethical, but I believe that much of what I say applies to the other areas of human value. A variety of factors have led to and reinforced this mistake. But first let us consider three examples that foreground the issue.

1. Gauguin: The example of the life of this French painter has recently figured in several writings of moral philosophers who discuss what is referred to as the "overridingness thesis." (I summarize this discussion later.) Gauguin, with some remorse, left or, to put it less neutrally, deserted his family in order to travel to Tahiti to devote himself to a kind of painting that he evidently believed he could succeed at only in that island environment. Many people, even those who could not themselves possibly turn their backs on familial obligations, appreciate, even admire his decision. How, as the philosophers who discuss this example so intriguingly put it, can one admire Gauguin's immorality?

2. A Goldfish Painting: I have been told that a Canadian artist creates bright and extremely interesting pictures by first dipping goldfish into pots of primary colors of paint and then placing them onto canvas surfaces. Their flipping about, at first frenzied and then sporadic as they die, produces unusual spatial, linear, and color effects. Some people, when told about the artistic procedure, insist that knowledge of it does not modify their positive aesthetic experience of this artist's work. Others—and my informal survey indicates that they constitute a majority—insist that it does change their aesthetic experience. Many members of both groups take a nonjudgmental attitude toward the responses of others. "Maybe it makes a difference to you, but it doesn't to me; that's okay—to each his own." "Yes, I can see that it might not make a difference to you, but it certainly does to me." However, some representatives of both groups view members of the other group with suspicion; they feel either that soft hearts let concern about a few cheap goldfish get in the way of a satisfying aesthetic experience or, on the other hand, that detachment from or disregard for the artistic process precludes an appropriate response.

3. Goody Two-Shoes: This character from children's fiction was probably created by Oliver Goldsmith, though there is some question about this. Few people have actually read the book that describes her life and urges young readers to model their own after it. Nonetheless, being a "goody two-shoes" is a fairly well-known epithet in popular English-speaking cultures; it is usually applied to someone who is shal-

low, mindlessly follows conventional moral rules just for the sake of following them, has no fun, seeks approval from authority figures, and is generally self-righteous and boring. A goody two-shoes cares more about the appearance of being good than about really doing the right thing. (This is why it would be a serious error to say that, for example, Mother Teresa was a goody two-shoes.) Having read the story about Goody, I believe that she has gotten a lot of bad press. (My critics will say that this is because I am a goody two-shoes, no doubt.) She devoted her life to helping and educating those less fortunate than herself. She was genuinely grateful for the smallest gifts, for getting two shoes instead of just one shoe, for instance. She married, came into a fortune, and shared it with others. Admittedly, she led a pretty boring life. But in many ways it was an admirable, if rather conventionally admirable, life. Is Goody more or less admirable or valuable than Gauguin or the artist who sacrificed goldfish to what she perceived was a greater artistic end?

Both popular and theoretical attitudes have supported the view that when one takes the aesthetic point of view moral considerations are to be put aside, and vice versa, or that aesthetic and moral values differ essentially in metaphysical or epistemological respects. In everyday discourse, it is not difficult to find apparently noncontradictory conjunctions of positive aesthetic and negative moral terms, or negative aesthetic and positive moral terms. There are handsome rascals and beautiful devils. People can be sloppy but kind, selfish but graceful. Who is so foolish or naïve as to believe that a course in drawing or art history makes one more virtuous, or that saints tend to create great works of art?

At the theoretical level, some philosophers (the eighteenth century abounds with them) have insisted that special psychophysical faculties function in aesthetic experience or judgment. Hume, for example, believed that judgments about the beautiful could be explained in terms of the operation of a special sense of taste. Deciding that a rose is beautiful depends on the proper operation of this sense, just as deciding that a rose is red depends on the proper operation of humans' color vision. Hutcheson posited two "internal" senses, one for moral and one for aesthetic judgments. And Kant, of course, carried the separation even further, by insisting that in aesthetic experiences, pure and practical reason play no role whatsoever.

Twentieth-century aesthetics has been marked in many circles by a drive to free aesthetic value of any dependence on the moral. There has thus been a strong formalistic strain that severely limits the properties considered aesthetically relevant. Formalists insist that only such features as color, shape, line, or volume in painting, rhyme, rhythm, or metaphoric images in poetry, and so on for the other arts are the proper focus of aesthetic attention and the true cause of a genuine aesthetic response. (See chapter 2 for a discussion of why I think aesthetic relevance extends beyond formal properties.) In contrast to nineteenth-century naturalism, utilitarianism, or romanticism, where maxims like "Beauty is as beauty does" were commonplace (and a motto Goody Two-Shoes would certainly have endorsed), critical schools of the twentieth century often dismissed any reference to artistic intentions or moral messages as distracting and out of place in aesthetic judgments.

Responding in part to nonobjective, "contentless" developments in art history, formalists seem intent on granting equal status to works that could not depend on derivative value arising from considerations of truth or goodness. "Separate but equal" is one way of articulating their view that works of art with no discernible moral value may be worthy of aesthetic praise.

Moral value has rarely been thought to depend on such formal features as beauty or gracefulness or harmony or dramatic rhythms.[2] And this attitude exemplifies a strong strain in moral philosophy (and perhaps Eurocentric cultures generally), namely, the inclination to consider moral concerns as more important than aesthetic concerns. However, "separate but maybe not always superior" is a way of expressing a growing worry among some moral philosophers, who increasingly, if sometimes grudgingly, admit that perhaps aesthetic value does not always take a back seat to moral value.

Previously, when I introduced the example of Gauguin's alleged "admirable immorality," I referred to a controversy in contemporary moral philosophy that addresses this question of whether moral value always supersedes aesthetic value, a debate over what is called the "overridingness thesis." A survey of some of the most widely discussed articles on this topic shows that some theorists are willing to grant status to some aesthetic considerations at least equal to that of some moral considerations. However, in doing so, they reinforce the separation of the two and hence further entrench the mistake of so doing. Nonetheless, the debate itself can point in the direction of correcting the separatist error, and it is primarily for this reason that I shall discuss it here at some length.

In a 1978 paper "Are Moral Considerations Overriding?" Philippa Foot discusses D. Z. Phillips's view that moral considerations must be the most important sort for anyone who cares about morality.[3] Foot believes that this is simply false—that moral considerations are not always more important than other kinds of interests. A sizable financial cost, for example, will not be overridden by a small moral concern such as the fact that someone might feel minor embarrassment. Often, people say that they know what they are doing is wrong but still think it must be done—to save one's family or even to give themselves pleasure, for instance. Though they do care about morality in general, in specific cases they will not even feel very much remorse.

Foot was among the first to claim that moral considerations do not always override; later writers are interested in cases in which putting other types of considerations first actually seems admirable. They focus on cases of what they call "admirable immorality," such as Gauguin's decision to put his painting before his family. Michael Slote's paper on this topic is, perhaps, the most influential.[4] He wants to show "that common [nonphilosophical] sense is right to reject the proposed limits on what is a virtue or personal good."[5] In particular, he wants to show that there are admirable though immoral character traits and virtues. Do not confuse this, he warns, with cases of admiring admirable traits in overall immoral people or actions. Admiration for daring robbers is not a case of approving an immorality, for the daring can be separated off; we can imagine the same trait put to an admirable, moral end.

Slote has in mind a radically different case—one first presented by Bernard Williams in his paper "Moral Luck."[6] Williams there talks about Gauguin's decision to desert his family and go to Tahiti to paint. (Williams, incidentally, thinks that the only thing that justifies Gauguin's decision is "success itself."[7] I shall discuss this claim later.) Slote insists that Gauguin's single-minded devotion to an aesthetic good, with the result that he hurt his family, cannot be separated off the way that the robber's daring can, for single-mindedness *demands* neglecting many considerations, including moral ones. Such devotion is a good that seems to entail wrongdoing, in a way that daring does not demand doing evil things.[8]

Artistic single-mindedness is not a generally good thing, Slote says, for there is no reason to expect that its general consequences will be worthwhile. "Gauguin's single-mindedness is thus, if anything, a morally *un*justified motive or character trait, and any virtue we find in it, any admiration we feel for it, is predominantly *not* of a moral kind."[9] Thus, Slote thinks that admiration of Gauguin's Tahiti venture is a genuine case of admiring immorality, that is, an example of overriding the overridingness thesis.

Owen Flanagan identifies three versions of the overridingness thesis:

- Strong: Immoral behavior as such is sometimes admirable.
- Weak: Sometimes certain nonmoral features of immoral actions are admirable, as are some features of persons that are contingently associated with the commission of immoral acts.
- Intermediate: Sometimes certain admirable features of persons are "intrinsically connected" with immorality. Such features cannot be admired without that admiration also accruing to or carrying over to the immorality.[10]

Slote, Flanagan says, denies the strong thesis, thinks the weak thesis is obvious, and so argues for the intermediate thesis. Although Flanagan does not buy the overridingness thesis, he does think there are no cases that satisfy the intermediate thesis. Three things need to be satisfied, he claims, for the intermediate thesis to be satisfied:

1. Immorality has occurred.
2. Traits of the agent are admired.
3. These traits are "intrinsically connected" to the immorality.

It is easy, he thinks, to imagine disagreement about the first and second, because admiration for particular character traits is invariably conditioned. The traits cannot be excessive, for instance. Furthermore, on certain moral theories, the acts associated with the traits may be moral, not immoral.

Even supposing that 1 and 2 hold, there are three senses of 'intrinsic connection'.

- The action would not have been immoral without a particular trait's entering into it. (For example, it is because Gauguin craved fame that his leaving is immoral.)
- No token of an action type could occur without a token of that trait's figuring in the action's production. (Gauguin would never have left if he had not craved fame.)
- Possession of a trait is sufficient for immorality. (Gauguin's craving for fame is sufficient to make us disapprove of him.)

The last, Flanagan says, is clearly false; there are no examples of immorality that results simply from defects of character. There are so many examples of the first that it will not serve to distinguish between Gauguin and a daring robber. So the second must hold—but it does not, unless it is terribly watered down, that is, unless it is interpreted as claiming that artistic passion is necessary for the kinds of immorality caused by artistic passion.

Admiration of character traits, Flanagan writes, is based on "the views we have about over-all personal bearing. . . . The wily spy has an admirable trait relative to his job description, but this very same trait, if it carries over to his family life and friendships, will quite possibly end up implicated in an immorality."[11] While this may be true of the wiliness of a spy, it is not true, I think, of the single-mindedness that one may admire in Gauguin. It is precisely the "carryover" effect that matters here. If Gauguin were not passionately single-minded in ways that affect *all* of his life, one would not forgive, let alone admire, his willingness to desert his family and live with his guilt. I shall return to this point later.

Flanagan concludes that the overridingness thesis will not be shown wrong via admirable immorality. Like Foot, he prefers a view that identifies acts as genuinely immoral, but nonetheless necessary or at least justifiable. He also agrees with a position that Susan Wolf takes in her paper "Moral Saints," that being thoroughly good is incompatible with our idea of a desirable personal life.[12] (Here we see the relevance of Goody Two-Shoes.) Wolf writes that a person may be *perfectly wonderful* without being *perfectly moral*. Wanting to be a good cook, for example, will get in the way of being a moral saint.

Flanagan thinks that the possibility of wonderful though not thoroughly moral lives shows that the overridingness thesis is wrong with respect to what is morally *ideal* and even with respect to what is morally *required*. It is wrong here because "qua philosophical thesis it lacks content and does little action-guiding or dispute-resolving work."[13] It is no help in a society where there are disputes about what constitutes morality and about what is morally required. Wolf reads incompatibility between what is morally ideal and personally ideal in terms of differing points of view. Flanagan prefers to attack the overridingness thesis via a "direct assault on moral realism."[14] We can, he thinks, talk about the good life—"about actual and possible worlds and the visions of humans flourishing therein"[15]—without talking about "the moral" per se or thinking that it is primary.

Flanagan's hunch that some people might not agree with Slote's moral assessment of the examples he discusses is borne out by Marcia Baron.[16] In particular, Baron does not conclude that the agents discussed really feel that on the whole they are doing the wrong thing. Surely she is correct that Gauguin felt some justification for going to Tahiti. I will spell this out in more detail later. For now, I want to suggest that Gauguin is choosing what appears to him to be a more *meaningful* life—and recognized that remorse was part of the price he had to pay because it is never possible to "have it all." What finally shows up the overridingness thesis, I believe, is the existence of real dilemmas, where we recognize that not everyone will choose the same thing, and that different choices can be justified. (See chapter 6.) A cook who says, "Don't you see—I had to try to prepare the perfect meal?" may be admired for single-mindedness if the choice entailed hard work, dedication, and sacrifices. He or she will probably not be admired if the outcome was sought for merely material gain or short-term gratification. Further, as Baron says, we admire single-mindedness only if it knows some bounds. And those bounds are moral. For example, most people would not admire a cook who killed for fresh eggs, or Gauguin if he had killed for art supplies. So, like the daring of the robber, even single-mindedness can be separated off.

Richard McCarty also represents the group that Flanagan predicts will not accept Slote's analysis. He believes that Slote has not proven that admirable immorality negates the overridingness thesis but only that it may be difficult to *understand* how an immorality can be admired by someone who thinks the overridingness thesis is true. McCarty argues that, strange as it may seem, Kant's moral theory can explain how someone who adheres to the principle that moral considerations are always primary could still admire Gauguin's desertion of his family. According to McCarty, the Kantian notion of enthusiasm—sublime commitment to some good characterized by single-minded pursuit of that good—accounts for admiration that is not inconsistent with an inability to justify the desertion on moral grounds.[17] McCarty also believes, "Contrary to Slote's suggestions . . . admitting the possibility of . . . contra-moral virtues does not require rejecting morality's overridingness, provided we take a suitably broad view of the scope of morality."[18] I shall argue later that it is a suitably broad view of ethics that is required—one that points at how aesthetics and ethics are connected.

All of the discussants we have looked at separate the moral from other considerations, particularly, for our purposes, from aesthetic considerations. Whether they deny the overridingness thesis, as Foot and Slote do, or accept it by enfolding other considerations into a broad view of morality, as Flanagan, Baron, and McCarty do, they still put the moral and the aesthetic into distinct and disparate categories. This, I believe, is at least sometimes a mistake, and it is a mistake that incorrectly points to a separation between moral and aesthetic experience and value. Our experiences, our encounters with and in the world, and the decisions we make as a result do not typically come in separate packets, with the moral, aesthetic, economic, religious, political, scientific, and so on serving as viewing stands distanced from one another so that we look at the world first from one and then from another standpoint. I do not claim that aesthetic experiences or considerations are never separable from other sorts. What I insist is that it is *not a requirement* of the aesthetic that all other interests or concerns are blocked off or out.

There are, undeniably, situations in which things true of an object, perceiver, or context result in an experience in which one type of consideration wipes out all others. Moral, aesthetic, economic, scientific, and other considerations—all of these individually are potentially so important that on specific occasions one may be unable even to think about any of the others. Concern for a child may blind one to economic or aesthetic or political aspects. Aesthetic interest may erase concern for the pain of goldfish. And so on for all the others.

A comparison of the famous duck-rabbit figure helps here. The figure itself, the background, interests, psychology, or physiology of the observer, or the context of

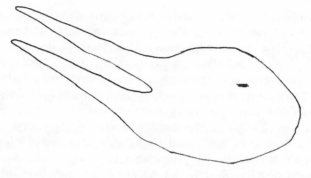

FIGURE 1

viewing may make it impossible for an observer to see the rabbit. But, of course, this is not the only possibility. Usually the situation with which we are more familiar—that in which we shift rather easily back and forth between the duck and the rabbit—obtains. Similarly, the blocking of the aesthetic by the moral, or vice versa, is not the only possibility. At will, we may sometimes consider first the moral features of something, then the aesthetic, and then the moral again. (And other aspects—the economic, parental, etc.—are possible candidates here; I am limiting myself to the aesthetic and moral.) One assesses Gauguin morally and then aesthetically. One looks at the goldfish painting first in terms of formal features and then considers the moral aspects of its production. These are different, and sometimes separable.

In part I, I defined 'aesthetic' in a way that highlights differences between the aesthetic and the moral.

A is an aesthetic property of O (an object or event) if and only if A is an intrinsic property of O and A is culturally identified as a property worthy of attention (i.e., of perception and reflection.)

Aesthetic experience and aesthetic considerations, it follows, will be directed at these intrinsic features, understood epistemologically as explained in part I. Formal and expressive properties like color or treatment of nature or the speech act performed by a protagonist are paradigmatic instances of the aesthetic.

Typically, moral considerations turn toward extrinsic features, the consequences or principles being followed. These are features that cannot be directly perceived in a person or in the action that he or she performs. It might seem to follow that, as with the duck-rabbit, where you cannot see both animals simultaneously, a shift from the aesthetic is required before one can see the moral, and conversely. But this inference does not hold, I believe. What is wrong is the claim that when one looks, reads, or listens to works of art or aesthetic objects, the only genuinely aesthetic experiences are those solely or exclusively directed at intrinsic features. Or, to put it another way, it is false that the intrusion of any other kind of consideration necessarily destroys or dilutes an aesthetic experience. Although attending to intrinsic features considered worthy of attention within a community that shares cultural traditions is a necessary and sufficient condition of aesthetic experience, it does not follow that attending to or reflecting upon other features at the same time dilutes or erases aesthetic experience. Thinking that it does is one version of the separatist mistake—one upon which is based the strong formalist view that insists that genuine aesthetic experience is necessarily devoid of any and all attention to features that go beyond an object's immediately presented properties.

A weaker version of the separatist mistake admits that the aesthetic-moral is not like the duck-rabbit, that is, agrees that there is not anything like a gestalt shift involved, but still insists that the aesthetic and the moral are completely different—analogous more to size and color properties. Of course, on this view, one can see both that something is red and that it is tall at the same time, but nonetheless one can always think of the one property wholly independently of the other. Likewise, one might notice simultaneously that an action is graceful and evil, but one will be wholly able to abstract the gracefulness from the evilness. I believe that even this weaker version is wrong.

The incorrectness of both versions of the separatist mistake becomes clearer when one considers an interesting case: sentimentality. I discuss this fascinating "ethico-aesthetic" concept in chapter 9. Here, it is interesting chiefly because works like *Goody Two-Shoes* are precisely the sort often described as sentimental, and people who are called goody two-shoes often suffer from some of the defects associated with sentimentality. We use 'sentimental' to describe both people and artworks, and I shall argue that when we do we apply moral and aesthetic considerations simultaneously. Works of art are judged to be sentimental because of content, facts about the artist, effects on the audience, or formal properties that they possess. All of these judgments demand reference to what are typically taken to be moral principles or consequences and also to intrinsic properties of the object. One must know, for example, something about how people react to death or unrequited love before one can decide that these topics are being treated sentimentally in a song or novel, and this takes us beyond the song or novel per se. Moral uses of 'sentimental' depend on what is typically taken to be aesthetic considerations, for attention must be given to intrinsic features—*how* something is done, as well as *what* is done. The superficiality or excess that often marks sentimentality resides in intrinsic features of a person or her or his actions. It is not enough to know that Goody Two-Shoes expressed gratitude for having two shoes, not just one, to accuse her of being sentimental. Intrinsic qualities—degree or means of expression, for instance—must be given due attention, and extrinsic features such as the appropriateness of her response to the situation are also relevant. Evaluation of Goldsmith's portrayal of Goody as sentimental or not also requires attention to both what he tells us and how he presents it—to form and content at the same time. If the aesthetic and moral were separable, two different sets of criteria would be involved in each sort of assessment. If version one of the separatist mistake were correct, something like seeing the duck-rabbit figure (where we look first at the duck and then at the rabbit) would characterize our judgings: we should be able to notice that something is morally sentimental or aesthetically sentimental, but not notice both simultaneously. If the second, weaker version of the separatist mistake were correct, we should be able to consider moral sentimentality wholly independently of aesthetic sentimentality and vice versa. However, to use 'sentimental' we *must* look at intrinsic and extrinsic features at the same time. Form and content in this case cannot be pulled apart.

The separatist mistake is generally reinforced by members of both sides of the overridingness controversy. The very question "Do considerations like x always override considerations like y?" makes sense only if x and y are always separable. If they are not, the question is misleading. One way of avoiding the mistake is to see that admiration is often not purely moral *or* aesthetic, but an aggregation of both. And I shall argue later for an even stronger point: admiration should not be segregated, for this precludes a rational life.

Before getting to that, however, I want to discuss aestheticians who have made the separatist mistake, for it is not only moral philosophers who have muddied the waters. Art theorists in the first quarter of the twentieth century argued for a strong formalist position—one that insists that aesthetic experience totally excludes concern with anything except manifest properties of objects or events. In particular, they insisted that moral considerations be separated from aesthetic ones.[19] These strong formalists have recently undergone severe criticism by myself and others, and I have already shown why I think this criticism is well founded. However, two respected aesthetic theorists from the last quarter of the twentieth century, Peter Lamarque and Stein Haugom Olsen, present a weaker version of a view that insists on the difference between and separation of the aesthetic and the moral. They argue that the aesthetic value of narrative fiction (and, by implication of other art forms) is different and separable from any moral value that might attach to it. They do not deny *that* content matters to an aesthetic experience (as strong formalists insisted), but they do put a limit on *how* content can matter. Literature is not disconnected from truth and knowledge of the world, but there is nothing integral to the value of literature that "makes expression, embodiment, revelation, etc. of truths indispensable to their value."[20] Works of literature are, of course, *about* something, and what they are about matters to the reader's experience. But this "aboutness" is of a special kind, one that has to be explained not in terms of matching the world but in terms of thematic content and structure that is within the work itself. "We must avoid the trap of aestheticism, which cuts off fiction (or art) from the world, but we must also avoid the indulgent pursuit of special kinds of reference and truth."[21]

This special feature of narrative fiction follows, these authors argue, when one correctly understands the character of this linguistic entity and persons' responses to it. Writing and reading fiction are interrelated practices that involve following "the conditions governing the way descriptions are presented, the purpose they seek to fulfill, the responses they elicit."[22] Writers present word sequences that invite readers to intentionally make believe that they are being told something about people who may or may not exist, and both authors and readers recognize that there is no engagement of "standard speech act commitments [involving] inferences from a fictive utterance back to the speaker or writer, in particular inferences about beliefs."[23] The fact that as readers we know that we are not supposed to infer anything about the world or form any new beliefs shapes the response that we have. We "entertain" statements made about people and things, but we do not make any judgment about their truth or falsity, according to Lamarque and Olsen. We recognize that an act of creative imagination produced the story; we "construe" passages—recognize that the elements go together in a unified, patterned way. We even find some of them of great human interest. But all of this is achieved without commitments on the part of the creator or the reader to any assertions being made about the world.[24]

In chapters 10 and 11, when I come to discuss that nature of narrative art and its relation to ethics, I will say more about Lamarque and Olsen's theory of narrative. Here, I want to concentrate on their insistence on the separability of fictional value from truth or moral insight. They grant that part of the value of fiction (and art) is its human interest—and this interest is directed to what they call the "themes" of narrative literature. These are organizing propositions that create intelligible patterns of events and situations. Lamarque discusses these themes more explicitly in his paper "Tragedy and Moral Value," where he again warns that "the search for moral wisdom in the great works of tragedy . . . can become just another form of appropriation, losing sight of what is truly distinctive about tragedy conceived as literature or art."[25] Again, his fear is that the special value of literature will be overlooked: the value that resides at least as much in the response to the mode of telling as in what a story is about. Moral principles become literary themes when they are tied to a particular work and its specific features. Their importance and value are as organizers of intrinsic properties of the work rather than as asserters of independent moral truths about the world, he insists. It is the former that enhances understanding of a work and sheds light on specific elements. A radical difference between themes and assertions calls for radically different kinds of assessment.[26]

My quarrel with Lamarque and Olsen stems not from their claim that works are organized by themes but from their claim that something cannot simultaneously be a theme and an assertion. Why must there be a radical difference? Why cannot one, as I proposed in chapter 2, go back and forth and back and forth between a work and the world? Interpretation, they propose, is a matter of applying concepts to works in such a way that themes are both discovered and constructed; it does not go the other way. That is, they think that aesthetic response does not involve applying concepts uncovered in works to the world. "A literary work 'implies' general propositions only in the sense that the practice of literary appreciation makes use of such propositions to organize into an intelligible pattern the events, and situations described in literary works."[27] I certainly agree that attention must be paid to the work, but I do not see why this precludes also paying attention to the world. We expect to find themes in narrative fiction, but I think another part of our expectation (though admittedly one that we recognize may not be fulfilled) is finding themes that have some relevance to the world. Works can help us to find intelligible patterns in the world. It may not be a defining property of 'art' that it includes content that engages us with the world as well as the work, but that it can be and is a property of some artworks remains a possibility. Finding intelligible patterns in one place not only does not preclude finding them in other places but also makes it more likely. I will discuss this in detail in later chapters—both the fact that it does happen and how it happens.

However, an example of the connection between themes and assertions might help here. Consider the ways in which two poets describe flight:

> Casting the body's vest aside,
> My soul into the boughs does glide:
> There, like a Bird, it sits and sings,
> Then whets and combs its silver wings;
> And, till prepared for longer flight,
> Waves in its plumes the various light.
>
> —Andrew Marvell

> He rises and begins to round,
> He drops the silver chains of sound,
> Of many links without a break,
> In chirrup, whistle, slur, and shake.
> For singing till his heaven fills,
> 'Tis love of earth that he instills,
> And ever winging up and up,
> Our valley is his golden cup.
> And he the wine which overflows
> To lift us with him as he goes.
> Till lost on his aerial rings
> In light, and then the fancy sings.
>
> —George Meredith

Surely the assertions made here point to different but equally true things about birds and flying and the human longing to join them, among other things. Would the language be so admirable, would the themes that bring the parts into a coherent whole work as well, were the claims made about the real world false? I think not. Furthermore, Ralph Vaughn Williams's musical version of Meredith's poem relates to both the real world and to the poem; in both cases, correspondence to things outside the work contribute to the successful patterns created within the work. In chapter 10, I will give examples of ways in which the success of some artworks depends on the correctness of the moral claims therein.

Lamarque and Olsen sometimes talk as if they themselves want it both ways. They distinguish what they call "internal perspectives" and "external perspectives." In the first, one reflects on fictional characters as persons; in the second, one identifies them as characters per se.[28] But they admit that these perspectives interact. They also acknowledge that great artworks embody themes of perennial human interest. I fail to see how something that embodies perennially interesting human themes could not stimulate a response to not only intrinsic properties of a work but also thought about the world which generates that very interest. Artworks engage us often by presenting content that interests us as human beings. Fair enough—but built into the very notion of human interest is a concern with the world, as well as with the work.

Themes, they argue, are not asserted, so "the question of truth is separate from the question of intelligibility."[29] But we are not simply after intelligibility. Consider the theme that they attribute to *Middlemarch:* "The best human hopes and aspirations are always thwarted by forces beyond human control." Suppose we substitute 'never' for 'always' in this generalization. As a theme per se, it would still be as intelligible; but if Eliot had used it *Middlemarch* would have been a very different work—no better, probably, than *Goody Two-Shoes.* To object that this substitution results in a less "interesting" work would be only question-begging. It is difficult for me to imagine a great work of art that had as its theme human hopes and aspirations never thwarted. This is precisely one of the reasons for denying the separability of moral and aesthetic value.

Of course, one might *ironically* begin a novel with a line to the effect that human hopes are never thwarted by external forces. But recognizing irony will not be a matter simply of reading what follows; it will also involve the reader's recognition that things in the real world contribute to its being a false sentence used ironically. Again, the work-world fit goes both ways. The appropriateness of form to content is not a positive value of literary works only because it demonstrates how effective authors can be at fitting patterns and meanings. Part of what we value, in some artworks at least, is the efficiency or cleverness with which a relatively ordinary but truthful claim is made. Consider Robert Frost's description of the leaves of early spring: "Nature's first green is gold." In one sense, this is hardly an original thought; most of us have noticed that special shade of green that graces early foliage. What makes Frost's words noteworthy and delightful is not just the fact that these words fit into a pattern that unites it with other lines of the poem—although they do. It is satisfying in itself, because it so aptly describes something that is true of the world and something that we have noticed is true of the world but have not been able to describe so well ourselves. I do not see how recognizing the truth of the claim could distract us from recognizing the aesthetic merit of the line. Quite the contrary— the former draws attention to the latter. As Malcolm Budd writes, "Artistic value does not exist in a watertight compartment impermeable by other values. . . ."[30]

Jerrold Levinson provides a powerful example of the way in which knowledge of the real world is relevant to the interpretation of the rap song "High Rollers." It is impossible to see how one would relate to the song at all if one did not have knowledge of the kinds of things Levinson points to in the work:

> Any adequate interpretation of the song would have to take into account (1) the import of the vocal delivery at various places, for example seductive and sinuous at the start, taunting and cynical on the rhetorically posed 'right?' near the end, (2) the comically exaggerated colours in which the pusher is painted (e.g. as 'a titan of the nuclear age' or one who 'eats fly guys for breakfast'), (3) the animalistic painting at the end of each stanza, which evokes the hunger for material goods of pushers and those who envy them, and (4) the abrupt way the music, with its standard pulsating bass rhythm, cuts off after prefacing the final refrain ('you wanna be a High Roller') with a warning about watching one's back, suggesting sonically the kind of termination one can expect if one chooses that path. All of these features seem to point toward the net force of the song being one of counsel against the lure of pusherdom.[31]

Attention to and sensitivity to aesthetic features, crucial though it is, would not result in a very full appreciation of the work if one lacked knowledge about the world of drug dealing. As Levinson puts it, "[W]ith art we appreciate the *unique way* in which the artwork embodies and carries its message."[32] But we also pay attention to whether the work has gotten the message right or not, and this is impossible without knowing whether the message is true or false and does or does not capture important, correct insights about the world.

Lamarque and Olsen stop short of strong formalism precisely because they admit that content and form merge. Once this admission is made, it is hard to keep people from thinking about truth and morality while they read, I think. They agree that "we identify 'large' themes in daily life, and they tend to be literary themes. We then tend to view reality in artistic terms, either in terms of a particular work to which we have given some attention, or in terms of an artistic technique that we have come to appreciate."[33] This comes very close to my notion of going back and forth between works and the world; if one is willing to allow that people reflect on the world in terms of art, why not allow that they also reflect on art in terms of the world? The fear that somehow concerns with truth and goodness will dilute or confuse literary value with other sorts is misplaced. Blurring the line between artworks and the world is exactly what is called for, I think. Immediately following the passage just quoted, Lamarque and Olsen add, "However, seeing life in terms of art is an optional extra. . . ." Quite the contrary, I believe. It has been and continues to be at the core of aesthetic value.

As Ronald W. Hepburn writes, "We particularly cherish the presentation of a perspective that we can make our own, 'inhabit,' see as sustainable, as capturing what seems to us to be the truth about the world."[34] Part of art's power resides as well in its power to modify our grasp of reality and even partially to constitute it, he thinks. This is certainly true of many readers' experiences. It supports the view that theorists who insist on a separation of the moral and the aesthetic make a mistake. In an attempt, perhaps, to solidify the position of artistic value, they deprive it of that which gives a great deal of art, at any rate, a great deal of value to a great many people. If separatists have made a mistake, the right way of accounting for the nature and value of the aesthetic must be a nonseparatist, integrational direction. To this right way, we now turn.

SIX

Serious Problems, Serious Values

Aesthetic Dilemmas

Aɛsᴛʜᴇᴛɪᴄ formalists, I have said, are motivated by a desire to give the aesthetic its proper due. One cannot help sympathizing with them. D. Z. Philips's attitude that whoever cares a whit about morality will always put it first is not at all uncommon. Too often we are told that aesthetic considerations are "extras"—luxuries to be indulged in after real concerns have been taken care of. Classes in the arts are often the first to be cut when retrenchment strikes schools systems. Bands and ceramics courses are "frills," compared with language and mathematics skills, it is assumed. I believe that separatists both in ethics and in aesthetics have reinforced these attitudes—in spite of the fact that the latter are usually so intent on doing just the opposite. Showing the connections between ethics and aesthetics will go some way toward remedying the situation, I think. I will say much more about this later. But first there is another strategy for showing that aesthetic values are really important, serious values.

People who argue that the aesthetic and the moral are totally separate and distinct claim that several essential differences create and maintain that separateness.[1] Behind the reasons given often lies the attitude that somehow aesthetic concerns are just not as serious as other concerns. For example, Stuart Hampshire, attempting to support his assertion that "there are no problems of aesthetics comparable with the problems of ethics," has called artistic problems "gratuitous." Unlike the moral problems that confront us every day and demand a response, aesthetic problems do not seem to impose themselves on us in any comparable way.[2]

Although Hampshire himself takes aesthetics and art very seriously, his remarks give aid and comfort to those who consider art a frill and think that aesthetic considerations are rather far down on the list of those things that individuals and societies should attend to. Who really cares whether concert halls or theaters stay open? Faced with problems of poverty and illness, what real difference is made if a museum has funds to support a controversial exhibit? Could anyone seriously believe that teaching dancing is as important as teaching reading? When moral issues are settled, the worst seems to be over; aesthetic choices just don not pack the same wallop. Moral values are really serious; aesthetic values often appear less central to the pressing concerns of everyday life.

The overridingness debate that we examined in the last chapter is one manifestation of this attitude. In this chapter, I want to argue a more general point: there are some aesthetic problems that are marked with a kind of seriousness that characterizes some moral problems, or, to use Hampshire's language, there are some aesthetic problems comparable in an interesting way to some moral problems, namely, exhibit the sort of features that one kind of moral conflict exhibits. The sort of conflict that I have in mind is that which is often referred to as "a dilemma." In our moral lives, we often face agonizing choices when moral principles that we find equally compelling come into conflict, or when a single moral principle requires that we perform two actions, both of which cannot possibly be performed. I have to decide whether to be kind or honest. Or kindness demands that I do one thing for Dick and another thing for Jane, and it is impossible to do both. In this chapter, I want to see whether in the aesthetic arena there is anything analogous to these agonizing ethical problems. In other words, are there aesthetic dilemmas?[3]

There are two sorts of "tests" for determining whether a conflict is a moral dilemma: a logical test and an emotional test. If there are genuine aesthetic dilemmas, one would expect positive results when these two tests are run on aesthetic conflicts.

The logical test focuses on an agent's confronting separate, mutually incompatible or contradictory actions, both (or all)[4] of which are covered by competing moral requirements, neither of which is the clear winner.[5] The competing moral requirements create a logical puzzle. Using simple, straightforward rules of logic and apparently true statements, including the standardly accepted moral principle that "ought implies can," a contradiction arises: One is obligated to do A and one is not obligated to do A.[6] If a conflict is such that resolution is impossible, we have a full-fledged dilemma. Unlike the case of helping the homeless or teaching illiterates, where one might conceivably do both, in dilemmatic situations it is impossible to satisfy two (or more) different obligations. "One but not both" is, as it were, built in. The now-classic example is *Sophie's Choice.*[7] Sophie is presented with two alternatives—she can save her son or she can save her daughter—but the *or* is exclusive; she cannot do both.

The logical (or incompatibility) test is often paired with an emotional test. Here, a conflict becomes dilemmatic when one realizes that whatever one chooses, one will not "feel right" about it. This emotional remainder has been variously described as "guilt" or "remorse" or "regret." In Sophie's case, the emotional remainder is so intense and agonizing that she eventually commits suicide. No assurances from friends or loved ones—"You did the only thing you could in the circumstances," for instance—provided relief.

Recently, moral philosophers have been split on whether moral dilemmas actually exist. Some believe that the logical test is wrongly construed, others that once an adequate moral theory is discovered the conflicts will disappear. Full discussion of this debate is not necessary here. Suffice it to say that most nonphilosophers are surprised when told about the controversy. "Of course they exist" is the typical response, a response often followed by stories of personal experiences. (In chapter 11,

I shall discuss ways in which such stories figure in ethical deliberation.) The commonsense attitude seems to be that anyone who has lived long enough will realize that life is so complicated that no a priori principle could rank different sorts of considerations or differing moral requirements. Any principle that Sophie might have articulated in advance could only be repugnant: "Always choose a son over a daughter" or "Always give precedence to your youngest child" or "When faced with such a choice, flip a fair coin" or "First choose the girl and next time the boy."

Although I tend to side with those (both philosophers and nonphilosophers) who believe in the existence of genuine moral dilemmas, I do not believe that this issue must fully be resolved to consider the possibility of the existence of aesthetic dilemmas. What cannot be denied is that some serious moral conflicts are marked by at least apparent incompatibility and intense emotional remainder. This intensity is one reason that the moral is granted such seriousness and importance. If one can show that there are aesthetic conflicts that also exhibit incompatibility and remorse, regret, or guilt, then there is support for the view that aesthetic values, like moral values, are really serious. For simplicity's sake, I shall continue to refer to these conflicts as 'dilemmas'.

Although common sense points in the direction of the existence of moral dilemmas, there is, I think, not much in the way of common sense at all in the case of aesthetic dilemmas to give us direction. After all, if a composer says, "I have a dilemma—I could end the sonata I am composing in this way or that, do A or not-A, but not both," one might easily and simply respond, "Where's the contradiction? You can just write two different sonatas; this isn't like Sophie's choice at all." And there doesn't seem to be any obvious candidate for an emotional remainder that has anything like the force of guilt or remorse. Martha Nussbaum expresses this attitude clearly and forcefully when she writes,

> Works of art are precious objects, objects of high value. And yet it is a remarkable feature of our attention to works of art that it appears to spread itself smoothly and harmoniously. I can, visiting a museum, survey many fine objects with appropriate awe and tenderness. I can devote myself now to one, now to another, without the sense that the objects make conflicting claims against my love and care. If one day I spend my entire museum visit gazing at Turners, I have not incurred a guilt against the Blakes in the next room; nor have I failed in a duty toward Bartok by my loving attention to Hindemith. To live with works of art is to live in a world enormously rich in value, without a deep risk of infidelity, disloyalty, or any conflict which might lead to these.[8]

But are these intuitions correct? Are there no real contradictions? Is there never an aesthetic emotional remainder? Only a close look at actual cases—that is, at candidates for aesthetic dilemmas—will tell.

Many of the following examples were suggested to me in private conversations, with both philosophers and nonphilosophers, artists and nonartists. I will not even attempt to provide a rigorous taxonomy. I have, instead, grouped the examples into rough categories of occasions on which different kinds of agents must make a decision. Some of the cases are more like morally dilemmatic situations than others.

Artistic Choices

Artists must constantly make choices with respect to the medium in which they will work and the goals they want to achieve. Should a particular area be red or blue, a poem in pentameter or hexameter, a composition divided into three or four movements? How should a given work end? The film classic *Casa Blanca* is legendary with regard to its ending; two different ones were, in fact, shot. Several years ago I was fortunate to hear the British composer John Casken refer to what he readily described as "a dilemma."[9] Working on a song-cycle for baritone and orchestra, using the words of the poet Rodney Pybus, Casken was "stuck" on what to do with the line "Let me be whale and graze through unfenced acres of blue." The composer had to choose between having the music fit into the context of the music that had just preceded this passage or providing a more literal sound imitation of "grazing" and "unfenced." (I have, of course, simplified the example.)

In these cases of artistic choices, the logical test does seem to be met in one sense. An artist cannot do both A and not-A, at least not in the same work. He or she can, however, create different works. (Both the book and the film versions of *The French Lieutenant's Woman* by John Fowles actually include two endings in one work, but this, of course, is an exception.) Like those theorists who maintain that moral dilemmas are really just not-yet-solved conflicts, one might be strongly inclined to treat all of these examples as problems that, once solved, will be felt to be "correct." "I've finally got it right," one can imagine the composer saying, with relief. "I've managed to alter the preceding passage so that literal imitation does not sound jarring." There simply does not seem to be anything here like the emotional remainder that we find in moral dilemmas—nothing that would qualify as aesthetic remorse.

The author Joseph Heller insisted to me that although moral dilemmas are commonly the subject of literary works (his own *Catch 22* being the classic case), he never heard anyone speak of aesthetic dilemmas. Anita Desai reflected that she could not think of anything in her own creative process that she would refer to this way. Given that so much contemporary fiction deals with writers' lives, one would expect somewhere depictions of how awful it is to have to choose between endings or when to reveal what or which genre to choose. Novels often deal with what we might call "mixed choices"—for instance, aesthetic-moral choices in which an artist must decide between his or her work and parenting or aesthetic-economic choices about making fine art or money. But I know of no counterexamples to Heller's and Desai's intuitions.

Emily Dickinson refers to dilemmas in several of her poems. Here is one example.

> If I could tell how glad I was
> I should not be so glad—
> But when I cannot make the Force,
> Nor mould it into Word,
> I know it is a sign
> That new Dilemma be
> From mathematics further off
> Than from Eternity.

Two dilemmas are described here. The first asks whether one should have an experience or write about it. One cannot do both; just as it is not possible to play tennis and at the same time write about playing tennis, one cannot be glad and write about being glad simultaneously. This is not an unmixed dilemma, that is, a choice between two aesthetic actions; I confess I do not know quite how to describe it. The second asks how, having decided to write, one can find and shape the words. This is an aesthetic problem (like whether to use red or blue) where one feels that though not yet discovered, a correct solution does exist. Hence it is not a real dilemma.

I am inclined to conclude that artistic choices are problems or conflicts, all right, but not genuine dilemmas.

Presenters' Choices

Art presenters (people who administer or direct museums, theaters, concert halls, publishers, etc.) must obviously make choices about what to provide their audiences. Though many of the conflicts they confront are "mixed" (given limited resources, they often have to choose between crowd-pleasers or avant-garde experiments, between quality and quantity, for instance), there are here some genuine aesthetic conflicts that are at least candidates for dilemmas. Which of two equally beautiful works from a permanent collection or repertoire should be put before the public at a given time? Again, the logical test is met, but only because the decision is space- and time-bound. One feels again that one can make up later for what one does not do now: Bach in the first week, Bartok in the second; King Tut this year, Ming Dynasty next; African American writers in this anthology, Asian American writers in the next. Or one can follow a "mostly Mozart" strategy, and sprinkle contemporary music among the classics in order to invite a range of aesthetic experiences. Even in the case of nonrepeatable presentations such as jazz performances or concerts featuring artists who are not likely to ever work together again, the problems seem, under fuller scrutiny, to be only contingent. Although, of course, practical concerns such as financial constraints can be daunting, there appears to be no dilemma in theory. Again, one might ask, where's the real remorse?

However, a recent presenter's choice does strike me as more dilemmatic. Picasso's famous *Guernica* was returned in 1981 by the Museum of Modern Art in New York to the Prado Museum in Madrid because the artist himself had expressed his wish that the work be displayed in that Spanish museum once the country was no longer a dictatorship. He wanted it to be housed under the same roof with such painters as Titian, Dürer, Rubens, Velázquez, and Goya; his wish was at last fulfilled. In 1992, however, the painting was moved to the nearby Queen Sofia Center of Art, Madrid's first museum devoted to modern art. It is in such a context that the painting actually belongs, decided the Prado's board of directors. The modern center is near the Prado (a five-minute walk) and hence close to the art historical setting Picasso hoped for. But is it close enough? Since a painting cannot be in two places at the same time, the logical test for a dilemma is met. The board of directors did report that their decision was a painful one, and to those who would feel bad no matter where the painting was finally located, the emotional test seems to be met. One might move the painting back and forth—but only by risking severe damage. Here, I think, we have something that at least approaches a genuine dilemma.

A concern related to the "In which museum?" problem is the "In a museum or not in a museum?" question. This is an issue that has arisen recently, for example, with respect to quilts. Long ignored as "women's work," quilts have at last been duly recognized as a genuine art form largely because they have begun to appear prominently in major museums of fine art, where it is clear (in cultures that have museums) that attention is to be given to certain intrinsic properties. Not everyone celebrates this fact, however. Many radical feminists argue that displaying quilts out of the context for which they were originally created diminishes, even erases, their aesthetic value. The true aesthetic worth of quilts, they assert, can be fully experienced only when they are viewed on beds, preferably keeping bodies warm, better yet when the viewer knows that this piece of material came from Aunt Clarice's blouse, that piece from Uncle Owen's overalls. Removing them from the bedroom amounts to acknowledging and acceding to the power of usually white, usually male museum directors who assume that only they can decide what counts as art. Suppose a curator invites me to display my mother's quilt in a museum. Surely there are good reasons to do so—the aesthetic properties will be accessible to many people under excellent conditions of viewing and preservation. But there are also good reasons for not turning it over to such an establishment: the viewing conditions will be of the wrong sort—on a wall, not on a bed. And museum preservation practices fly in the face of the fact that quilts are meant to wear out through use; this is part of their value, and full aesthetic experience demands awareness of this feature. Perhaps it is too strong to say that I will feel guilty or remorseful no matter which alternative I choose; but there will be some regret. Thus the logical and emotional tests for being a dilemma do seem to be met.

Ordinary or Everyday Aesthetic Choices

Which wallpaper should I put in the bathroom? Should there be a fountain or a grove of trees in the town square? If I am to be marooned on a desert island, which ten books, musical compositions, or paintings should (would) I take? Some of these cases can be handled easily by the "one—now, the—other later" strategy or by a majority vote. Even tossing a coin does not carry the repugnance it does in the Sophie example. Someone who felt remorse about a wallpaper choice would be, I think, considered ill, not aesthetically sensitive or meritorious. Again, my hunch is that cases like these are not strong candidates for aesthetic dilemmas.

Extraordinary Aesthetic Choices

The "desert island game" does suggest a more serious set of candidates, however. This example is similar to the "burning museum game" with which we aestheticians often confront our students. Suppose you are in a museum when a fire breaks out, and you can carry out only one (the "not-both" condition) artwork. Should you take a Rembrandt or a Picasso? The logical incompatibility is built in, and I believe there will also be an emotional remainder. Though not as excruciating as Sophie's forced decision about which of her own children to save, feeling regret when one cannot save both works of art that one values equally would surely be more appropriate than in the trivial wallpaper case.

Norman Bowie has suggested that the burning museum game would be more interesting if additional choices are added.[10] Suppose one had to choose between saving *Guernica* or one's son, or the painting or a museum guard, or the painting or a museum guard dog. The fact that people of good faith might find at least some of these decisions excruciating suggests again that the moral does not always easily trump the aesthetic.

Interpretative Choices

One nagging problem in philosophy and the theory of art has always been the problem of the status of interpretations. Is there one and only one correct interpretation of a given work of art, or are there several equally and perhaps incompatible good interpretations? Clearly, there is a close analogy here with problems in the moral realm. Is there one and only one right thing to do in every situation, or are several equally right and sometimes incompatible actions possible? In both the moral and aesthetic cases, belief in an all-encompassing theory that will cover all contingencies requires that one deny the existence of dilemmas. Critical literature, as well as moral philosophy, abounds with ongoing disputes over particularly troublesome cases, with some people arguing that harder work will eventually yield a general theory that will cover all situations and others insisting that the human condition makes faith in such progress ludicrous. Just as some writers hold onto utilitarianism in ethics, for example, in aesthetics some believe that there are general principles that settle disputes. For example, intentionalists hold that the intention of an artist, if known, yields the one and only correct interpretation of a work. Obviously, such theorists resist acknowledging dilemmas. But needless to say, there is no greater agreement on the general truth of intentionalism than there is on utilitarianism, or with any other aesthetic or moral theory thus far proposed.

Another way of dealing with contradictory interpretations (e.g., Henry James's *The Turn of the Screw* is a ghost story and is not a ghost story) is tantamount to denying the logical incompatibility, namely, to accepting a theory that enables one to have it both ways. One might take a relativistic stance: "*The Turn of the Screw* is a ghost story for Dick, who loves supernatural thrillers, and *The Turn of the Screw* is not a ghost story for Jane, who loves psychological thrillers." There is no contradiction here. Or one might (as I have, in fact, done in my own interpretation of the novel[11]) claim that James wrote an ambiguous work that, like a duck-rabbit figure, can be read in two ways. But again, many theorists will not agree that competing interpretations can be dispensed with so easily. (I myself think that *The Turn of the*

Screw is a very special case; by no means can all puzzling artworks be handled in this way, i.e., with what might be called an "ambiguity solution.")

Still, those who recognize a logical incompatibility between two interpretations are not likely to feel regret or guilt or remorse when they opt for one interpretation over another—or decide not to make a choice at all. Because of this, I do not think that interpretative choices involve one in a real dilemma.

Evaluative Choices

Your mission is to judge an art contest (poetry, singing, ceramics, etc.). You can give only one blue ribbon, and hence the logical test is met. There may be some single-dimensional aesthetic judges who believe that some intrinsic features of works always override (e.g., paintings of ducks are always better than paintings of fruit, or songs in minor keys are always superior to those in major keys), but I know of no serious critic or philosopher of art who takes such a position. George Dickie has proposed a matrix system for evaluating art, but even his system allows for ties.[12]

Nonetheless, the emotional remainder test seems not to be met in evaluative choices any more than it is in interpretative choices. (One might, of course, feel moral remorse because a virtuous person fails to win the blue ribbon, but this is not aesthetic remorse.) Like feeling no guilt when listening to Bach rather than to Bartok, one just does not have to decide which of these composers wins. Indeed, we often eschew questions about which master is best because they seem pointless. Even if I am supposed to award a prize, I can refuse or insist on a tie. Sophie cannot refuse to pick just one child—or at least cannot do so without that decision's being itself agonizing.

Tanya Rodriquez has pointed out to me that some people do sometimes report feeling guilt about their preferences.[13] One might feel bad about the fact that one prefers Stephen King to Leo Tolstoy. I myself have discussed what I call "the purple loosestrife problem," where in spite of knowing that it endangers the wetlands where it occurs, one finds the plant beautiful. (See chapter 12.) One might feel guilty about this. But these examples, I think, are cases of "aesthetic incontinence," not aesthetic dilemmas. Like moral incontinence, where one knows what the right thing to do is but does not want to do it, a correct theory is acknowledged that settles the question of what one should do. One is not torn between two horns of a dilemma that consists of choices that seem equally right or wrong but simply fails to respond appropriately to the single thing that one readily recognizes should be done.

Restorative Choices

I have saved for last the set of examples that I believe most clearly constitute genuine dilemmas. They preclude the "you—can—always—make—another—one later" solution to incompatibilities and, for anyone who cares at all about such things, leave a significant emotional remainder. The most celebrated of the restorative choices in recent history is undoubtedly the cleaning of the ceiling of the Sistine Chapel, but there are others. Particularly acute are those surfaces on which one painting has been done on top of another, and decisions about whether to rebuild or leave a ruin. In Crete, for example, there has been a controversy about how to treat historical sites—to rebuild and even repaint the stones, as has been done at Knossos, or simply to excavate the ruins, as has been done at Phaistos. No matter which set of experts and politicians wins, something becomes inaccessible or is lost, and in some cases lost forever. There are documented restorative disasters. In June 1992, in as careful a place as the Louvre, Veronese's *Marriage at Cana* was ripped in five places while undergoing restoration. It is unlikely that it can be completely repaired. Critics of what they describe as a "cleaning frenzy" in today's museums have even formed the Association to Protect the Integrity of Artistic Heritage.[14] Even "wallpaper decisions" that I dismissed as trivial earlier may assume an urgency if issues of restoration are involved.

Comparable cases exist with respect to environmental decisions about land reclamation and restoration and use. Should a dam be built at a site that boasts unique rock formations that will be lost or at another site where forest acreage will disappear? There is a "heated" controversy over whether controlled burning in some areas should be carried out, or whether naturally occurring fires should be allowed to follow their own course without interference.

The logical test is met in these cases, for one cannot, at least with existing technologies, have it both ways. And disappointment—I think in some instances actual remorse—may be felt. Some "clean-don't clean," "rebuild-don't rebuild," and burn-don't burn" proponents probably feel so strongly that theirs is the correct way to go that there is, for them, no sorrow. I know some people who now refuse to go to the Sistine Chapel because they feel it has been ruined forever. But many of us are of two minds, and people of good aesthetic faith will be differently inclined—and will feel that no matter what decision is made, restorative choices will occasion doubt and regret. Even the staunchest advocates of cleaning the Sistine ceiling supported extensive photographing of the dirty one before the cleaning began, as in frustration one grasps at straws in an effort to have it both ways.

In presenting the "desert island" choice, I deliberately equivocated on 'would' and 'should'. Even if one is reluctant to go from the former to the latter in this game—agree that one can decide for oneself what one *would* take but decline to say that there is anything that one *should* take—there are other cases where the move seems more natural:

- How would/should you interpret a particular artwork?
- To which work would/should you give the blue ribbon?

And certainly the move seems appropriate in:

- What would/should one do to the Sistine Chapel?

Should, of course, implies the existence of an obligation. It is obligations that generate dilemmas by creating logical incompatibilities. If there are aesthetic *should*s, there must be aesthetic obligations. And if there are aesthetic obligations, aesthetic dilemmas become possible.

In the context of relating moral and aesthetic value, I believe there is a parallel to moral obligation in the aesthetic realm.[15] The resistance to accepting the notion of aesthetic obligation rests, I believe, on our feeling that while it is bad or wrong to fail to recognize and act on our moral obligations, there is nothing comparable to this in aesthetic conflicts. Where is the badness or wrongness, one might object, in the aesthetic realm? Can it really be wrong not to notice the sunsets or fail to read poetry or listen to jazz? It seems quite reasonable to claim that

I. If S fails to consider moral features, then S is bad.

But it seems less reasonable to claim that

II. If S fails to consider aesthetic features, then S is bad.

But if we replace 'bad' in II with 'leads an impoverished life', then I think we get a much more reasonable assertion.

IIa. If S fails to consider aesthetic features, then S leads an impoverished life.

The problem now is that I loses much of its force.

Ia. If S fails to consider moral features, then S leads an impoverished life.

Our moral actions, our failures to be morally sensitive, affect others in a way that aesthetic insensitivity seems not to, and hence more than the quality of one's own life is at stake.

Ib. If S fails to notice moral features, then S hurts others.

But not,

IIb. If S fails to notice aesthetic features, then S hurts others.

Similarly, there is an asymmetry when one assumes a deontological moral theory.

Ic. If S fails to notice moral features, then S will fail to do his or her duty.

But not

IIc. If S fails to notice aesthetic features, then S will fail to do his or her duty.

However, if one believes it is one's duty to lead as full and rich a life as possible, something that I do not consider farfetched—indeed, I believe it is true—then IIc is no longer odd. And even IIb will be true in some cases. Failure to consider the aesthetic features of the Sistine Chapel—to demolish it to build a parking ramp, for example—would hurt others. Thus both I and II may be true.

Readers can substitute features in either statement that they think appropriate, such as duty or pain in I, color or expression in II. Although I is clearly true, it will strike many readers as odd to be told, following II, that anyone has an *obligation* to consider the colors of a sunset or the expressiveness of a Beethoven symphony or the graceful lines of a statue or the contorted movements of a dance. But the strangeness diminishes when one claims that one is obligated to consider the intrinsic properties considered worthy of attention in a culture when deciding what to do with the paintings in the Sistine Chapel.

Some may object that it is a *moral* obligation in the case of the Sistine Chapel—that one has a moral obligation to posterity to preserve objects that will enrich others' lives, not an aesthetic obligation. But suppose we have a case where we believe the moral value of two options is equivalent. Say we have a canvas on which two beautiful paintings have been placed, one on top of the other, and that people's lives will be equally enriched if either is saved, or equally harmed if either does not exist. For aesthetic reasons alone, one must then make a choice. I do not believing a coin-tossing strategy would be satisfying here, anymore than it is in the moral realm. Ultimately, of course, we are concerned with how people's lives will be affected—what will make their lives meaningful or worth living. The fact that there are hard aesthetic choices—ones involving incompatibility and emotional remainder—shows what a serious, important role aesthetic experiences have in creating such lives.

SEVEN

Aesthetics: The Mother of Ethics?

BOTH strong and weak formalists who insist on the separation of ethics and aesthetics exhibit, I have suggested, a zeal for establishing a rightful place for the latter. Some theorists express a similar zeal in maintaining not only that the moral does not always come first but also that actually it comes second. I believe that this is also a mistake—another version of the separatist mistake—but it is one that takes us further toward a correct integrationist view.[1]

In his Nobel laureate address in 1988, the poet Joseph Brodsky said, "On the whole, every new aesthetic reality makes man's ethical reality more precise. For aesthetics is the mother of ethics."[2] Many philosophers of art have struggled to convince others that aesthetics and ethics are connected; some of us have gone so far as to claim that aesthetic and ethical values are, at least sometimes, equally important and serious. That was the topic of the last chapter. But few go so far as Brodsky does in this remark. One might even construe it as hyperbole. Another author, André Gide, when asked in an interview what morality is, responded, "A branch of aesthetics."[3] One senses that Gide was trying to be outrageous or cute. I think Brodsky, however, was quite serious. What could it possibly mean to say that aesthetics is the *mother* of ethics? In his lecture, Brodsky did not spell out in any detail what he meant, but the phrase enthralls me and I believe that consideration of possible interpretations of it sheds light on the extent to which aesthetics and ethics are integrated.

The history of Western philosophy does not offer many theories in which aesthetics is prior to ethics. Plato, of course, tells us that beauty and goodness are ontologically equivalent. Hence, neither can be construed as the "mother" of the other. And when at the level of human experience the aesthetic is embodied artistically, it is strictly inferior to ethics for Plato. Even when our friend Aristotle gives artistic value its due, it does not for him become superior to or prior to ethical value. At most, they are equal, as they are for his medieval champion, Thomas Aquinas, who ascribes ethical value to doing, aesthetic value to making. Though goodness and beauty for him are manifestly different in human experience, Aquinas, like Plato, does give them ontological equality. But when he discusses the conflicts that may arise when one tries both to do good and to create beauty, he acknowledges that art can have both positive and negative effects on our moral life. These are determined extra-aesthetically, by the degree to which art leads one to God; thus, in this sense goodness finally takes the primary role. In later centuries, when beauty and goodness are related—when beauty is as beauty does, for example—the moral almost always takes precedence. D. Z. Philips's attitude, encountered in chapter 5, that moral considerations override all others, has been prevalent.

Western philosophy offers us plenty of systems in which the ethical and the aesthetic are firmly separated. Kant's is the most influential. It is against such views that I (and many others) have argued. The formalism that has its roots in the Kantian separation of the aesthetic from the ethical and cognitive has led, as Mary Devereaux succinctly observes, to precluding a full understanding of artworks, confusing the interests of the dominant group with universal interests, and disguising the actual standards of evaluation that are employed.[4] Referring to such formalism as "radical autonomism," Noel Carroll has recently argued that it fails to recognize that a great many works of art become intelligible only when the audience provides appropriate moral emotion and evaluation.[5] Failure to elicit proper moral response, he argues, can be an aesthetic flaw. I shall discuss Carroll's view more fully in a later chapter. For now, suffice it to say that even those of us like Devereaux and Carroll who insist on a deep connection between aesthetic and moral values rarely go so far as to say that the aesthetic is in some sense *prior* to the ethical. There may be assessments that require *both* aesthetic and ethical reflection simultaneously. In chapter 9, I shall offer sentimentality as just such a concept. But in this and similar cases, the ethical and the aesthetic seem to be on equal footing. Neither is the mother.

Mark Packer has recently argued that some evaluative notions used morally are, in fact, aesthetic. He gives several examples of conduct that is deemed offensive, even when no threat of pain or infringement of rights exists. Suppose, he says, that we could use DNA painlessly extracted from cows or chickens to create rib eye steaks or boneless breasts. Since no animal would suffer, vegetarian arguments against eating such meat would lose their force. And suppose, further, that we could produce and serve human flesh in the same way. Does all moral offensiveness disappear? Packer answers, "No." But the offensiveness, outrageousness, or at the very least the inappropriateness herein must lie in aesthetic evaluation, since no issues of pain or rights are involves. He says, "Our consumption of human flesh . . . [or other] real life instances of harmless offense, such as incest between consenting adults, are instances of behavior that are found unacceptable in virtue of the actions themselves, i.e. for aesthetic reasons."[6] Negative response to harmless offensiveness is, he thinks, more widespread and common than we have realized.

Packer calls this an "aesthetic approach to morality," and there are ties, I think, to views that I shall discuss later. But even if he provides a way of giving priority to aesthetics over ethics in some specific moral responses, there is still a historical and conceptual dependence of the former on the latter, rather than the other way round. Outrageousness, for example, even if one agrees that it is *now* primarily an aesthetic response, is a vestige of a moral response that originated because of deleterious effects, according to Packer. Pains or rights infringement may get separated off (nothing may feel pain if I eat DNA-produced roast human thigh) but the principle against doing it remains, as does the emotional aversion. So, implicitly for

Packer, the ethical does retain its priority. And he admits that his analysis seems to fit only some ethical notions (like offensiveness), not all; thus, it cannot serve as a general argument that supports the priority of aesthetics over ethics.

Julia Driver points to another area in which morality and aesthetics are intertwined. Sometimes she argues, "Being good is . . . a matter of looking good."[7] There is a grain of truth in the intuition that an act may be immoral or moral if it is not morally valuable in itself but only resembles an action that is morally valuable, because others, upon seeing it performed, may imitate it. For example, if we see Caesar's wife (or anyone who is supposed to have integrity) acting badly, we may conclude that it is okay for us to behave similarly. (This intuition was expressed over and over again during the recent impeachment crisis in the United States.) It is such an intuition that keeps those of us who support animal rights from wearing even fake fur; we don't want to be taken as someone who supports wearing fur coats, for that might make it more likely that someone will see me doing it and think it is all right for them to wear real fur. Thus, Driver might have uncovered another area in which we, as Packer puts it, approach morality aesthetically. But again, this is at most a special case, and although appearance is crucial, the ethical is not superseded, for it is the appearance of being ethical that matters; the ethical thus remains prior.

There have been theorists who have thought that there is a causal connection between aesthetic and ethical experiences. Leo Tolstoy, for example, insisted that genuine artistic expression is a matter of transmitting feelings and thereby spiritually uniting communities. People who really participate in real art are morally improved. Urban designers from Thomas Jefferson to Jane Jacobs have argued that beautiful cities make for better citizens. When the Baltimore Aquarium opened a new Caribbean Reef exhibit, the curator said she believes that when people see how beautiful the ocean ecosystems are, they will be more likely to take action to protect these environments. Indeed, many ecologists do report that the beauties of nature initially drew them to their specializations.

Unfortunately, we can find a plethora of counterexamples to the claim that aesthetic experiences make people morally better in general. SS officers in Nazi concentration camps often arranged concerts performed by prisoners. People who love to visit forests on weekends often leave litter behind, and there is little evidence that artists are typically kinder or more generous that nonartists. As Alan Goldman puts it, "For every Verdi there is a Wagner."[8]

Even if it were true that people for whom aesthetic activity plays a significant role in their lives were more ethical than others, the priority of the aesthetic would still not be established. Advocating city beautification via claims about the moral benefits presupposes ethical preferences. Saying that more fountains and neater streets will make better neighbors presupposes a theory of what makes citizens "better." Just as claiming that eating more salmon makes one healthier depends on a particular concept of health, valuing beauty as a means to goodness presupposes a concept of moral goodness. Theories of artistic genius that attribute special ethical insights to art makers, even if true, also presuppose a concept of what it means to be ethical. Thus, even those theorists who have claimed a causal connection for art and the aesthetic on the one hand and ethical action on the other do not provide a way of giving the aesthetic the role of *mother*.

Brodsky himself makes some causal claims in his Nobel laureate address. On that occasion, he said,

> I have no wish to . . . darken this evening with thoughts of the tens of millions of human lives destroyed by other millions. . . . I'll just say that I believe—not empirically, alas, but only theoretically—that, for someone who has read a lot of Dickens, to shoot his like in the name of some idea is somewhat more problematic than for someone who has read no Dickens. . . . A literate, educated person, to be sure, is fully capable, after reading some political treatise or tract, of killing his like, and even of experiencing, in so doing, a rapture of conviction. Lenin was literate, Stalin was literate, so was Hitler; as for Mao Zedong, he even wrote verse. What all these men had in common, though, was that their hit list was longer than their reading list.[9]

Brodsky here echoes a position taken by Wayne Booth in *The Company We Keep*.[10] The books we read, like the friends we surround ourselves with, say much about what kind of people we are. But I think that Brodsky is doing more than making a causal claim when he says that aesthetics is the mother of ethics. As he himself says, he is not making an empirical claim; he has a conceptual connection in mind. What he seems to be after is a strong sense in which the ethical comes into existence only when an aesthetic system is already established.

Perhaps Brodsky was influenced by another European literary artist and theorist, Friedrich Schiller, whose book *The Aesthetic Education of Man* by its very title suggests a central role for the aesthetic in broader human development. Two human faculties, Schiller claims, sensation and reason, have too often been thought at odds by philosophers. Reason has usually been awarded the higher status. But, Schiller fears—anticipating, perhaps, the theories of Bernard Williams—that when reason is deprived of sense or feeling, the self is coerced; one acts to do the right thing as if with clenched fists. Art can reconcile reason and feeling, for it is there that one freely acts to do what is aesthetically pleasing. This is, Schiller scholars have pointed out, analogous to Kant's moral ideal, in which one freely, disinterestedly does one's duty.[11] This, they say, is in fact what Kant must have meant when he said that beauty is the symbol of the good. For Schiller, however, reason is not separated from feeling in a judgment of beauty; rather, they are in harmony: "Athletic bodies can, it is true, be developed by gymnastic exercises; beauty only through free and harmonious play of the limbs. In the same way the keying up of individual functions of the mind can indeed produce extraordinary human beings; but only the equal tempering of [all human powers creates] happy and complete human beings."[12]

Schiller calls the working together of sense and reason the "play drive." Education should seek to reinforce this drive—to produce people who derive pleasure from sensation, which is developmentally prior in human beings, when it works in partnership with reason. The priority of sensation and the delight attending it begins to sound like the kind of priority Brodsky wants. Unfortunately, I find Schiller's writing so difficult that it is, for me, suggestive at best. One finds mottoes, for instance, "Aesthetic education is education from the aesthetic through the aesthetic to the aesthetic," but not a clear way to explain, let alone accept, how for him aesthetics might be the mother of ethics. Thus, we must, I think, look elsewhere for a possible interpretation of Brodsky's metaphor.

American philosophy does serve up one person who could provide the strong prior role for aesthetics over ethics that Brodsky indicates. Charles Peirce describes aesthetics as the "science of ideals, or of that which is objectively admirable without any ulterior reason." In a letter to William James in 1902, he describes how he came rather late to a recognition of the unity of the sciences of logic, ethics, and aesthetics, and of the way in which "logic must be founded on ethics, of which it is a higher development." "Even then," he admits, "I was for some time so stupid as not to see that ethics rests in the same manner on a foundation of esthetics—by which, it is needless to say, I don't mean milk and water and sugar."[13] Just exactly what he does mean—in this as elsewhere in his dense, obscure writings—is not completely clear. Logic, he says, rests on ethics because the question "What is the end of reason?" is an ethical question. Ethics, in turn, rests on aesthetics because answering the question "What conduct will achieve certain ends?" requires first answering the question "What are or should our ends be?" And this last question can be answered only in terms of intrinsic desirability—an aesthetic matter, he thinks. Or, to put it another way, the question "What makes an ideal ideal?" requires aesthetic evalution: "An ultimate end of action deliberately adopted—that is to say, *reasonably* adopted—must be a state of things that *reasonably recommends itself in itself* aside from any ulterior consideration. It must be an admirable ideal, having the only kind of goodness that such an ideal *can* have; namely, esthetic goodness. From this point of view, the morally good is a particular species of the esthetically good."[14]

However, the sort of value that Peirce has in mind is profoundly influenced by Kant and is a view in which the aesthetic is grounded in formalistic pleasure. In Peirce's description of how human understanding of the world arises out of humans' experiences in the world, he presents his tripartite distinction between firstness, secondness, and thirdness. Firstness is the quality of the felt world—the world as inner, subjective experience. Secondness is the relation of "bumping up against the world"—the sensation of self coming up against nonself. Thirdness is the representation of generality—the human experience of making predictions. Aesthetic theory belongs to firstness. When he discusses this aspect of experience, he gives the following examples: the taste of quinine, the color of magenta, the tragicness of *King Lear*. These are, of course, not just pleasures or pains, but they are nonetheless inner feelings. Peirce says we cannot really use worlds to name them, because this in itself would be artificially to divide up firstness by selecting only certain aspects of it. Experience of this sort is "so tender that you cannot touch it without spoiling it."[15] There are clear connections here to Kant. Thus, the priority Peirce gives to aesthetics depends on his separating the feeling from the object of the feeling. Ultimately, then, Peirce gives priority to the aesthetic only by separating the aesthetic completely from the ethical. This is something that I have shown I am loath to do. It is, I have argued, a misguided way of conceiving of aesthetic value.

If this is what Brodsky meant by the aesthetic being the mother of ethics, I want none of it. It is—excuse me—throwing out the baby with the bathwater. And I do not think that Brodsky wanted this either.

A more promising source for a view that might provide an interpretation of what it could mean to put aesthetics first is an interview given by Michel Foucault for an Italian magazine, *Panorama*. The interview is suggestively titled "An Aesthetic of Existences," and implicitly rests on his general theory of the way in which human practices and institutions define us as individuals, as communities, and as individuals-in-communities—how names name, for instance. He suggests that lives can be construed as works of art. For example, the differences between the moralities of antiquity and of Christianity, he says, are differences in "styles" of liberty. The former was "mainly an attempt to affirm one's liberty and to give to one's own life a certain form in which one could recognize oneself, be recognized by others, and which even posterity might take as an example."[16] Thus, an "elaboration of one's own life as a personal work of art . . . was at the centre . . . of moral experience" in antiquity. For Christians, "morality took on increasingly the form of a code or rules."[17] But both can be construed formally—and hence aesthetically. In our own age, as codes are increasingly questioned—both in particular and more generally (by Bernard Williams, for example) in terms of the role they actually play in moral experience—we are increasingly, Foucault suggests, seeking a new form, a different "aesthetic of existence."

Foucault does not, in this interview, provide the details of what such searching or choosing might entail, and I do not want to attribute to him a view in which aesthetics is in some sense the mother of ethics. But suppose one gives more emphasis than may typically be given to the term *form* in Wittgenstein's phrase "forms of life." Suppose that one chooses the form one's life should take before deciding on the content. That is, suppose one opts for the form Foucault ascribes to antiquity—decides that what matters is living according to patterns that can be recognized by other members of one's community as representing a particular type of person or character. Or suppose one opts for a life in which one demonstrates that one is following a code. *Which* patterns or *which* code is not as important, one might imagine, as the fact that one exhibits the style appropriate to patterned or coded (or some other, maybe even any other) behavior. Form would in this sense be prior to content, and hence aesthetics might be construed as prior to ethics.

Something along these lines is, I think, proposed by Charles Altieri in his book *Canons and Consequences*. He sets out to bridge the Kantian gap between universal ethical principles and concrete moral problems, and turns to expression of the sort one finds in art for a solution.

> The fullest social uses of art have less to do with exposing the historical conditions of their genesis than with clarifying how the arts help us understand ourselves as value-creating agents and make possible communities that can assess those creations without relying on categorical terms traditional to moral philosophy. . . . Persons appeal to communities not because their deeds meet criteria for rationality but because the deeds embody specific features of intentionality that an agent can project as deserving certain evaluations from those who can be led to describe it as the agent does.[18]

Expression properly understood accounts for a strong sense of artistic presence in works that draws viewers to go beyond the manifest properties to make "expressive implicatures" that allow speakers "to project certain qualities of their own act as significant aspects of the message."[19] We call attention to the way we speak, as well as to what we say. We project purposiveness into the world, thus contributing to the creation of a "public theater" where we act and react to constitutive acts. Like Charles Taylor, Altieri believes that in acting, we present a certain kind of self that reflects second-order values. We take both first- and third-person stances whenever we enter complex personal and social relationships. Similarly, self-assessment is carried on in terms of traditional forms. These forms come to us from art, which provides "a range of projective sympathies so that we come to appreciate what is involved in given choices."[20] Expressive patterns constitute a grammar for action and for evaluation of action. A basic question is "How will others see me?" But we cannot answer this question without knowing the grammar by which others see us. And this we learn from art, according to Altieri. One might interpret him as saying that lives are presentations whose intrinsic properties, within specific communities, become representations.

If Foucault and Altieri insist on a separation of form and content, then I want no more of them than I do of Kant, Schiller, or Peirce. If they claim that one can choose bare form apart from content, if I am supposed to be able to choose to express myself as a code follower and then choose the code, for instance, then I believe the claim is a reductio ad absurdum. For it is impossible to understand what it is for something to have the form of a code without understanding concepts such as the function of a code, which ultimately requires general and probably specific ethical concepts. But I do not think that this is what they claim. Rather, they represent the ethical and the aesthetic as essentially intertwined, and perhaps a clearer sense of Brodsky's mother metaphor begins to emerge. In the mother-child relationship, the members are not ontologically equivalent, nor are they conceptually separate, nor is the first causally related but separated from the second. Rather, they are conceptually related, and the causal connections are continuous and in both directions. I shall return to this idea shortly.

The Foucault-Altieri way of connecting aesthetics and ethics turns to art as a course for the construction of the individual and of communities. Many postmodernists have given a great deal of attention to the role of art in the development of individual and community identities. Sharon Welch, for instance, insists that solidarity grows in part from listening to stories.[21] Humans are moved not only by better arguments but also by "more richly textured narratives." She calls this "transformative communication." But she admits that aesthetic objects are only one source of it and thus, like most postmodernists, views the connection between aesthetics and ethics synchronically rather than in terms of conceptual or causal priority.

In the analytical philosophical tradition, writers such as Hilary Putnam and David Wiggins[22] argue that art plays a crucial role in developing meaningful lives. Wiggins builds on Richard Taylor's use of the Sisyphus myth to explain how value must be added to one's life, either by providing an external purpose (I am pushing these stones uphill to help build a beautiful temple) or by producing an appropriate inner psychological state (I somehow get an injection of something that produces happiness as I push my boulder). Value, according to Wiggins, does not exist independently of human existence; it is invented. In science, it makes sense to seek for a truth, at least in the Peircean sense in which truth exists as an ideal—the eventual agreement of all rational people. In ethics, all rational people will not ever agree about the single best invention of what counts as a meaningful life. But this does not mean that invention is wholly arbitrary or that all ways of inserting value into one's life are equal. Invention must be, as Wiggins puts it, "assertible"; that is, like assertions, the choices one makes about the best kind of life to lead must call for justification. One product of invention, literature, offers alternatives, he says, and we can learn from art which ways of constructing meaningful lives are assertible. In *Anna Karenina,* for example, Tolstoy represents Levin's life as more assertible than Anna's. We as readers may disagree. But we realize that different rational agents invent differently. Thus, aesthetic objects are a major source of teaching us how to be inventive. They may not be the only source—Wiggins does not discuss this. Whether aesthetic objects can be devoid of ethical content or whether, even if they could, they would create ethics is another question. Perhaps Wiggins's view is a version of the causal theory. I am inclined to think it is subtler.

The notion of *invention* is clearly related to imagination—a human faculty that has often been viewed with fear and suspicion in philosophy but that recently is getting a better rap. Sabina Lovibond, for example,[23] believes that it is central to ethics, for it is required if we are to do the necessary work of projecting the good situations that we want to bring about. Mark Johnson makes similar claims. In his book *Moral Imagination,* he argues that our key moral concepts are metaphorical, both theoretically and practically. "Acting morally requires acts of imaginative exploration of possibilities open to us in morally problematic situations."[24] We select and then organize significant details on the basis of narratives provided by our cultures. We criticize ourselves and others by pointing out that certain details have been ignored in making decisions, or that the order of the actions is wrong: "Living a fulfilling life in accordance with some notion of human flourishing is one of the chief problems we are all trying to solve. We each want very badly for our particular life stories to be exciting, meaningful, and exemplary of the values we prize. Morality is thus a matter of how well or how poorly we construct (i.e. live out) a narrative that solves our problem of living a meaningful and significant life."[25]

In this statement, we find a number of aesthetic concepts, for example, *exciting.* Like John Dewey, Johnson believes that the artistic can give experience coherence by unifying it. Hence, moral development can entail aesthetic development. "The aesthetic dimensions of experience—including imagination, emotions, and concepts—are what make meaning and the enhancement of quality possible (or correlatively, the disintegration and impoverishment of experience)."[26] Aesthetic skills provide us with the necessary moral skills of discernment, expression, investigation, creativity, and interaction of materials, forms, and ideas.[27]

Several years ago, R. W. Hepburn and Iris Murdoch urged a view of moral philosophy that would capture concerns similar to Johnson's. (More recently, a growing number of moral philosophers have come to share their attitude, but I think insufficient attention has been given explicitly to Hepburn and Murdoch's work. The extent to which I have been influenced by their insights will become more important in chapter 11, when I describe ways in which the role of narrative in morality specifically points to one kind of deliberation in which ethical and aesthetic merit necessarily come together.) Using autobiographies as data, Hepburn described an ethic based on "inner vision" rather than on a morality of choices made in specific circumstances. Some people describe their lives, and what they have tried to do with their lives, in terms of what Hepburn calls "personal myth." These stories involve "interlinked symbols, not rules, a fable, not a sheaf of principles."[28] On such a view, evaluating lives morally employs such concepts as coherence, comprehensiveness, vividness, and harmony. Murdoch, too, proposes a view of morality different from the standard one in which moral differences are based on "differences of choice, given a discussable background of facts."[29] This different ethic, she thinks, accounts for the following.

> When we apprehend and assess other people we do not consider only their solutions to specifiable problems, we consider something more elusive which may be called their total vision of life, as shown in their mode of speech or silence, their choice of words, their assessments of others, their conception of their own lives, what they think attractive or funny: in short, the configurations of their thought which show continually in their reactions and conversation. These things, which may be overtly and comprehensibly displayed or inwardly elaborated and guessed at, constitute what, making different points in the two metaphors, one may call the texture of a man's being or the nature of his personal vision.[30]

This texture of being expresses a person's moral nature and demands a vocabulary and methodology not provided by an ethic based solely on independent choices.

Cora Diamond continues this line of thought by insisting that what Murdoch calls "texture of being" is precisely what novels give us. (And, I would add, other kinds of art as well.) A morality based on forms of social lives includes, for example, Henry James's interest in the kind of furniture people have.[31] This seems exactly right to me; it accounts for my sympathy with Mrs. Gereth's assessment of the moral character of her hosts in his novel *The Spoils of Poynton,* based on the fact that she finds it impossible to sleep because of the way they have wallpapered the guest room. It also explains the unease I feel about having laughed with Mrs. Gereth at the hosts' poor taste when I am caused to reflect, later in the novel, upon what such aesthetic-ethical assessment, amounting as it does to snobbism, can entail. The question, Diamond argues, is not how art helps me to understand an issue more clearly (e.g., whether I should talk behind my hosts' backs about how badly they have decorated their home and what it implies about their shallow moral character) but, as Diamond puts it, "How is it that *this* (whatever feature of the novel it may be) is an illuminating way of writing about *that* (whatever feature of human life)?"[32] Just as seeing a connection with ethics requires that one have a view of aesthetics that differs from formalism, seeing a connection with aesthetics requires that one have a different way of thinking about ethics.

But in saying that the moral entails the aesthetic, or in identifying an aesthetic dimension to moral development and assessment, Johnson, Hepburn, Murdoch, and Diamond do not, I think, go as far as Brodsky—at least if what we take Brodsky to be saying is that the aesthetic necessarily comes first, that there is no ethics without aesthetics in the sense that first we become aesthetically skilled and only then does moral development begin. But does Brodsky mean this, or does he come closer to views in which aesthetics and ethics are not related in terms of *causal* priority but in terms of woven *interdependence?*

In the theories I have mentioned, we find two main ways one might posit a connection in which priority is given to the aesthetic over the ethical. I do not have a wholly satisfactory terminology but, for lack of anything better, will use the following.

1. Formalistic Priority. According to this view, in making a moral decision, one first chooses style and then content.
2. Psychological or Behavioral Causal Priority. The strong version of this view asserts that one who fails to engage in aesthetic activity will not be a moral person. The weak version asserts that people who engage in aesthetic activity are more likely to be moral people.

Both, I believe, should be rejected, and if either is what Brodsky means in saying that aesthetics is the mother of ethics, then he is wrong. But a third kind of connection has also been suggested.

3. Conceptual Interdependence. To understand morality and thus become a mature person, one's action must have both appropriate style and content, and this requires aesthetic skills. In this third position, neither the aesthetic nor the ethical is prior, so if priority is required for motherhood, Brodsky's metaphor is not apt.

In the Nobel laureate address and elsewhere, there definitely are statements that are consistent with both the formalistic and psychological or behavioral causal views. Brodsky maintains that evil is "bad style."[33] In an essay on Stephen Spender, he says that we recognize character traits from an individual's "metier."[34] That we are aesthetic creatures before we are ethical creatures, he insists, is shown by the way that we are directed by our aesthetic instincts. Babies go to their mothers rather than to strangers for aesthetic, not moral reasons.[35] "If in ethics not 'all is permitted,' it is precisely because not 'all is permitted' in aesthetics, because the number of colors in the spectrum is limited."[36] Brodsky championed poetry-for-the-people and supported federal subsidies for distribution of inexpensive paperback books because he thought a civilization in which art becomes the "property or prerogative of a minority" is doomed.[37] Politicians "should be asked, first of all, not how [they imagine] the course of [their] foreign policy, but about [their] attitude toward Dickens," because like the envoys he describes in his late poem titled after a Balkan dance, "Kolo," too little Dickens may lead to too much time spent "contemplating new ways of creating symmetry in a future cemetery."

I have far more sympathy with the psychological view than with the formalist view. On those days when I can still muster up some optimism about teaching, I even believe that bringing students to love Henry James or Bach or Michelangelo will make them morally better. I certainly wish we would hear more discussions of

David Copperfield during election campaigns. But I think that the third way of connecting aesthetics and ethics—one that demands a conceptual interdependence—is closer to the truth, and more likely to give an interpretation to the mother metaphor that enriches the study of both ethics and aesthetics.

In the Spender essay, Brodsky says, "You can tell a lot about a man about his choices of an epithet," for "Living is like quoting."[38] But epithets are chosen not just because they fit the space on a piece of marble or granite. Quotation is not just repetition of rhythms and rhymes. We repeat not just the way something is said but the sense or content of what is said as well. This conception of morality is basically Aristotelian, and the idea is to imitate the behavior of people we believe are virtuous in order to become virtuous ourselves. Martha Nussbaum asserts that Greek drama foregrounds this connection between what is done and how it is done.

> Content is not separable from its poetic style. To become a poet was not regarded by the Greeks, nor should it be regarded by us, as an ethically neutral matter. Stylistic choices—the selection of certain metres, certain patterns of image and vocabulary—are taken to be closely bound up with a conception of the good. We, too, should be aware of these connections. As we ask which ethical conception we find most compelling, we should ask what way or ways of writing most appropriately express our aspiration to be humanly rational beings.[39]

Brodsky would agree completely and would add, I think, that such choices extend to life in general. Not only must one make aesthetic choices when one attempts to create art but also one must do it as one attempts to become a moral individual. Becoming virtuous involves more than imitating what people do; it involves quotation: attempting to copy the *way* those we admire act. The dancer and the dance cannot be torn or told apart.

The reason that André Gide could play *enfant terrible* by saying that ethics is a branch of aesthetics is that aesthetic decisions so often seem not to pack the punch that ethical decisions do. As Stuart Hampshire has written, artists' choices seem "gratuitous."[40] Even Alan Goldman, with whom I find myself almost always agreeing, has said that "aesthetic disagreements do not involve so broad and direct conflicts among important interests" as do ethical disagreements.[41] But the views of Foucault, Altieri, Wiggins, Hepburn, Murdoch, and Diamond belie this view. For them, the aesthetic is not always gratuitous, let alone frivolous. Aesthetics can become as important as ethics not because making an ethical decision is like choosing wallpaper but because it like choosing one story over another. The story one chooses is a life story—hardly a gratuitous matter. I shall return to this sense of ethical deliberation in a later chapter.

In her paper "Taste and Moral Sense," Marcia Cavell seems initially to agree with Hampshire. She writes, "As moral creatures we have to think of the effects of our actions on ourselves and others; we have to make difficult decisions which require us to consider and reconsider our commitments and often to sacrifice one moral good for another; we are confronted with problems in such a way that even to attempt to avoid them is to incur responsibility. To these dimensions of concern and obligation there is nothing parallel in the activity of the artist qua artist."[42] And one assumes she thinks there is nothing parallel in the activity of aesthetic viewer qua aesthetic viewer. But she thinks Hampshire overstates his case, and in arguing for a revision she comes closer to something like the conceptual interdependence view. As in aesthetic judgments, there are many moral judgments that do not involve references to principles, she asserts. Furthermore, neither aesthetic nor moral judgments concern themselves with "an object or event in isolation from the environment and other events."[43] Moralists and art critics have a great deal in common, she asserts. In moral judgments, "We don't so much justify our judgments as explain them in much the same way as the critic explains why a character is badly drawn, or how a musical passage is more or less banal than it seemed on a careless listening, or why a poem is false or sentimental."[44] We point to details, give new emphasis to them, and show new patterns and relationships between them. Moral sensitivity develops in particular contexts. We have to pay attention to the tone with which something is said, as well as to the content, and to the relations between the speakers, or to meanings of other words spoken earlier or later.

A similar observation is made by R. M. Hare in *Freedom and Responsibility*, though like Cavell, he ultimately seems to want to keep the aesthetic and the ethical distinct. Moral ideals, he observes, have a close resemblance to aesthetic ideals, as can be seen in the following example.

> The leader of a Himalayan expedition has the choice of either leading the final assault on the mountain himself, or staying behind at the last camp and giving another member of his party the opportunity; yet it is easy to suppose that no argument concerned with the interests of the parties will settle the question—for the interests may be precisely balanced. The questions that arise are likely to be concerned, not with the interests of the parties, but with ideals of what a man should *be*. Is it better to be the sort of man who, in the face of great obstacles and dangers, gets to the top of the nth highest mountain in the world; or the sort of man who uses his position of authority to give a friend this opportunity instead of claiming it for himself? These questions are very like aesthetic ones. It is as if a man were regarding his own life and character as a work of art, and asking how it should best be completed.[45]

Decisions like this do seem to involve the sort of thing that Cavell rightly attributes to art criticism.

When one attends to relationships and patterns of expression, one relates and arranges specific things. Attention to fit and implications challenges one to attend closely to a variety of elements, and challenges one to develop powers of perception, reflection, and imagination. In this way, music and abstract art have as much to offer ethics as do narrative and representational art. Both aesthetic and moral sensitivity are demanded in making judgments such as "This situation calls for bold action" or "This situation calls for subtlety." Great music, as well as great literature, helps one to learn to make such distinctions. Many of my students seem to model their lives on soap operas. I think I did, too, at that age. But I unabashedly assert now that there are better models for meaningful life stories than *Stella Dallas* or *Melrose Place*. Most Bach fugues offer more toward becoming a reflective, mature agent than do most country-western hits.

At the same time, one must be careful not to interpret the notion of judging lives like works of art in separatist, formalist terms. One does not decide what sort of person to be simply in terms of rhythms or shapes or fit of images. There is an interdependence between what have typically been taken as ethical considerations on the one hand and aesthetic considerations on the other. One may remain undecided even after all the matters of interests or rights are settled; nonetheless, we will not choose between the alternatives in ignorance of matters of interests and rights.

But if aesthetics and ethics are equal partners, what happens to the mother metaphor? Is there any way of holding on to it if we give up the view that aesthetics comes first, as I think we must finally do?

To answer this question, we have to ask ourselves what work Brodsky intends the metaphor to do. The answer is straightforward: he wants to convince his audience of the importance of art. My readers, I am sure, share this goal with me and would like from such a metaphor help in convincing others of the importance of aesthetics. The truth of the statement that aesthetics is the mother of ethics depends on the truth of the premises on which it rests. The argument goes something like this:

1. Mothers are valuable to their children.
2. Aesthetics is the mother of ethics.
3. Therefore, aesthetics is valuable to ethics.

Also presupposed is a belief in the value of ethics. So aesthetics is valuable to something of value. And the first premise, "Mothers are valuable to their children," when filled out, produces the real argument:

1a. Mothers are valuable to their children when and because the relationship that exists between the mother and child provides the child with something of value.
2a. Aesthetics is the mother of ethics and does relate to it in a way that provides it with something of value.
3a. Therefore, aesthetics is valuable to ethics.

The value derived from the relationship does not require biological or ontological priority. Rather, the special relationship calls attention to two features that will help us convince others of the importance of aesthetics. First, in the mother-child relation, each member is defined in terms of the other. Second, it is a relationship in which nurturing and mutual concern are, ideally, long and deep.

Are aesthetics and ethics defined in terms of one another, and does nurturing take place? Is what characterizes the relation between them such that one might look to aesthetics to try to better understand the nature of ethics? I think the answer to all of these questions is affirmative. In later chapters, I shall provide specific examples of the nature of the mutual influence of the one on the other. The importance and seriousness of aesthetics is manifest when one sees what it has to offer ethics (and other disciplines): a kind of attention and understanding that is not gratuitous.

Still, the mother metaphor is troubling because we are left with a relationship that emphasizes a one-way direction, and I believe this makes it misleading. The only way that one can say that aesthetics comes first by definition is in terms of barren formal properties or patterns. This I reject. I would prefer a metaphor that emphasizes the conceptual interdependence and mutual nurturing without any con- notation of priority. Friendship or siblinghood would be better. But the point Brodsky makes when he says, "Aesthetics is the mother of ethics" seems weakened when we replace it with "Aesthetics is the friend of ethics" or "Aesthetics is the sib- ling of ethics." Neither connotes the depth or longevity of parenthood or child- hood. (By childhood, I mean the relation one is in for life with one's parent, not simply the period of one's youth. Unfortunately, there seems to be no good word to capture responsible, caring "offspringhood.") The fact that much is lost when the metaphor is revised in itself supports the centrality of metaphors—an aesthetic concept really—to human life.

And the mother metaphor is gendered. How different would Brodsky's point have been had he said that aesthetics is the *father* of ethics! There are certainly tasks conventionally associated with motherhood that I do not want to include. Suffice it to say that if his mother metaphor demands accepting traditional views of moth- ers as illogical servants happy to remain in the background and gaining satisfac- tion from washing and ironing others' clothes so that they will look good, I want none of it.

What I really want is a way of construing aesthetics that will make clear that it is important, serious, and integrated with general human values in a binding, in- fluential, and deep way. I attempt to provide it in the next part of this book.

PART III

Integrating Aesthetic
and Moral Value

What happens when someone looks at a brightly colored abstract painting and learns that it was produced by dying goldfish? There is, I think, no single correct answer to this question. People respond differently to aesthetic objects—to objects that possess intrinsic properties of the sort considered worthy of attention in their communities. One mistake often made by aestheticians (by both strong and weak formalists certainly) is thinking that theirs is the right way to respond, perhaps the only way that counts as responding in a genuinely aesthetic way to objects and events. I do not want to repeat this mistake. What I insist is that we not dismiss a priori as nonaesthetic those experiences that involve both attention to the work and attention to the world at the same time.

There are several things that might happen, several reports that might be given, when individuals who have been enjoying the bright painting learn how it was made.

1. "I am so taken by the colors that I don't even think about the fact that I am look-ing at something made by dying goldfish." In this case, one's moral experience is overridden by aesthetic considerations. Indeed, one might not even have a moral response.
2. "All I can think about is those poor fish—I can't even concentrate on the colors." Here, one's aesthetic experience is overridden or precluded by one's moral con-siderations.
3. "First I think about the fish and feel repelled, but then I think about how lovely the colors are." One shifts back and forth between moral and aesthetic considerations, has first a moral and then an aesthetic experience.
4. "I was enjoying the painting; but now that you've told me how it was made, I don't enjoy it quite so much; the lines look creepy rather than playful." Here, one's aes-thetic experience, while not, perhaps, wiped out completely, *changes*. The aesthetic does not give way to the moral in the sense of being overridden by it (as it is in the second case), but the colors and shapes no longer please one as much as they did before.

All of these cases are quite possible, I believe. Some people's aesthetic experience may remain the same. They do not find it artificial, unrealistic, or contrived to be told, "Just forget about the goldfish and look at the wonderful squiggly colors." But the fact is that some people are unable to forget. They say the following sort of thing: "When I look at the painting, I see the colored marks [a perception of an intrinsic property] made by dying goldfish [a consideration of an extrinsic fact about the painting]. And this latter consideration makes it hard for me to enjoy the colors that I continue to look at. I do not, in fact cannot, treat it the way I treat a duck-rabbit figure. That is, I cannot just look at the marks per se and have a pure aesthetic experience and then just think about the dying goldfish and have a pure moral experience."[1]

As I said before, I do not want to dictate what counts as the one and only correct kind of aesthetic experience, for I think these differ tremendously between individuals and, certainly, between cultures. What I do insist is that perception and/or reflection on intrinsic properties is a necessary condition. For me and for some others (but by no means all), the actual perception of some works changes when we are given certain bits of information. The reflection or conception obviously changes. Hence, the overall experience changes. We look for positive features that we did not look for before— instances of an intriguing use of perspective or application of an interesting color theory or expression of democratic values—or, negatively, we notice how boring the composition is or we scrutinize it for and find traces of sexism, fascism, or sadism, for instance. Often, the level of pleasure changes, though the experience remains one that we want to call 'aesthetic'. This suggests that aesthetic response is a result of aggregate rather than separate perceptions.

Perceptual experiences like those of the duck-rabbit figure are rare. So, I think, are occasions in which we neatly shift back and forth between exclusively moral and exclusively aesthetic experiences. When we are looking at, say, a painting of a horse, we do not look first at a horse

and then at the horse shape on the canvas. Those who have learned to "read" the marks immediately see a horse. There are not two acts of seeing here the way there are two acts of seeing in the duck-rabbit case. Seeing the horse in the horse shape (and vice versa) is what Richard Wollheim calls "the two-foldedness of seeing-in." Seeing a horse in marks on a page is an experience that has two aspects, but, as Wollheim writes, they are "two aspects of a single experience that I have, and the two aspects are distinguishable but also inseparable. They are two aspects of a single experience, they are not two experiences."[2]

I believe that my thinking about the goldfish painting is also a two-folded experience—one that involves distinguishable but inseparable components. It is wrong to assert that considering goldfish marks *as marks* and *as marks made by dying goldfish* implies that there must be two different experiences, one aesthetic and one moral. To repeat, most experiences do not come neatly parceled in that way.

What advice are we being given, or what are we being asked to do, when urged, "Don't let your moral considerations get in the way of your having an aesthetic experience"? Is it on a par with "Don't let the duck get in the way of the rabbit"? If so, it applies to relatively few experiences—those where a doubling or shifting is involved. The advice is quite unclear when it amounts to being told "Don't let seeing the horse get in the way of your seeing the horse shape," or vice versa. One may see a drawing of a horse and, for some reason, stop looking at the drawing—think about childhood pony rides or sexual theories of teenagers' fascination with stallions. But as long as we continue to look at the horse, we continue to look at the horse shape. Surely, looking closely at the horse (attending to the intrinsic properties of the drawing) does not preclude our looking at the horse shape, or vice versa.

Similarly, moral considerations do not necessarily block aesthetic experiences. Indeed, as in the case of sentimentality (discussed in detail in chapter 9), the aesthetic and the moral may be mutually dependent. Philipa Foot characterizes moral considerations as those relevant to moral judgments.[3] Any statement that can be shown to be directly or indirectly relevant to a moral judgment is a candidate—something as obviously relevant as pointing out that an action is a case of breaking a promise or as apparently irrelevant as being done on a Friday. A story can be told that makes the particular day of the week extremely important. As I argued in chapter 2, anything can also be aesthetically relevant, as long as it reports about or draws attention to an intrinsic property aesthetically and communally valued. "It was painted in Canada" or "The paint was applied by dying goldfish" can do this. They can also serve at one and the same time as a moral consideration and as an aesthetic consideration. Knowing something about goldfish may change the way we perceive or reflect upon the paint, and something about the paint may modify our moral appraisal. But no gestalt or mode shift is required here. Being applied by goldfish is not relevant exclusively to a moral judgment, and being frenetic is not relevant exclusively to an aesthetic judgment.

In this part, I shall examine some specific ways in which the aesthetic and nonaesthetic are connected, particularly at ways in which aesthetic and ethical concerns are integrated. I shall discuss what makes for "an aesthetic life." I shall also show how one term of assessment, 'sentimental', provides a case study for the interconnectedness of aesthetic and ethical evaluation. I shall conclude this part with two essays, one on art and moral lessons and one on a kind of ethical deliberation in which aesthetic attention is at the core. I hope that these specific examples of the integration of moral and aesthetic concerns and values will provide the best foundation for coming to recognize the general inseparability of these two core elements of humanity.

EIGHT

The Aesthetic Life

Aᴇsᴛʜᴇᴛɪᴄ experience, as I have defined it, involves attending to—perceiving and reflecting upon—an object or event's intrinsic properties considered worthy of that attention within a community into which one has been socialized. These experiences, I have argued, are not necessarily—indeed, are rarely—"pure" in the sense that one's attention is aimed only at aesthetic properties. One can look at a painting or landscape, listen to a song or poem and, while paying due attention to shapes or rhythms or repetitions, also think about grandma, sex, oppression, or anything else. As long as one continues to perceive or reflect on aesthetic properties, one is having a genuine aesthetic experience. Aesthetic values are different than, but they are not necessarily separate from, other values.

Still, some people's lives include more occasions of aesthetic attention than do the lives of some other people. Stated simply, "the aesthetic life" is one in which attending to intrinsic properties valued in one's culture because they repay that attention plays a significant role in one's life, both quantitatively and qualitatively. In this chapter, I shall look at a literary depiction of someone who leads such a life. I shall show in detail what it entails and suggest how even those whose lives are what we might call "very aesthetic" still lead lives in which the aesthetic is integrated with other values, in particular, with ethical values.[1]

Anthony Powell's work has been looked at carefully by relatively few critical scholars, in spite of the fact that he was called "the most elegant writer presently working in the English language."[2] I am surprised at how little he is read, at least in the United States. (A few friends have greeted my interest in Powell with surprised glee—as if they, too, are struck with how few fans Powell has. Ted Cohen, for example, shares my high opinion of Powell.) He is a splendid writer, often entertaining, always a skilled craftsman. His earlier novels (*Afternoon Men*, 1931; *Venusberg*, 1932; *From a View to Death*, 1933; *Agents and Patients*, 1936; and *What's Become of Waring*, 1939) are short satiric and ironic comedies dealing mainly with Bohemian life in London in the 1920s. His later fictional work is a twelve-volume tour de force (*A Question of Upbring*, 1951; *A Buyer's Market*, 1952; *The Acceptance World*, 1955; *At Lady Molly's*, 1957; *Casanova's Chinese Restaurant*, 1960; *The Kindly Ones*, 1962; *The Valley of Bones*, 1964; *The Soldier's Art*, 1966; *The Military Philosophers*, 1968; *Books Do Furnish a Room*, 1971; *Temporary Kings*, 1973; *Hearing Secret Harmonies*, 1975)[3] in which the narrator, Nicholas Jenkins, attempts, with varying degrees of success, to make sense of life as *A Dance to the Music of Time*.

Both the earlier and the later works are populated by many characters. Manageable in the short, independent novels, they become so numerous in the interwoven novels of *Dance* that several critics are dubious about anyone's being able to keep them straight. Had I read them as they were published, with years and the novels of other writers in between, I am sure it would have been impossible for me to keep track of all of the minor characters. In 1960, *Time and Tide* published a cast of characters for "readers who find it difficult to remember from book to book details of family and other more tenuous relationships between characters who have a habit of popping up surprisingly in the most unexpected places."[4] The entries provide the following kinds of information: "McReith, Lady (Gwen): friend of Babs Templer and Jimmy Stripling; goes to bed with Peter Templer when staying in the Temper (senior) house. . . . Tolland, George: son of Lord Warminster; was in Coldstream for some years then went into city. Very correct." More recently, Hilary Spurling has complied a book-length guide to the plots and characters of *Dance*. It also includes an index of books, paintings, and places referred to.[5] (And as we shall see, the fact that there are so many details is an important factor in depicting the aesthetic life of the protagonist.) Even with these guides, there are loose ends, and it is not always clear what functions certain minor characters serve. Nonetheless, the popping up in unexpected places is, as I hope to show, essential to the theme of the work.

Powell is by no means universally acclaimed. His novels have been described as "contrived,"[6] as "pseudo-Proustian and "blandly snobbish."[7] The early novels were described as telling "about 'twentyish emancipation, silly parties at which drunks behave stupidly, ambitious young men on the make for daughters of fox-hunting families, all with an air of slightness and couldn't-care-less."[8] And *Dance* has been scorned in a similar vein: "To begin with, each character is introduced as he first appears to the narrator, who immediately speculates for three or four pages on the probable nature of a character who is blond, has small ears, and wears a black overcoat. The overcoat then says a few desultory words, whereupon the narrator takes several pages of pain to modify his original opinion in the light of the additional evidence."[9] Like all parodies, these have some truth in them. But it is simplistic to describe Powell's work in these terms; it amounts to painting in colors far too crude what is an enormously subtle picture of life. It is also to overlook what Powell suggests about how sensitivity to detail in art and a corresponding attention to details in real life are integrated. Powell's "easy modulations," as John Russell has called the novels,[10] capture intricacies of human behavior and interaction, parallel to those in aesthetic objects, in a profound and original way. And Powell's focus on ritual and the attempts of people to play chosen roles, ultimately provides a genuinely metaphysical, epistemological, ethical, and aesthetic interpretation of life.

It is hopeless to try to provide a synopsis of the twelve novels that make up *Dance to the Music of Time*. They follow Nicholas Jenkins from his school days to late middle age. Friends such as Peter Templer, Charles Stringham, and Hugh Moreland appear and reappear as Time pipes the tune to which life steps, and as an early-encountered nemesistic enigma, Kenneth Widmerpool, and a veritable army of eccentrics continually distort the dance in which Jenkins would prefer to join. Even the work's theme is difficult to state simply; it is best exemplified by a few key passages in the novels themselves.

In the very opening passage of the first volume, *A Question of Upbringing*, the world is described as a stage on which a few actors are observed. Of course, this technique is not original with Powell; what is special about his treatment is that the narrator's seeing the world in this way is itself a primary subject of the work. And, as I hope to show, Powell's way of seeing others see the world is one of the things that makes him so interesting philosophically, and it provides us with one way of seeing what is special about the aesthetic life and its relation to an ethical life.

> The men at work at the corner of the street had made a kind of camp for themselves, where, marked out by tripods hung with red hurricane-lamps, an abyss in the road led down to a network of subterranean drain-pipes. Gathered round the bucket of coke that burned in front of the shelter, several figures were swinging arms against bodies and rubbing hands together with large, pantomimic gestures: like comedians giving expression to the concept of extreme cold. One of them, a spare fellow in blue overalls, taller than the rest, with a jocular demeanour and long, pointed nose like that of a Shakespearian clown, suddenly stepped forward, and, as if performing a rite, cast some substance—apparently the remains of two kippers, loosely wrapped in newspaper—on the bright coals of the fire, causing flames to leap fiercely upward, smoke curling about in eddies of the north-east wind. As dark fumes floated above the houses, snow began to fall gently from a dull sky, each flake giving a small hiss as it reached the bucket. The flames died down again; and the men, as if required observances were for the moment at an end, all turned away from the first, lowering themselves laboriously into the pit, or withdrawing to the shadows of their tarpaulin shelter. The grey, undecided flakes continued to come down, though not heavily, while a harsh odour, bitter and gaseous, penetrated the air. The day was drawing on. (*QU*, p. 1)

Looking on the scene brings forth images of the ancient world in Nick's mind, and this classical imaging makes him think of Poussin's painting, *The Seasons*.

> For some reason, the sight of snow descending on fire always makes me think of the ancient world—legionaries in sheepskin warming themselves at a brazier: mountain altars where offerings glow between wintry pillars; centaurs with torches cantering beside a frozen sea—scattered, uncoordinated shapes from a fabulous past, infinitely removed from life; and yet bringing with them memories of things real and imagined. These classical projections, and something in the physical attitudes of the men themselves as they turned from the fire, suddenly suggested Poussin's scene in which the Seasons, hand in hand and facing outward, tread in rhythm to the notes of the lyre that the winged and naked grey beard plays. The image of Time brought thoughts of mortality: of human beings, facing outward like the Seasons, moving hand in hand in intricate measure: stepping slowly, methodically, sometimes a trifle awkwardly, in evolutions that take recognisable shape: or breaking into seemingly meaningless gyrations, while partners disappear only to reappear again, once more giving pattern to the spectacle: unable to control the melody, unable, perhaps, to control the steps of the dance. (*QU*, pp. 1–2)

Thus, there is a kind of aesthetic stream of consciousness leading from the theater to painting to memories of boyhood: "Classical associations made me think, too, of days at school, where so many forces, hitherto unfamiliar, had become in due course uncompromisingly clear" (*QU*, p. 2).

Powell sees life aesthetically, and so do many of his characters, most especially Jenkins. A close look at what this means reveals the extent to which this involves ethical as well as aesthetic response to the world. My reason for saying that Powell's is an aesthetic view of life is not that he wants or tries to turn life into art. What he wants to do, I think, is to show how life is already, or at least can be handled like, art. Understanding life is a matter of using artifices to arrange it. One cannot grasp the patterns and hence the full meaning of them at the moment of encounter. One must reflect on experiences over time if arrangements are to be discovered and in turn inform later experiences. Specific works of art are sources for reflection on the sensual and abstract intellectual qualities of life, as well as on the content and meaning of their messages. Like the dancers in Poussin's painting, the characters in Powell's *Dance* move in and out to the music of Time. There are patterns to the movements, but these patterns are not always clear to the dancers; they become clear only if reflected upon. Life is like a ball—"dance-tune following dance-tune, and partner following partner" (*BM*, p. 60). As the characters in this extended novel dance to Time, and to other external forces, Jenkins see the patterns more and more clearly. Other characters, failing to reflect, miss them. Jenkins's relative success depends on his experiencing life aesthetically, as a work of art. As his interests change and as he matures, he sees more, just as one sees more in a painting as one looks at it again and again, and just as one sees different things as one changes oneself, as one is "reconstructed socially," as it were. (See chapter 1.) If one matures, one's viewing matures. But motifs are repeated. The novel ends with a reiteration of the opening winter bonfire metaphor. "The smell from my bonfire, its smoke perhaps fusing with one of the quarry's metallic odours drifting down through the silvery fog, now brought back that of the workmen's bucket of glowing coke, burning outside their shelter" (*HSH*, p. 271). And "even the formal measure of the Seasons seemed suspended in the wintry silence" (*HSH*, p. 272).

For Jenkins, experiencing life aesthetically primarily involves two sorts of activity. First, he uses specific works of art as sources of comparison and contrast as he reflects on what is going on around him. Second, he discovers patterns that serve, as they do in works of art, to organize the details of life. There are literally hundreds of examples in Powell's writing, both fiction and nonfiction, of the use of artworks to describe people, places, and events. In the early novels, they are usually brief. A young woman is described as an Eve by Tintoretto,[11] another is described as striving "to resemble an early John painting."[12] And characters are placed within scenes described in artistic terms: "In the break between the high ground the sky above the horizon was marked with strips of light where the sun was drawing water. These broad rays stretched up to the gap in the clouds, which parted to receive them in the neat formality of a canvas background, an Assumption scene or baroque ceiling."[13]

In his *Memoirs*, Powell describes real people and places as if they were artistic creations (both real and fictional). The Sitwells are "tall fair attenuated courtiers from a mediaeval tapestry."[14] And people play stage roles. "Henry Yorke, as opposed to Balston—almost literally carrying a spear when the curtain goes up on him—enters the stage with a speaking part."[15] At Miramere, "rocks and marine vegetation, absolutely clear in [the water's] depths, recalled—seemed to embody—those other contrasted blues of Manet's melancholy solider, glancing down at his rifle."[16]

Kingsley Amis describes this as a "practice whereby all manner of paintings and sculptures got brought in to provide decoration and imagery, the fictitious ones so vividly that one could hardly credit not having come across [them] in some municipal gallery; and the real ones with such insistence that one wondered at times whether Mr. Powell might not have been intending finally to pass under review the entire corpus of Western visual art."[17] I think Amis has missed the point of the "review." It is not just for decoration or imagery but important in itself.

Most of the references to specific works of art, as in the earlier novels, are used in *Dance* by the narrator to describe persons, places, things, and events, and by Powell to portray Jenkins as a person who views the world in these terms. In Jenkins's eyes, interior decoration becomes artistic creation, as do people. "Middle-age caused him to look more than ever like one's conception of Colonel Newcome, though a more sophisticated enterprising prototype of Thackeray's old warrior" (*SA*, p. 195). People are molded and carved: "Short, square, cleanshaven, his head seemed carved out of an elephant's tusk, the whole massive cone of ivory left more or less complete in its original shape, eyes hollowed out deep in the roots, the rest of the protuberance accommodating his other features, terminating in a perfectly colossal nose that stretched directly forward from the totally bald cranium. The nose was preposterous, grotesque, slapstick, a mask from a Goldoni comdedy" (*MP*, p. 8). Autumn is described as gold leaf falling from a mosaic (*BM*, p. 224), women have pink, silky Renoir skin (*AW*, p, 34), and, with time, Jenkins's military experiences come to resemble Trajan's column (*BFR*, p. 1).

The dance motif from Poussin's painting in the opening passage recurs throughout with lovers changing partners, friends rhythmically appearing and reappearing. In many places, Powell has all of this happen with a stage setting complete with scenery and lighting. Searchlights seeking out the enemy appear to have been arranged in a "deliberately regulated unison" (*SA*, p. 11). But the main thrust of the theatrical imagery is not simply to present all the world as a stage. It is primarily intended to emphasize the importance of role playing in human action. One's role is crucial, for it establishes one's position in any given dance. Some people are conscious of their roles; others are not. And this makes a crucial difference for Powell—both in plot development and, I shall argue later, in distinguishing the aesthetic from the nonaesthetic life.

Again and again, people are described as *assuming* a role—attempting, successfully or unsuccessfully, to perform well in roles that they have chosen for themselves or, in some cases, have had thrust upon them. "Life is full of internal dramas, instantaneous and sensational, played to an audience of one" (*LM*, p. 43). Backstage, after attending the theater with Moreland, Jenkins gets "the impression that the action of the play was continuing its course even though the curtain had come down" (*CCR*, p. 45). Isobel (we find out relatively little about this woman, who is Jenkins's wife, but we do learn that she shares his way of viewing life) re-marks at a party that there are "odd scenes in the next room" (*CCR,,* p. 173). To some extent, this is explainable in terms of people's need for drama in their lives. But to a far greater degree, it is due to their wanting to lead a life patterned on one that they have identified as desirable: powerful, influential, colorful, profound, and so on. "Members rose suddenly from the sofa and cast himself, with a startling bump, almost full length on the floor in front of the fireplace: exchanging in this manner his Boyhood-of-Raleigh posture for that of the Dying Gladiator" (*QU,* p. 181). People try to appear in ways they believe appropriate, and often their strategy for doing this is to imitate the ways in which they believe certain model characters—often literary or artistic or operatic—would behave. When Widmerpool disrupts a dinner, Matilda's face assumes "a look of conventional stage surprise, one appro-priate to an actress, no longer young, playing a quizzical role in comedy or farce" (*HSH,* p. 109). General Liddament, hoping to appear with the air of a scholar, dresses like shepherd in an "idealized pastoral scene" (*VB,* p. 94). All of these ac-tions are accomplished by, and require, due attention to the intrinsic properties of the actions and images one presents.

The novels set during World War II provide several instances in which life imi-tates art, with characters dressing up in costumes. When Jenkins first enters the army, he is assigned to a company headed by Captain Rowland Gwatkin who mod-els himself on a Kiplingesque version of a dedicated officer. (In chapters 10 and 11, I shall explicitly discuss the ways in which taking moral models from art supports my contention that the aesthetic and the ethical are integrated.) Initially, he is suc-cessful, appearing "almost to perfection in the part for which he had cast him-self" (*VB,* p. 12). But as the war progresses, as this movement of the dance becomes increasingly complex and demanding, the role Gwatkin has chosen becomes out-dated in modern warfare, so he fails to fit in.

Jenkins worries a great deal about what the soldier's role should be; this is a cen-tral theme of *The Valley of Bones, The Soldier's Art,* and *The Military Philosophers.* Jenkins never really fits in either, not because he chooses an outdated role, but be-cause he is too conscious of those features of army life so limited to simply dress-ing up that he cannot do enough to get more fully into character. One of the most elaborately layered figures occurs at the beginning of *The Soldier's Art* (the title it-self supports the point I am making), when Jenkins goes to buy a greatcoat at a shop that, appropriately for the metaphor, sells both army uniforms and theatrical cos-tumes. The shopkeeper mistakes him for an actor and is concerned with aesthetic, not military, effects. The antithesis here between the aesthetic and the military sym-bolizes other tensions for Jenkins.

> [In the background] two headless trunks stood rigidly at attention. One of these effigies wore Harlequin's diagonally spangled tights; the other, scarlet full-dress uni-form of some infantry regiment, allegorical figures, so it seemed, symbolising du-alisms of the antithetical stock-in-trade surrounding them . . . Civil and Military . . . Work and Play . . . Detachment and Involvement . . . Tragedy and Comedy . . . War and Peace . . . Life and Death. . . . (*SA,* p. 1)

The shopkeeper's mistake is natural enough since Jenkins is not himself sure of what he is doing. It is not that he lacks the right perceptual or reflective skills. Cues must not be missed, even for a walk-on part. Not missing them requires the kind of attentiveness that is characteristic of Jenkins. But he attends to the "wrong" features, and so misses a chance for a big part on the military stage.

Characters of *Dance* can be classified according to those who do and those who do not experience life aesthetically. The less likable characters are attracted to inferior works of art, those whose features are gross, not subtle; correspondingly, they miss the subtleties of life. Bob Duport, the husband of Jenkins's first mistress, notices a picture in the more sensitive Charles Stringham's room, but his criticism is superficial. He attends only to content, not to the way that content is presented. "I've never seen a jock on land, or sea, sit a horse like that" (*QU*, p. 191) exhausts the scope of his perceptiveness.

Jenkins's friends are more inclined to make sensitive aesthetic judgments and to see the world in terms of more sophisticated art. The writers Quiggan and Members (not friends, exactly, but more attractive than unattractive, I think) tend to describe people as Jenkins does. "'You must admit,' said Members looking round the room, 'it all looks rather like that picture in the Tate, of the Sea giving up the Dead that were in It'" (*BM*, pp. 242–43). Peter Templer compares Mrs. Erdleigh, a seer, to the title character of Rider Haggard's *She*. And Jenkins's best friend, Moreland, spends most of his time engaging in conversations about art.

But for Jenkins (and other characters treated sympathetically by Powell), seeing life aesthetically is not just a matter of seeing life as a series of artworks. Jenkins also discovers the patterns that organize life. And this discovery of the patterns in life parallels that used by attentive viewers when they contemplate works of art. It is not only what is discovered that matters but also the fact of the discovery itself. Seeing life on the model of patterned dances and paintings gives it order and coherency; just as looking at a painting involves actively fitting the parts together, so life's pieces must be related by an active perceptive and reflective effort. In *Dance*, it is common to find Jenkins explicitly trying to do exactly this: "Although . . . the scene occurred within a framework on the whole commonplace enough, the shifting groups of the party created, as a spectacle, illusion of moving within the actual confines of a picture or tapestry, into the depths of which the personality of each new arrival had to be automatically amalgamated; even in the case of apparently unassimilable material such as Mr. Deacon or Gypsy Jones" (*BM*, p. 101).

Just as works of art are at once a device and a theme for Powell, so are patterns. Repetitions and associations are not coincidental. The dance metaphor is one way of suggesting structures that "draw attention . . . to that extraordinary process that causes certain figures to appear and reappear in the performance of one or another sequences of what I have already compared with a ritual dance" (*BM*, p. 175). The role playing that we have already seen Powell employing to indicate character traits he also uses to establish the existence of patterns. People position themselves to accommodate the parts others play or attempt to play, and to force the accommodation of others. Or they fail to position themselves correctly and disrupt an established and seemingly successful pattern. Responding to Nick's invitation to dine, Stringham says, "Dining with you would spoil the rhythm so far as I'm concerned" (*SA*, p. 78). Unusual happenings become, through repetition, usual; for instance, Jenkins finds himself with what would be incredible frequency—were it not for credible patterns—helping someone put someone else to bed. The reader comes to know that a knock of the door means the arrival of Widmerpool at what would otherwise be implausible times. And oddball eccentrics become, paradoxically, alike, because they interchangeably fit into similar positions in a choreographed sequence.

An obvious question that philosophers will raise—a version of the realist-nominalist debate—is where these patterns ultimately should be said to exist. Are they in the real world, having an independent existence of their own, or do they exist dependently in the mind of the observer? There are plenty of passages supporting affirmative answers to both questions, but at the end of the day I think Powell's position is reflected in one of his earlier novels, *From a View to Death*. One of the characters there is reported to have "gazed into the sky for a few seconds, and then with a sweeping gesture conveying in its scope, rage, despair, thwarted ambition, contempt, defiance, disbelief in the goodness of human nature, and a stumbling hope in some pantheistic creed, he indicated the house with his unnaturally long forefinger" (p. 67). Now no gesture could possibility do all that unless the viewer actively read a great deal into it. On the other hand, certain things must be true of the gesture—the gesture must have certain intrinsic properties that can be perceived and reflected upon—if it is to be read as despairing, for instance, rather than gleeful, just as it can be said to point in the direction of the house only if, in fact, it does point that way. Not all interpretations of the world are equally valid; they will be more or less adequate depending on how well they fit particular, independently existing events. This supports the role for truth about the real world that I argued for earlier when I criticized Lamarque and Olsen for insisting that such truth is not aesthetically relevant. We must know a great deal about the world to know exactly what themes and patterns organize parts of artworks. The world does not present its patterns ready-made, nor can just any old pattern be made to fit it. The same is true for works of art, and the bases for the fits are connected. The successful, sympathetically presented characters in *Dance* are those who make the best fits. The patterns with which we inform the real world necessarily leave something out. Outside realities preclude our having the degree of control of real life that artists have in the creation of their imaginary worlds. However, formation of patterns does provide us with some measure of control in experience.

> On the stage . . . masks are assumed with some regard to procedure; in everyday life, the participants act their parts without consideration either for the suitability of scene or for the words spoken by the rest of the cast: the result is a general tendency for things to be brought to the level of farce even when the theme is serious enough. This disregard for the unities is something that cannot be circumvented in human life; though there are times when close observation reveals, one way or another, that matters may not have been so irreconcilable at the close of the performance as they may have appeared in the Second Act. (*QU*, p. 52)

Jenkins repeatedly tells us how the appearances of things change as he becomes more experienced. This is to be explained both in terms of his coming to see the world more on its own terms and in terms of his growing skill at constructing patterns which make it more coherent. Arrangements strike him later in life that he missed in his schooldays. He sets out actively "to connect together a few additional pieces in the complex jigsaw" (*TK*, p. 8). Chance encounters provide a new way of "blending disparate elements" (*CCR*, p. 29) but only when he has learned how to manipulate those elements.

Placed in the foreground in Jenkins's narration, then, and the basis of my saying that his is an aesthetic life, is his organization of experience in and as artistic and patterned structures. I want now to compare this kind of perceptive and reflective attitude toward life with one that is unaesthetic. As I indicated earlier, examples of individuals leading this sort of life are provided by the characters that Powell treats unsympathetically. This comparison should allow us to uncover even more about what it is that aesthetic people have, do, or see that unaesthetic people fail to have, do, or see.

If in *Dance* Jenkins has the major role, the second role goes to Kenneth Widmerpool. A combination of appearing never to have any business where he is—being out of step in the Dance—and yet advancing in the world's affairs makes his an unaesthetic life. If Jenkins's life is one of aesthetic reflection, Widmerpool's is one of unaesthetic action.

Jenkins meets Widmerpool in school, where the latter is a misfit. Jenkins first hears of him through anecdotes and, when he encounters him out for a run, knows who he must be immediately. Widmerpool's run, on a rainy afternoon, voluntary, and is in itself notable. None of the other boys is odd enough to run of his own volition on a cold, damp day. (We must remember that these novels were written before such running became de rigueur.) Jenkins is at once struck by "something comfortless and inelegant in his appearance" (*QU*, p. 3). 'Inelegant' is clearly a negative aesthetic term; 'comfortless' becomes one in the novels' context. Widmerpool is not comfortable, not at ease in his environment. Nor are others made to feel comfortable in his presence. His own chosen roles often fail to succeed, and he disrupts the successful movements of others on life's stage. His utterances are noisy and awkward; he even wears clothes uneasily. Indeed, one of the legends surrounding him deals with his badly fitting overcoat, and the term 'a widmerpool' comes to mean 'an inappropriate or obtrusive garment', as in, "I'm afraid I'm wearing my widmerpool socks to today." Thus his very name comes to be a derogatory aesthetic term.

Widmerpool, the inelegant plodder, is contrasted with Jenkins's more graceful and stylish school chums, Charles Stringham and Peter Templer. All turn up later in his life, but Widmerpool, as a kind of nemesis, is encountered more regularly than the others. Though just one example of the way people reappear in our lives, as if in preordained patterns, Widmerpool is a paradigm example of the fact that "certain acquaintances remain firmly fixed within this or that person's particular orbit; a law which seems to lead inexorably to the conclusion that the often repeated saying that people can 'choose their friends' is true only in a most strictly limited degree" (*BM*, p. 127). The reader, like Jenkins, is initially misled into thinking of Widmerpool as simply a loser, a foolish plodder, of all Jenkins's early acquaintances the one least likely to succeed. But succeed he does—in the material world's terms. As a man of action, and through the kind of dogged single-mindedness he demonstrates by running on a miserable afternoon, he gets several important jobs in the business world, rises in the army and government, and lands a cabinet post.

Thus, Jenkins and we readers are forced to alter our initial impression. Though the pathetic, inelegant image never disappears, it is tempered by one that is far more dangerous and frightening. His absurdity, like that of characters similar to him, is combined with the sinister. Widmerpool is placed in authority in wartime. His first appearance in a military uniform (costume), which, of course, does not fit well, "struck a chill through [Jenkins's] bones"(*KO*, p. 134). And well it might, for Widmerpool's plodding self-absorption has disastrous results: among other things, he bears a great deal of the responsibility for the deaths of Stringham and Templer. The lack of perceptual and reflective skills that mark aesthetic attention has ethical repercussions. (Notice here how Widmerpool exhibits a kind of single-mindedness that is not admirable. This suggests that Michael Slote was wrong to distinguish single-mindedness from daring on the grounds that the former is generally admirable, the latter only admirable in those cases where it characterizes an otherwise admirable action. See chapter 5.)

One of the characteristics of the person of action as represented by Widmerpool, in contrast to the person of reflection as represented by Jenkins, is self-absorption. Widmerpool fails to notice anything that does not involve him. Jenkins remembers all kinds of things about Widmerpool—things of the sort that Widmerpool never remembers about Jenkins. But Widmerpool, instead of finding Jenkins's memory remarkable and admirable, seems to expect that others pay him this kind of unreturned attention. Self-absorption is a source of the kind of power Widmerpool possesses. Jenkins "felt in some manner imprisoned by [Widmerpool's] self-preoccupation. He positively forced one to agree that his own affairs were intensely important: indeed, the only existing question of any real interest" (*LM*, p. 56). And, at times, this single-minded decisiveness is grudgingly admired by Jenkins: "I almost admired him for making so little effort to conceal his lack of interest in my own affairs, while waiting his time to demand something of myself" (*KO*, p. 222).

It is not surprising that one who fails to see or to remember what does not involve him also fails to see the world in terms of works of art. Widmerpool does not read novels, look at paintings, or care for music. Thus, women will not appear to him as Renoirs or skies as Monets. He even chides Nicholas for his own enjoyment of reading. "It doesn't do to read too much. . . . You get to look at life with a false perspective. By all means have some familiarity with the standard authors. I should never raise any objection to that. But it is not good clogging your mind with a lot of trash from modern novels" (*QU*, p. 134). But as Joseph Brodsky might put it, too short a reading list is associated with what amounts to too long a hit list. Furthermore, his failure in particular to read a specific modern novel written by one of the other characters, X. Trapnel, is particularly ironic when Widmerpool's wife leaves him for this author. Obviously, it is Widmerpool whose perspective is flawed. He fails to notice any of life's subtle patterns, and again this is a contrast to Jenkins, whose imagination, however, is stronger than his will. For Widmerpool, maturity plays no role in discovery or enhanced sensitivity. His oversimplification of the world's structure, if it brings him success in practical affairs, is ultimately displayed as an unsatisfactory way to live one's life. He consistently fails in relations with other people. He is miserable, though on occasion he appears so out of touch with the world that he seems not to realize just how miserable he actually is. Caught up in, and substituting, fads and fashions for enduring patterns drawn from developed reflective skills, Widmerpool ends his life in a ridiculous commune, groveling before a despicable guru.

Widmerpool's failures can, I think, be traced to his tendency to get power by manipulating inadequate pictures he has of the world (the gross patterns that are all he is capable of noticing or applying). They are inadequate because they are not pictures which result from sensitivity to people or events. Like other unsuccessful characters in *Dance*, Widmerpool chooses roles for himself that do not suit him or the Time. His past—his father was in the fertilizer business—he assiduously attempts to hide, and likewise he hides from his own nature. But his very attempt to avoid ridicule seems to draw it to him: thrown bananas land on his head, a young debutante dumps sugar on him, he marries a woman who seems to have married him only to have someone to "dump on" generally. The roles he chooses even seem to necessitate his making an absurd figure of himself. Not comprehending subtle, intricate moves of the dance he is part of, he intentionally wills himself into stereotypical parts—and the result is that he becomes, in government life, for instance, a "political cartoon" *(BFR,* p. 49).

Widmerpool does have, as I have indicated, some measure of success. He is certainly not a stupid person, nor is he always ineffectual. He sees some things that Jenkins misses. But his ability to do this is based on a kind of obstinacy that Jenkins later learns accompanies the lust and quest for power that often mark a person of action. As Widmerpool moves up in the world, Nick lags behind, and the former criticizes him for it. The reader, with Jenkins, is constantly reminded that Widmerpool is getting somewhere while Jenkins seems to stay in one place. But the degree of success Widmerpool achieves is bought by remaining "one of those persons capable of envisaging others only in relation to himself" (*BM*, p.271). As a man of action rather than reflection, he notices only those properties of the world immediately directed at his own ends. I asserted before that some characters are more conscious of the roles that they play than others. But it is more complicated than this. Both Jenkins and Widmerpool are aware of their roles. Here, the difference is that Jenkins is interested in the playing out of his role within a larger pattern; Widmerpool is interested only in the self-interested goals which might be achieved through the assumption of one role rather than another. He is preoccupied with manipulating others in order to control the world but without an awareness of his effects on others. There is for the Widmerpools of the world none of the delight felt by the Jenkinses in the discovery of patterns, no aesthetic pleasure taken in the world. But the consequences of failure to reflect upon the world extend beyond aesthetic pleasure. Those who fail to perceive patterns fail to form meaningful relationships with others; again, we see that aesthetic and ethical skills are integrated.

The theme of action versus reflection, will versus imagination, is central to *Dance*. Those who live the life of action, we have seen, miss important patterns. But Powell is conscious of a tension between action and reflection; too much reflection also takes a toll. For one thing, those who lead too reflective a life sacrifice the power that the world often tells us is so important. Robert Morris writes that *Dance* is based on this theme, "a dualism fundamental to human nature, yet peculiarly symptomatic of the twentieth century: a dualism that sets in opposition the man of will and the man of imagination, the power-hungry and the sensualist."[18] Indeed, this theme is already present in some of the earlier novels. The title *Agents and Patients* bespeaks concern for the same theme. But the line from a Wesley sermon from which the title is taken ("So in every possible case; He that is not free is not an *Agent*, but a *Patient*") also suggests that the message Powell sends must not be oversimplified. It cannot, for example, be captured easily in the dictums "Reflection is better than action" or "A life of power is less rewarding than a life of thought." If the aesthetic is to nurture the ethical, the ethical must also nurture the aesthetic.

One difficulty is with understanding the very term 'power'. In *Dance*, unsympathetic characters like Widmerpool who seek and achieve power make power itself, and the action associated with it, unattractive. But in the line from which "agents and patients" is borrowed, it is clear that action is a necessary condition of freedom, and hence is something obviously desirable. There is not a rigid dichotomy between action and power on the one hand and art and reflection on the other. Everyone must act, and action, if it is to be successful, requires reflection. But actions and their contexts also shape reflection—focus attention on what matters, for example. Many of the weaknesses in the characters of Powell's novels are traceable to the absence of reflection or action or to too much attention on the one rather than on the other. Nicholas Jenkins, who we have seen is primarily a reflective person, is too often indecisive. "Meanwhile, the question of whether or not to introduce Gwinnett to Pamela, without saying some preliminary word first, was becoming more urgent than ever. Thinking about allotropy was no help" (*TK*, p. 99). But *thinking* about allotropy is precisely the sort of thing that Jenkins does in such situations, and introductions are left to others to make—to those who have not sufficiently reflected on the situation and hence are likely to mismanage them. The tendency to hesitate too long because of complex reflection keeps him from succeeding as a soldier, or in any other roles that require immediate action.

> My own guilty feelings . . . came back to me, those sudden awarenesses at military exercises of the kind that, instead of properly concentrating on tactical features, I was musing on pictorial or historical aspects of the landscape; what the place had seen in the past; how certain painters would deal with its physical features. That was just what was happening now. Instead of trying to comprehend in a practical manner the quarrymen's proposals, I was concentrating on The Devil's Fingers themselves. (*HSH*, p. 161)

Reflection seems sometimes to preclude desirable action, but lack of it even to make action possible.

To the extent that action is required for survival, and indeed for the creation of works of art, the power to act is desirable. Thus, Powell does not simply disparage power. Rather, he is critical of power that is directed at manipulating or controlling the world—power in terms of worldly or material success. Powell favors a life in which the ability to reflect aesthetically—to concentrate on valuable intrinsic properties—is sought in preference to skills which lead to action when that action, as he seems to think is usually the case, lacks any such concentration. In his *Memoirs*, he praises Constant Lambert and suggests that his genius can be partially explained in the following way. "Lambert inwardly inhabited, often outwardly expressed, a universe in which every individual, every action, was instantly appreciated in terms of art" (Vol. 2, p. 61). Clearly, he could here be describing Nicholas Jenkins. Even with his indecisive shortcomings, Nick's life is a good one—though lack of action keeps him from being a genius. A combination of action and reflection is required, but for Powell reflection gets first place. Again and again, he contrasts those who are apt to notice and reflect upon the world with those who are not—those who are primarily concerned with what action might be performed. One of the strongest of these passages describes an occasion when Jenkins and Quiggans (a leftist editor-writer-politico) come together in a country cottage. Jenkins admires the landscape, while Quiggans bemoans the fact that it has not been agriculturally developed. This leads Jenkins to speculate that Widmerpool might not have noticed their surroundings at all. "Widmerpool would genuinely possess no opinion as to whether the view from the cottage window was good or bad. The matter would not have the slightest interest for him. He would be concerned only with the matter of who owned the land" (*LM*, p. 108).

In the final novel, *Hearing Secret Harmonies*, a young hippie wears a T-shirt with the single word *Harmony* on it. This is what the leader of the communal group to which she belongs says they are seeking. Nick says to the leader, "Harmony is not easy to define." When the leader responds, "Harmony is Power—Power is Harmony," Jenkins asks, "That's how you see it?" The leader's simple answer is "That's how it is" (*HSH*, p.12). Though not accepting the group's strategy for achieving it, I think Nick does agree with the slogan. Harmony—elements fitting together in appropriate and pleasing patterns—is achieved by reconciling oneself to one's role and striving for control not of others or the world, but of oneself as one seeks integrity and meaningful relations with family and friends. Reflection is good in itself, but it is also good because of the quality of life one can achieve by it. Those who, like Widmerpool, strive for power to control fail to achieve a meaningful life and fail to achieve the power to enjoy life. The insight Jenkins has, his ability to experience the world aesthetically, does bring him, in the end, what he mainly wants: sensuous and cognitive satisfaction.

Dance repeatedly demonstrates that it is "no good battling against Fate, which, seen in right perspective, almost always provides a certain beauty of design, sometimes even an occasional good laugh" (*VB*, p. 234). At most, we can hope not to control the world, but to modify our own approach to it. We can attempt to see the humor or beauty in it or to play our roles, as the character Trapnel does, with panache. Trapnel, a writer whose involvement with Widmerpool's wife, Pamela, has disastrous results, is introduced to the reader as one who is fully aware of the limitations the world places on what roles we can take on and what we can do with them. He has written a highly regarded novel, the title of which he has taken from a Egyptian in Cairo hawking, "Camel rides to the Tomb." "I grasped at once that's what life was. How could the description be bettered? Juddering through the wilderness, on an uncomfortable conveyance you can't properly control, along a rocky, unpremeditated, but indefeasible track, towards the destination crudely, yet truly, stated" (*BFR*, p. 109). Recognizing this, he eschews the melancholy (something Jenkins can never quite rise completely above) for a "panache which played a major part in Trapnel's method of facing the world" (*BFR*, p. 121). For example, he always travels by cab; even when he himself has no money, he manages to get others to handle it. He even manages to borrow fare from Widmerpool, who is particularly exasperated by any lack of practicality, particularly lacking in panache.

Modeling our lives on art and furnishing not only our rooms but also our lives with books and other works of art provide satisfaction, satisfaction of the sort which the artworks themselves provide. We are then in a position to enjoy our lives and the patterns we find therein, just as we enjoy uncovering patterns in works of art. Life is itself "worth attention" (*HSH*, p. 29) for those who approach it aesthetically—for those who hope "to construct one of those formal designs in human behaviour which for some reason afford an obscure satisfaction to the mind: making the more apparent inconsistencies of life easier to bear"(*LM*, p. 66).

The kind of enjoyment or satisfaction afforded by what I have called "the aesthetic life" is, I think, best suggested by a character who says, "Action is, after all, exciting rather than interesting" (*VB*, p. 107). The aesthetic life may be, after all, interesting rather than exciting. People of action not marked by reflection are stimulated only by what they think will be exciting. People of reflection, on the other hand, who find the ordinary extraordinary, are stimulated and delighted by what is basically interesting. Their pleasures may be tamer, but Powell believes that they are richer and more likely to bring the good life.

One of the ways in which this lesson is taught is by inviting the reader to become an aesthetic type. Frederick Karl says, "As the series continues, the reader becomes increasingly aware of the music itself, of the frequent variations and modulations on a basic theme, of the counter-pointing of motifs and characters, of the rich harmonic chords suggested by the author's close orchestrations."[19] Not all readers will notice these. Most features yield themselves only to a reader's sustained attention. But giving such attention to artworks, as to life, shapes both the aesthetic and moral life. I will say more in subsequent chapters about how aesthetic attention affects us morally. Only readers who share Jenkins's compulsion to attend to intrinsic properties and seek and form patterns in them have any hope of enjoying them.

> I could not help pondering once again the discrepancy that existed between a style of
> painting that must have been unfashionable, and at best aridly academic, even in [Mr.

Deacon's] early days; and its contrast with the revolutionary principles that he preached and—in spheres other than aesthetic—to some considerable extent practised. I wondered once again whether this apparent inconsistency of approach, that had once disconcerted me, symbolized antipathetic sides of his nature; or whether his life and work and judgment at some point coalesced with each other, resulting in a standpoint that was really all of a piece—as he himself would have said—that "make a work of art."(*BM*, p. 8)

It is the Jenkinses of the world, not the Widmerpools, who puzzle over this kind of thing—and delight in the puzzling. Ultimately, the good life, one in which goodness and beauty are integrated, requires such attention.

I think, then, that the aesthetic life as presented in *Dance* can be briefly stated in this way: A person leads an aesthetic life if he or she, through perception and reflection, tries to organize life in terms of patterns of intrinsic properties similar to those displayed by works of art, and delights in this reflection for its own sake. "Reflection for its own sake" is by no means a new notion, but suggesting what in particular it amounts to in life, as well as in art, constitutes Powell's profound contribution. It advances our understanding of the aesthetic. But more remains to be said about how such a life, how such an understanding of the aesthetic, reveals deep connections between the aesthetic and the ethical.

NINE

Sentimental Art and Sentimental People

She was dead. Dear, gentle, patient, noble Nell, was dead. Her
little bird—a poor slight thing the pressure of a finger would
have crushed—was stirring nimbly in its cage; and the strong
heart of its child-mistress was mute and motionless for ever.

—Charles Dickens,
The Old Curiosity Shop

Oscar Wilde is reported to have said that "one must have a heart of
stone to read the death of Little Nell without laughing." Wilde's aphorisms often
contain an element of surprise: as with many jokes, we expect one thing but get just
the opposite. Here he bursts our complacent bubble of belief that sensitive people
cannot keep from crying at such sorrowful events as the death of poor Little Nell.[1]

But appreciation of Wilde's claim does not entail a complete reversal of belief.
That is, we do not suddenly come to believe that genuinely sensitive people will find
Little Nell's death funny. Part of what makes Wilde's remark "work" is that there is
something funny *and* tragic about this death. We realize that in some ways it is appropriate even for people without hearts of stone to laugh at the death of an im-
possibly good child. At the same time, we still find something odd about such
laughter.

Wilde sharply criticized Dickens's sentimental lapses. The depiction of Little
Nell's death in *The Old Curiosity Shop* was such a lapse, he thought, and was certain to make only sentimental people cry or, if a nonsentimental person were to
have a lapse, to cry only sentimentally. What this means and its implications for
both aesthetics and ethics is the subject of this chapter. I will try to show that when
we see why, when, and how sentimentality creates bad art and bad people, we will
see another deep connection between the aesthetic and the moral.

In earlier chapters, we examined the separatists' claim that ethical and aesthetic
experiences and values are independent and that assessments of the one should not
be confused with assessments of the other. Wilde in many writings expressed this
attitude. He believed that morality and art should be kept distinct (although, as we
shall see in the next chapter, he himself was not immune from combining the two).

People who laugh at Little Nell's death are aesthetically correct, and anyone morally offended by such amusement makes a mistake. But if it is a mistake to let ethical considerations affect one's aesthetic judgments, and vice versa, how do we account for the fact that reasonable, even ethically and aesthetically sophisticated people, repeatedly make such mistakes?

The fact that people describe things in ways that are ethically positive but aesthetically negative and vice versa does seem to support the view that there is a fundamental difference between aesthetic and ethical values. A person can be kind, but sloppy; an action can be cruel, but gracefully executed; there are obscene, well-composed photographs; a march that incites a riot may have dramatic rhythms—indeed, the violence induced may be partially caused or intensified by them. Even the most central terms of ethics and aesthetics, 'good' and 'beautiful', often appear quite separate, for there seem to be many things that are beautiful though bad, good though ugly. Nonetheless, I have been arguing that the moral and the aesthetic cannot always be pried apart, and sentimentality provides a clear case study for one evaluative term in human discourse that proves that this is so.

'Sentimental' comes from '*sentire in mente*', literally, *feeling in idea*, and is a relative newcomer to English, dating back only to the eighteenth century. According to Allen B. Sprague, the earliest undisputed use of 'sentimental' is in a letter to Samuel Richardson from Mrs. Balfour (Lady Bradshagel) dated 1749: "What in your opinion, is the meaning of the word *sentimental,* so much in vogue among the polite? . . . Everything clever and agreeable is comprehended in that word. . . . I am frequently astonished to hear such a one is a *sentimental* man; we were a *sentimental* party; I have been taking a *sentimental* walk."[2] In spite of its initial use to refer to "everything clever and agreeable," 'sentimental' quickly took on derogatory connotations.[3] In a 1785 issues of *The Lounger,* Henry Mackenzie wrote, "In morals as in religion there are not wanting instances of refined sentimentalists who are contented with talking of virtues which they never practice, who pay in words what they owe in actions."[4] Thus, in only one generation, the term took on its contemporary tone, perhaps most aptly expressed in Wilde's famous description of a sentimentalist as one who "desires to have the luxury of an emotion without paying for it. . . . Even the finest and most self-sacrificing emotions have to be paid for. Strangely enough, that is what makes them fine. The intellectual and emotional life of ordinary people is a very contemptible affair. . . . And remember that the sentimentalist is always a cynic at heart. Indeed sentimentality is merely the bank holiday of cynicism."[5]

Still, like Lady Balfour, one must be astonished at the frequency of the use of 'sentimental'. In book titles, for example, there are sentimental journeys, sentimental revolutions, sentimental collections, sentimental centuries. Sometimes its use indicates disapproval, but not always. When Kermit Roosevelt wrote about a "sentimental safari" that he took to Africa, he described a journey taken with the purpose of retracing one of his grandfather's trips. It was to be not just a safari, but a safari with feeling. Perhaps there is a suggestion that the author was indulging himself, but he was certainly not confessing to evil or vicious actions.[6] Sentimentality can even be viewed positively. One drama critic cited a play's failure to provide a "sentimental tug" as a cause of its failure.[7] And in some cases, it is not clear whether sentimentality is good *or* bad. Following a rather tear-jerking report, I heard an exchange between two television newscasters that went something like this:

A: (Choked up) Sorry—I'm just so sentimental.

B: Nothing wrong with that.

A: Oh, I know, I'm glad.

If A is truly glad, does he lie when he says, "Sorry"? It appears that just as the edge is taken off our admiration of the man who laughs at Little Nell's death, so an edge is taken off our contempt for the anchorman who cries at a sentimental report.

Even when used negatively, accusing people of being sentimental is not on a par with accusing them of displaying other vices. Unlike being cruel or insensitive or selfish, describing someone else or oneself as sentimental is on a different level. For example, if you say, "I'm so sentimental," my reaction is likely to be quite different than if you say, "I'm so cruel (selfish, insensitive)." If you say, "Joe tends to be sentimental," I may say, "Nothing wrong with that," a response I will never give if you say, "Joe tends to be cruel." Similarly, I am more inclined to read a novel that someone has told me is sentimental than I am to read one advertised as brutally pornographic.

Nonetheless, 'sentimental' is used most often in straightforward negative assessment, both ethical and aesthetic. American policy in East Asia has been described as "sentimental imperialism," where this was identified as "cold war zeal [that cannot] substitute for realistic knowledge."[8] When a pilot of a hijacked airplane seeking landing rights in Beirut argued that a person on board had suffered a heart attack, he was told that there were people all over Lebanon dying. "Don't get sentimental on me," he was admonished by an official in the control tower. The "Helga paintings" of Andrew Wyeth have been accused of sentimentality, with no indication from critics who describe them this way think that there is "nothing wrong with that." Although displayed at several American museums, the Metropolitan Museum of Art in New York City refused to host an exhibition of them. The director, Phillippe de Montebello, declined on the ground that such sentimental works belong on greeting cards, not in New York museums of art.[9] The critic Hilton Kramer gave the following assessment of Wyeth's work: "It's provincial, it's sentimental, it's illustration and it's without substance. In my opinion he can't paint. They are just sort of colored drawings. It's one of those illustrated dreams that enable people who don't like art to fantasize about not living in the 20th century."[10] Though not everyone by any means agrees with this view (several museums did, after all, mount the show), such accusations are not lighthearted. Looking back at the exchange between the television newscasters, it is hard to imagine this one:

Wyeth: Sorry, I'm just so sentimental, so provincial and without substance.

Kramer: Nothing wrong with that.

Wyeth: Oh, I know. I'm glad.

Many authors describe novels as sentimental when they hold fast to a determined belief in the innate goodness of the human heart that expresses itself in such things as reformed rakes, profound sacrifices, the ultimate triumph of justice and virtue, or early deaths that prevent loss of innocence.[11] Heroines are consistently delicate, self-effacing, dutiful, conventional, and more comfortable facing death than a breach of decorum. Instead of babies being born, cherubs appear. The physical world is described in ways that always cooperate to present pictures of innocence, melancholy, or tenderness—or all of the above. Landscapes feature pale moons (full when necessary), purple mists, and weeping willows. The epistolary form is a particularly popular sentimental device because it allows for the detailed laying out of feelings; teardrops can blur the ink at appropriate spots, and unfinished sentences can easily be used to suggest death or suicide. Sculpture that is patriotic and pretty is open to the charge of sentimentality, as are songs that have such titles as "Mary's Last Words," "The Inebriate's Lament," "The Parting Requiem," "The Sailor's Grave," "My Mother's Bible," and the ever popular "Old Folks at Home." Their rhythms and harmonies are predictable and simplistic.

Critics debate whether Laurence Sterne's novel *A Sentimental Journey* is sentimental or ironic. In either case, one of the effects of his immensely popular novel was to turn sentimental journeys and books relating them into something of a fad. Marked by reminders to the reader that the authors were sufficiently (or abundantly) sensitive and by a whole range of stylistic gimmicks, one discovers that, no matter where the journey is taken, authors, "never failed to find virtue in distress or some ill-treated animals in need of help."[12] According to Marjorie Bowen, one such treatise was written by Guillaume Raynal, who undertook to write a history of the New World that would show how corrupt Europe was, compared with the land inhabited by the Noble Savage. In about a year, he put together the *History, Philosophical and Political, of the Establishments and the Commerce of Europeans in the Two Indies*. Written in French and published in The Hague in 1770, it was essentially a fashionable travel book that "gave abundant opportunity for the shedding of those tears and the heaving of those sighs every educated person was eager to shed and heave."[13] Populated by savages, money-grubbing explorers and traders, and ill-used cows and servants, it presents the world as a battleground between the right and evil practices of humankind. Though immensely popular, this book and others like it did not, of course, prevent the exploitation of the New World and its inhabitants by the criers and sighers. Such inconsistency of expression and action is a main reason for their being considered sentimental.[14]

There have not been many philosophical discussions of sentimentality, but there have been enough to show what some theorists think it entails and to suggest why they think it is bad to be sentimental.[15] One of the earliest and most extensive discussions of sentimentality in the twentieth century is that of I. A. Richards, a writer whose interests are primarily aesthetic, not ethical. Sentimentality, according to Richards, is a question of appropriate response. Vaguely, it indicates that something is wrong with the feelings involved; more precisely, it suggests that "emotions are too easily stirred. . . . All our emotional susceptibilities may be more or less affected, but the results are most marked with those which we can luxuriate in, those which do not obviously endanger our self-esteem."[16] In literature, this is marked by use of conventional or "stock" metaphors and other stylistic devices that invite proportionately stock responses. The causes of sentimentality, whether defects of the reader, of the work, or of both, vary. It is often the result of inhibition, Richards thinks. Writers and readers focus on one aspect of a thing or situation because they are afraid to think of others. Childhood or war is most easily thought of in terms of innocence and camaraderie, for instance. In other cases, readers seem to be afraid of expansive emotional responses and so blame poems as sentimental not when "its victims have too much feeling at their disposal, but . . . too little; they see life in too specialized a fashion and respond to it too narrowly."[17]

One of the best things about Richards's discussion is his explicit recognition that 'sentimental' is a term that can describe both aesthetic objects and moral agents. This follows from the fact that there are both good and bad poems and good and bad readers of poetry. Thus, good poetry can be read well or badly, as can bad poetry. Readers, as well as what they read, are open to assessment. Stock metaphors can generate stock responses, but so can nonstock metaphors if the reader's response is shallow. (There may even be some excellent readers who respond nonsentimentally to stock metaphors, one assumes.)

We do not often think that calling someone a good or bad *reader* is an *ethical* assessment. However, I think that in the case of sentimentality we begin to see that it can be. Too little feeling, too shallow feeling, overindulged feeling, or inappropriate feeling cannot be evaluated merely in terms of features of an object responded to. I shall develop this point later in this chapter.

Michael Tanner has provided one of the most detailed analyses of sentimentality.[18] He is primarily interested in the conditions under which we predicate sentimentality of people. Everyone seems to agree, says Tanner, that sentimental feelings are cheap, too easily come by, and directed at unworthy objects. But he believes that Richards's explanation in terms of crude and inappropriate response to a situation is not adequate, for sometimes, as in music, there is no "situation." Furthermore, he thinks that inappropriateness and crudeness do not explain why Victorian treatment of the death of a child is often sentimental. Nor are all inappropriate responses sentimental: Othello's jealousy, for example. Even "too easy" does not always apply, for sometimes sentimentality leads to suicide, hardly an easy response.

Tanner prefers an analysis in terms of a dislocation of feelings from their objects that is characterized by "auto-generation." Since the feelings are generated by the feeler, self-deception and dishonesty are often involved. Thus, they often contain an element of illicit pleasure. What results is feelings that have "lost touch with their origins in insidious and dangerous ways."[19] Inappropriateness results because sentimental people do not act on their feelings in ways that would probably make them go away. Instead, they seek satisfaction from doing things that make it likely that the feelings will continue.[20]

But, Tanner warns, we must be careful with 'appropriate' here. Some people act appropriately, given their sentimental feelings; for example, those who are sentimental with regard to snails refrain from stepping on them. Such cases make it clear that "all such predications are made on the basis of a set of standards regarding the relationships between feelings, attitudes, beliefs and actions which will necessitate . . . a full account of our deepest moral commitments."[21] Not surprising—for sentimentality provides a clear case of the inseparability of ethics and aesthetics.

Mary Midgley suggests that the instrument of what Tanner calls the auto-generation of feelings is a misrepresentation of the world that distorts expectations and perpetuates fantasies such as totally good and innocent children.[22] Though harmful, she argues that the opposite of sentimentality, brutality, is far worse because it indulges intrinsically harsh feelings. The actions associated with the latter have far worse consequences for other people on the whole than those associated with the former.

Mark Jefferson believes that although sentimentality is sometimes thought of as just silly, it, like brutality, should be generally construed as pernicious.[23] He thinks that Midgley's view of sentimentality as a kind of misrepresentation for the sake of self-indulgence is too broad, for this alone does not explain why it is bad. Daydreaming and some moviegoing involve misrepresentation for the sake of self-indulgence, but these are not really dangerous, nor are we even inclined to think of them as unethical. Perniciousness enters when there is a "sustaining fantasy."[24] We become attached to certain beliefs, and when these prevent us from having a true picture of the world, they become dangerous. By emphasizing sweetness, dearness, littleness, blamelessness, and vulnerability, one views the world simplistically. The distortion is aggravated when one can sustain the "sweet" belief only by making something else appear worse than it is. The distortions are, in a sense, multiplied. Tanya Rodriquez pointed out to me that a good example of this is the image of Aunt Jemima that formerly appeared in advertisements for food products. Her smiling wholesomeness invited "sweet beliefs" that veiled a whole range of oppressive practices.[25] One was invited to believe that all black women were ready and willing to assume servile roles.

One of the fullest discussions is found in Anthony Savile's *The Test of Time*, in which he makes the following claims about sentimentality that lead to his definition:

1. There is no distinct feeling or content of thought that passes under the name 'sentimenality'; it is a mode of feeling rather than a kind of feeling.
2. Sentimentality is always open to criticism; there are no situations the proper perception of which demands a sentimental response.
3. The desire under whose guidance sentimental thought is conducted is not the desire for belief. If it were, falsity or lack of sufficient evidence would capture the essence of sentimentality. They do not. For example, if I believe falsely or unjustifiably that my brother has died, my response is not (necessarily) sentimental. However, sentimentalizing is active, not passive, and sentimental responses tend to resist correction of the thought upon which they are based.
4. One desire under whose guidance sentimental thought is conducted is the desire to have enjoyable emotions.
5. Another is the gratifying image of the self as compassionate, righteous, or just, that is thereby sustained.
6. Sentimentality requires idealization of an object.

The resulting definition is this: "A sentimental mode of thought is typically one that idealizes its object under the guidance of a desire for gratification and reassurance." Sentimental artworks will either display or evoke such modes of thought.[26] For example, they will display inflated language, vague cliches, stock metaphors, and the like.[27] As we shall see later, these stylistic features, as well as the characteristics that mark sentimentality as a mode of feeling, are the focus of attention when we judge art and people as sentimental.

This survey of the uses and analyses of 'sentimental' point to a variety of properties that it is used to pick out. They do not lend themselves to a neat taxonomy; there is significant overlap both semantically and syntactically; there are even some positive items present. But the following lists help to remind us of the sorts of features the concept includes.

Ethical

Excessive, compassionate, innocently self-indulgent, shows feeling, misrepresentative, unrealistic, deceptive, self-deceptive, fantasizing, idealistic, lacks substance, childish, romantic, prevents thinking, sheds tears easily, escapist, feminine, utopian, ignores reality, humanitarian, provides motive for moral improvement, nostalgic, belief in innate human goodness, hypocritical, stifling, inhibitive, confused, mentally lazy, benevolent, inappropriate, self-gratifying, auto-generative

Aesthetic

Excessive, insubstantial, unrealistic, trite tricks (e.g., pretty colors, unfinished sentences to refer to death), stock descriptions, language avoiding reference to real world, circumlocution, inflammatory language and style, clichés, euphemisms, images that tug at feelings, overused vocabulary ('tears', 'sighs', 'faints', 'purple mists') vague, unfocused, confused, crude, impure, unduly gratifying and reassuring modes of thought and expression, imprecise

At the very least, these lists show that Richards was correct when he said that 'sentimental' is vague. Furthermore, when you ask someone for the opposite of 'sentimental', the response is likely to be only 'unsentimental'. Wilde thought the opposite was 'cynical', but we have also been offered 'brutal', 'deep', 'sincere', and 'genuine'. All of these oppose only some features that 'sentimental' is used to call attention to.

The ethical list includes quantitative, cognitive, and developmental features. That is, some features have to do with how much, how little, or how intense a response is. Others concern the deceptive or unrealistic nature of an attitude or belief. Still others relate to the extent to which moral development is exemplified or implied. Some, of course, overlap all of these crude categories.

The aesthetic list is similarly vague. It includes features having to do with both what is presented and how it is presented. Some features suggest something about the kind of person likely to create the object being described. Others concern the kind of person likely to respond to the object.

We need to remind ourselves that both lists include positive, negative, and possibly neutral terms. 'Idealistic', for example, is neither positive nor negative when taken out of context, I think. When sentimentality implies sensitivity—that is, when it simply refers to the presence of sentiment (as it seems to have done in its earliest uses)—it is all right to be sentimental. This is, of course, particularly the case for those moral theories in which sentiment is also the ground for morality. It is also positive when it refers to feeling (even an excess of feeling) that results in admirable action. Geoffrey Atkinson writes, "More than one of the sentimental authors . . . confessed that they had grown more compassionate after having suffered themselves."[28] When sentimentality is connected with humanitarianism or motivation for a good act or maturing moral development, it is positive. I know of a company that manufactures electronic medical devices that annually invites people who have benefited from their products to visit the company and tell the employees how important their work is. Often, the stories they tell are designed to leave no dry eyes in the audience. Sentimental? Probably. But at the same time, this is undoubtedly a useful ritual.

Less positive, but not yet fully negative, are those uses of 'sentimental' that are connected with innocent self-indulgence. Tears shed at the death of Little Nell (in private or with a consenting adult) hurt no one else. Nostalgic trips taken to one's childhood neighborhood or to retrace the steps of a favorite relative are not in themselves bad. It is only when such activities are undertaken with excess or, for example, to avoid other responsibilities that they become negative. Similarly, some sentimental activity seems to provide a protective function: it allows therapeutic escape from pressure or from an unrelenting onslaught of the world's problems. James Serpell, for instance, argues that pet owners, even if open to the charge of sentimentality, derive deep and meaningful medical and psychological benefits from their involvement with their animals.[29] Just as one of its opposites, cynicism, may, by emphasizing the negative, protect by keeping one from being duped, cynics take a "bank holiday" from the distressing side of life when they allow themselves occasional sentimental indulgences. Again, this defense becomes immoral when it becomes habitual, for then it begins to involve self-deception and other character flaws.

Most of the features on the ethical list are negative, however, and concern a gap between feeling and appropriate belief or action. Sometimes one's response displaces or replaces what one should really feel—as when grief replaces guilt or when one's response deceives oneself or others or moves others to action one is not ready to perform oneself. As Mark Jefferson writes, one voluntarily attaches oneself to beliefs that warp expectations (both others' and one's own), lead to oversimplification, and through maintaining a particular picture of the world, prevent one from considering other, possibly more appropriate or effective views of the world.[30] Inconsistency between feeling and action is typical of many persons accused of being sentimental. Mrs. Long's criticism of Raynal is apt here. Though an ardent verbal supporter of Rousseau's back-to-nature views, Raynal "continued to enjoy as far as his means allowed him the benefits of that civilization he so wholeheartedly condemned."[31] A kind of dissonance marks awareness of sentimentality in oneself or others. V. S. Naipaul portrays one such occasion—a party like those many my age attended in the 1960s where political songs were played on the latest stereo equipment: "It was make-believe—I never doubted that. You couldn't listen to sweet songs about injustice unless you expected justice and received it much of the time. You couldn't sing songs about the end of the world unless—like the other people in that room, so beautiful with such simple things: African mats on the floor and African hangings on the wall and spears and masks—you felt that the world was going on and you were safe in it."[32]

Virtually all the features on the aesthetic list are negative. However, we did encounter an example in which the additions of a "sentimental tug" would have improved a play. Although Saville may be correct that we typically do not invoke sentimentality, there may be times when such admonitions as "He would have benefited from being a bit more sentimental" are not nonsensical. When a work of art evokes feelings as part of its intention, sentimentality in the sense of drawing on the compassion of the audience can be a good-making characteristic. Or when 'sentimental' refers, as it sometimes does, to the content of works of art, there is some possible benefit, especially that connected with therapeutic escapism, humanitarian urges, or development of moral sensitivity—and now we begin to see how closely related the ethical and aesthetic are in the case of sentimentality. Artworks that tug at feelings do sometimes elicit these.

There are a few neutral aesthetic features. There is nothing wrong per se with colored or pretty drawings, for instance. It is only when these are connected with lack of substance that an aesthetic vice results. Depictions of death, landscapes dotted with weeping willows and pale moons, and stories in which virtue triumphs are not bad in themselves. But artists must take care when using them. They easily become defective when they are associated with trite, facile, or false representations. Death depicted by use of unfinished sentences or human passion described with circumlocution easily results in a sentimental work, as do stock vocabulary, metaphors or syntax used to describe genuine and profound experiences; all are aesthetically impoverished. Typically, these are tied to the general sins of deceptiveness or misplaced or undue idealism—to children who are thoroughly innocent or women who perform no bodily functions other than weeping, fainting, and blushing, for example. "Sweet beliefs," as Tanner describes them, are too often false, even dangerous, beliefs.

Given that there are positive, neutral, and negative features on both the ethical and aesthetic lists, it is now time to think in more detail about what it is that turns these into good- or bad-making properties. Let us go back to three examples: the sentimental newscaster, the sentimental pilot, and the person who laughs at the death of Little Nell.

1. The anchorman chokes up when a story is shown and apologizes for being so sentimental. The co-anchor says there's nothing wrong and then the emotional man

admits that he is actually glad that he is sentimental. Clearly, if "Sorry, I'm so in-dulgent, self-deceiving, insincere, trite, etc." were what he meant by 'sentimental', it would not be all right. It must in this context mean that his show of emotion in-dicates appropriate compassion. It indicates the ability to feel, probably deeply, and hence there is "nothing wrong" with it. The co-anchor applauds the readiness or ability to show feeling, particularly in this set of circumstances—in front of a large audience when cool, objective reporting is supposed to be the rule. The behavior would be censurable if one had reason to believe that the newscaster had been duped (had been drawn into an exaggerated or shallow piece of reporting about suffering innocent children) or if one believed that he never acted appropriately when these feelings were aroused, for example, never donated time or money or supported legislation to help suffering children. (The Ted Baxter character on the old Mary Tyler Moore show was such a person.) Sentiment, as required for moral-ity, is all right unless it is indulged in and never results in the action called for. Here, it is all right if the feeling shown is real. As members of the audience who do not know the newscaster, we cannot know if the feeling is real, or if the man is chari-table. Part of what counts as evidence for deciding that the feeling is or is not sen-timental is knowing whether a person is ready to act; since we do not have this bit of knowledge, we cannot judge whether he is being negatively sentimental.

2. The sentimental pilot is ready to act. He wants permission to land to get medical care for a passenger who may die, and there is nothing culpable about this as such. When the official in the control tower says, "Don't get sentimental on me," the pi-lot is accused neither of failing to feel nor of failing to act on his feelings, but of failing to think broadly, for failing to have a realistic picture of the world. If he had such a view, even if he were himself moved by the impending death of a person for whom he has some direct responsibility, he might not expect others to be so moved. The tower official may also be suggesting that even if the impending death really bothered the pilot, he should have done or do something about the hun-dreds of people dying all over Beirut and the rest of the world. Primarily, however, the official implies that *he* cannot be moved by one sick passenger when there are more demanding needs to attend to—and he criticizes the pilot for failing to have realized this.

3. Should one laugh or cry at the death of Little Nell? There is nothing laughable per se in the death of a sweet, innocent little girl who has dedicated her life to caring for her grandfather. Typically, crying is exactly the sort of emotional response ap-proved or expected in such a situation.[33] However, identifying the appropriate re-sponse to depictions of death in art demands answering more questions: is crying over Nell acting as if Dickens's *depiction* of her death is like things genuinely wor-thy of tears? Laughing is admirable if it shows that one is not manipulated by an inferior description of a serious event. The person who cries at trite, stock depic-tions has been taken in by them and, to that extent, is as sentimental as the depic-tion itself. This can be excused only if it is neither a form of self-indulgence nor deception and does not take the place of other appropriate action. We may want take a holiday from the real woes of the world, and the indulgence may be justi-fied and even necessary if it is occasional and not habitual.

At the same time, seeing sentimentality for what it is, and hence laughing at it, is also appropriate. Dickens's presentation of Little Nell's death is laughable. The pas-sages in which her death is intimated are full of features found on the list of things that make something aesthetically sentimental. There are trite phrases, clichés, inflated vocabulary, stock metaphors, and more. Nell feels "involuntary chills" when she comes to the house where she will die.[34] The child is "riveted" to the spot, though she "knows not why." She observes that it is a "place to live and learn to die in."[35]

Dickens is at his worst when he describes this good character's demise. Indeed, he is generally cleverer when he deals with "bad guys" than with "good guys." (Perhaps writers always have a harder time creating convincing thoroughly good characters.) Consider the passages in which the deaths of sweet Little Nell and the evil Quilp are described:

Nell

She was dead. No sleep so beautiful and calm, so free from trace of pain, so fair to look upon. She seemed a creature fresh from the hand of God, and waiting for the breath of life; not one who had lived and suffered death. . . . She was dead. Dear, gentle, patient, noble Nell, was dead. Her little bird—a poor slight thing the pressure of a finger would have crushed—was stirring nimbly in its cage; and the strong heart of its child-mistress was mute and motionless forever.

   Where were the traces of her early cares, her sufferings, and fatigues? All gone. Sorrow was dead indeed in her, but peace and perfect happiness were born, imaged in her tranquil beauty and profound repose. . . . She had never murmured or complained; but, with a quiet mind, a manner quite unaltered—save that she every day [had become] more earnest and grateful to them—faded like the light upon a summer's evening.[36]

Quilp

Another mortal struggle, and he was up again, beating the water with his hands, and looking out with wild and glaring eyes that showed him some black object he was drifting close upon. The hull of a ship! He could touch its smooth and slippery surface with his hand. One loud cry now—but the resistless water bore him down before he could give it utterance, and, driving him under it, carried away a corpse. It toyed and sported with its ghastly freight, now bruising it against the slimy piles, now hiding it in mud or long rank grass, now dragging it heavily over rough stones and gravel, now feigning to yield it to its own element, and in the same action luring it away, until, tired of the ugly plaything, it flung it on a swamp . . . and left it there to bleach. And there it lay, alone. The sky was red with flame, and the water that bore it there had been tinged with the sullen light as it flowed along. The place the deserted carcass had left so recently, a living man, was now a blazing ruin. There was something of the glare upon its face. The hair, stirred by the damp breeze, played in a kind of mockery of death—such a mockery as the dead man himself would have revelled in when alive—about its head, and its dress fluttered idly in the night wind.[37]

Why is it so hard for even as skilled a writer as Dickens to portray good people and their deaths without slipping into sentimentality? In answering this question, we see that understanding the use of 'sentimental' points to the connection between the ethical and aesthetic components of sentimentality. Instead of being separate, *both* aesthetic and moral features must be considered before one can correctly ascribe 'sentimental' to something.

Although the description of her demise is full of clichés and stock metaphors, we cannot account for the sentimental nature of Little Nell's death simply in terms of such trite devices. After all, newspaper death notices resort to the same tools without suffering such an accusation. Their use alone does not constitute a sufficient condition for sentimentality. It must be coupled with an unrealistic picture—in this case both of children (even good children) and of death. Dickens would have us accept a child not only who is uncomplaining but also whose only displayed emotions are increasing earnestness and gratitude. There are no signs of suffering. The innocent little bird, who stirs nimbly rather than fluttering clumsily in its cage, provides the only trace of action in a scene of otherwise undisturbed tranquility.

Even had he succeeded in avoiding the trite phrases and images, Dickens could not write in a way that would convince us that death and dying are like this, for they are not. Even people who die surrounded by loved ones and favorite pets sometimes moan, produce a death rattle, or exhibit signs of pain or at least sickness. At the very least, the onlookers suffer. Death is, in reality, much more like Quilp's, where the transition from person to corpse is pronounced. To ignore this is, at best, disingenuous. Thus, recognizing the sentimentality of the passage describing Little Nell's death requires attending to aesthetic properties, but in addition it requires that we think about death. Ignoring its real nature results in a depiction that is laughable rather than moving or even interesting. Once we begin to consider the *deceptive* nature of depictions, we have entered the moral realm.

One certainly finds trite phrases and stock devices in the Quilp passage: "flaming red skies," for example. But the frequency of these is not nearly so pronounced as it is in the Nell passage. Quilp's death comes in a few short paragraphs; Nell's takes several pages and thus a plethora of clichés contributes to the representation's becoming more and more maudlin. Where vivid phrases like "left there to bleach" and "sullen light" make up for Dickens's resort to "flaming red skies," no such striking images color the picture of Nell's death.

Ethical evaluation is the assessment of someone's character or behavior in terms of the effects it has on human well-being or in terms of the behavior's compliance with dictates of conscience or principles governing human beings' treatment of one another. Aesthetic evaluation, we have seen, assesses something in terms of its capacity to produce delight when intrinsic features of it, traditionally identified as worthy of attention, are the object of perception and reflection. In the case of 'sentimental', both types of assessments are involved. Although I have provided lists of aesthetic and ethical features, such division can be very misleading: it might lead someone to think that 'sentimental' can be used only ethically or only aesthetically.

In fact, aesthetic ascription of 'sentimental' requires ethical assessment, and vice versa.

First, let us examine the ways in which the use of 'sentimental' to perform aesthetic functions—mainly negative assessments—involves ethical considerations. A work of art may be judged to be sentimental because of its content, the artist, effects on the audience, or formal qualities. All depend on both reference to consequences or moral principles and to intrinsic properties of an object or event.

Content

When 'sentimental' aptly characterizes a work of art that deals with the death of innocents, devotion beyond the call of duty, virtue miraculously rewarded, the incredible return of a pet, and the like, it is because the people, actions, or situations themselves exhibit features such as overabundant sighing and shedding of tears, idealization, and implausibility. In this case, a work of art is aesthetically sentimental partly because its content is ethically sentimental. Whether a work is believable or unbelievable cannot be directly perceived the way rhythm or harmony or color can. Judging whether Little Nell's death is realistically depicted demands that we compare it to deaths outside the novel. It is not merely that the description of death is false (many false descriptions are not sentimental); rather, it is that the description is shallow, insincere, dishonest. Someone who found the description accurate would not be likely to deal adequately or appropriately with death. We have seen that aesthetic properties are such that direct inspection of an object or event is a necessary condition of knowing whether that object or event has the property in question. In the case of sentimentality, one must, in fact, inspect the object or event, but while one does so, one must also think about other things. One perceives the sentimentality in the object while one conceives the content.

Artist

When 'sentimental' is used to describe an artist, something is usually being said about his or her shallowness, self-indulgence, hypocrisy, misrepresentation, insincerity, and so on. All demand ethical assessment of the artist as a human being. An author who describes death only as Dickens does in the Little Nell passage may fail to stack up morally. The fact that Dickens also treats death as he does in the Quilp passage, plus knowledge about his efforts at reforming British industrial society, helps to protect him from the criticism of being generally sentimental. Instead, we probably decide that he had trouble avoiding it when dealing with the death of sweet little girls.

Audience

If a work causes the audience to respond with shallowness, self-indulgence, and the like, it and the members of the audience are sentimental. Again, this requires evaluation in terms of moral values. We expect profound works to have a deep and lasting effect on readers—to make it somehow less likely that they will respond emotionally to a story about a dog's death and proceed immediately to kick the neighbor's pet. As I said previously, even profound works may have a sentimental effect in individuals who are morally shallow. But making this judgment will require looking at aesthetic and moral properties of both works and the individuals involved.

Formal Qualities

Since formal qualities are intrinsic—there in the work to be perceived directly—it is harder to see how this kind of sentimentality requires ethical analysis. I have argued that it was largely the formalist movement in the twentieth century that was responsible for the insistence that ethical and aesthetic assessments are distinct. Therefore, I must show that even the formal features on my aesthetic list do not result in an aesthetic judgment without ethical considerations.

In 1904, *National Magazine* announced that it would spend $10,000 to collect "heart throbs," selections that had touched the hearts of its readers.[38] There is a sense in which all one needs to do is scan the titles of the published entries (just *look* at the titles) to suspect that most are sentimental:

A Tribute to a Dog
Mother
The Returned Battle Flags
Today!
At Home
Almost Home
Build a Little Fence
A Look at Life
A Lonesome Boy
The Old Canoe

But one must read the poems themselves to know for sure. One must discover if the vocabulary is trite or the metaphors stock, and so on, but one must also consider more than the words alone. One must see if there is a fit between the words and what is described, whether it be death, mothers, flags, or canoes.

There is a mix of aesthetic and ethical considerations here, as there was in the case of sentimental content, artists, and audiences. One must perceive and reflect upon the object itself, of course, to have an aesthetic experience. But it is impossible to put aside the ethical, to ignore aspects of human action and experience in the real world. If one were to put these aside, 'sentimental' could no longer function aesthetically.

A more difficult question is the reverse: How do ethical uses of 'sentimental' depend on aesthetic considerations? Here, I claim that when 'sentimental' functions ethically, attention must be given to intrinsic features of the object under evaluation. Considerations of principles or consequences alone will not suffice. Something is sentimentally defective in the ethical sense when it is superficial, indulgent, facile, stock, or false. But all of these attributes can be ascribed only when one sees *how* something is done, not merely *what* is done. Just as we cannot tell from intrinsic features like title or use of particular phrases that something is aesthetically sentimental, knowledge concerning extrinsic features alone, such as what someone does, will not permit us to conclude that something is ethically sentimental.

Consider again the pilot who is accused of being sentimental. Even if we know that he is lying about being concerned, or that he does not act to help dying people generally, we cannot conclude that he is sentimental. That would equally be evidence for saying that he is cruel or mean-spirited. Deceptiveness and failure to act according to generally accepted moral dictates is not equivalent to sentimentality. As Savile says, sentimentality is a *mode* of action or feeling, not an action or feeling itself. One cannot go from a report about what was done or its consequences to the claim that it was sentimental. Suppose we learn that the pilot is crying; we cannot conclude that he is being sentimental until we also know that he is crying sentimentally. This requires, I believe, that we inspect him directly. Are his tears "crocodile tears"? Is he trying to control himself, or is he too easily giving in? Like doing something gracefully or beautifully, doing something sentimentally depends on intrinsic features of the situation—acting excessively, insincerely, indulgently, shallowly, relying on trite tricks to feign feelings, using inflated vocabulary and tones of voice, and the like.

Indeed, the judgment that something is ethically sentimental demands that we assess it in ways comparable to those in which we assess works of art. This becomes apparent when we consider how our pilot could be defended against the charge of sentimentality. Essentially, I believe, it would have to be shown that he did not do things tantamount to giving a bad performance. (Here one is reminded of how performing well contributes to the good aesthetic and ethical life as portrayed by Anthony Powell.) To display sentimentality is to act in ways that are unconvincing, to indicate that one is insincere or self-indulgent or inconsistent. It is not an accident that 'melodramatic' is so often associated with 'sentimental'. Melodramas are unbelievable, shallow, and facile—with the result that they are funny when they should be sad.

When the control tower officer sneers, "Don't get sentimental on me," the pilot might, of course, point out that in his spare time he is active in volunteer work that is intended to help the sick and dying. But we are more likely to conclude that he is not sentimental if he responds like this: "Look, I'm not being sentimental. I'm not beating my breast or crying crocodile tears. All I said was, 'Request permission to land. Have passenger with heart trouble.' I was not excessive or imprecise. I did not use inflated vocabulary or stock metaphors or clichés. I did not say things like, 'Of course, I don't care about myself' or 'Since human life is such a precious thing. . . .' I simply did my duty."

Sentimentalists are exposed for what they are precisely when they are "bad actors." And the recognition that something is a poor performance requires attending to aesthetic properties—those intrinsic properties that a culture deems worthy of attention. In this case, it is features associated with literature (language used) and theater (gestures) to which the pilot points.

In a column about the 1988 U.S. presidential debates, Ellen Goodman worried that voters had "become so sophisticated about the backstage politics that we can no longer see [them] like voting audience, but only like drama critics."[39] Though I think she is right to be concerned with analysis primarily in terms of candidates' being "well-rehearsed" or delivering effective one-liners, it is hard to see how one could recognize the sentimentality that often marked these performances (and especially the vice-presidential debates that year) without being a kind of drama critic. The manner of talking about care of the aged or patriotism, for instance, matters at least as much as what is said.

If the aesthetic and the ethical were truly separate, then judging that something is aesthetically or ethically sentimental should involve two different meanings of the term, two different sets of criteria for application, or two different and separable ways of looking at something. A situation like seeing the famous duck-rabbit figure, where we can see either a duck or a rabbit but not both at the same time, should obtain. We should be able to see that something is ethically sentimental or aesthetically sentimental, but not as both simultaneously. However, in order to use 'sentimental', we have to look at all features of an object or situation at the same time. Form and content, once again, cannot be pulled apart.

If ethical ascription of 'sentimental' requires aesthetic assessment and aesthetic ascription of 'sentimental' requires ethical assessment, then ethical and aesthetic judgments are not completely distinct. What is demanded, then, is a holistic view of human value. The edge is taken off one's approval of the man who laughs at the death of Little Nell and disapproval at one who cries because we recognize that both responses play roles in the overall assessment of something's value. Both the aesthetic and the ethical are part of what I think is best understood as value grounded in one's conception of the meaning of life.

Norman Dahl argues that a meaningful life is one that it is rational to want to live.[40] I believe that it is rational to seek a life in which both aesthetic and moral goals play a significant part. Separatists have often tried to give equal or superior status to the aesthetic by giving it its own realm. But by detaching it from other human concerns, they achieve for it only an inferior position.

In Flaubert's *Sentimental Education*, Frederic, having achieved his sentimental education, is unable to respond as he should to a riot in Paris: "The drums beat the charge. Shrill cries arose; and shouts of triumph. The crowd surged backwards and forwards. Frederic, caught between the two dense masses, did not budge; in any case he was fascinated and enjoyed himself tremendously. The wounded falling to the ground, the dead lying stretched out, did not look as if they were really wounded or dead. He felt as if her were watching a play."[41] Watching life as if it were only a play, as if were a purely formalistically valuable object, does not constitute a wholly meaningful life. The separatist view implies that there is nothing wrong with considering only formal features. But in many cases, there is something amiss with doing this; one, at least, would fail to be able to uncover sentimentality. This is why some people cannot fully admire the person who laughs at Little Nell's death. They worry that compassion when needed to motivate appropriate moral action is missing, that such a person might be equally dispassionate when genuinely tragic death is encountered.

The separatist view may also lead one to fail to see that works of art have profound ethical consequences—the topic of the following chapters. Greuze's sentimental paintings are bad not just because they are hypocritical. Bruce Lebus has argued that his "harmless" paintings of women may contribute to making violence against women more acceptable.[42] Though the jury is still out on the empirical truth of such claims, sentimentality may be connected to pornography in some instances. At the very least, sentimental works contribute to what Wilde described as the "contemptible" emotional lives that many people lead. Little Nell's death is not just funny. It lacks both aesthetic and ethical depth of the sort that sustains attention. No long-term delight or satisfaction is forthcoming. It does not stand either the moral or the aesthetic test of time.

Ultimately, I believe, describing someone or something as 'sentimental' involves making decisions about how one should lead one's life. It is simultaneously an observation about what moves one and what one is moved to do, about how deeply one sees and feels, about how much effort one is prepared to spend. Thinking, feeling, attending, perceiving, reflecting—all characterize human response; all are involved in coming to the conclusion that something or someone is sentimental. There are undoubtedly other terms that are like this: sincere, interesting, compelling, moving, poignant, uplifting, inspiring, insightful, compassionate, amusing, significant, meaningful, sleazy, obscene, genuine, powerful, belligerent, strident, aggressive, offensive, clever, bombastic, pretentious. Detailed analyses are required of each, of course; but my hunch is that, like 'sentimental', applying any of these concepts will necessitate an integration of moral and aesthetic considerations and values.

TEN

Art's Moral Lessons

I AM by no means alone in thinking that there is a closer relation between aesthetic and ethical values than has often been asserted. Colin McGinn, for instance, criticizes analytic moral philosophers for their failure, in investigating the nature of moral language, to focus on a sufficiently broad range of discourses. Rather than looking simply at individual moral statements or simplified moral arguments that lend themselves to uncomplicated syllogistic form, more attention should be given, he suggests, to larger texts—to parables, short stories, novels, and films, for instance. Stories and films such as that about Frankenstein's monster (which McGinn himself analyzes) help to sharpen and clarify ethical issues. At the same time, narrative artists must structure their creations according to aesthetic criteria.[1] McGinn is one of a growing number of philosophers who share this attitude about the importance of thinking of ethics broadly enough to attend to aesthetic as well as moral features and values.

Jerrold Levinson, in the introduction to his important new anthology on aesthetics and ethics, describes three ways in which aesthetic and ethical inquiry proceed together. The first is to investigate areas of commonality between aesthetics and ethics. The second is to look at ways in which aesthetic and artistic pursuits have ethical ramifications. The essays in his volume, he asserts, deal with one of these. I am interested in the third inquiry that he identifies, which is aesthetic issues in ethics. Or, more precisely, I am interested in the ways in which aesthetic and moral properties and judgments relate to and depend on one another. This third concern obviously depends on the other two, and so in what follows I will naturally refer to them.

I strongly agree with those who have argued for what Berys Gaut has described as *ethicism*, the thesis "that the ethical assessment of attitudes manifested by works of art is a legitimate aspect of the aesthetic evaluation of those works, such that, if a work manifests ethically reprehensible attitudes, it is to that extent aesthetically defective, and if a work manifests ethically commendable attitudes, it is to that extent aesthetically meritorious."[2] Fortunately, the list of persons who have come in recent years to sympathize with this position is getting longer every day, and it is not possible to discuss or even to list them all. I shall begin by discussing representative theorists who investigate commonalities of ethics and aesthetics and the ethical ramifications of aesthetics before moving on to my main thesis in this chapter: it is the integration of aesthetic and ethical properties that accounts for art's success in teaching moral lessons.

I am less interested in this book in the problems and presuppositions that aesthetics and ethics share than I am in how their differences nonetheless preclude their separability. However, their commonalities do reinforce the attitude I am advocating—one that leads one to hesitate before too quickly assuming that ethical and aesthetic values exclude one another, and that both, in turn, differ essentially from the scientific. In Levinson's anthology, Richard Miller and Peter Railton both make strong cases for putting moral and aesthetic judgments on a par with scientific judgments with respect to being objective. Miller's strategy is to characterize the former in such a way that they compare favorably with science vis-à-vis playing a meaningful and important role in rational discussions; at the same time, he recognizes that aesthetic and moral judgments cannot attain the kind of universal truth to which science rightfully aspires. He calls the objectivity to which ethics and aesthetics can aspire "appraiser-independent truth."[3] Our practices in all realms—scientific, moral, and aesthetic—allow for, even depend on, the belief that claims in each area are not always limited to the perspective of the viewer; all human beings share capacities to detect properties that others perceive, and shared data about these properties can result in agreements. This is the case in ethics and aesthetics, as well as science. But we do not and cannot hope for universal agreement in ethics and aesthetics; here, the possibility for rational dissent always remains. "Someone lacking our elementary moral [or aesthetic] inclinations can deny what we mean by 'justice' exists, while someone lacking even a provisional inclination to respond to experiences with our elementary physical and psychological ascriptions could not even discern what we mean."[4] I am not convinced that someone who lacked my most basic moral views would, in fact, understand how I interpret 'justice'. But this aside, I think Miller is surely right that shared sensory and reflective mental capacities, influenced, as I have insisted, by social and cultural construction, do often, at least, lead to agreement in aesthetics.

Peter Railton makes an even better case, I think, for his claim that both moral and aesthetic values lie at "the intersection of the subjective and the objective."[5] Value judgments are subjective in the sense that in the absence of human preferences they would not exist; they are objective in the sense that they do, in fact, refer to objects in such a way that the judgments "approximate features of the world."[6] Building on David Hume's explanation for the possibility of standards of taste, Railton argues that judgments of taste reflect shared human sentiments—a "conformity between objects and [human] faculties."[7] There is broad agreement among people about many ethical and aesthetic questions, and where people do not agree, they can often be brought to perceive what others, especially experts, perceive. Railton finds community value in this agreement, for the fact that individuals share aesthetic preferences creates "a gratifying confirmation and bond" between them that would not be possible if a match between human faculties and objects' properties were missing. Not everyone responds exactly the same way to chocolate or to Homer, but agreement is sufficient to allow for rational discussion and a hope that others may come to share our aesthetic and moral interpretations and evaluation after engaging in such discourse.

Commonalities between aesthetic and moral judgments could exist, of course, without its being the case that they are inseparable. Stronger links between the two are forged by considering ethical ramifications of the aesthetic and, even more important, the ways in which these ethical concerns affect aesthetic value. In the context of criticizing Lamarque and Olsen's position that ethical truth is not part of aesthetic evaluation, Stephen Davies has shown that the application of advice found in fiction in the real world, such as Polonius's admonition in *Hamlet*, "Neither borrower nor lender be," belies their claim.[8] Davies is certainly correct to point out that we use and refer to artworks in everyday ethical discussions. If I say, "That's good advice," I don't mean that one should never lend or borrow—for I do both and think both are sometimes crucial for sustaining relationships and communities. But still, I think it may be good advice in some contexts—to a young person who perhaps needs some rules or guidelines as he or she learns how to deal with specific situations. Furthermore, ethical discussions often take place within contexts of a great deal of shared knowledge. My son, for example, knows that I try to be generous and that I applaud his generous nature. Now, if I say that line to him, knowing also that he knows *Hamlet* and knows that I know *Hamlet*, then my quoting this line takes on a whole new meaning. It may mean something like "Be careful, you're dealing with a flaky friend who may not return your lawn mower in good condition." But, of course, we need to do more than show that we use artworks in ethical discussions to prove that there is a deep connection between aesthetic and ethical value and to show, further, that they are sometimes inseparable. Someone might even go so far as to agree with Jenefer Robinson's assertion that we learn important lessons about human conduct from art via emotional responses that "change my conceptions and my focus of attention [in such a way that] sentimental education occurs"[9] but still insist that ethics and aesthetics are essentially different.

T. J. Diffey, like some others we have come across, believes that what members of the audience bring to artworks matters much more than what they learn from the object. No truths, specifically ethical truths, "belong peculiarly to works of art."[10] Like Lamarque and Olsen, he believes that assuming an "aesthetic stance" requires putting aside questions of whether assertions in an artwork are true or false. Otherwise, we risk losing what is essentially aesthetic. As Lamarque has put the worry, "The danger of the search for moral wisdom in the great works of tragedy is that it can become just another form of appropriation, losing sight of what is truly distinctive about tragedy conceived as literature or art."[11] I have insisted that the two are not necessarily exclusive. We can, as in the example of "Neither borrower nor lender be" go back and forth between considering its role in the play and its application in the real world. But what is needed, if we are to show that ethics and aesthetics are sometimes inseparable, is not just the possibility of going back and forth but the necessity of considering both intrinsic aesthetic properties and extrinsic ethical features simultaneously. Karen Hanson has put the issue very nicely: "Is moral criticism of art a thing apart from aesthetic criticism, with moral concerns trumping aesthetic ones, or not reaching their rarefied heights, or coequal but simply different? Or should we expect a merging of moral and aesthetic values in our judgments about art? Or does art possess immunity from ethical criticism, existing on an altogether different plane?"[12]

One proof that moral criticism of art is not a "thing apart" from aesthetic criticism would come from showing that an ethical weakness in an artwork is an aesthetic weakness. This is precisely the project of several contemporary theorists, who hope to prove that the aesthetic impact of a work is diminished if it is ethically flawed. Berys Gaut agues that it is the nature of works of art to engage our imaginations and to prescribe attitudes to accompany those imaginings. Certainly, those attitudes are open to moral assessment. "If a work prescribes a response that is unmerited, it has failed in an aim internal to it, and that is a defect."[13] And it is an aesthetic failure. One way in which responses are unmerited is in being unethical. A work that intentionally invites us to respond favorably to horrible violence, for instance, creates a mismatch (at least, one assumes for people lacking sociopathic or psychopathic tendencies) that is at once, Gaut maintains (if I have understood him correctly), aesthetic and ethical. If our responses "are unmerited because unethical, we have reason not to respond in the way prescribed. Our having reason not to respond in the way prescribed is a failure of the work"—an aesthetic failure.[14] Eva Dadlez makes a similar point. Works of art, if they are to be aesthetically successful, must lead us to entertain the thoughts they raise "seriously and compassionately." If one cannot do this, if indeed one's beliefs—in particular, moral beliefs—make it impossible to respond to intrinsic properties at all, then a work fails aesthetically.[15] Hanson points out that power and grace are at once intellectual, moral, *and* aesthetic qualities. "Art marked by bigotry and superstition is art deprived, to that extent of power and grace."[16] This, of course, robs them of *aesthetic* value, and hence a moral failure, as Gaut says, becomes an aesthetic defect. Bigoted works may have other powerful features—but their overall value is diminished when crude, weak, or dangerous thought processes are represented and viewers are asked to participate in them.

"Our impressions of human life are picked up one by one; and remain for most of us loose and disorganized. But we constantly find things in literature that suddenly coordinate and bring into focus a great many such impressions," writes Northrup Frye.[17] Noel Carroll has expanded and refined this view and calls it "clarificationism." Like me, he rejects the formalistic position that he calls "autonomism,"[18] the view that aesthetic evaluation precludes ethical, or any other, assessments. Although formalists are right to point to the fact that art is absorbing, "just because we value art for the way it commands our undivided attention does not preclude that some art commands our attention in this way just because it is interesting and engaging cognitively and/or . . . morally."[19] Carroll gives too much away, I think, by his use of the phrase "undivided attention." Something can be very absorbing without its being the case that one's attention is "undivided." In the latter part of the quoted sentence, Carroll grants this, I think; attention can be engaged cognitively *and* morally *while* aesthetic. He uses a much more felicitous phrase when he writes that one would have to be "willfully blinkered" to miss the fact that artworks are often intended precisely to engage our moral interests. Formalists do ask us to wear blinkers whenever we want to have an aesthetic experience—when in fact, I insist, the very value of much art depends on us having as much peripheral vision as possible.

Artworks, Carroll asserts, present "narratives of human affairs."[20] (I will say more about narrative in the next chapter.) These are necessarily incomplete, so readers and viewers must fill in gaps. This engages cognitive and moral imaginations, as well as aesthetic imaginations. The filling in is possible because authors and readers share beliefs and emotions, including moral emotions such as contempt or disgust for certain kinds of behavior. The reason that Carroll thinks that the process involved is one of clarification is that he believes that the cognitive, emotional, and moral lives that viewers bring with them to artworks have already been acquired; thus, works do not provide new material but rather occasions for deepening what we know and feel already: "Clarificationism does not claim that, in the standard case, we acquire interesting, new propositional knowledge from artworks, but rather that the artworks in questions can deepen our moral understanding by, among other things, encouraging us to apply our moral knowledge and emotions to specific cases. For in being prompted to apply and engage our antecedent moral powers, we may come to augment them."[21] Narratives show us things in such a way as to "strike home." They encourage the audience to connect already held beliefs in new ways and thus to grasp the significance of what, in a less vivid sense, we already know. Eileen John describes this as engaging in a kind of "thought experiment," where, using beliefs and emotions already in our repertoire, we broaden "the conditions or application of a concept."[22] Conceptual questions are, in her view, clarified by being brought to the surface. Carroll, John, and the others I have discussed here recognize that people for whom art is very important (certainly no less important than it is for formalists) have a natural tendency to discuss works in ethical terms, and this cannot be ignored without diminishing the value of art.

One of the metaphors that reappears throughout the writings of members of this group of theorists who recognize the ethical ramifications of the aesthetic is the "showing" metaphor. Art, especially narrative art, they assert, *shows* readers what is morally salient in the lives of the characters whom the reader is asked to imagine. This is, of course, a gloss—but it will suffice for what I want to discuss here. And although it is not always explicit, a kind of Aristotelian view of virtue lies behind the explanation of why art can therefore be morally valuable. If morality is a matter of exhibiting virtue and if one acquires moral understanding and habits by following examples of virtuous behavior rather than by simply trying to apply moral principles, then anything that *shows* such behavior will be morally valuable. This is true of both virtuous people and of stories about virtuous people (or their opposites, of course), for both invite (or discourage) imitation.

Aristotle himself, of course, recognized the power of drama to force us to imagine what happens to people of certain kinds in certain circumstances. Many contemporary ethicists follow this line of approach. Fiction approached seriously demands that one imagine what happens when one does or does not tell the truth, share things, or persevere in the face of daunting obstacles or conflicts. We might put it this way: art, at least the narrative arts, can teach us moral lessons. However, the theorists who have skillfully demonstrated this typically do so by discussing the *content* of those narratives. Rob van Gerwen, for instance, talks about ways in which films that idealize or romanticize the psychopathic serial killer, because they are not true to the world, are failures. Martha Nussbaum brilliantly describes the way in which Greek tragedy asks the audience to consider how or whether human happiness might be possible in a world in which much of what happens is beyond an individual's control. Several writers discuss the novels of Henry James or George Eliot in terms of how their novels present a vivid picture of how lack of self-knowledge influences human relationships. I do not want in any way to belittle or undermine the importance of the contributions of these theorists. However, if one is to explain how art, or at least the narrative arts, uniquely play a role in the development of moral understanding, it seems to me that we must attend not only to the content of such works but also to *how* they contribute to moral development—that is, to the particular properties works of art have that make it possible, even likely, that the kind of *showing* that is at its heart will be successful.

If mimicking virtuous people—real or fictional—is at the heart of moral development, then one must pay close attention to the properties of their actions, to how they act as well, as to what they do. Attention must be paid both to ethical properties and to aesthetic properties. Earlier, I offered the following definitions:

A is an aesthetic property of x if and only if A is an intrinsic feature of x, and A is culturally identified as a property worthy of attention (i.e., of perception or reflection).

A is an intrinsic property of x if and only if direct inspection of x is a necessary condition for verifying the claim that x is A.

In imitating, humans must duplicate at least some of the intrinsic properties, often some of the very ones that are valued aesthetically in their communities. People who produce imitations of virtuous or nonvirtuous people must attend to the requirement that aesthetic properties contribute to and are appropriate to their actions. Aesthetic properties are not frills or add-ons that make moral lessons more palatable. As Joseph Brodsky suggested, the style and métier of individuals' behavior is at the core of what they do and who they are. Attending to this plays a crucial role in moral development and in what we construe as good or meaningful lives.

Some works of art (and I emphasize *some*) have a moral content, and sometimes we accept, or at least do not dismiss outright, the moral perspective presented or represented. The task is to see how the aesthetic properties of those works contribute to the ethical success of the work. Two general questions cry out for attention here: what does it mean to say that a work of art has moral content and what constitutes ethical success? I'm not going to try to give an adequate answer to either here. 'Having a moral content' covers a variety of artistic types. Didactic fiction has moral content by definition. But even nondidactic narratives present what Peter Kivy, borrowing from William James, has called "live hypotheses" about what might constitute a good life.[23] Or we might view some fictions as "case studies," whose moral content consists of the presentation of moral exemplars. By ethical success, I will simply rely here on what other ethicists have elsewhere suggested: fiction is ethically successful if it succeeds in stimulating serious moral thought, brings one to put oneself in others' shoes, increases moral understanding, broadens moral perspective, introduces or deepens reasonable moral guidelines, instantiates correct moral principles to the extent that these exist, or contributes to moral development. (I will say more about this later and in the next chapter.)

I want to go beyond the view that asserts that aesthetic experiences contribute to the good life. I want to look at how the aesthetic is part of the very meaning of 'good' in the phrase 'the good life'. That is, does our moral use of the word 'good' ever include aesthetic properties; does describing the good life, or at least *a* good life, require aesthetic considerations? If the answer is yes, as I think it is, then moral philosophers should pay as much attention to aesthetics as aestheticians have in recent years paid to ethics.

There are at least four questions that those of us interested in the connections between ethics and aesthetics must address:

1. Can moral success contribute to aesthetic success?
2. Can moral failure contribute to aesthetic failure?
3. Can aesthetic success contribute to moral success?
4. Can aesthetic failure contribute to moral failure?

As Levinson rightly points out, most philosophic attention has been given to the first two questions. I think the fact that the answer to question #1 is obviously yes is one of the things that had led many of us to give an affirmative answer to question #2. It is much harder, I think, to show that questions #3 and #4 must sometimes be answered affirmatively. This list does not exhaust the possible ways of connecting aesthetics and morality; one might ask, for instance, whether aesthetic failure ever contributes to moral success. Mary Devereaux, for example, considers how aesthetic success in *Triumph of the Will* contributes to its moral failure and hence ultimately to overall aesthetic failure.[24] But I will concentrate on the role of the aesthetic in moral success and failure.

Rob van Gerwen has suggested that Berys Gaut's question, Can something be aesthetically good if it is morally bad? should be interpreted in this way: Can something be *artistically* good if it is morally bad? because both of those theorists concentrate on the art. But van Gerwen also maintains that the substitution is required because 'aesthetic' refers to formal properties—properties not involved with what works are *about*. On his view, furthermore, art is open to moral criticism because it is artistic action that produces works of art, and all human actions per se are open to moral criticism.[25] But I construe 'aesthetic' more broadly than van Gerwen (and I think than Gaut, but I am not certain of this). I agree with Mary Devereaux, who points to two ways of interpreting 'aesthetic'. The first is to say that there is more to art than beauty and form. The second is to say that "whenever we respond to a feature that makes a work the work of art it is" we are responding aesthetically. She opts for the second.[26] This is very close to the characterization I proposed of "aesthetic" as any intrinsic feature of an object or event identified culturally as worthy of perception and reflection. I hope to go further than van Gerwen and Gaut. Not only do I want to give a positive answer to the question about the connection of artistic success or failure and moral success or failure but also I hope to be able to give positive answers to these questions when 'aesthetic' is substituted for 'artistic'.

So I shall take it as proven that ethical successes and failures can be aesthetic successes and failures, and turn to the questions of whether aesthetic successes and failures can contribute to moral successes and failures. We need to uncover and discover when and how aesthetic success makes ethical success more likely. This requires, I believe, looking at specific examples. In chapter 9, I concentrated on a specific property that shows the integration of aesthetic and moral assessment—sentimentality. Here, I want to begin with a specific work, and a very simple one at that. As lovers of art, we aestheticians tend to discuss the most difficult and complex cases—*The Turn of the Screw, Middlemarch, Triumph of the Will, Silence of the Lambs,* and the like. But I am going to start closer to the beginning with an artwork that has moral content in the sense of intentionally and explicitly contributing to moral development—to teaching a moral lesson, if you will.

I should repeat that my claim is modest. Some works of art have a moral content, and of those, some would not be morally successful if their aesthetic properties were not what they are. James C. Anderson and Jeffrey T. Dean criticize Noel Carroll and Berys Gaut for too readily inferring from examples where ethical flaws are aesthetic flaws that the connection is universal. They rightly cite cases where alien moral perspectives are entertaining.

> There are also cases in which it is arguably part of the project of the work that it explores the boundaries of the moral and the aesthetic. Peter Greenaway's film *The Cook, The Thief, His Wife and Her Lover,* while perceptively written, lushly filmed, and beautifully scored—in short, artfully crafted and aesthetically potent—is also relentlessly brutal and morally cynical. In this instance, one could make a case for the claim that the contrast between the film's richly detailed and highly aestheticized formal features and its preoccupation with moral baseness is intentionally provocative, specifically designed to play on the tension between moral and aesthetic value.[27]

Although these authors themselves sometimes move too quickly—for example, state that *Triumph of the Will* is "doubtless a classic case of moral and aesthetic value going their separate ways,"[28] when in fact Mary Devereaux has shown that it is not doubtlessly so at all—they are correct in drawing our attention to the fact that moral and aesthetic judgments often differ, and that one sometimes even overrides the other. Many works, furthermore, do not have a moral content; indeed, some art forms per se may, as Peter Kivy insists for pure music, preclude it.[29] Some abstract visual art seems to make no moral claims, to present no moral perspectives. The truth lies somewhere in between: sometimes aesthetic and ethical values go hand in hand. Some works are such that the choice of aesthetic properties is not driven by aesthetic goals alone; the choice is shaped by moral ends. (Here, as we have al-

To "look good" and to "be good" have traditionally been held to be two very different things. By and large, philosophers have seen aesthetic and ethical values as fundamentally separate. In this work, Marcia Muelder Eaton introduces a bold new notion of merit in which "being good" and "looking good" are integrated into one.

In contrast to other more formalist philosophers of art, who argue that aesthetic experiences exclude other kinds of outside influence, Eaton believes strongly that the nature and value of the aesthetic cannot be understood in isolation from a wide range of human endeavors and institutions. Aesthetic experiences, she says, are inevitably tied to a community or a context—be it historical, cultural, or attitudinal. But if the aesthetic is socially constructed, then surely moral properties, particularly concerns about truth and goodness, must thus be a component of the aesthetic. Eaton develops this idea of the inter-relatedness of aesthetic and ethical values throughout the book and brings it to bear on long-standing issues in the philosophy of art. The latter part of the book examines the consequences of this integration for educational, environmental, and community policy.

Eaton's book is at the cusp of a new wave of aesthetic theory and will appeal to scholars and students of aesthetics as well as to philosophers of moral and ethical theory.

ready seen, I differ significantly from the position taken by, for example, Lamarque and Olson; and I shall have more to say about this later.)

As I said earlier, many writers have used the metaphor of 'showing' to describe what fiction does. In discussing this, in laying out his theory of "clarificationism," for example, Noel Carroll brilliantly explains what this entails. But—and this is typical of philosophers who take the ethicist position—he does not have much to say about why or how showing proceeds. Even when he gives us detailed analyses of the filmic properties of movies, he only implicitly demonstrates the connection to ethical success or failure. I believe that explaining *why* art is in the business of showing us things and *how* it does this contributes to an understanding of the nature of both the aesthetic and the ethical.

If fiction "shows" us things, the properties of a work of fiction must contribute to showing those things. In aesthetic experiences, certain intrinsic properties are the focus of attention; they are, thus, the ones that are salient or are made salient to us by others. Sometimes properties of the world stand out only when others help us see them, or help us to see them in new ways, to re-interpret them, as it were. The narrator in Charles Frazier's novel, *Cold Mountain* provides the following example. "Swimmer had looked out at the landforms and said he believed Cold Mountain to be the chief mountain of the world. Inman asked how he knew that to be true, and Swimmer had swept his hand across the horizon to where Cold Mountain stood and said, Do you see a bigger'n?"[30] Artworks often, by drawing attention to properties and hence making them salient, also make it possible to attach meanings to those properties—like being the biggest makes it obvious that a mountain is the "chief." Successful showing depends on including properties that allow readers to "see" what is going on and what these goings-on imply.

My simple example is Watty Piper's children's book *The Little Engine That Could*.[31] I choose an example from children's literature that, at least for American readers, is a classic and at least for me was central to my moral development. I believed and, heaven help me, continue to believe, that what it shows about the world is true. For those readers whose childhood was not enriched by this particular work, the story is this: A small train engine of very limited power confronts a task (crossing a mountain) that requires tremendous strength and effort, neither of which the engine initially believes she possesses. (Trains, like ships, are feminine in English, so I do not think much can be made of the issue of gender here.) However, she becomes convinced that she should try and, telling herself repeatedly, "I think I can, I think I can, I think I can," undertakes the task and succeeds.

The moral lesson is simple: perseverance always wins. But the lesson has a far better chance of being accepted if it is "shown" in a story form, not merely "told" via the explicit statement. (I think the fact that as children many of our moral lessons, and other lessons, are presented in story form makes it natural that as adults we associate the story form itself with morality. But this is another topic.) Piper, as moral teacher, chooses narrative but then must also discover ways of vividly showing via his choice of aesthetic properties the truth or power of the lesson. One such property is the use of lists that emphasize by cataloging. A train is carrying a load of wonderful things—that is, of things likely to be considered wonderful by children. Piper cannot simply say, "A train was pulling a load of wonderful things," if he is to succeed in showing. He must give lists of specific things that children will visualize and find appealing. Nor does he just say, for example, the train was carrying toys. He provides a list of specific toys and describes them in some detail: toy animals such as giraffes with long necks and Teddy bears with almost no necks at all, dolls with blue eyes and yellow curls or brown eyes and brown bobbed hair, and "the funniest little toy clown you ever saw." There are airplanes, tops, books, puzzles, and jackknives. (Perhaps knives would be left out if the story were written for American children today, since their inclusion in the list might preclude a positive response.) Children are shown enough specific examples to allow them to visualize and continue to fill out the train's wonderful load in their own imaginations.

Another property used by Piper is repetition—a property we also, of course, find, though more subtly, in adult fiction. Listing is itself one kind of repetition. Another is Piper's use of the repeated-question form so typical of children's literature: the same question is asked of many different people, animals, trees, and so on before a solution is found. Here, the train in trouble repeatedly asks for help from a shiny new engine, a big steam engine, and a rusty old engine, all of whom refuse to help. Finally, she asks for help from the Little Blue Engine—the one that finally saves the day. (Notice that Piper chooses blue—a color that, at least in the Christian art historical tradition, symbolizes goodness. This may be another example of the way in which aesthetic choices contribute to ethical enterprises; however, I admit that it may be a bit of a stretch to claim that Piper was intentionally exploiting religious symbolism in producing his moral tale.) Piper goes beyond showing the train asking for help from other engines: the other engines are described in ways that show the world more forcefully, given the moral lesson he wants to teach. The shiny new engine is carrying passengers—adults, presumably—and the steam engine is pulling cars loaded with machinery. Both adults and machines are associated in children's minds with potentially dangerous power and thus contrasted with the safety of toys and distinguished from the Little Blue Engine that succeeds in getting the precious load across the mountain. Space prevents my going more fully into an analysis of the author's choice of aesthetic properties in such a way that the moral lesson is shown and, at least in my own case, instilled in the reader. One might discuss why, for example, it is the toy clown that takes a leadership role in stopping the various engines, or investigate the character of the language used by the different engines that Piper offers to intensify the images he provides. But the clearest instance of a successful choice of an aesthetic property is the repetition of the statement "I think I can." The very rhythm of this phrase suggests the turning of a train's wheels. Parents learn to read the words appropriately—slowly as the Little Blue Engine begins the journey, more quickly as she reaches the goal. Finally, the phrase becomes the triumphant "I thought I could"—repeated six times as the story's climax.

My claim is that without aesthetic success this story would not be the moral success that it is. Children would not only not see what the author intends to show but also would not request that the story be read over and over to them so that what is shown has an even greater chance of being convincing. Like adult works to which we are drawn again and again, children's stories whose rereading and retelling are demanded are more likely to affect beliefs about the world and possibilities for successful interaction with and in it.

Showing is successful when vivid, memorable images are created by foregrounding features, by using words and patterns that enable readers to form these images. Authors must attend to questions of accessibility—what images are likely to be formed, given the age, gender, social status, and other characteristics of the reader? What properties are likely to encourage, even require, readers to fill in more details for themselves and to do the kind of "hands-on work" that is more likely to lead to learning than activities that consist simply in being told something? Originality, novelty, and spectacle all contribute to evoking thoughts and emotions likely to have a lasting effect on the reader. As Leo Tolstoy advised, art must be clear;[32] authors must provide clear examples of principles that they hope will inculcate moral lessons via vivid instantiations. "Push harder, push harder, push harder" might exemplify the will to exercise power, but it is not as effective as "I think I can, I think I can, I think I can" for exhibiting perseverance. Readers must, in the end, be able to match their experiences to the fiction; otherwise, to use Carroll's terms, narratives could not clarify what we already know. Finally, the aesthetic choices made by artists must be such that the attention of the audience is drawn to the work and sustained.

I noted previously that Anderson and Dean point to the possibility of fiction that engages precisely by presenting the reader with moral perspectives that are alien. But it is interesting to note here that some aesthetic properties can be used only to enliven moral perspectives that one hopes to inculcate or reinforce. One could not use the rhythm of the wheels of a train to intensify the message of giving up—"I think I can't, I think I can't, I think I can't." Indeed, it would amount to a contradiction. The rhythmic repetition necessarily indicates sustained effort, with an accompanying belief in the possibility of success. The message one wants to project dictates the intrinsic properties that one can use.

I have chosen *The Little Engine That Could* as my first example because, admittedly, it is such an easy case. I think it is fairly representative of much children's art, but even in this genre there are many subtler cases—stories where it is not so easy to show how aesthetic properties nurture moral lessons. A more sophisticated tale is one of Oscar Wilde's children's stories, *The Selfish Giant*. Again, I choose it because I loved it myself as a child—and, of course, like to think that I learned the lesson of unselfishness as well as the lesson of perseverance! Wilde does not rely on obvious rhythmic phrases that contain an explicitly stated moral lesson; there is nothing comparable to "I think I can, I think I can, I think I can." There are no long lists of good things or bad things that bring home the point. But there are certainly other aesthetic strategies that work to instill the belief that it is better to be unselfish than to be selfish.

Here is a quick summary for those unfamiliar with the tale. A giant owns a beautiful garden. While he is away on a trip, village children enter the garden and play happily in it. When the giant returns, however, selfish as he is, he runs the children out of the garden, builds a high wall around it, and posts a sign, Trespassers Will Be Prosecuted. Winter comes to the garden and will not depart, even though in other parts of the village, the seasons follow their normal cycle; this, of course, puzzles the giant and makes him unhappy. One day, he is awakened by sweet music and sweet smells. He discovers that a small boy has sneaked into the garden and climbed into a tree to play and sing, and the tree has burst into blossom. The giant realizes that it is his selfishness that has prevented the return of spring. He tears down the wall and invites the children back, and all is beautiful again. The little boy, however, seems to have disappeared. He returns many years later, with "wounds of love" (stigmata) and accompanies the giant to the garden of Paradise. The moral lesson is clear: Unselfishness is rewarded; selfishness is not.

I read this story in my family's set of *The Book of Knowledge*. There were no illustrations, and this, coupled with all the years between then and now, makes it impossible for me to duplicate my childish experiences as I reread the tale in the Scholastic edition so beautifully illustrated by Lisbeth Zwerger. Her drawings certainly help to intensify the moral message while at the same time softening, with her gentle pastels and graceful flowing lines, even the scariest parts of the story. I had also forgotten the stigmata part—perhaps it was not included *The Book of Knowledge* version—and I find it a bit jarring. Nonetheless, the story can still bring tears to my eyes. (Is this a case of acceptable, even admirable, sentimentality?)

Wilde's descriptions are, one might say, soft as well. The beauty of the garden is a delicate beauty of pinks and pearls. Thus, Wilde presents a conventionally frightening character, a giant, in a nonviolent manner, making him less scary and probably making his conversion more believable. Like Piper, Wilde uses images that children can imagine vividly. Enough details are provided to engage the imagination while leaving it free to do the pleasant work that filling in the gaps in artworks invites. The giant is not just away, he is off visiting "his friend the Cornish ogre."[33] And, like Piper, Wilde relies on association of ideas. In the very title of the tale, a giant, a usually scary thing, is associated with selfishness—the trait we are being taught is bad. The explicit expression of selfishness, "Trespassers Will Be Prosecuted," challenges young children to ask what that means. (Indeed, much of the vocabulary used is challenging but not overwhelmingly difficult and hence engages rather than defeats interest.) Once learned, another scary thing (being prosecuted) is associated with the giant's selfish action. When flowers see the sign, they retreat into the ground. Selfishness gives pleasure only to cold, bad things—snow, frost, rattling (noisy, hence possibly frightening) hail, and the destructive, howling north wind. Only when the giant's heart melts, with the result that he becomes unselfish, will these unpleasant things also go away. Music (singing birds) is associated with happy play, and it is a sweet song that rouses the giant and wakens his unselfish side. Once he has become unselfish, even winter loses some of its sting, for the fact that it is a temporary part of the cycle of the season means that it can be viewed as "merely the Spring Asleep"—a time that provides the flowers a chance to get some much-needed rest.

We are not told explicitly that once the garden has been opened (the wall is torn down) and flourishes again that everyone lives happily ever after. The implication is, however, that even after the giant's death, the garden will remain available for public recreation. And as winter has become less threatening, death itself is not presented violently, but softly. It is definitely sad—this emotion must be roused for the story to pack its full wallop, I believe—but not scary. The giant is admitted into another, even more beautiful garden, the garden of Paradise. A rewarded death, appropriately described in the Wilde's language (the giant is "all covered with white blossoms"), helps to make unselfishness heroic.

I believe that the strategies demonstrated so successfully by Piper and Wilde are used by creators of art for adults. Jenefer Robinson, in her paper "L'Education Sentimentale," points to ways in which salient textual properties make a moral difference, and, in fact, she shows how repetition of a rhythmic phrase in Edith Wharton's *The Reef* works to arouse and organize the reader's emotions in much the same way as the repetition does in *The Little Engine That Could*. Here the phrase "She doesn't want you, doesn't want you, doesn't want you" recurs in the mind of one of characters as he rides a train.[34] But, of course, many other devices than repetition or listing are used. Rhythms are created more subtly, by presenting stories—within stories, for instance. Works, as Richard Eldridge says, make us enter "deeply and fully," but to do so they must have intrinsic properties as well as subject matter that grab us.[35] Suspense in films is created not just by making us fear that there is someone in the dark house into which an unprotected woman is about to enter but by making us wonder just what that someone is like and likely to do. Doubt is created in Henry James's *Turn of the Screw* by his use of "backing off" phrases in the governess's narrative ("It seemed to me at the time that" instead of "I knew that," for instance) that make us question whether what she experiences is real or imagined by her.[36] Portrayal of the complexity of the human condition requires an integration of aesthetic properties and moral subject matter that is itself complex. As in children's literature, adult art can successfully advance moral development only if it is at once challenging and convincing. The aesthetic properties must be sufficiently memorable to have an effect on one's moral life that lasts after a book has been put down or after one has left the museum or auditorium.

Of course, the quality or type of moral lesson provided by some works of art intended for adults is different from that of children's art. Some works may bring us to believe that we can change our lives, make or do things better. Even reading *The Selfish Giant* as an adult may reinforce our determination to try to be less selfish. But typically, the moral lessons in adult artworks are more sophisticated that this. Rather than presenting straightforward moral principles, they are "higher level" lessons—general lessons about, for example, the role of moral principles per se in our lives. We learn not that we must work harder to be unselfish but that we must do more in the way of making "an honest effort to do justice to all aspects of a hard case, seeing and feeling it in all its conflicting many-sidedness."[37] Instead of being encouraged to "Persevere!" or "Be Unselfish!" we may be taught that perseverance sometimes requires selfishness or that people of good faith might not always act as we would act in the face of similar conflicts. But for us to be taught this, the artists must use properties that *show* people of good faith, and what we are shown must evoke emotions and thoughts that bring the conflict home. The adult book might very well be *The Little Engine That Couldn't*—but failure will have to be made acceptable or understandable via properties of the protagonist or situation that make for tragedy rather than pathos. When a viewer or reader responds with repulsion to aesthetic properties, moral lessons will, of course, not be instilled; when one believes that "people just aren't like that," the lesson won't take.

One of the moral lessons of sophisticated art is that one must work to develop perceptive and reflective skills. Aristotle taught that virtue depends on refined skills of both sorts. Art teaches this in part by demonstrating that one must work to develop those skills. Works of art will teach this only if they themselves require such work. The complex sentences of Henry James's show, clarify, and teach how complex human relationships are, how difficult (perhaps even impossible) it is to see and know what we need to see and know to avoid misunderstanding others, ourselves, and the situations in which we interact. One can almost at random pick a sentence from his fiction that *shows* how difficult it is to make sense of the lives of others and of oneself. Here is a case in point: "I verily believe it hung in the balance a minute or two that in my impulse to draw him out, so that I might give him my sympathy, I was prepared to risk overturning the edifice of my precautions."[38] The reader is forced to reread many of his sentences to figure out what is going on, what is being said. Without this, the point about the world's complexity would be less forceful.

Literature (and there are analogues in the other arts) teaches us that we must pay close attention, that we must "treat apparently idle incidents in a story as not at all idle," as Eileen John puts it.[39] The fact that maturity requires moral principles that are often anything but straightforward can be reflected by convoluted sentence structure and unusual vocabulary. Consider Iris Murdoch's "The absence from his life of ordinary norms of politeness was taken as a sign of deeper moral anarchy."[40] The moral message of this sentence cannot be stated simply; it requires a sentence that does not lend itself to easy diagramming. The aesthetic properties and moral content are inseparable.

This point is made by Hugo A. Meynell in a passage that deserves extended quotation, for it exemplifies how philosophical writing also is characterized by an integration of style and content.

> If, and in so far as, one tends to come to knowledge of the truth to the degree that one attends to the data of experience, to the degree that one understands a range of possible explanations for it, and to the degree that one judges that possibility to be the case which is best supported by the data of experience; and if, and in so far as, the appreciation of works of art . . . essentially involves exercise of the conscious capacities of experience, understanding, and judgment; appreciation of works of art is conducive to knowledge of the truth. And if, and in as far as, one tends to come to know and do what is good to the degree that one exercises these conscious capacities in establishing what makes for happiness and fulfillment in people, and acts accordingly; and if, and in so far as, the appreciation of works of art essentially involves these capacities: appreciation of works of art is conducive to the knowing and doing of what is good.[41]

Meynell obviously believes that the antecedents are true. The moral lessons of art are often lessons about what is required for adequate moral perception and vision.

Most of my examples have been literary. But the other arts are as rich a source for the integration of ethical and aesthetic success. A painting such as Pieter Brueghel the Younger's *108 Proverbs* presents an abundance of images that depict Dutch sayings and moral tales such as "She comes carrying water in one hand and fire in the other" and the story of belling the cat. He does not just make these visual, however. Their arrangement and the overall composition are part of the message: life is complicated, even contradictory, and cannot be captured in any or even all of the slices of life represented. The didactic paintings of Jan Steen use some of the same devices—cluttered form and content to show that life is messy, but (or thus) full of delight. His *The Merry Family* (reproduced on this book's jacket) is a study in contrasts. A family is clearly having a wonderful time, eating, drinking, and making music. But an explicit warning appears on a piece of paper tacked to the back wall: "As the elders sing, the children pipe." Though the scene is on the whole wholesome, there is a clear message that if moderation is not observed, things could quickly degenerate into immorality. The aesthetic properties emphasize this: neatly arranged objects in the back of the room are contradicted by a disarray of objects on the floor in the front. The eye of the observer easily, harmoniously moves from the face of one family member to another—but a little too fast, reinforcing the message that things might quickly get out of hand. Steen leaves it ambiguous as to whether a child is blowing bubbles or smoking a real tobacco pipe. The perspectival lines of the floor and table edge lead the eye to a woman's bosom—just a bit too exposed, again in contrast to the modestly dressed older woman seated next to her. Like her blouse, a cloth that is supposed to protect an expensive Persian rug that served as a status symbol on middle-class Dutch tables is disheveled. The host, clearly the founder of the feast, who should be setting the best example, has put down his violin (considered a dignified instrument) and instead of concentrating on the music is about to take a big drink of what looks like geneveer (Dutch gin). Thus, the music is left to the younger people, who are playing more suspect, vulgar instruments, the flute and the bagpipe. Off to the left, a young boy (the one whose pipe content is unclear) stands outside the house but participates through an open window. Is he a neighbor? Is this a sign that the entire community, not just this particular family, is at risk? The arrangements, juxtapositions, and contrasts invite the viewer's imagination to fill in what they are singing, drinking, and doing with their pipes. The intrinsic aesthetic properties cannot be separated from the moral message.

Though the ethical content of some of Jan Vermeer's and Norman Rockwell's paintings are superficially alike, the intrinsic properties of their works makes all the difference. Rockwell's works are "childish" and for that reason work better with the morally immature than do Vermeer's. It is intrinsic properties as well as subject matter (use of light, relation of shapes, ambiguities) that made it possible for a war crimes judge at the World Court in The Hague to report that it was the Vermeers in that city's Mauritshuis that regularly restored his faith in humanity. We saw in chapter 8 how Anthony Powell uses a painting of Poussin as the thematic metaphor for the nature and meaning of life. In both the painting and the novels, Powell shows his moral message: "Partners disappear only to reappear again, once more giving pattern to the spectacle: unable to control the melody, unable, perhaps to control the steps of the dance."[42] Patterns exhibited in the properties of the novels and paintings deepen and clarify their ethical content.

Picasso's *Guernica* shows what it states. The distorted shapes and rhythms express the horrors of war.[43] Of course, the intrinsic properties of this great work do not, as E. F. Granell has pointed out, directly refer to war, at least not in the traditional ways.

> This scene is far from representing a battle. There are no opposing factions. Several domestic objects and a few obsolete and broken weapons have nothing to do with modern warfare techniques. Uniforms are nowhere in evidence. Nor are there any other kind of tools suitable for war. Certainly, it has been argued, that the scene so depicted is one of violence, and it has been stated repeatedly that this violence is the consequence of a great commotion caused by a bombardment. But it could also be argued that *Guernica* represents an accidental fire taking place in the house; or a death in the family, the calamity of a hurt beast, or any other sort of unfortunate daily happening.[44]

Deciding whether Granell is right demands close inspection of the painting itself, of course. I disagree with his view; I believe that only something more than an "unfortunate daily happening," even one as tragic as a home burning down, is consistent with the distortions, the restriction of color to black, whites, and grays, and the clutter of shapes. Picasso is saying something about a particular event that exemplifies a general moral failure.

Käthe Kollwitz handles the horrors of war differently from Picasso, and the properties of war that she makes salient depend on salient intrinsic properties of her works (see, for example, figure 2). In her sculpture *Vater und Mutter*, 1954, parents grieve at their child's tomb. Originally, she intended to include the child, a war victim, but decided that this would make the work too reminiscent of a pietà and thus would make death seem heroic—a message about war that she was loathe to convey. The intrinsic property (in this case, a property made present by an absence) is crucial to the success of her moral lesson.

Any art form that is communicative (and this is all of them, after all) has the capacity to convey a moral message and hence teach a moral lesson. Dances or mimes that present tales with moral content use intrinsic properties appropriate to or required by the message in ways similar to many of the literary strategies I have mentioned: repetition, complexity, tempo. Valerie A. Briginshaw contrasts the different interpretations that Margot Fonteyn and Natalia Makarova have given in the second act of *Swan Lake*.

> Fonteyn's performance is speedier, particularly in the pirouettes and fouettes, which come towards the end of the duet. Fonteyn appears to perform a greater number of fast, whipping turns and to perform them more quickly, conveying a more passionate and desperate mood, which contrasts with Makarova's considered intensity. . . . In Makarova's interpretation Odette's feelings seem to be conveyed most clearly in the phrases of elongated arabesques and deveoppes which assume greater importance, whereas in Fonteyn's performance the pirouettes and fouettes appear to have more emphasis, stressing the ecstatic elements of the relationship.[45]

FIGURE 2 Käthe Kollwitz "Mourning Parents," Ruins of St. Alban's Church, Cologne, Germany. With permission of Käthe Kollwitz Museum, Cologne, Germany, and VG Bild-Kunst, Bonn, Germany.

Whether individuals are motivated by a mixture of hope and despair or by ecstasy matters greatly to making sense of what they do, and hence to a moral assessment of their actions. Any art form (and this includes all of them) that contains allusions, representations, emotional expressiveness, and imagery lends itself to comparative and contrastive response. Even nonnarrative dances can present a moral outlook. Christine Lomas, for example, explains how the work of a community dance group, Jabadao, in England uses "disenfranchised" dancers—the elderly or the disabled, for instance—to make a statement about the way such groups are devalued in contemporary British culture.[46] The absence of high, graceful jumps or pirouettes from their performances refers to those very features of classical dance, and in doing so provides an example of the inseparability of the intrinsic and the extrinsic, the aesthetic and the ethical.

Some musical works can, in spite of Peter Kivy's strong arguments to the contrary, present moral lessons; for example, some integrate confident, bold faith in outcomes, and others are more tentative. Kivy certainly agrees that music with words can have ethical content. Songs intended to bind communities—national anthems or school songs, for example—must have appropriate intrinsic properties. The moral lessons Mr. Rogers presents in his songs must combine intrinsic musical properties with intrinsic properties of words in such a way that they emphasize or make accessible the lesson he wants to give. Malcolm Budd provides examples of musical features that might lend meaning, and hence moral meaning, to compositions: momentum, anticipations, forward and backward references, contrasts, pauses, explosions of sound, juxtaposition, leaps, violent rhythms, syncopation, drama, organization, interlocking, reconciliation, wit.[47] It may be difficult, even impossible, for pure music (music without words or dance) to teach moral lessons. But even here we hear 'sentimental' applied (to Pachelbel's *Canon*, for instance), and I argued in chapter 9 that this term cannot be applied without an integration of aesthetic and moral properties. Music certainly can connect to what Graham McFee calls "life-issues or life situations,"[48] and life situations are certainly often moral. I shall say more in the next chapter about another way in which even pure music might have ethical connections.

It is true that in art, life, even complicated human life, is presented with a clarity that is lacking in ordinary experience. "[There is] something about the real quality of human nature, when it is envisaged, in the artist's just and compassionate vision ... [that has] a clarity which does not belong to the self-centred rush of ordinary life," writes Murdoch.[49] But the fact that the rush of life is distilled in art does not imply that art is separate from life. What it means is that the thoughts and emotions of people can be evoked vividly and in such a way that applications to real moral life are encouraged. Just as it is more likely that a child will remember "a visit to his friend the Ogre of the North" longer than "a trip out of town," so intrinsic features of adult art, when vivid and memorable, can alter our moral views and attitudes, as well as clarify them. Richard Eldridge convincingly describes how *Pride and Prejudice* suggests a type of marriage that is untraditional but possible. And he shows how this requires successful juxtapositions of various sorts of marriages and mastery of literary techniques such as the short half-sentences that Jane Austen puts in the mouth of Mrs. Bennett to show "a distracted and disintegrated mind ... circling through its persistent obsessions with money and appearances."[50] Eva Dadlez points out, "Even the descriptions of an omniscient narrator can have stylistic features that determine what states of affairs are included in the world of a work."[51] It makes a big difference, for instance, whether the narrator says, "The Dog came up to Spike and barked, so Spike knew it was time for her supper" or "The dog importuned Spike for her supper." Mary Devereaux analyzes the intrinsic properties of *Triumph of the Will* that make that film such a troubling case of the combination of beauty and evil. Even the use of a particular medium, as John

Berger so brilliantly argues in *Ways of Seeing*, can carry a moral message in its aesthetic effects.[52]

Obviously, many more case studies must be provided, both from art and from real life, before we aestheticians can convince moral philosophers that the study of ethics is not complete without due attention to aesthetic matters. Many writers have shown how aesthetic properties contribute to a theme. Lamarque and Olsen do it brilliantly in *Truth, Fiction, and Literature*. I disagree, however, with their insistence that these themes do not make real assertions about the real world but matter only because they provide an aesthetic coherence that unifies a variety of textual properties. I believe, on the contrary, that real-world relatedness is precisely what makes many works important to us. I see nothing inconsistent between creating a text with aesthetic coherence and moral value.

Moral philosophers have always used literature in their work and hence have acknowledged, at least implicitly, the importance of narrative. But, like most aestheticians, they have tended to concentrate on content. Extending the discussion to form and realizing, finally, that content and form, like ethics and aesthetics, are inseparable would do much to firmly establish a place for aesthetics at the center of philosophy.

Many more detailed analyses of artworks remain to be done to show exactly how intrinsic properties integrate with moral content to teach moral lessons. Even more must be done to prove that aesthetic failures lead to moral failures in art. An even more difficult task yet will be showing that this applies in real life—that our personal aesthetic failures, at least some of them, lead to moral failures. Does showing that we are virtuous (so that others may imitate us) require that we give attention to things like rhythms or to creating vivid images? Must we, as writers such as Iris Murdoch and Richard Eldridge assert, attend to creating well-wrought narratives out of the actions that constitute our lives? Must I worry not only about being a good parent, spouse, or friend but also about doing it gracefully? Must I not only try to avoid being a racist but also avoid doing it in a boring way? Must I not only be unselfish and persevere but also do it vividly and memorably and beautifully?

I shall end this chapter with a quiz: How would you show in an adult artwork that perseverance always wins? My hunch is that one could not do this, since most adults have already learned that it does not. But one might show that perseverance sometimes wins, even in the most unlikely circumstances. Or one might show how people cope, more or less successfully, when perseverance does not pay off. But doing this will require much more than simply saying it. One will have to *show* these things in ways that engage adult thoughts and emotions. Such moral lessons will be successful only when readers are encouraged via intrinsic properties that integrate with moral content in such a way that the audience proceeds to fill in details and otherwise engage in the perceptive and reflective skills that lead us from the work to the world and back again many times.

ELEVEN

Deliberation Aesthetic and Ethical

TEACHING moral lessons is one contribution that aesthetic objects and events can make to ethics, and we have seen that thinking about how this works shows how firmly integrated ethical and aesthetic considerations can be. Obviously, however, there is more to ethical or aesthetic perception and reflection in the arts than teaching moral lessons. In this chapter, I want to discuss how art figures in what I will call "deliberation aesthetic and moral" and argue that here again we find a deep connection between the moral and the aesthetic, one that implies a kind of merit that is also at once aesthetic and moral.

Once again, I want to consider how "real people" use art. I begin with an excerpt from a letter from a friend, Mary Macdonald McCray, responding to a description I gave her of the work I was currently involved in.

> In my own head the highest form of art is this: first, the art validates something I have thought, felt or sensed. It makes me feel very human. I look at the painting and think, yes, I have seen that, or, I have felt just like that. If it is an abstract line I equate it with some of the practices of modern jazz where each instrument has a chance to show off the technique or virtuosity of the player. . . . Second, the work of art makes me start thinking, or imagining, or, yes, it teaches me something, although that may not be its primary characteristic. I do think that the best artists are not seers, but are more sensitive to the actual times in which they live. Because of this it makes people like me (who are struggling) read their novel, or view their art and think, "Aha—yes, that is the way it is. Why didn't I think of that?" Some think that great artists are really ahead of their time, but I think they are really just more attuned; most of us have on blinders.

I quote my friend's remarks because I think they express an attitude about the role that art plays in our lives that is typical, or at least not unusual, for persons in the culture to which Mary and I belong. The view is shared, as we shall see, by several philosophers of art. But, as we saw with both strong and weak formalists in the chapter on the separatist mistake, many theorists would deprive art of this function. I hope in this chapter both to capture how many thoughtful people connect art to their struggle for ethical understanding and to show how this activity further demonstrates important connections between ethics and aesthetics.

I discussed in chapter 7 the suggestion that has been made by some moral philosophers that we broaden our view of ethics. It is too narrow a view of both ethics and aesthetics that has been responsible, I believe, for the attempt to cordon off value realms in human experience. A theorist such as Richard Posner, who, we have seen, worries that moral considerations are "distractions" from genuine aesthetic value, make the common mistake of associating moral merit with moral content or consequences. But he takes this position because he makes an all—too frequent error, one that is implicit in the following remark: "The moral content of a work of literature is merely the writer's raw material. It is something he works up into a form to which morality is no more relevant to the value of the sculptor's clay than a building material is relevant to the artistic value of the completed sculpture."[1] This rather glib attitude results from a formalist insistence on the separation of aesthetic and economic value. Only a philistine, it is often held, would say that a golden statue is aesthetically more valuable than an identical one made of clay. Mainstream art critics and their followers contemptuously dismiss the riffraff who want to know how much a painting would sell for as they stroll through museums. But the fact is that throughout much human history, the raw materials from which objects are made have been part of the overall aesthetic value. This has been true of the use of gold leaf or rare shells. Preciousness and rarity, if not economic value per se, are often part of what is valued aesthetically. And the moral nature of works, properly construed, is also often part of what I call merit aesthetic and ethical.

Philosophers have, of course, always been in the business of proposing models for ethical reflection. Many of the models they have proposed are directed to decision making, to providing rational strategies for answering the question "What should I do?" Often, but not always, this is a question about the right course of action to take, as it were, "here and now," though the here and now may be more or less close at hand. Should I have an abortion? Should I tell her the truth? Should I give money to the Red Cross or to Oxfam? The strategies that moral philosophers suggest for answering such questions usually include general principles that direct moral reasoning (Seek to maximize happiness or Do your duty). What in this situation must I do given rule R or principle P? They also often include analyses of the logic of ethical reasoning. Thus, Aristotle asserted that moral decision making comes as a result of applying a practical syllogism; more recently, many moral philosophers have provided other models for moral logic that do or should lead us to our decisions.[2] Directions for answering the question "What should I do?" differ tremendously; what they all have in common, however, is the view that this is the central question of moral philosophy. Recommendations for how best to teach moral lessons can probably most appropriately be seen as relevant to this kind of question, and I have already indicated how important I think art can be here. (You should persevere, or Share your garden with others.)

Another question, however, has been taken by other philosophers as the key issue: "What sort of person should I be?" This was Socrates' worry, and it is a worry that many others have shared. Many people do take seriously the challenge to "choose something like a star" but are not quite certain how to proceed in an attempt to aim for more from life than a big house or a secure job. In trying to sort this out, both ethical and aesthetic concerns are involved. In earlier chapters, I have shown how the value of art is tied to this type of concern. Metaphors encountered earlier—Murdoch's "the texture of being," for instance—point to this general question, one that addresses not particular actions but the overall character of one's life. Richard Eldridge articulates a human concern that I think is a version of this question that connotes its urgency. "How . . . are we to go on as persons to manifest and sustain our being in the world? From what landmarks in our courses can we take our bearings?"[3] Though this question clearly involves answering questions about what to do "here and now," it also demands more than that. It also, as Eldridge explains, requires thinking about "what it is to lead the life of a person, and to lead it well."[4] I shall in this chapter say more about how I believe art and morality come together in humans' struggles to deal with this question.

But there is another kind of question—one that moral philosophers have not exactly ignored, but one that often is implicit rather than explicit in ethical writing: "How can we make sense of how people treat one another?" This is very vague, and I can only hope that what I am after in this articulation of the query will become clearer as I discuss it. It is a question not so much about what one should do or be, but about why people do what they do—where the "people" may, of course, include oneself. "How could someone do something like that?" "What could have gotten into me?" Reflecting on such questions is, I believe, a much more prevalent form of what I am calling "deliberation aesthetic and ethical" than has often been recognized in philosophy. And the attempt to make sense of it all often stimulates and is stimulated by engagement with aesthetic objects and events.

Peter Lamarque and Stein Olsen, we saw in chapter 5, worry that readers have a dangerous tendency to confuse moral and aesthetic value. In the course of their discussion, they criticize in particular theorists such as Martha Nussbaum, who insist that literature can do important philosophic work. They are suspicious of this thesis: "Some literary works make a contribution to moral reasoning and must therefore be considered as an integral part of or necessary adjunct to moral philosophy. The features of these works that make them valuable as moral philosophy are identical in part with those features that make them valuable as imaginative creations, that is, as literary works. The function they serve in moral philosophy could not therefore be served by any other kind of text." They charge, "The questions of whether their moral value is part of, or integral to, their aesthetic value is simply not raised or not considered."[5] I think, as a matter of fact, that Nussbaum does explicitly deal with this. In any case, in this chapter it is my intention to show explicitly how moral and aesthetic value are integrated in ethical deliberation, understood as the attempt to deal with questions about how one should generally lead one's life and as an attempt to make sense of the human moral condition.

Before I turn to that task, however, an aside is in order. Currently, it is very popular to describe individuals' encounters with works of art as "make-believe." The intelligent, clever work of Kendall Walton in this regard has been justifiably influential. At the same time, I fear, it has lent support to some theorists who are friends of the separation of ethics and aesthetics, for if we are only making believe when we experience objects and events aesthetically, then additional work is required to show how art is relevant to real life.[6]

I do not claim that we never make-believe or play "Let's pretend" with respect to artworks; I only insist that it is not the only thing we do. One powerful objection to the view that in experiencing art we imagine possible worlds and imagine ourselves in them comes from Susan Feagin, who argues that the presupposition that art and reality are separate simply does not always obtain. Walton's theory, she objects, clearly does not handle the experiences that many people have in front of, say, an altarpiece. An artwork often acts not as the occasion for make-believe but as a substitute, as "something that can function, in material respects, as what it represents, does or did."[7] Substitutes "extend the power of the original,"[8] and to insist that worshipers at an altar engage in some kind of make-believe diminishes both the viewer and the viewed, she rightly claims. Noel Carroll also objects to describing engagements with art solely in terms of make-believe. Our response to Oedipus surely, he thinks, is one of pity, not self-recrimination.[9]

I agree with these objections. What they suggest is that experiences of art (narrative art in particular) construed exclusively as make-believe create too wide a gap between art and real life. The very phrase 'make-believe' suggests something unreal, remote, detached. The uses of art are many. I am intent, of course, on making sure that nothing is done that creates an a priori separation between the aesthetic and the moral in general, and between art and moral development more specifically—where that development involves both learning moral lessons and engaging in ethical deliberation construed broadly. We may imagine that we are a character in a book, for instance, and what it might be like to act some way. But we may also ask ourselves whether we might *in fact* be someone like this, whether the reasons we get into the trouble we do might really be that we are like this character. We imagine not that we are so-and-so but whether if we acted like this we might find ourselves in a comparable mess. As E. M. Dadlez points out, make-believe at most only correctly characterizes some of our activities with regard to works of fiction. We participate, but our imaginations are engaged cognitively and empathetically,[10] not simply in the ways of pretense.[11] Taking works seriously "involves a whole complex of mental states and events, a pattern of thoughts, desires, reflections, suppositions, evaluations, responses, and frequently feelings and emotions."[12] What is correct about make-believe theories is that they capture the fact that our encounters are active, not passive. But constructions need not result only in games of pretense. 'Make-believe' is too reminiscent of 'distance'.

So now we turn to the combined roles of aesthetics and morality in "real" ethical deliberation. One of the things art sometimes provides is specific examples of individuals whom we would like to emulate. Just as David Copperfield chose Roderick Random, we might decide to try to be more like The Little Engine or an unselfish giant or a character from a Jan Steen painting who seems to fully lust for life. Sometimes, as Joseph Brodsky said, "Living is like quoting."[13] This is the sort of thing that I discussed in the chapter on art and moral lessons. Here, I am after broader applications—not trying to decide specifically what artistic character one will model one's life after, but more generally the sort of characteristics one wants to develop.

Many advocates of the arts have described how works can develop skills necessary to a rich aesthetic and moral life. These skills relate to my definition of art as an object of attention. One must pay attention to objects and events if one hopes to have an aesthetic experience, and the attention one learns to pay is similar to sensitive observation of the sort required in moral scrutiny. One's perceptive abilities are refined by art, and one's reflective enterprises are deepened. One learns that signs and clues must be sought deliberately and painstakingly. As Martha Nussbaum both asserts and exemplifies, features of artworks "both show us and engender in us a process of reflection and (self-)discovery that works through a persistent attention to and a (re-)interpretation of concrete words, images, and incidents. . . . Every horizontal link contributes to the depth of our view of the particular, and every new depth creates new horizontal links."[14] For this to work, of course, the signs, the clues, the links must be there. Only works that bear close attention will engage attention for more than a fleeting moment. The study of ethics brings to the foreground features of the human situation that must be attended to and the connections between them. Art does this as well, and it does it by requiring many of the skills necessary for "reading" the features foregrounded. Just as moral rules can be taken not as laws that determine whether acts are right or wrong but as guidelines for identifying salient features of moral actions, so artworks can be construed not as telling us what is right or wrong but with identifying salient features. They do this not just by presenting subject matter that possesses those salient features but by also possessing themselves properties that one must perceive—and that often one must work to uncover.

Aristotle's ethics recognized the role of these "aesthetic skills"—perceptive and reflective abilities. One must be careful, however, not to commit the separatist mistake; mature perception and reflection involve ethico-aesthetic or aesthetico-ethical skills. They go together. To stem the tide of separatism, I shall introduce the admittedly clumsy term *aes-ethical* and abbreviate it in two other terms, *DAE, deliberation aesthetic and ethical* and *MAE, merit aesthetic and ethical.*

Nussbaum's succinct characterization of Aristotle's view emphasizes the connection between aesthetic and ethical skills and supports our thinking in terms of the aes-ethical. For Aristotle, she writes, ethical knowledge "consists above all, in the intuitive perception of complex particulars. Universals are never more than guides to and summaries of these concrete perceptions; and 'the decision rests with perception.' Perception, furthermore, is both cognitive and affective at the same time: it consists in the ability to single out the ethically salient features of the particular matter at hand; and frequently this recognition is accomplished by and in appropriate emotional response as through intellectual judgment. Aristotle repeatedly emphasizes that correct perception cannot be learned by percept, only through and in one's own experience."[15] One of Nussbaum's great contributions to the study of ethics has been her insightful analysis of ways in which literary works help us to develop the perceptive and reflective skills we need to discern the salient properties required for ethical knowledge. One of the ways we do this is through responding to art and reflecting upon our responses to art. As I hope I have shown, the kind of perception required to recognize that acts are sentimental—reflection that integrates the ethical and the aesthetic (see chapter 9)—is one sort or facet of this kind of ethical knowledge. Art serves to provide occasions for ethical deliberation that sometimes leads to such knowledge.

But in trying to decide what kind of person one should be, we also look for alternative answers, and the ways in which artworks present possibilities have been identified by several writers as a central aesthetic value. This, I suggest, is another source of the integration of the aesthetic and ethical. Aristotle, again, was one of the first to point out that literature shows us what happens when people of a certain kind act in certain ways. Related to looking to the arts for specific role models and aes-ethical talents, one reason people value art is that it invites openness to consideration of various courses of actions, various choices of the sort of person reasonable people may want to be. In particular, the narrative arts, integrating form and content, show what might be possible and show how one considers possibilities. Art, as my friend Mary wrote, helps us to remove our blinders.

We have already encountered a fictional depiction of how art provides a resource for trying out possibilities in the work of Anthony Powell. But he is by no means alone in describing how trying on roles can be a stage in moral development. V. S. Naipaul provides another example in his novel *A Bend in the River*, when the protagonist describes a young friend.

> I could see him now trying on various characters, attempting different kinds of manners. His range was limited. For a few days after [his mother] came to town, he might be the son of . . . the *marchande*. He would pretend to be my business associate, my equal, might make inquiries about sales and prices. Then he might become the young African on the way up, the lycee student, modern, go-ahead. In this character he liked to wear the blazer with the *Semper aliquid Novi* motto; no doubt he felt it helped him carry off the mannerisms he had picked up from some of his European teachers. Copying one teacher, he might, in the flat, stand with crossed legs against the white studio wall and, fixed in that position, attempt to conduct a whole conversation. Or, copying another teacher, he might walk around the trestle table, lifting things, looking at them, and then dropping them, while he talked.[16]

One can imagine that had this young man, like David Copperfield, read the same books, he, too, would have gone through a Roderick Ransom stage.

But the ethical deliberation that art often invites goes beyond the invitation to "try on" different roles. Richard Posner maintains that literature's value cannot reside in its moral content because works "often invite a variety of incompatible moral responses."[17] But, on an extended view of ethics, it is precisely this feature than makes the moral such an essential part of the aesthetic value of a work. Considering alternatives is a necessary part of mature ethical deliberation.

An excellent example of DAE constituted by consideration of alternative viewpoints comes from the pen of someone who was both a first-rate literary artist and practicing philosopher—Iris Murdoch. An expert in the ways in which philosophers have discussed comparative strengths and weakness of both ethical principles and the logic of ethical argument, Murdoch also, I think, sees ethical deliberation in the broader sense of asking questions about how to lead one's life and how to make sense of moral and immoral and amoral behavior generally. Here is a passage in which she exemplifies precisely the particular value that art can have with respect to opening us to possibilities. One of the characters in her novel *The Message to the Planet* does what I believe art often invites attenders to do.

> The mere thought of Marzillian *talking* to Marcus, probing him, theorising him, investigating his childhood and so on made Ludens shudder with disgust. And then there was the other doctor whose appearance Ludens had not liked at all. The place reeked of drugs and expertise and mental care . . . the whole scene was awful, the risks were terrible. Marcus would play chess with Mr. Talgarth, bridge with the doctors and Camilla, chat with the other inmates in the common room, become a well-known habitue of the swimming pool.
>
> Here Ludens suddenly checked his thoughts and actually stopped his fast walk abruptly. Well, why not? Might Marcus *enjoy* some human companionship in this comfortable expensive place? . . . He thought, I'm being possessive, I'm being jealous, my old vice. I want Marcus to myself, I want to be the only one he talks to. But suppose he were to stop wanting solitude, or to spend all his time thinking? Suppose he became soft and corrupted? But that's nonsense, he's incorruptible. . . .[18]

Ludens, the protagonist, "checks himself"; his thoughts turn from one possibility to another. He demonstrates an openness to competing explanations of the actions of himself and others. The style Murdoch employs emphasizes the particular kinds of thought processes that often characterize such deliberation. The sentences are short and choppy; the punctuation used signals rapid mental transitions from one alternative to another. As we saw in the last chapter, successful artists master stylistic devices required by the ideas being presented and re-presented.

Good art can stimulate the very kind of "checking" Ludens exemplifies on the part of readers or viewers. We see alternative actions and life choices, travel among them ourselves as we attend to the artwork, and check to see whether we are moving too quickly to judgment. Ludens represents to the reader what, I suggest, readers are invited and encouraged to do themselves as they engage with art. As R. W. Hepburn writes, "Art can be presented as inculcating that open, exploratory attitude to new possibilities of experience, and as overcoming views of human possibility that are limited by what is filtered through a restrictive and crude set of popular concepts."[19] That this activity does not always result in improved moral character must be acknowledged; but so must the fact that it can and does sometimes make a contribution.

Like me, Gregory Currie sees this activity as being at the core of the value of art. Imagination can be a source of knowledge and, in particular, a source of knowledge about how to act to achieve proper moral goals. As I shall argue later, I also think it can be a source of satisfying our need for understanding the human condition. What Currie calls "projective imagination" enables us to put ourselves into the minds and shoes of others, a crucial step in ethical deliberation. We consider, construct, and respond to a variety of alternatives and outcomes. In reading fiction, we "try out" moral choices. Our moral failures are often a matter of poor planning because we fail to "anticipate circumstances, the consequences of actions, the reactions of others."[20] Artworks can help us to remedy this situation.

And they can do this with respect to assessing individual lives (both our own and others') and in understanding and judging interpersonal relationships and communities. Artworks motivate specific inquiries by, as Richard Eldridge puts it, urging us to "read cooperatively and in responsiveness to the criticism of our lives that may be implied in opposing narratives of development." What is demanded of us, at least by works of art that invite sustained and serious attention, is a "way of reading that is alert to both the partiality and the genuineness of achievements or self-understanding and value on the parts of protagonists."[21] I referred earlier to his discussion of Austen's *Pride and Prejudice*, as presenting alternative views of marriage, and of the possibility of a marriage that might allow for respecting the lives of both parties. Austen succeeds, he thinks, in drawing the reader to see this institution alternately as a "blending of individuality and society, energy and discipline, innovation and tradition" or

> inevitably and predominantly the arena for the perpetuation of exploitation and possessiveness. . . . In doing things, she would educate us to a sense of our best real possibilities. What prevents us from receiving this education, and what keeps us locked in our ambivalence, is the strength of the prior conceptualizations of marriage that we bring to the work. In order to see how we might be educated by *Pride and Prejudice* away from these prior conceptualizations and toward an appreciation of marriage of a certain sort as a materially realizable ideal, we need first to articulate and acknowledge those prior conceptualizations.[22]

We must, as Murdoch says, "check ourselves," and art is often the occasion for bringing this about.

Artworks can not only ask us to examine our lives and our relationships within communities but also make us consider the very limits of what might be possible for life itself. Many works of science fiction, I think, do this by causing us to ask, for example, to what extent we are ready to grant rationality and other aspects of humanity to entities. This is why we take seriously even what we know to be literally false. Not only is it science fiction that does this but also myths do it. Knowing full well that we are dealing with the mythic, we assess some as shallow, some as serious. The basis of this assessment, according to Hepburn, is the worthiness or unworthiness of our own response. We are, as he puts it, invited "to see *this* in light of *that*."[23] When seeing this in terms of that, whatever that may be, rewards such seeing, we consider valuable the object or event that brings it about.

Art not only expands our repertoire of beliefs concerning what is possible but also expands our emotional repertoire. Jenefer Robinson thinks they go together; as we read, we form "emotional conceptions" that involve desires, values, goals, and interests, as well as beliefs. I showed in the last chapter how cleverly she describes how specific features of works bring this about. E. M. Dadlez calls this "empathetic engagement" and insists that it is "ethically significant precisely because it allows us to explore experiences we have not had from perspectives that are not wholly our own but that we can make our own."[24] I suggest that a combination of beliefs and emotions that result from a consideration of possibilities plays an important role in our deliberations about meaningful lives. At least some people strive to discover the best way or at least one of the best ways of living. They accept the challenge to, as it were, "choose something like a star." But being told to aim high is not enough; what a "star" might consist in will have to be filled out *aes-ethically*, and artworks are primary resources. Martha Nussbaum puts this point beautifully in explaining why she thinks Greek tragedy and philosophy serve us so well in answering the human need for confronting and remaining open to possibilities.

> That I am an agent, but also a plant; that much that I did not make goes towards making me whatever I shall be praised or blamed for being; that I must constantly choose among competing and apparently incommensurable goods and that circumstances may force me to a position in which I cannot help being false to something or doing some wrong; that an event that simply happens to me may, without my consent, alter my life; that it is equally problematic to entrust one's good to friends, lovers, or country and to try to have a good life without them—all these I take to be not just the material of tragedy, but everyday facts of lived practical reason.[25]

And, that it is the material of both art and life is the reason that art is so important in the lives of ordinary people.[26] It is not just a matter of pointing out what people have done in the face of conflicts; it is also a matter of an artist's coupling this with aesthetic properties that embody them. Nussbaum shows how, in *Antigone*, the words used pick out these features of "the ethical world," just as we saw in discussing moral lessons in art how aesthetic features contribute to the success of the lesson.

> To the ordinary member of this play's audience [the labels used] pick out *distinct* and *separate* features of the ethical world. One and the same action or person will frequently possess more than one of the attributes picked out by these words ['just', 'unjust', 'friend', 'foe,' e.g.]—since in many cases they go together harmoniously. But they can be present separately from one another; and, even when co-present, they are distinct in their nature and in the responses they require. Many friends will turn out to be just and pious people; but what it is to be a friend is distinct from what it is to be just, or pious. The ordinary expectation would therefore be that in some imaginable circumstances the value named by these labels will make conflicting demands. Friendship or love may require an injustice; the just course of action may lead to impiety; the pursuit of honor may require an injury to friendship. Nor would each single value be assumed to be conflict-free. . . . In general, then, to *see* clearly the nature of each of these features would be to understand its distinctness from each other, its possibilities of combination with and opposition to each other, and, too, its opposition within itself."[27]

Not only does reflecting on the nature of, say, friendship not get in the way of focusing on the words used but also the two necessarily go together and enhance one another. This is DAE.

Many aesthetic theorists have used the term 'entertain' to describe the thought processes involved in scrutinizing artworks: Noel Carroll, Susan Feagin, Peter Lamarque, Stein Olsen, Peter Kivy, Malcolm Budd, Jerrold Levinson, Patricia Greenspan, Jenefer Robinson. It is a felicitous term. As we entertain thoughts, the thoughts shape the attitudes that color the activity of entertaining itself; the two cannot be prized apart. The way one entertains is determined by the thoughts one has because the thoughts one has in the "entertaining mode" will differ from those one might have when one engages in a different kind of activity. When one looks for possibilities, one is likely to have thoughts one will not have when one is, for example, trying to discover how to install a garage door opener. There are other words and phrases that capture facets of the entertaining activity: contemplate, consider, inspect, scrutinize, reflect on, puzzle over, wonder about, let one's imagination play freely, question, explore. But 'entertain', because of its relation to 'entertainment', carries with it the implicit value that we find in engagement with works of art and aesthetic objects. We *enter* into the object of attention, art or life, by attending closely to certain of its intrinsic properties, and the attention is repaid.

Rob van Gerwen uses an equally felicitous term, *intimation*,[28] though I have pressed him to change its construal slightly. Van Gerwen believes that the relationship between artworks and viewers is one in which properties of the object "intimate" or cause an imaginative act on the part of the viewer. He insists that the intimation is something that the object, not the viewer, does. Entering a work via empathetic imagination, we perceive properties, where for van Gerwen perception involves both sensation and imagination.[29] The intimation of the work is what accounts for the fact that people become engaged with—that is, intimate with—works of art. Since I view aesthetic properties as intrinsic but not supervenient—as much in the viewer as in the object—I would like 'intimate' to refer not only to what a work does but also to what the viewer does. One infers or fills in or interprets and thus becomes intimate (adjective) with the object. Properties of the object steer—'intimate' as a verb—our intimations, of course, but aesthetic response is active, not passive. Both the thoughts and emotions that result from attention to intrinsic properties valued in our community for the delight which they are capable of producing bring us close to, intimate with, an object or event.

The most important way that consideration of possibilities involves aesthetic perusal—attention to intrinsic properties that are considered worthy of perception and reflection in a community—arises from the fact that possibilities are engaging just in case they are, as it were, considered possible. That is, something about the way in which the most obviously and outlandishly false scenarios are presented must make them "acceptable." Acceptability depends less on truth or even plausibility, I think, than it does on coherence. Parts must fit together in an ordered pattern so that what happens next can be related to what went before. Aristotle's criterion of organic unity—that everything that is necessary happens and that everything that happens is necessary—may be a bit too strong, but it certainly captures the essence of narrative. One of the most important ways in which ethics and aesthetics come together into an aes-ethical deliberation involves narrative: what happens and the way it happens—content and form, as it were (with all the usual caveats about not thinking them separable)—come together. Patterns cannot be constructed from just any old parts. Parts must be chosen so that the pattern will emerge, and, of course, only some patterns can emerge. Unless there is this coalescence, possibilities will not play a role in serious ethical deliberation. Proust, for example, could not have made his point about the way in which memory works without showing it—without choosing intrinsic properties that would instantiate the very pattern that he was in a sense asserting existed in the mind. Frequently in literature (and the other arts), sequential patterns—narratives—provide instances of the integration of the ethical and the aesthetic.

All ethical deliberation arguably involves what amounts to storytelling. Even when one attempts to come to a decision about what particular action to perform in a specific set of circumstances, one imagines scenarios about various possible consequences. But I am less interested in this than I am in the ways in which storytelling or narratives play a role in evaluating lives as more or less meaningful and in trying to generally make sense of the human condition. Peter Brooks writes, "Our lives are ceaselessly intertwined with narratives, with the stories that we tell and hear told, those we dream or imagine or would like to tell. . . . We live immersed in narrative, recounting and reassessing the meaning of our past actions, anticipating the outcome of our future projects, situating ourselves at the intersection of several stories not yet completed."[30] Telling life stories, or at least stories about segments of lives, is an enormously important part of our relationships, both with friends and with strangers. "The very possibility of moral assessment seems to be bound up with the idea of ongoing character. We do not know how we would talk about an agent who kept improvising himself from moment to moment and was never willing to identify himself with any general commitments,"[31] Nussbaum correctly observes. Acts must be joined together for us to make sense of personhood at all. No story, no meaning. In a very real sense, whether a life is meaningful depends first and foremost on there being a story to be told. The more coherent and interesting the story, the more likely it is that we will judge a life meaningful.

Perhaps the shortest life narratives appear on tombstones. Usually, we are given only the dates of the start and finish, and a line or two: "Beloved mother," "Taken too soon," "A hero." Famous people get more. Charles Burney's epitaph in Westminster Abbey exemplifies how important intrinsic properties (the aesthetic) combined with moral traits can be.

> 1726–1814. Who, full of years, and full of virtues, the pride of his family, the delight of society, the unrivalled chief, and scientific historian of his tuneful art! Beloved, revered, regretted, breathed, in Chelsea College, his last sigh! Leaving to posterity a fame unblemished, raised on the noble basis of intellectual attainments. High principles and pure benevolence, goodness with gaiety, talents with taste, were of his gifted mind the blended attributes; while the general hilarity of his airy spirits animated, or softened, his every earthly toil; and a conscience without reproach prepared in the whole tenour of his mortal life, through the mediation of our Lord Jesus Christ, his soul for heaven. Amen.

"Amen" to a life of "blended attributes."

An even more vivid example of the ways in which existence of a narrative and meaningfulness come together in healthy human lives is provided by Oliver Sacks, a neurologist famous for his stories about his patients.

> We had at first thought in narrow, chemical terms, believing that it would be sufficient to animate the patients chemically with L-DOPA, and then let them go. But L-DOPA,

it was soon clear, was only the beginning. What was then necessary, after the first excitement had come and gone, was "reality," the sense of a real life, an identity: it was necessary for them to find or make a life with purpose and meaning and individuality and dignity.

This, it might be said, is true of us all, but it was especially clear in these neurologically damaged patients, who had so little of the normal resilience the rest of us have, and so great a tendency to disintegrate physiologically. These patients had an exaggerated need to find ways of centering and organizing their so greatly disturbed physiology. Thus studying them, in their extremity, made clearer what is needed and sought by us all.[32]

Sacks also provides an example that shows that McFee rather than Kivy may be correct about the power of music to deal with life issues. "One . . . postencephalatic patient, a former music teacher, said she had been 'demusicked' by her disease; but, even before L-DOPA, she would suddenly recover herself, albeit briefly, if she was 'remusicked.'" Like literature, music can provide the coherence that yields patterns that affect and influence human lives. Though not narrative per se, any arrangement that invites forward and backward reference might contribute to the structural skills we need in DAE.

What is "sought by us all" is what I shall sum up in the phrase "the urge to narrative."[33] It is motivated by a variety of human impulses. The narrator in Ford Madox Ford's brilliant novel, *The Good Soldier*, says early on: "You may well ask why I write. And yet my reasons are quite many. For it is not unusual in human beings who have witnessed the sack of a city or the falling to pieces of a people to desire to set down what they have witnessed for the benefit of unknown heirs or of generations infinitely remote; or if you please, just to get the sight out of their heads."[34] Or we tell tales, as this narrator does, to make sense of and hence deal with what has finally been revealed to him about his wife and friends. Mr. Rogers advises parents that "What is mentionable, is manageable," and that one should thus tell children as much as they want to know. This is not all that far from psychotherapy, which is often based on the view that what is tellable is treatable. We yearn to be able to say, on balance, that what we have done fits together. In her novel *The Laws*, Connie Palmen's protagonist tries to make sense of the way in which an astrologer friend sees the world. "Life had to free him from his horrible isolation by incorporating him in a big story and thus prove to him the necessity of his existence."[35] Not everyone, of course, needs so big a story as that which connects us with the stars, but we do need a story. At the end of the day or of all of our days, we want nothing crucial left undone or unsaid. In chapter 7, I mentioned Michel Foucault's claim that the ancient Greeks sought a morality that would enable individuals to recognize and be recognized as having a certain kind of identity (in that case, one involving a particular sort of liberty).[36] Though the Greeks may have sought an especial moral system, the desire to present ourselves and see others as individuals with an identity that can be read across time was by no means uniquely Greek. We also saw in chapter 7 how important both Charles Altieri and Mark Johnson think providing narratives and grammars of narratives are for creating meaningful lives. I do not pretend that the idea is new with me; what I hope to emphasize is the extent to which recognizing the importance of narratives for moral-ity points to the inseparability of ethics and aesthetics.

Something akin to what Aristotle was after in his phrase 'organic unity' is today expressed by people who say that they want to rid their lives of "excess baggage." This, I think, expresses the urge or longing to have a life that lends itself to crisp as well as rich narrative. Well-being, in the Greek sense of not simply feeling happy but of "being well" or living well, where 'well' is MAE, demands life with a purpose, a life in which a sense of unity or identity draws together the parts. Finding this de-mands aesthetic sensitivity, that is, skills at perceiving patterns, coherence, fit, har-mony, and proportion. We often get this from art.

Mark Bernstein construes 'well-being' phenomenologically in a subjective sense, as the way someone feels "from the inside." He distinguishes this from ob-jective accounts of moral value that point to something else important to human beings, namely, the value of their lives, the meaningfulness of their lives as con-nected sentential experiences.[37] While I favor the Greek sense of 'well-being', the distinction Bernstein makes is important. There is a difference between judgments one makes about one's life in terms of the pleasure or pain one feels at the moment and the judgments one makes about one's own and others' lives in terms of ex-tended series of events. Bernstein thinks the latter are "non-experiential." I disagree; I believe that we do have a sense or experience of patterns of events that make up our life stories. Moreover, we feel an urge to create these narratives. Bernstein con-trasts individual states of feelings viewed from inside (this is the well-being he thinks serves as the criterion for moral demarcation and enfranchisement) and classes of states viewed from the outside (this is what he takes to be the objective meaningfulness of lives). He does not talk about the fact that, in addition, perhaps in between, we have beliefs about our individual inner states and about the causes of those inner states. These beliefs affect both individual states and classes of states, I suggest. If I believe I am or have been deceiving myself, then it diminishes both my present pleasure and the overall meaningfulness of my existence. Bernstein says, "Neither authenticity nor veridicality contribute to personal well-being."[38] But I think they do precisely that by determining how good or how bad one's nar-rative is. One's inner life is not unaffected by an awareness of what has gone before and what may happen later. Palmen writes, "The sixties gave me the impression of being untrue, a phony scene in the stage play of life. This untruth was an intoxica-tion and everybody lived in the stirring compulsion of the lie. This lie was the de-nial of the twentieth century and it penetrated the bodies, the gestures, the rela-tionships and particularly it penetrated the skin of language."[39] If Palmen raises our blinders, brings those of us who lived in this period to share her sense, our nar-rative is, to that extent, spoiled.

But Bernstein is certainly correct to associate meaningfulness with classes of states rather than with individual states. As Sarah Conly asserts, part of what makes life meaningful, beyond our attachments and achievements, is a "certain coher-ence," and "ordered arrangement" of these things. "To be a mere bundle of emo-tions and interests in not enough. . . . [We need] a general harmony of orienta-tion—on the whole, our dispositions, goals, etc. must not be inconsistent."[40] David

Novitz discusses ways in which art connects to life precisely because it provides such coherence; art and life are mutually constructed through, among other things, narratives, he correctly observes.[41] Both constructions require what are usually taken to be aesthetic skills, but what I am urging are better recognized as *aes-ethical* skills: the ability to perceive and reflect upon the intrinsic properties of objects and events, to recognize and construct patterned collections of them and the states in which they inhere, and to connect these to properties and patterns in the world of human action and interation. "In order for a life to feel meaningful it needs what has been called a certain narrative structure. We seek a comprehensible pattern within a life, where its actions and events have an internal relationship which gives them significance."[42] And Conly is correct: we "feel" this. We sense that what we are doing "fits," and this demands attention to more than just the pleasure or pain one feels at a given moment. Conly asks why the death of a guerilla fighter is judged meaningful, whereas death by falling into an uncovered manhole is judged absurd. Her answer is that the latter has "no place within the plot."[43] Moral principles themselves work, are not alienating, just when they can be integrated into one's narrative, she correctly suggests.

Ted Cohen has discussed a phenomenon that is related, I think, to the urge to narrative: the desire for intrapersonal consistency. We expect others to be consistent in their aesthetic preferences; that is, if a person gives a reason for liking something, we expect that it will be a reason for his or her liking similar things. We also expect this of ourselves. We seek out explanations for our own preferences when we want to believe in our own coherence "even though one might know that the sought generality is forever out of reach."[44] I suggest that we do this partly because the very sense of there being a self requires consistency across preferences. Desiring consistency is a part of the urge to narrative; we want our states to fall into harmonious patterns.

Art teaches not just particular moral lessons but provides a coherence of the sort that we long for in our own lives. Eldridge's question "How—with what capacities, concerns, tasks, and self-understandings as persons in the world—do we go on?"[45] is, after all, a question about narrative (though not only about that, of course.) Asking how "to go on" is asking how to arrange events so that the outcomes will be acceptable and also so that the arrangement of events itself will be acceptable. It is a question about *how* to arrange *what* we do—where what happens as we go on depends on what has gone on before and what we anticipate will come later. Eldridge takes a very strong position when he insists that "such generalizations about our capacities as there can be will emerge only as we show ourselves to ourselves through the work of reading."[46] This leaves no room for illiterates or for those who find resources in places other than texts, and thus I think it is too strong. But there is no question that artworks can help. Without narrative models of some sort, it is hard to imagine how people would learn to shape their lives in the kind of coherent pattern that yields meaning. Art displays narratives, exposes us to the very nature of narrative, helps us to conceive possible ways of constructing our own life stories, invites us to entertain and intimate (in the verbal sense that I have suggested) alternatives. Pursuing ideas in art requires attending to the course of events and reveals strategies for making this course coherent. We see how resolution of conflict and tension might be possible. This is why some possibilities are more enthralling than others. Again, I turn to Martha Nussbaum for an example.

> The *Antigone's* choral lyrics have an unusual degree of density and compression. Each has an internal structure and an internal set of resonances; each reflects upon the action that has preceded; each reflects upon the preceding lyrics. Already, then, we find that to interpret fully any single image or phrase requires mapping a complex web of connections, as each successive item both modifies and is modified by the imagery and dialogue that has preceded. But once we mention that the succeeding item modifies the preceding or deepens our reading of it, we must then acknowledge that the web of connections to be drawn is much more complex still: for the resonances of a single item will be prospective as well as retrospective. An image in a lyric must be read not only against the background both of dialogue and of lyric that has preceded, but ultimately, in the light of events and lyrics yet to come. An intrinsically optimistic statement . . . may be undercut or qualified in the light of later occurrences of the same images or words. . . .[47]

Each action is shaped by remembering what has happened and imagining what might come. We learn very early to try on narratives through role playing: "You be Batman, I'll be Robin," "You be the teacher, I'll be the student," "You be the cop, I'll be the robber." And we try on narratives by engaging with works of narrative art. But we are not making-believe, or not merely making-believe; we are engaged in imagining how behavior and interactions serve to satisfy the urge to narrative. The skills we develop are the DAE skills needed for an important kind of ethical activity.

We engage in such deliberation not only because we want to create lives that are meaningful but also because we want to uncover meaning; that is, we feel the urge to make sense of what goes on around us. There have been many theories about why earliest humans painted scenes on the walls of caves. It is not unlikely, I think, that they were at least in part telling stories about themselves and their world; they were not just hoping to manipulate that world but to come to have a fuller explanation of it.

If we are lucky, we find the lives of others endlessly interesting, though puzzling—perhaps so interesting because so puzzling. I have insisted that ethical deliberation takes forms that go well beyond the models that philosophers have usually discussed. Some of these occasions of ethical deliberation are precisely those that make connections between aesthetic and ethical values apparent. Using syllogistic argument is not the only way, or even, probably, the most common way in which ordinary, everyday moral discussions proceed. I have, I hope, shown that consideration of possibilities of the sort stimulated by art is another way in which people engage in moral reflection. These possibilities contribute to satisfying the urge to create narratives that make meaningful lives possible. Undue concentration on providing lists of principles or strategies for decision making has unfortunately de-emphasized an important kind of ethical activity, one that might be called the "He Said, She Said" model of ethical deliberation. This form of working to understand the human condition by rehearsing what has occurred begins in childhood and is fully developed by the time we become teenagers!

Aristotle says there are two goals of human endeavor. At the beginning of the *Metaphysics,* he says all people want to understand the world; at the beginning of the *Nicomachean Ethics,* he says that all people want to be happy. The sort of ethical deliberation we engage in when we are trying "to get a handle" on the human condition displays both desires. "He said then she said then he said then she said . . . then she left" is deliberation aimed at an understanding that ideally contributes to human happiness. As I. A. Richards writes in *Principles of Literary Criticism,* "Everybody knows the feeling of freedom, or relief, of increased competence and sanity, that follows any reading in which more than usual order and coherence has been given to our responses. We seem to feel that our command of life, our insight into it, and our discrimination of its possibilities, is enhanced."[48]

In the last chapter, we considered Noel Carroll's view that art provides occasions for moral clarification. But he emphasizes clarification of one's own ethical positions. The extended sense of ethical deliberation that I am concerned with here aims at a broader understanding. Nussbaum explains Aristotle's notion of *katharsis* also as a kind of clarification, but in the sense in which water can be clarified: "the removal of some obstacle (dirt, or blot, or obscurity, or admixture) that makes the item in question less *clear* that it is in its proper state."[49] We often find ourselves in a state of puzzlement that demands this kind of clarification; but it is one that invites revision as much as refinement.

Recently, I participated in a conversation that is (to me at least) a clear instance of the sort of ethical deliberation I am trying to get at. My husband and I had dinner with two close friends whom we had not seen for a few years. (I will change names of locales and "characters" to protect the innocent and, perhaps, the guilty.) Dinner conversation covered food, recent and upcoming travels, music, housing costs, families, and similar topics. At one point, I turned to Fred and asked, "By the way, have Robert and Anne separated?" "I hope so," Linda said before Fred had a chance to reply. Fred smiled a bit knowingly and said, "Before I answer, I'd like to know why you ask." Fred knew that I had not seen Robert and Anne as Robert had only very recently returned from a half-year's studying in Paris. I explained that we had heard that Robert had gone to Paris without Anne, and that in the past he had refused to travel much at all, and never without Anne because she suffered from depression and he was unwilling to leave her alone with the children for long periods. Thus, we had been a bit surprised that he had gone alone. However, when we had last seen the pair, about three years before, Anne had begun taking anti-depressants and was feeling much better. In fact, I remarked, instead of being rather quiet and withdrawn, she had been "hyper," and I rather preferred her earlier self. So, I reported thinking, perhaps she had decided to remain at home with her children while Robert was gone for half a year. On the other hand, Joe and I knew that Robert had had a tough time of it during Anne's extended mental illness, and we suspected that perhaps his unhappiness, once she was better, had led him to decide to leave her. We had also learned that, on returning, Robert had taken a visiting position some distance from his home and was living away from his family, at least during the week. Joe also explained that he had written to Robert just before he left for Paris, but had had no reply. He was afraid that he had done something to offend Robert, since in fact he had declined to do a favor Robert had asked for, but we all agreed that Robert was not the sort of person who would be angry about such a thing. Fred then explained that he had seen Robert just a few days before and that Robert, when asked about his time in Paris, said that he wasn't sure whether he had enjoyed himself or not. It turned out that once Anne was feeling better, Robert himself became depressed and, although he had begun taking medication himself just before leaving for Paris, the medicine had not begun to work until only very recently. Fred reported that Robert reported that he now thought he was probably happier in Paris than he had realized while he was there. Yes, he was living away from home during the week now, but he was returning for weekends, and he proposed that he, Anne, Linda, and Fred get together some weekend soon. This led Fred to believe that although there might be some trouble, at least there was no official separation. We all then engaged in a discussion of why so many wives we knew were unhappy and even mentally ill. Was it because intelligent women had been placed in traditional roles of stay-at-home wives and mothers and were incredibly frustrated? We agreed that Robert, an unusually sweet man, deserved a better life than he had had, and that, away from Anne, he had always seemed more enthusiastic and generally brighter than when he was with her. Linda, in particular, thought that Anne was not much fun to be with either before or after medication, and looked forward to spending more time with Robert on his own, should it come to that.

I have probably told you more than you wanted to know—or, for some of you perhaps, less. I provide this scenario because it is of a sort with which I am certain you are familiar. Certainly, there is no crisp narrative here. I expect that you have participated in such a conversation within the last week, if not within the last twenty-four hours. It goes most often by the name "gossip," of course. (Women are supposed to engage in it more often than men, but studies indicate that this is not the case.)[50] What is the purpose? Surely not to come to any immediate decisions about what we should do or even about what advice we should give Robert or Anne. Though Linda made at least implicit moral judgments, the rest of us did not really claim that Robert or Anne was good or bad, should or should not do such and such. We puzzled together over their lives and the lives of similar couples. But notice that even in this run-of-the-mill exchange, attention is given to how to "go on." For example, Fred does not tell us what he knows until Joe and I have had a chance to tell him and Linda what we know. The flow would have been spoiled had he revealed too much too soon.

Such gossip is, I insist, a common form of ethical deliberation. I think the form is found not only in conversations with friends and colleagues but also in many other venues where people are trying to make sense of their world: on talk shows or in therapists' offices, in newspaper articles or pop psychology books, for example, where stories are constructed in the attempt to understand or explain some human conundrum. To a great extent, the study of history engages the same kind of ethical deliberation. My father, a history professor, confessed that he was drawn to this discipline in large part because of the scandals it offered; he loved sharing them with his students and demonstrating how crucial they were to an understanding of humanity. The extent to which ethics is the mother of history is, however, the topic for another book.

There are dangers with using the term 'gossip' to refer to serious ethical deliberation, for we often use the term in a derogatory way, one that demeans the conversations in which it flourishes. (Indeed, all the synonyms the thesaurus provides are negative.) I am well aware of these dangers but hope that by now the reader is sufficiently convinced of my belief in the positive power of the arts that I need not worry that he or she will think I intend to demean narrative as mere negative gossip. Some studies of gossip explicitly point to the fact that "positive gossip" or "praise gossip" exists.[51] ("Did you hear that Christine got her promotion?" "As usual, he acted like a gentleman.") Others point to the helpful informative content that such talk often contains.[52] ("Did you hear that the co-op has gotten in some great sweet corn?") Sticking with the term 'gossip' is useful, I think, because it emphasizes the connections between the lives of real people and the arts. Often, the stories provided by the arts, particularly literature, of course, parallel and intertwine with the storytelling—that is, the gossip—we engage in as we attempt to understand the human situation. But a more felicitous term has been suggested by Jorg R. Bergmann, who, in his study of gossip, refers to it as a communicative genre that "reconstructs" the world.[53] (Another reconstructive conversational genre is Monday-morning quarterbacking.) I prefer the phrase "*constructive* communicative genre," for imagination as well as memory, and prediction as well as reporting, are so important. Though not aimed at decision making or evaluations per se, this kind of ethical deliberation contributes to the social construction of cultural mores. Discussing the behavior of others, and knowing that others will undoubtedly discuss our own behavior, is one way in which many communities and cultures prescribe and proscribe individual and group actions. (This is a primary function of gossip per se, according to most theorists of gossip.) While art is only one resource for such deliberation, it is a particularly good resource, largely because aesthetic properties combine with the ethical to produce a more vivid, engaged, intimate experience.

Human relationships and circumstances, like artworks, call for interpretations that depend on skills of imagination as well as a repertoire of one's own experiences to call on. The skills we use in working to unravel puzzles about other people are applied to artworks, and, vice versa, the skills we develop in learning to interpret artworks are applied to life. This is another instance of the "back and forth" attention between art and life that I have referred to earlier. Gregory Currie writes, "The imagination that helps us to see through a moral issue or to make a moral choice is the same mental mechanism deployed when we read or—if we have the right talents and inclinations—create fictional works. There are not two things, a moral and a creative imagination, but rather one thing put to different purposes. Indeed the purposes themselves are inextricably intermixed"[54]. One purpose, as Noel Carroll correctly asserts, is clarification, but explanation and revision and honing of imaginative skills are also goals. To use a metaphor from an earlier chapter, in this sort of deliberation, DAE, aesthetic attentiveness "nurtures" ethical sensitivity and vice versa.

Works of narrative art, I suggest, can be thought of as well-constructed gossip or, more precisely, as a case of the communicative constructive genre that exhibits MAE—merit aesthetic and ethical. They present us with scenarios that, when successful, evoke an interest in the characters not unlike that we have in some of the people we encounter in the real world, particularly friends and family. My mother, brother, and I used to announce with glee that we had a "starkness" to share with one another. A starkness was a particularly good piece of gossip, usually one that was sufficiently shocking to be "really stark." We had a high standard of what counted as a genuine starkness as opposed to a run-of-the-mill bit of gossip. Some works of narrative art certainly qualify as starknesses. They engage us not just by providing a possibility to entertain and intimating a story that might be believed, but by enthralling us, by inviting—indeed, demanding—that we use our imaginations and the other "four wits" to fill in details and provide our own possible interpretations. Narrative artworks are like extended pieces of gossip that sustain attention when they are good. As Anthony Powell wrote in *At Lady Molly's*, constructing narrative design out of human behavior affords us "an obscure satisfaction . . . making the more apparent inconsistencies of life easier to bear."[55] When they are really good, our interest does not disappear when the story is over or when we turn away from the picture. We continue to think about the characters, speculate about what might have happened to them later, and compare and contrast them to people we encounter in the real world. What was it like to live with Mr. Rochester as his wife? Did the peasant never see Icharus? How is Isabel Archer like my friend Annie?

Unlike everyday gossip, narrative artworks have, of course, a much tighter structure. As Currie says, this makes "it easier for us to weave together a complex pattern of complex imaginings by laying out a narrative; they give us, through the talents of their makers, access to imaginings more complex, inventive and colourful than we could often hope to construct for ourselves. Sometimes, by artfully withholding crucial bits of narrative information, they can, like inspiring sports coaches, bring us to the point where we can make imaginative leaps for ourselves."[56] Good readers are often good gossipers, successful at DAE, precisely because they learn to become inventive and colorful in conversation. Ethical deliberation of this sort, then, not only takes on the artistic qualities of patterned construction but also is marked by vivid images, a build up of suspense, amusing depictions, and the like; that is, it is marked by aesthetic properties—intrinsic properties considered worthy of attention in a community. Thus, we may well call this deliberation aesthetic and ethical.

One of my continuing worries has been whether there is such a thing as an aesthetic obligation, and I believe that my reflections on this important kind of deliberation have allowed me to uncover one. I shall end this chapter, then, with a discussion of a brilliant piece of fiction that demonstrates, I believe, that there sometimes exist moral obligations to construct narratives about our own and others' lives. If I am correct, this is an example of an OAE, an obligation aesthetic and ethical: there is a requirement to construct a well-formed, enthralling story that provides a possible and reasonable and charitable interpretation of a human situation.

The novel is William Maxwell's *So Long, See You Tomorrow.*[57] Like all great artworks, this one is difficult to summarize. One of the engaging features of the book is that the narrative is not a straightforward "first this happened, second this, third that, . . . with this outcome." Instead, the events are organized in a back-and-forth pattern. Thus, the plot does not lend itself to a few simple sentences. I quote from the back jacket cover.

> On a winter morning in the 1920's, a shot rings out on a farm in rural Illinois. A man named Lloyd Wilson has been killed. And the tenuous friendship between two lonely teenagers—one privileged yet neglected, the other a troubled farm boy—has been shattered. Fifty years later, one of those boys . . . tries to reconstruct the events that led up to the murder. In doing so, he is inevitably drawn back to his lost friend Cletus, who had the misfortune of being the son of Wilson's killer and who in the months before witnessed things that Maxwell's narrator can only guess at.

Cletus's father has been the lover of Wilson's wife; town gossip about the affair thus provides a ready explanation for the motive for the murder. But details are missing and can never be recovered. Cletus and the narrator have not been close friends in the sense of sharing their troubles with one another. They meet and play together for a short time at the site of a house that is being built for the narrator's family. They do not go to each other's homes; they do not socialize at school. They simply spend time together climbing on the structure, balancing on beams, exploring newly created spaces, "risking our necks and breathing in the rancid odor of sawdust and shavings and fresh-cut lumber." "Boys don't need much of an excuse to get on well together, if they get on at all. I was glad for his company, and pleased when he turned up the next day."[58] They quietly value companionship, saying little. "When the look of the sky informed us that it was getting along toward suppertime, we climbed down and said "So long" and "See you tomorrow," and went our separate ways in the dusk. And one evening this casual parting turned out to be for the last time. We were separated by that pistol shot."[59] After Cletus's father becomes a murderer, the companionship disappears, along with the companion. News of the killing, of course, provides a "starkness" for discussion in the small town. But although the protagonist misses Cletus's company, his own troubles keep him from thinking very much about him. "I knew it was a most terrible thing that had happened to Cletus and that he would forever be singled out by it, but I didn't try to put myself in his place or even think that maybe I ought to find out where he lived and get on my bicycle and go see him. It was as if his father had shot and killed him too."[60] And this imaginative failure leads to a moral failure that troubles the narrator and eventually leads him to attempt to fulfill an OAE.

As the narrator grows older, for a variety of reasons he becomes a bit less withdrawn, a bit less self-protective. He learns (and the reader learns or relearns or has emphasized) an important moral lesson about possibilities in human relationships. His family moves to Chicago, where his uncles help him to adjust. They un-expectedly give him some pocket money and surprise him by taking him in a cab to his new home so that he can see the sights more easily than he would have from the elevated railway. "As I looked out of the window at Sheridan Road they looked at me, and were so full of delight in the pleasure they were giving me that some fi-nal thread of resistance gave way and I understood not only how entirely generous they were but also that generosity might be the greatest pleasure there is."[61] But he still has a great deal to learn. Some days later he begins the year at a new school and, to his great surprise, sees Cletus in the hallway.

> He didn't speak. I didn't speak. We just kept on walking until we had passed each other. And after that, there was no way that I could not have done it.
>
> Why didn't I speak to him? I guess because I was so surprised. And because I didn't know what to say. I didn't know what was polite in the circumstances. I couldn't say *I'm sorry about the murder and all that,* could I? In Greek tragedies, the Chorus never attempts to console the innocent bystander but instead, sticking to broad generali-ties, grieves over the fate of mankind, whose mistake was to have been born in the first place.
>
> If I had been the elderly man I am now I might have simply said his name. Or shaken my head sadly and said, "I know, I know. . . ." But would that have been any better? . . .
>
> I think now—I think if I had turned and walked along beside him and not said anything, it might have been the right thing to do. But that's what I think *now*. It has taken me all these years even to imagine doing that, and I had a math class on the sec-ond floor, clear at the end of the building, and there was just barely time to get there before the bell rang.[62]

But he does learn to imagine, and he feels compelled to right the wrong he feels, as an older man, that he must right. He does it through reconstructing what might have been Cletus's story—knowing full well that it is only one possible construal of the events.

> If I knew where Cletus Smith is right this minute, I would go and explain. Or try to. It is not only possible but more than likely that I would also have to explain who I am. And that he would have no recollection of the moment that has troubled me all these years. He lived through things that were a good deal worse. It might turn out that I had made the effort for my sake not his.
>
> . . . Except through the intervention of chance, the one possibility of my making some connection with him seems to lie not in the present but in the past—in my try-ing to reconstruct the testimony that he was never called upon to give.[63]

So the protagonist calls upon himself to give the testimony, to speak for Cletus, to tell what might be Cletus's story. In so doing, he helps to heal himself, but he also fulfills what he feels is a keen obligation to Cletus. He comes to recognize that "there is a limit, surely, to what one can demand of one's adolescent self,"[64] especially from a wounded adolescent. But part of the impact of the story comes from affecting readers, who, though to some degree wounded themselves, realize that they could have done better. To rid himself and Cletus of guilt becomes somewhat possible through the construction of a narrative, though limits are placed on how much healing can be accomplished in a world in which one will inevitably feel some guilt, even about those things over which one has little or no control. The protagonist seeks to reach a point where "instead of being stuck there he could go on and by the grace of God lead his own life, undestroyed by what was not his doing."[65] But reaching it demands at least an attempt to atone by telling another's story as well as one's own, and to show that and how our stories are common and connected.

In recent years, moral philosophers have increasingly discussed the role of ethics in improving and maintaining human relationships. One of the ways in which we seem to do this is by telling stories that explain ourselves to each other and thus make it possible to do exactly that. Respecting the personhood of others is a necessary condition for healthy communities. The narratives that we construct for ourselves and for others contribute to the sense of identity that this entails. Thus, there is a very real sense in which this constitutes an obligation. And, of course, the obligation is not simply to tell any old story—one must tell a good story. One must be faithful to facts as one perceives them; one must achieve an authenticity that demands due attention to the intrinsic properties of the telling. Doing this successfully means that the aesthetic "nurtures" the ethical. One must integrate the moral and the aesthetic to fulfill the ethical-aesthetic obligation of telling the interesting and illuminating stories about others that, as Richard Eldridge puts it, allows us to "go on." One is obligated to engage in "gossip" of a certain kind—the kind that makes deliberation genuinely deliberation aesthetic and ethical.

PART IV

Consequences

Formalist theories have exerted tremendous influence well beyond art theory and criticism. Belief in the separation of aesthetic and moral value permeates other academic disciplines but also public policy making. The theory that I have presented in the earlier chapters belies this separation. If correct, it has important implications for practical matters. As I have considered the connections between aesthetic and ethical values over the past several years, I have engaged in the kind of "back-and-forth" reflection on art and life that I have insisted here characterizes most people's experience of both. In considering practical issues such as environmental aesthetics, public policy, and education, especially arts education, I have become increasingly convinced that art, when forced to stand alone, is often sterile.

In this part, I propose the consequences that an integrated theory of value has for several "big" questions: how do we produce and maintain sustainable environments and communities, and what role does education have to play in these efforts?

I start at the "macro" level—with Nature—and move through communities to the "micro," how education that emphasizes merit aesthetic and ethical can affect the lives of individuals. Environmental aesthetics demonstrates clearly how essential a contextual view and attitude is: there is no way to create, maintain, and regenerate sustainable environments without due attention to science, ethics, politics, economics, religion, aesthetics—indeed, to all human areas of human endeavor. Merit aesthetic and ethical is at the heart of those beauties we treasure in a nature increasingly affected by culture.

Art advocacy often takes the form of insisting on ways in which good art makes for better citizens. I have shown in earlier chapters why I think such assertions are misleading and often just plain false. However, a more modest claim is true: some art, some artforms, and some aesthetic activity can contribute to sustaining communities. But they can do so only when they are contextualized, that is, when art is seen as crucially integrated with a wide range of human pursuits.

Advocates of arts education also sometimes overstate their case—claim that art classes produce better scores on math or science tests, or serve to prevent students from dropping out of school. Evidence for this is thin. Nonetheless, when one understands what I have called merit aesthetic and ethical, important consequences follow for what arts education should entail and how and why it should be at the core of each person's course of study.

TWELVE

Aesthetics and Ethics
in the Environment

Aesthetic experiences of nature, and the role they play in making lives worth living, are at least as important and central as those experiences that have as their focus works of art.[1] Kenneth Clark has gone so far as to say that the key term 'beauty' may for many people have its foremost application in nature. "Almost every Englishman, if asked what he means by 'beauty' would begin to describe a landscape—perhaps a wood with bluebells, and silver birches, perhaps a little harbour with red sails and whitewashed cottages; but at all events a landscape."[2] In the last chapter, I suggested that there may be something morally suspect about individuals who do not take an adequate interest in the lives of others. Many people also intuitively sense that something is morally lacking in people who do not cherish aesthetic experiences of nature. Immanuel Kant insisted that we "require" others to take an interest in nature, indeed, that "we regard as coarse and ignoble the habits of thought of those who have no feeling for beautiful nature."[3]

In this chapter, I present an argument that I developed as I worked with an interdisciplinary team of scholars, artists, and practitioners who met for two years to discuss cultural ecology—the study of the interaction between scientific and human phenomena in the environment. One of the remarkable things about these discussions was that from the outset there was no question on the part of scientists, social scientists, policy makers, and designers that ethical questions underlie everything we do. What *should* be done shared the spotlight with what *can* be done. It was also acknowledged that human aesthetic values have played a major role in landscape management—and thus are open to the same ethical scrutiny that agricultural or forestry practices must undergo. Only an aesthetician who believed that aesthetic experiences are not and cannot be separated from other human experiences could have contributed, I think, to our ongoing workshops. A formalist who insisted that the aesthetic is solely concerned with apprehension of formal properties would not have lasted. In what follows, the deep connections between ethics and aesthetics will sometimes be made explicit but will always be implicit.

Almost every country has some legislation that has established national preservation zones, regulates waste, punishes littering, and so on. These laws often refer to what the U.S. Environmental Policy Act of 1969 refers to as "aesthetic amenities." In increasing numbers, individuals spend weekends and vacations in places that they consider naturally beautiful. Residents of our ugliest cities treasure the presence of trees, squirrels, and birds in their everyday experiences.[4] Ecologists often report that what first led them to their specialty was an aesthetic experience of nature. From being intrigued by beautiful butterfly designs to delighting in the smell of a forest interior, what drives people who study the environment is a profound concern for what Aldo Leopold calls the "integrity, stability, and beauty of the biotic community."[5]

It is sometimes claimed that evaluating nature is inappropriate—that all biosystems are valuable intrinsically and that ranking one above another aesthetically is misguided, for there is nothing ugly in nature.[6] But such a view makes rational decision making with regard to managing and preserving natural environments impossible. At most, it could apply only to "pristine" environments, and the number of these decreases daily. It also flies in the face of the fact that people do rank natural sites and that these preferences seriously affect ecological processes.

As a philosophical aesthetician concerned to show connections between aesthetics and ethics, landscapes and environmental values provide a sterling example of the intersection. The continuum from individual experiences to public policy making through ecological sciences provides a wealth of examples of the impossibility of separating kinds of judgments and values when one attempts to understand experiences of nature. Aesthetic experience, I have argued, is marked by perception of and reflection upon intrinsic properties of objects and events that a community considers worthy of attention. I have also insisted that anything that draws attention to these properties is aesthetically relevant. Furthermore, communities, not individuals responding in isolation, determine what is worthy of attention and how aesthetic attention becomes directed to aesthetic properties. And when one comes to ask the central question that shapes ecology and environmental policy—how we can create and maintain biosystems that are sustainable—it becomes quickly apparent that ethical values (and political, scientific, religious, economic values) are essentially integrated with a community's aesthetic values. We also begin to uncover another "aesthetic ought:" Creating sustainable environments necessitates asking not just what people do find beautiful but what they should find beautiful. This is a major consequence and a happy one, I think, of a theory like mine that allows for and insists on a connection between ethics and aesthetics.

Allen Carlson has suggested a model of nature appreciation that is, in my opinion, the most promising so far articulated if one's goal is to produce, protect, or preserve environments that are both beautiful and healthy. In a seminal essay in 1979, "Appreciation and the Natural Environment," he asserted that we know fairly well how to go about appreciating paintings or piano performances—that is, we know what we should attend to and what we can disregard. (The "we" here is, of course, culturally bound.) In large part, he thinks, this is because these objects and events are human creations whose production we understand. But, he asks, what of those "unproduced" natural objects and events that we admire?[7]

Carlson identifies two models for nature appreciation that he thinks have figured both in theory and in practice in central ways: the nature-as-object model and the nature-as-scenery model. In the first, people interpret and evaluate parts of nature as if they were artworks. But, he says, this approach treats natural objects as if they were self-contained entities and not as what they really are: parts of a larger organic whole. When we look at a rock as if it were a piece of sculpture, we see interesting shapes or pleasing light-reflecting planes, but we may miss seeing how these properties are related to the forces in the natural environment that shaped them. If aesthetic appreciation is of *nature*, the viewer must be aware of *natural* connections, and treating natural objects solely as artworks is inadequate to this task, Carlson argues. Many theorists share his view; some actually see dangers in looking at natural objects as if they were works of art. The landscape architect John Tillman Lyle complains that, for most people, "shelter [is] separated from its environs and, in large terms, from the processes of global ecosystems and its heat balance. In the twentieth-century city, people . . . think of landscape as the frame around a picture . . . rather than as the source of life."[8] The result is that we become oblivious to nature and thus a threat to it.

Similarly, the scenery model, according to Carlson, distorts or leaves out what is special in nature. By emphasizing qualities that are related to prospect, such as coloration and overall design, nature is viewed as if it were a static unity. I shall say more later about the ways in which this bias has worked against the production of sustainable landscapes.

What Carlson believes is necessary is a model of appreciation that emphasizes both nature and environment and allows for an involvement of all the senses and of cognition as well, in particular, scientific understanding of ecological forces and processes. In Carlson's view, instead of a creative act guiding attention (as it does in our experience of a painting or a piano performance), it is knowledge of nature that should guide an aesthetic experience of nature. "If to aesthetically appreciate art we have to have knowledge of artistic traditions and style within those traditions," he writes, "to aesthetically appreciate nature we must have knowledge of the different environments of nature and of the systems and elements within those environments."[9] Appreciation based on knowledge is the only way to avoid aesthetic omissions and deceptions, he thinks.

Like Leopold, Carlson also insists that sound aesthetic views will shape ethical views about how to manage environments.

> We do not aesthetically appreciate simply with our five senses, but rather with an important part of our whole emotional and psychological selves. Consequently, what and how we aesthetically appreciate cannot but play a role in the shaping of our emotional and psychological being. This in turn helps to determine what we think and do, and think is correct for ourselves and others to think and do. In short, our aesthetic appreciation is a significant factor in shaping and forming out ethical views.[10]

Carlson's outlook is precisely the sort needed not only for understanding at least many occasions of the appreciation of nature but also for establishing and maintaining sustainable landscapes. It thus lends itself to exhibiting how ethical and aesthetic values converge.

What counts as *sustainable* has, of course, been variously interpreted by ecologists and public policy makers. A United Nations panel defined it as follows: "A sustainable condition for this planet is one in which there is stability for both social and physical systems, achieved through meeting the needs of the present without compromising the ability of future generations to meet their own needs."[11] Although sustainability became an increasing problem for the globe in the twentieth century and promises to be a crisis in the twenty-first, ours is not the first degenerative civilization. In the sixteenth century, Easter Island underwent a devastating deforestation when its inhabitants cut down trees in order to move huge stones from the interior to the coast to create the awesome statues still standing there. A thriving civilization was reduced to subsistence level.[12] The fact that at least some of its members must have realized to some extent what was happening without desisting in the practices bringing it about strikes one with an eerie sense of familiarity.

I have asserted that aesthetic value is a matter of that which sustains attention. Great works of art and beautiful landscapes repay prolonged and repeated perception and reflection. Kenneth Clark puts it this way: "I fancy that one cannot enjoy a pure aesthetic sensation . . . for longer than one can enjoy the smell of an orange, which in my case is less than two minutes; but one must look attentively at a great work of art for longer than that, and the value of historical criticism is that it keeps the attention fixed on the work while the senses have time to get a second wind."[13] Aesthetically relevant information (which we saw in chapter 2 is anything that draws attention to intrinsic properties considered worthy of that attention) helps to sustain perception and reflection; indeed, it not only sustains it but also "regenerates" it. When one learns something that directs perception to or stimulates reflection on an aesthetic property of an object or an event, the rich experience that results may well lead someone to seek more information about it. New knowledge redirects attention, which motivates a desire for more knowledge, which redirects attention, and so on and so on and so on. Thus is attention *sustained*. We protect artworks to which we want to give repeated attention—put them in museums, record and write scores for them, print or memorize them, for example. Through art education and criticism, we provide the background necessary for delighting in the intrinsic properties our community deems valuable. Aesthetic sustainability exists when cultures provide for repetition of aesthetic experiences over the long haul, as it were. Artworks engage a sustained aesthetic when they repeatedly support and invite aesthetic experiences.

This is true for landscapes as well as for artworks. Building on the UN's definition of 'sustainability', in aesthetics we require landscapes that repeatedly support and invite aesthetic experiences. Obviously environments, like artworks, must exist to be experienced at all; thus, they must be *physically* sustained. But aesthetic sustainability goes beyond this. Institutions and practices must be in place that invite attention to intrinsic properties that yield aesthetic satisfaction once the culture has identified them as worthy of attention. Just as critics and educators help to sustain and regenerate attention to artworks by discussing them in a variety of ways that may direct attention to aesthetic properties, so ecologists provide information about ecosystems that may direct attention to aesthetic properties of the landscapes—or to intrinsic properties that may become valued within a community and thus become aesthetic properties. This is why Carlson's cognitive aesthetic model of nature appreciation is so powerful. Not only does it provide an explanation of why knowledge plays a key role in the enjoyment of nature but also it suggests why his model *should* be the one that guides aesthetic education.

First, knowledge sharpens aesthetic experience, both of art and of nature. Understanding a system enables one to perceive elements of the system and their relationships. Mushy, desultory responses become more vivid and focused. As Ronald Hepburn has pointed out, perceptions can be attentive or inattentive, discriminating or undiscriminating, lively or lazy—just as thought can be.[14] Since thought and perception are components of aesthetic experience, sharper thought and perception make for sharper aesthetic experience.

Second, knowledge contributes to sustainability, for it not only sustains attention in the presentbut also makes one more aware of what may or must be the case if attention is to be possible at all in the future. Even a modicum of ecological knowledge—enough to see that a city park in an arid climate can be maintained only with enormous amounts of scarce water—will force one to admit that such a park is unlikely to exist in the future. What is ecologically bad begins to be seen as aesthetically bad.

Carlson's knowledge-based theory of nature appreciation is not without problems, however. Many theorists agree with the formalists whom we have encountered earlier and insist that all aesthetic experiences, including those of nature, are subjective responses disconnected and separate from intellectual or ethical concerns. When applied to nature, this view yields the argument that when one is enthralled with a landscape, one cares little about its biology or geology; indeed, if one takes a strong Kantian view, one does not even care whether it is real.

Even nonformalists sometimes object that Carlson's view undervalues the role of imaginative engagement with nature. Emily Brady thinks that Carlson's view precludes the flights of imagination that mark the delight many people take in nature. She agrees with Immanuel Kant's position that central to human aesthetic pleasure is what he called the "free play of imagination." As we saw in earlier chapters, aesthetic experiences are marked, he argued, by disinterestedness. We put aside ordinary scientific, ethical, or personal interests and respond to objects as we please. We allow our imaginations full rein and range. We are free to think of a tree as a person or an animal or a tower or a mountain or whatever. And this freedom gives us, according to Kant, tremendous pleasure. Brady agrees.

Like Carlson, Brady believes that basic distinctions between objects of art and objects of nature generate important distinctions between artistic and natural appreciation. "Various natural objects . . . lack a human maker, an artist, and also an artistic context in respect of the type of artwork."[15] In artworks, intentional acts of an artist give us clues that direct our attention and thus our imaginations. These clues and cues are not present in natural objects. Thus, the response is additionally free—free from any concern about what it is intended to express or how it should function as an object. To put it in my terms, there is nothing to guide attention to specific intrinsic properties. Distinguishing natural from artistic objects as she does, Brady is perhaps correct to point out that human responses to nature do not involve considerations about artistic intentions. But this distinction does not, I think, also entail that information about context is either nonexistent or irrelevant. Indeed, knowledge concerning how nature functions within a particular context is exactly the sort of thing that Carlson and I insist plays a major role in appreciation of nature. It is precisely a failure to understand the proper function of certain kinds of trees or forest soils, for instance, within their specific biosystems—that is, within their context—that has led to mismanagement of forests, for instance, even when providing aesthetic value has been one goal. (I shall discuss more such mistakes later.)

Brady is primarily interested in the special ways in which immersion stimulates imagination, for imagination, she thinks, "intensifies" experience. It plays exploratory, projective, amplifying, and revelatory roles, she says. Surely she is right about this. There are, admittedly, many positive roles that imagination can play in aesthetic appreciation of nature. I remember very well what was, when I was a child, a very small thicket (in memory, it is still very big, of course) that served as a jungle where we Midwestern Americans fought off a variety of animals and foreign enemies. What harm could there have been in thinking that dread poisonous tropical snakes lurked under the blackberry bushes? Or that not only an enemy soldier but also a tiger might at any moment spring from behind the elm tree? Who really cares that tigers and elm trees do not share the same biotic patches or that there were no tropical snakes for a thousand miles?

Surely rich imagination is just what is needed if we are to develop new metaphors for designing sustainable landscapes. The clichés that we have inherited from romantic and sentimental visions of the picturesque no longer work; indeed, they often work against development of ecologically sound landscape designs. New visions are required, and this does require creative imagination.

Such vision may come from what R. W. Hepburn calls "metaphysical imagination." Sometimes our aesthetic experiences of nature, he insists, involve more than perceptual or expressive pleasures. "We may experience a polar scene of ice and snow as revealing something fundamental (and no doubt grim) about how things really, or ultimately, are: something concealed from us in more familiar, temperate, farmed countryside. Or, in sharpest contrast, we may experience a nature whose poignant beauty on some occasion seems to speak of a transcendent Source for which we lack words and clear concepts."[16] Landscapes can be occasions of revelations of truth that go beyond rock structures or whether we need at least forty inches of rain annually to maintain a particular plant in the garden.

So what do I have against imagination or fiction in the appreciation of nature? Let me begin by quoting a couple of Brady's examples of her own imaginative flights.

> In contemplating the bark of a locust tree, visually I see the deep clefts between the thick ridges of the bark. Images of mountains and valleys come to mind, and I think of the age of the tree given the thickness of the ridges and how they are spaced apart. I walk around the tree, feeling the wide circumference of the bark. The image of a seasoned old man comes to mind, with deep wrinkles from age. These imaginings lead to an aesthetic judgment of the tree as stalwart, and I respect it as I might a wise old

sage. My interpretation of the locust tree is tied to its nonaesthetic qualities, such as the texture of the bark, as well as the associations spawned by perceptual qualities.[17]

And a second example: "A quick glance at a lamb reveals little except an acknowledgment of its sweetness. But the fuller participating of perception and imagination can lead to a truth about innocence. Contemplating the fresh whiteness of a lamb and its small, fragile stature evokes images of purity and naivete. It is through dwelling aesthetically and imaginatively on such natural things that we achieve new insights."[18]

Brady, we see, believes that aesthetic experience, interpreted in terms of imagination, provides us, as she puts it, with "insight" into the tree and the lamb. The cognitive model of aesthetic appreciation of nature in its restrictiveness precludes access to the richness of imaginative insight, she fears. These insights amount to what she refers to as "aesthetic truths," but she fails to adequately explain these. Furthermore, if there are aesthetic truths, there should also be aesthetic falsities. Brady does not give examples of these. She does, however, maintain that some imaginative responses are "appropriate," so perhaps aesthetic falsity is related to responses that are inappropriate. As an example of an inappropriate response, she points to actions that are "self-indulgent."[19] Appropriate responses involve what she calls "imagining well." Imagining well in turn "involves spotting aesthetic potential, having a sense of what to look for, and knowing when to clip the wings of imagination. This last skill involves preventing the irrelevance of shallow, naïve, and sentimental imaginative responses which might impoverish rather than enrich appreciation."[20]

The very notion of sentimentality, I argued in chapter 9, is at once ethical and aesthetic. Brady, of course, emphasizes the aesthetic, speaking only of the impoverishment of one's own appreciation. But there are moral consequences of sentimental responses to nature—ones that impoverish nature itself, not simply one's own experiences of it. Let us go back to Brady's own examples. Is responding to a little lamb with reflections on innocence or to a tree as a stalwart man or haggard witch appropriate? Are these responses such that they indicate a sense of what to look for? Do they avoid being shallow or naïve? When do we know that we have gone too far and need to clip imagination's wings? I see no way of answering these questions without relying on the kind of cognitive model that Carlson demands. Knowledge does not simply deepen the experiences that imagination provides. As with artworks, knowledge directs perceptions and actions—or should direct them if we hope to preserve and design sustainable landscapes. Concepts such as *imagining well* make no sense unless one knows what the object is that one is talking about. Something—in fact, as much as possible—must be known about the object and its context before one can distinguish healthy from unhealthy imaginings.

On the face of it, of course, it seems quite harmless, even charming, to think about trees in terms of human faces or lambs in terms of purity. But, in fact, imaginative flights—often directed by works of art (some of them very sentimental)—can and do lead to harmful actions. Fiction, for example, has played an important role in shaping the attitudes, images, and metaphors with which we approach na-

ture. Perhaps the most striking example of art's power to inform responses to nature is *Bambi*—a book written in 1923 by the Austrian writer Felix Salten. The Walt
Disney film version is a classic. Both the book and the movie contain much that is
beautiful and in other ways valuable. Many passages and images make it easy to understand why the literary classic has achieved such worldwide popularity that it is
hard for anyone to look at a deer and not see a Bambi. It has also made it incredibly difficult to look at a deer in terms that are true to it as an object on its own and
even more difficult to respond to it in terms appropriate to the role that it increasingly plays in the ecological systems it has come to dominate. In the United States,
most states' departments of natural resources have had as a primary goal preserving and providing deer in sufficient numbers to satisfy hunters. (Bambi lovers are
in complete denial about the extent of influence of hunting lobbyists in forest management, of course.) Landscape architects have tended to exacerbate the situation
with their preference for defined edges and have thus contributed to an increase in
forest edge. Such planning has been carried out with disregard for organisms other
than game animals and birds. The result has been an explosion in the deer population and a decrease in the population of several songbirds and tree species. We
are told, in fact, that in some areas deer have become vermin.

But how can one look at a deer or a picture of a deer and not imagine it as the
innocent, noble creature that Salten depicts? We tend to respond as the fictional account directs us to respond. In the book, we are given the following episode, for example. Bambi and his mother see a ferret kill a mouse. Frightened by the violence,
Bambi asks his mother if they will kill a mouse.

> "No," replied his mother,
> "Never?" asked Bambi.
> "Never," came the answer.
> "Why not?" asked Bambi, relieved.
> "Because we never kill anything," said his mother.[21]

This is valuable if one wants to teach children not to be violent, but totally misguided if one wants to teach children about the actual effect of overpopulation of
deer in the forest.

The prose of the story is often beautiful and does, as Brady hopes, heighten some
imaginative insights about the forest. There are beautiful inventories—ones in
which vivid images and metaphors certainly help children learn to observe details
and connect individual species into an organic whole. But Salten contrasts the gentle deer with the vulgar species that fight for food. Deer, we are told, never fight for
food, because there is enough for all. We are seduced into a sentimental image that
is hard to shake. Even in the presence of trees ravaged by deer who in their own way
do, indeed, fight for food, we continue to think of all deer as Bambi, the consequence being that forest managers find it difficult to convince the public that their
numbers should be severely decreased in some areas.[22]

In fiction, there is often a tendency to sentimentalize. There is also a tendency
to demonize. Both result in misconceptions. Just as there are lots of deceptively innocent creatures in the arts, so there are lots of monsters. One reason that it is hard

to get people to appreciate wetlands is that they have so often been conceptualized as "swamps" inhabited by various kinds of slime monsters.[23] Death by drowning in quicksand has been a common fear of children, even those of us who grew up in the heart of the U.S. corn belt. Should lions come to flourish in numbers great enough to threaten the environment, a hard sell will be required for the generation that watches *The Lion King* several times a year. In his book *Land Mosaics*, Richard Forman discusses the importance of protecting "keystone species"—species that play a central role in an ecosystem. One keystone species that he describes is the cassowary bird.

> This territorial bird, as tall as and able to rip the guts out of a man, is believed to be the only seed disperser for more than one hundred species of woody tropical rain-forest plants in Queensland, Australia. The bird normally inhabits large forests. Logging and fragmentation have eliminated the bird from several areas where only small remnants remain. Consequently, a progressive and massive loss of trees and other woody species can now be expected, unless the big bird can adapt or adjust its behavior.[24]

I would guess that if regional fiction describes the cassowary bird as a terrible monster, it will be harder to save this bird.

As I have already said, I do not want to claim that there is no positive role for fiction or for the imagination in general in developing a sound nature aesthetic. I do insist that it must be based on, tempered by, directed, and enriched by solid ecological knowledge that leads to ethical practices.

Noel Carroll worries that Carlson may have overintellectualized the human experience of nature at the expense of the importance of emotional engagement. Driving through the countryside would truly involve appreciation of nature only if one understood large-scale agricultural practices; responding positively, or at least profoundly, to a wildflower would necessitate knowing not only its name but also its evolutionary history. Carroll thinks that this leaves out one important kind of appreciation—the ordinary experiences we all have had standing near a raging waterfall or watching a bird in flight. It would seem that all we really need to realize is that the water is cascading or that some sort of bird is going somewhere. Carroll does not deny that there is always a cognitive element in emotional response. But, "it is far from clear that all the emotions appropriately aroused in us by nature are rooted in cognition of the sort derived from natural history."[25] He does not think Carlson's arguments need to be completely abandoned, but he does think that we must also accept nonscientific arousal in nature as genuinely aesthetic experience of it. Stan Godlovitch further worries that Carlson does not leave room for the "mystery" that he believes characterizes many of our experiences of nature.[26]

I certainly want to make room for the role of pleasure, imagination, emotion, metaphysical revelation, and even mysteriousness in the experience of nature; as I said earlier, this sort of awe often accounts for individuals' becoming interested in learning more about nature in the first place. Certainly, we all have had "wow" experiences in the absences of any, or much, information about what we see or hear or smell or feel; these are often the most memorable experiences we have and contribute significantly to the meaning of life. Are experts' experiences better than these?

I am reluctant to "rank" various ways of responding to nature. But even if it were possible to rank them, I see no point in, or necessity for, doing it in general. However, if we want to develop a basis for rational evaluation of a landscape's ecological sustainability, I am convinced that we must stress the cognitive. A patch of purple loosestrife, with its brilliant color, may cause a lot of pleasure. A fawn at a forest's edge may stimulate tender emotions, particularly for those of us who suffer from the Bambi syndrome—a tendency to sentimentalize this animal. A large expanse of closely clipped, deep green grass may cause soothing flights of imagination. But all of these objects threaten certain biosystems, and only someone whose aesthetic response is based on knowledge will act in ways that are sustainable ecologically and, ultimately, aesthetically. Even a theorist such as Emily Brady, who favors an imaginative model of nature appreciation, finally agrees that one's imaginings must take account of the integrity of the object. Hepburn also insists that imaginative metaphysical visions of natures be coherent and sustainable. I do not see how the concepts of integrity or coherence or sustainability can be explained or applied without relying on knowledge of the object and its relationship to other biota. This is what Carlson shows us.

My own view of aesthetic appreciation of nature, influenced as it has been by Carlson, relies, of course, on my own characterizations of the aesthetic and of aesthetic relevance. To repeat,

> A is an aesthetic property of O if and only if A is an intrinsic property of O and A is culturally identified as a property worthy of attention, i.e., of perception and reflection.

> F is an intrinsic property of O if and only if direct inspection of O is a necessary condition for verifying the claim that O is F.

But how can these definitions be brought into line with a cognitive theory such as Carlson's? Ecologists, as they come to understand the environment better, point to the kinds of information that one must have to understand how certain ecosystems work—to inconspicuous plants, to soil types, to underground drainage systems, to histories of fires and storms and other "nonperceivables." A couple of specific examples will help to indicate why this might apparently create a problem for me.

Increasingly, ecologists have become aware of what they call "edge effects." Landscapes consist of patches, each with its own biota, that interact with one another, particularly at the boundaries. Certain interior species flourish only when an appropriate distance from the edge is maintained. Harvesting trees via clear-cutting of patches has a disproportionate effect on these interior-loving organisms. If edges become overabundant, habitat for rare interior populations may lose out to species that are not threatened.[27] When departments of natural resources have as their primary goal maintaining large populations of game animals and birds that, as a matter of contingent fact, frequent forest edges, one effect has been a decrease in the number of interior songbirds. Knowing this, if you see a deer or grouse at a forest's edge, should you have a negative aesthetic experience—or at least try to restrain yourself until you know the status of the interior species? It seems that one cannot rely simply on direct inspection.

Ecosystem managers typically rally for native species, knowing as they do that importing exotic species to an area can often have devastating intrusive effects. Does this mean that one should feel aesthetic repulsion at the sight of a nonnative tree or bird? What about nonnative species that seem to fit right in, the way China pheasants have in the Midwestern United States? Must I feel guilt when I respond positively to seeing one of them along a Minnesota highway?

These examples involve properties that cannot be immediately seen or heard or otherwise perceived directly. In general, it is very difficult to say what ecological health looks like.[28] Many biosystems and landscape projects involve planning or thinking in terms of scales (both spatial and temporal) that go far beyond human experience, even as imagined. Aesthetic experience as I have characterized it, on the other hand, is immediate—focused on what is present in the moment. So how can one explain how knowledge concerning the nonperceivables that often determine ecological health is important, perhaps even necessary, for aesthetic appreciation of nature? The explanation is twofold, with the second being a special case of the first.

First, knowledge of certain nonperceivables is generally relevant, too, and hence a part of aesthetic experience, just as certain extrinsic features of objects and events can be relevant to experiences of intrinsic features of those objects and events. In chapter 2, I defined aesthetic relevance as follows.

> A statement (or gesture) is aesthetically relevant if and only if it draws attention (perception, reflection) to an aesthetic property.

Strictly speaking, an aesthetic property is intrinsic; roughly speaking, by reference to what draws attention to a valued intrinsic property, anything aesthetically relevant can be construed as an aesthetic property. Does it matter that a painting is located in a particular museum? Only when we know how knowledge does or does not causally affect one's perception or reflection can this question be answered. An extrinsic fact about a piece of music—being written in 1717, for instance—will be aesthetically relevant just in case knowing this fact causes the listener to attend to an intrinsic property of the music, its particular structure, for example. Knowing that a painting was made in Italy in 1540 will cause someone who is "in the know" to experience in a special way the glow around the head of a man who is attached to two pieces of wood nailed together in a **t** shape. When one has an aesthetic experience, there are always intrinsic properties of the object of the experience that one can claim to be attending to and that one believes are at least a partial cause of one's experience. But both the attention to the intrinsic properties and the directing of attention can themselves be caused by awareness of properties not intrinsic to the object.

Just as works of art must often be "read"—with extrinsic information determining the reading that results—so landscapes will be read in terms of the knowledge one brings to experiences of them. Even intrinsic properties (such as the soil type or presence of polluted groundwater) may not be directly perceivable without action that would seem extraordinary when viewing artworks—digging up the soil or conducting chemical tests. But the knowledge that a microorganism is present, or that drainage has been adversely affected, or that too many deer may result in too few songbirds may very well cause a viewer to perceive genuinely intrinsic properties that would otherwise be overlooked. Just learning the names of wildflowers (surely an extrinsic property) does sometimes make it more likely that one will see the flowers. As one learns more about the invisible things that make particular ecosystems healthy, landscapes begin to look more or less healthy. As aestheticians, I think we should concentrate more effort on determining the extent to which looking healthy and looking good or beautiful are related, and give more attention to specific ways in which knowledge influences particular aesthetic experiences. Thus, I want to suggest a second, more specific way of understanding how ecological knowledge directs attention to aesthetic properties and vice versa. This connection is related to the merit aesthetic and ethical that has been the topic of this book.

In a 1992 essay, "The Appearance of Ecological Systems as a Matter of Policy," Joan Nassauer insists that reliance on what is typically considered the picturesque in landscape design will not protect ecosystems. Designers must use "social signs" to indicate ecological function. "The general principle that we can use to guide design and policy is to label ecological function with socially recognized signs of human intentions for the landscape, setting expected characteristics of landscape beauty and care side by side with characteristics of ecological health."[29] The development of specific principles, I believe, challenges philosophical aestheticians to explain more fully what is involved in aesthetic landscape preferences and how it might relate to ethical ecological management. Thus, what I am exploring in this chapter is an extension and elaboration of Nassauer's general principle, which is related to contemporary cognitive models of nature appreciation of the sort that Carlson proposes.[30]

I referred before to scale as a problem that confronts us as we try to perceive ecosystems. One research team has written, "No issues attract as much attention within conservation biology as those connected with geographic scale and distribution: How large should reserves intended to maintain diversity be? How should they be arranged relative to each other? Should they be connected via corridors? Do species common within old growth require areas of some minimum size?"[31] Due attention to scale can produce the "problem of nonperceivables." When stretches of time and space become too big, human beings can no longer "see" them—and hence it is hard to conceive of how aesthetic experience at such scales is possible. This problem was recognized early by Aristotle, who pointed out that things too big or too small cannot be beautiful because they cannot be held in memory. Therefore, he insisted in *Poetics* that the action of a play must cover just the amount of time that a human being can take in (a day or so, he thought). More recently, John Lyle has acknowledged that the holistic treatment of landscape rarely works because "it is so difficult to see . . . a vast landscape as a whole."[32]

To some extent the problem of nonperceivability at large or small scales is handled by the general method I suggested earlier, whereby extrinsic information directs attention to intrinsic properties. But the scale factor in ecology also has important connections of a different kind to the aesthetic appreciation of nature. Ecologists must pay attention not only to different scales but also to different types or categories of landscapes. Obviously, what is studied in a desert will not be studied in an ocean. And increased awareness and understanding of the primary role of categories of scale and landscape type in ecology has suggested to me that aestheticians should pay closer attention to the role of scale and other landscape categories. This is both an aesthetic and an ethical *should*, or, as I called it in chapter 11, an obligation aesthetic and ethical that results in merit aesthetic and ethical. Formalists, of course, would dismiss any such advocacy. But when the goal is experiencing healthy, sustainable landscapes, category mistakes become aesthetic-ethical mistakes.

In discussions of works of art, we are accustomed to the fact that certain features are category-specific. Properties possessed by a measure of music will not typically be possessed by the work as a whole. What characterizes a line of a poem (having twenty-two syllables, for instance) will not typically characterize a stanza, and vice versa.[33] But observations "upscale" affect observations "downscale." The fact that it is an epic we are reading affects how we read individual lines or verses. We look for plot development in an epic, but not in a sonnet. The fact that something is called a "march" will determine how we emphasize the rhythm of each measure.

Category mistakes have consequences for the experiences of artworks. Someone who mistakes a satire for a serious political essay will miss or misinterpret many important intrinsic properties. Similarly, landscape-aesthetic category mistakes have consequences for the appreciation. Before I describe some specific landscape-aesthetic categories, I want to mention some of the mistakes (many of these have been acknowledged by landscape architects) that my proposal is intended to help avoid.

One of the most serious criticisms that has been leveled against conventional design practices is that designers have too often acted as 'beauticians," that is, as if their task were to "prettify" by covering up, not really altering, underlying flaws. This criticism is not just a recent complaint. At the turn of the twentieth century in the Midwestern United States, such landscape architects as Jens Jensen argued that Beaux Arts formalism or the romantically and sentimentally picturesque standards that had a grip on city planning should give way to more regionally appropriate styles. Thus, the Prairie School called for greater use of indigenous species and materials to express the spirit of the area. But the use of particular design principles may not be a mistake simply because of regional inappropriateness. It may result from what others have described as landscape architects' undue emphasis on "scenery." Clearly agreeing with Carlson, Paul Hellmund writes, "One of the traditional concerns of landscape architects has been preserving or enhancing views. But, narrowly pursuing visual goals by trying to capture or re-create static images can have tremendous costs, both financial . . . and ecological."[34] Hellmund is worried, for example, that trying to offer motorists beautiful vistas may threaten wildlife migration corridors. I would also like to suggest that there may be aesthetic costs when landscape architects treat all landscapes as if they were located within a single landscape-aesthetic category.

Another mistake is a tendency to leave human beings out of "nature." 'Natural' is, I believe, a term whose application changes when there is a shift in aesthetic category. What is natural on a farm will not be natural in a city, and what might be natural on both of these may not be natural in a desert or forest. J. B. Jackson has criticized the ways in which undisturbed, conventionally photogenic landscapes have been taken as the sole standard of ecological and aesthetic integrity.[35] He has also discussed Edgar Anderson's work on the effect of human beings on plants, not all of which has been deleterious. Sunflowers, for instance, which grow only in rather poor soil where grass does not overtake them, thrive in areas where humans have depleted nutrients. This provides an example of "how man has not only destroyed ecosystems but has also devised *new* ones."[36] Jackson's most famous nonconformist defense is of mobile homes—a human artifact that may be as natural in the landscape as the beaver dam, he insists. "Indeed, it almost seems as if those shortcomings which critics never tire of mentioning—the lack of individuality, the functional incompleteness, the dependence on outside services and amenities, and even the lack of such traditional architectural qualities as firmness, commodity, and delight—all are what make the trailer useful and attractive to many of its occupants."[37] But even those who are not generally put off by trailer courts will not relish them in a wilderness. What counts as "natural" depends on the category within which one is operating.

Another category-relative term is 'stewardship'. What counts as care for the land or sound management practice in a forest does not translate directly into care at the urban level. (I will say more about this later.) 'Biodiversity' is another ambiguous term. One often comes across it in the following sort of admonition: "We want to conserve all cultural approaches that are compatible with conserving biodiversity,"[38] and "Areas set aside to fulfill recreational or esthetic objectives do not necessarily meet biodiversity conservation goals."[39] But is the converse true? Too often, the unexamined assumption is that biodiverse environments will automatically meet aesthetic and ethical goals.

What I hope attention to landscape-aesthetic categories can do is to undermine the often too glibly held attitude that we all know and agree about what is good and beautiful in the landscape. Jackson and others have made us wonder about mobile homes and fast-food restaurants and Las Vegas. Leopold urged us to think not about "building roads into lovely country, but of building receptivity into the still unlovely mind."[40] But are all roads into lovely places then ugly? In his report of discussions with David Brower, an early leader of Friends of the Earth, John McPhee describes how Brower's early love of trains affected his aesthetic sensitivities: "A railroad over the Sierra is all right. It was there. An interstate highway is an assault on the terrain."[41] Are they really so different? John Lyle wonders why Dutch windmills are so lovely and power lines are not.[42]

Hepburn has urged, "If we wish to attach very high value to the appreciation of natural beauty, we must be able to show that more is involved in such appreciation than the pleasant, unfocused enjoyment of a picnic place, or a fleeting and distanced impression of countryside through a touring-coach window, or obligatory visits to standard viewpoints."[43] (The connections between ethics and aesthetics reverberate in this remark.) I believe that one component of progress in understanding more about such appreciation and hence of avoiding some of the mistakes described is a greater awareness of environmental aesthetic categories and aesthetic scales, and of the interactions herein of ecology, aesthetics, and ethics.

There are various ways of thinking about scale, of course. To ecologists and geographers, scale is a quantitative concept defined in terms of sheer numbers of organisms or patch acreage or mapping grain. Just as the set of intrinsic properties valued in a sonnet is not identical with the set of intrinsic properties valued in an epic (these artworks have different "scales"), so the set of intrinsic properties valued in a bonsai garden is not identical to the set of intrinsic properties valued in a vista from a mountaintop or airplane. Due attention to a rough continuum ranging from the microscopic to the macroscopic is essential. Awareness that one is judging a small, medium, large, or very large area is required if one is to avoid category mistakes.

Although size is relevant, aesthetic evaluation obviously goes beyond considerations of quantity. Another important, more traditionally entrenched aesthetic category is the perception of the purpose(s) behind the particular manipulation of a medium. (Obviously, there will be connections here to the ways in which artistic intentions point in the direction of the contextual nature of the aesthetic. See chapter 3.) Attention to purpose will be as important in assessing nature cognitively as it is in assessing artworks. Some landscape units are what they are almost completely as a result of an individual's or group's aesthetic intentions; in others, intentional design is a lesser factor in determining their constitutions. At each scale, the intention of the designer affects the aesthetic properties meant to be a focus of attention. Designing sustainable landscapes requires relating the geographer's and ecologist's attention to scale and biota that is so important to their work with the aesthetician's attention to category and manipulation of medium in an attempt to draw attention to intrinsic properties that reward perception and reflection.

Here are examples of categories that differ considerably from one another with respect to the extent to which their intrinsic properties are what they are as a result of the particular purposes of human manipulation and intervention:

1. Landscape art
2. Parks and gardens
3. Managed urban and suburban landscapes
4. Managed rural landscapes (especially farms, but also mines and other "worked" nonurban areas)
5. Relatively pristine managed landscapes
6. Relatively pristine unmanaged landscapes

Specific examples from each category will be discussed shortly. At the first level, we have discrete artifacts (objects and events) that have landscape elements as core components. At the final level, we have landscapes in which human manipulation drops out—though I describe them as only "relatively" pristine because such effects as acid rain and ozone depletion influence even the wildest environments. In between, and even within a particular level, a continuum of intent and possibility for control exists. Individual artists often have a greater control over what they produce and a firmer image of what they want to create than urban designers, farmers, or wilderness managers. But we need to bear in mind that "reading" intentionality into a landscape will be greatly influenced by cultural factors. For example, many people see a garden as more intentionally determined than a farm, though in fact the former may be more a matter of chance.

Each category has its own history—both natural and cultural—and these histories have a tremendous influence on the properties within these elements. Martin Warnke has described the ways in which political values can be read off landscapes.[44] For example, roads converge at castles, churches, and city squares, and the size of fields reflects equal or unequal distribution of wealth. Nonaesthetic values affect one's preferences. Do you see a castle or a church as a positive sign of stability or a negative sign of oppression? Curt Meine describes how the sociopolitical grid permeates the design and perception of many American landscapes.[45] Sociopolitical values affect, and are in turn affected by, aesthetic values.

This interdependence is also true of aesthetic and ecological values—or at least they *should* be, if we are to have sustainable landscapes and hence sustainable landscape aesthetics. For every site or design project, an aesthetic as well as an ecological inventory must be made. Other writers have proposed inventories, of course, but they have often been formulaic; that is, they have assumed that one can simply apply a list of a priori properties like "vividness" or "uniqueness." But categories are culture-bound and culturally constructed, just as aesthetic values are, as I argued in chapter 1. Descriptions of sites will vary to a greater or lesser extent from culture to culture, both temporally and spatially. For example, the presence of red barns in a rural setting is not universally valued. Just as one cannot expect all ecological features to be found at every site (the presence of a particular microorganism, for instance), so aesthetic categories and the properties relevant therein can be determined only after a site has been fully studied. Categories used elsewhere may provide guidelines but should never be simply reapplied without being "translated" for each new project. Even when one is deeply fluent in a culture and tremendously knowledgeable about the ecosystems in which one is working, one must constantly remind oneself that disagreement is possible. Individuals who share a culture often disagree and have themselves inconsistent goals.[46] Scientists also disagree, of course. The best assessments will be those produced through holistic, interdisciplinary work, where values are seen as integrated and inseparable.

Some examples will be useful, perhaps, but these can be regarded only as prototypes, since actual analysis must be site-specific. Even prototypes are local—for what counts generally as beautiful or healthy in one sociogeographical locale may not apply in others. In the upper Midwest of the United States, what people tend to like in medium-sized urban parks is serenity, clean water flowing in fountains, a variety of plants and flowers arranged in neat patterns, careful maintenance, and wildlife that is clean and nonthreatening; and what they tend to dislike is messiness, stagnant or dirty water, and "vermin."[47] I have put 'vermin' in quotation marks, for which animals are classified as such will differ from site to site. Rats, for example, are accepted, even enjoyed, in relatively pristine landscapes. In large, relatively pristine unmanaged landscapes, people want vast outlooks and majestic, sublime scenery and are irritated if there are too many other people around or if trails appear overmaintained. In wilderness areas, they even like what would count as "messy" undergrowth in residential gardens.[48] The presence of a windmill may enhance landscape at one point and diminish it at a different scale or at a different level of manipulation. Adding one will probably not enhance the beauty of a relatively pristine vista or even a postmodern city center. The fact that people treasure human-built structures along the Rhine River but not along the Colorado River is not inconsistent when one realizes that different sites are involved. The Rhine is much more urban than it is pristine. In aesthetics as in ecology, we must first be clear about the locale and the relevant positive and negative features if we are to avoid inappropriate, misguided, or even dangerous assessments and designs.

Previously, I referred to the fact that categories have a history. I want now to provide more detail about some examples to show the importance of reminding oneself continually about the appropriateness of the features one does or should attend to.

As with all art, twentieth-century landscape art changed dramatically from what may still be the vernacular stereotype of landscape art—a nineteenth-century Hudson Valley representation, for instance. Viewers must thus attune themselves to category shifts while remaining conscious of the artistic traditions in which artists work. In Mel Chin's *Spirit*, a barrel (symbol of commerce and/or the effects of alcohol abuse) precariously balances on a rope made of samples of vanishing indigenous prairie grasses. It derives its power not from the viewer's admiration of the picturesque but from the awareness of the forceful way in which Chin has symbolized the impact of European immigrants on the American prairie. Nonetheless, it still depends on the viewer's close attention to many intrinsic properties (shape, proportion, balance) resulting from as meticulous a manipulation of the medium as that found in nineteenth-century landscape paintings.

Other landscape works of Chin seem to me less clearly located in the category of landscape art. In *Revival Fields*, his interest in chemical pollution led to collaboration in 1990 with a soil scientist, Rufus Chaney. Though Chin did use some conventional design principles—circular plantings within a square, for instance—the main goal of this project was experimentation with "hyperaccumulators": plants that absorb large amounts of minerals and metals and thus act as toxic sponges to restore the soil in which they grow.[49] Chin and Chaney's field was not found in a museum but in a landfill. It no longer exists, and even when it did, it was very difficult to get to and to perceive. Enabling attention to intrinsic design properties was simply not the primary intention. It is difficult to do an aesthetic evaluation of such "works" when there is uncertainty about the category into which they fit; the ability to provide aesthetically appropriate descriptions is lacking. In some ways, Chin's work is rural, for the toxic metals absorbed in the plants were meant to be "harvested" or "mined." Perhaps another category needs to be introduced. (This has, after all, often happened in the history of art.) Or one object may need to be evaluated according to several different categories. For example, the environmental artist Lynne Hull's work *Raptor Roost* provides a roost for birds that will not electrocute them, and she does "hydroglyphs"—drawings in desert stones that provide water storage for animals. The shape of the roost or the delicacy of the drawing is aesthetically pleasing in the category of small or medium landscape art; the fact that habitat is sustained and often present will be characteristic of aesthetic pleasure within the category of larger parks or relatively pristine landscapes.[50]

Many works of landscape art move upscale or cross categories into the realm of parks and gardens, and vice versa. Indeed, Mara Miller titles her very interesting book on gardens *The Garden as Art*. She defines a garden as "any purposeful arrangement of natural objects (such as sand, water, plants, rocks, etc.) with exposure to the sky or open air, in which the form is not fully accounted for by purely practical considerations such as convenience."[51] This definition also covers parks. Both are marked by what she calls an "excess of form"—and this is what connects gardens to artworks. Biology and culture, she argues, intersect. Biology is "categorized" via culture.[52] Gardens and parks are often designed with wildlife habitat in mind, but the territory or corridor provided therein differs significantly from that which guides designers at the level, for example, of managed wilderness. (In this sense, National Parks are not "parks" at all, a fact that both aestheticians and ecologists should remember.) Ornamentality, such as that provided by topiary, for instance, is quite valuable in some kinds of city gardens and parks; it can easily become excessive in residential lawns and would be quite jarring in a relatively pristine landscape.

Urban landscapes are, of course, very mixed and perhaps can be fully comprehended only as such. Parks must coexist with landfills. (Indeed, some landfills have becomes parks, even golf courses.) Concrete jungles provide habitat for raptors. Within some residential lots, one finds native and exotic species. One simply cannot plan rationally for anything except a multifunctional domain. Though trees within cities certainly provide ornamentation and some wildlife habitats and corridors, it is unreasonable to expect them in the vast numbers or variety that will result in majestic forests. Safety contributes positively to aesthetic experiences of cities; it is not usually managed for in the same way in landscape artworks or pristine environments. Rutherford Platt's history of urban open-space paradigms shows how factors relating to aesthetic value have changed in North America over the past two centuries.[53] He identifies several paradigms that characterize nonnative settlements. They have overlapped but are roughly chronological: civic-agrarian colonial commons, picturesque parks, areas providing public health, cities beautiful with their monumental plazas, garden cities with greenbelts separating zones, preserved ecological sites within cities. None should be given automatic priority in urban planning; both vegetable patches and preserved wetlands clearly provide citizens with aesthetic opportunities. But it is crucial for both city planners and aestheticians to keep them straight. A single park zoned for both gardening and wetland might fail to achieve much success for either—unless it is designed to distinguish clearly and label coherently each category.

Of course, neither wetlands nor gardens are by any means the most typical urban landscape in an age when most open space in cities (at least in the United States) is devoted to parking lots and human corridors. Martin and Warner discuss the conflicting policies and values that create tensions in city planning.[54] As the fact that people value both wide and narrow streets shows, people like different things, depending on the context. Applying values from other categories must be done carefully and consciously. At the same time, undue observance of conventional or vernacular values (e.g., insisting that all city lawns be a uniform height, green, and edged with sidewalks and curbs) has also caused a great deal of environmental harm.

Nassauer's research on the aesthetic preferences of farm dwellers is very telling here.[55] Farmers tend to appreciate aesthetically landscapes that signal stewardship. Stewardship is not itself a sufficiently specific concept; caring by both fertilizing and refusing to fertilize are signs of stewardship to different persons. What is category-specific is the sort of care and control that is ecologically sound in specific biosystems. The fact that a city or rural resident exerts a great deal of effort does not in itself guarantee health. Signs of pollution are not always obvious; effects of fertilizers, irrigation, or overgrazing are not immediately or easily perceived, particularly by viewers whose only experiences of farms are those had speeding through or above the countryside. Rural dwellers themselves are often oblivious to the fact that what pleases them visually may hide or cover unsound ecological practices. Contour planting—a component of many farms still found lovely by many farmers—is usually accompanied by the unsustainable use of chemical fertilizers and weed killers. One problem for designers and philosophers is developing an aesthetic "language" that will communicate ethical ecological health within this as well as the other categories. Experimental farming techniques will not be seen as beautiful until ecologically valuable properties of landscape types are more readily recognized.

The term 'nature' for most people typically connotes relatively pristine landscapes. Vastness, majesty, vistas viewed from elevated outlooks—in general, "the scenic" is what people like. Even in areas that one knows are highly managed (such as national parks and preserves), one generally prefers as little trace of that management as possible. Some things, for example, clearly marked trails, will be acceptable within managed, but not within unmanaged, relatively pristine areas. There have been several excellent studies of the ways in which human perceptions and assessments of wilderness have changed across the centuries, and of how they differ geographically and culturally.[56] These changes can be read, for example, in tourism trends. There has been less study of what is valued in "nature" in rural or urban environments. Ecologists—largely for aesthetic reasons, I think—have tended to concentrate on relatively pristine landscapes and too often have assumed that what is beautiful there must be what makes for beauty everywhere else. City "beautification" has too often taken the form of planting along corridors whose concreted soil produces unlovely, usually soon dead, trees. Nassauer describes ways in which paradigms of "scenic beauty" have often widened the gap between vernacular conceptions of beauty and ecological conceptions of health.[57]

Most people assert that the presence of human structures in pristine landscapes, especially unmanaged ones, is a negative factor. But further investigation of this reinforces the claim that specificity of category is a crucial determinant of aesthetic appreciation of nature.[58] Most people admit that not every human structure in a relatively pristine landscape is distracting; coming across a log cabin is not upsetting in the way that coming across a fast-food restaurant would be—indeed, the cabin might heighten an already positive experience. What is the difference? The answer lies in fuller awareness of how what is "natural" is category-specific. Fast-food restaurants are "natural" landmarks that we expect and are therefore appropriate to, and even admired by some, at urban scales—those urban patches where the population of meat-eating, economically able bipeds has attained a certain level. Abandoned shacks in urban areas are eyesores. The occasional abandoned hut—but not a busy Pizza Hut—will be fine along a trail in relatively pristine landscapes. Thus, the term 'presence of human structures' is itself too vague to explain positive or negative aesthetic response. Attention to scale and to degree of manipulation is essential to making this term precise enough to guide planning.

I have talked about the mistakes that can be made if one fails to contextualize aesthetic values via category specificity. But how else might such attention be positively useful? If landscape architects are to take advantage of aesthetic preferences as they design ecologically sound landscapes, then they must make accessible the aesthetic properties people delight in.[59] Ecologically sustainable landscapes will be possible only if due attention is given to the cultural values that determine people's choices and actions. I suggested earlier that a general strategy for drawing attention to aesthetic properties consists of showing viewers how nonperceivables or factors in themselves not aesthetically valued are connected to the perceivable intrinsic properties that members of a community consider worthy of attention and reflection. I would now like to suggest another way in which designers might exploit aesthetic values—one that utilizes aes-ethical and ecological categories and one that underscores their relations.

In general, *showing* consists of using gestures, words, or signs that point to something and draw a viewer's attention. There are, of course, many theories of signifying. But most share the idea that there are "natural" signs (e.g., signs related causally to their referents: smoke signifies fire) or "conventional" (e.g., a word in a spoken language stands for something: 'cup' signifies something from which one drinks). Designers must use both kinds of signs. By having a certain kind of tree pointed out, one may look more closely to see if (or at least value the possibility that) a particular kind of orchid may be nearby, for some trees are natural signs of some varieties of orchids to people who have adequate knowledge of the biosystems in which they occur together. Nassauer's research is again helpful here, for she has proved that simply putting up a placard (a "conventional" sign) that says that an area is being cared for via certain conservation practices enhances the aesthetic value for most viewers.[60] Signs that simply let us know where we are ("You are now crossing the National Divide') provide frames that may enrich our aesthetic experiences.

In each aesthetic category, there are properties valued by members of a community: carefully laid out patches, vistas, winding roads, monuments, windmills, clearly marked trails, colorful forbs, bright lights. These clear indicators can be borrowed and used in a variety of environments to signify that designers have given attention to aesthetic values. Not every property is a clear indicator, of course. Silence may be a positive feature of a serene garden but not of an exciting city; it may even be a negative indicator in a forest where one had hoped to hear songbirds. Nor will all indicators cross categories. A mass of lights will not be appropriately borrowed from the city to signify aesthetic attentiveness in a rural or pristine landscape. A chaotic jumble of species valued at the relatively pristine level may not translate automatically to city parks. But clearly marked (e.g., "socially signed," to use Nassauer's phrase), a chaotic patch in a city's open space may come to have aesthetic value for residents if they read it as a sign of an attempt at achieving biodiversity within urban boundaries. Formal properties such as balance, color, or shape (valued at rather small scales, for instance, in residential yards) become signs of due attention to aesthetic amenities at larger scales, even in relatively pristine landscapes. Whether the signs actually work to enhance aesthetic experiences, of course, depends on the knowledge that the viewer brings to the site. Park boards that opt for less mowing will be reelected only if the public sees too much mown turf as a sign of an unhealthy ecosystem. A wetland initially read as a dirty swamp may be read as a park if there are boardwalks or species markers. The ethical and the aesthetic once again come together in the realization that responsible policy making is underway.

Artists are in the business of providing communities with new metaphors that challenge and hence broaden our comprehension of the world. Our attitudes toward nature are largely determined by the metaphors with which we conceptualize it, and many of these have come to us from the arts. We have the tree, the spring, the sea, the waters of life. We categorize in terms of light and dark, sun and moon, heaven and earth. We are warned not to lose the forest for the trees. We strive to reach rock bottom or to get at the root of a problem for ideas to blossom. Imaginatively developing new metaphors may indeed allow us, as it has sometimes been put, to "think outside the box." Fiction is of great use here. But this does not mean that there should be no restrictions on the imagination. As we have seen, fiction can sentimentalize and demonize, with serious harm resulting. If sustainable environments are the goal, then fiction must be at the service of fact.

I suggest that landscape designers can apply and introduce new metaphors, and that one way of providing new vision is by crossing categories. Once aesthetic and ecological studies have been produced that take careful account of the categories specific to a site, one is in a position to ask whether properties valued at other sites can fruitfully be borrowed and used. Like artists who expand languages by describing or portraying one thing as another (a petroglyph as water source, for instance), landscape architects may be able to expand their vocabularies and those of their patrons by borrowing clear signs from other categories. Of course, this will be successful only if we have a clearer understanding of the specific properties valued at each specific site and of what the clear indicators are. Incorporating the "messy" at smaller scales will work only when deep attention has been given to aesthetic values at the location of the particular design project.

There are dangers in borrowing. Signs can be confusing, even deceptive—as when a corporation announces that it is employing environmentally friendly safeguards when, in fact, it is not. We often have trouble knowing where we are. How many of us know the watershed or soil chemistry of our residence, for example? Honest, clear use of signs may help to alleviate the dissonance that characterizes so much of the contemporary human condition, especially when they inform us not just about the names of things but about the workings of an ecosystem as well. Details of a system that promotes category crossing for aes-ethical purposes remain to be worked out. It is an area in which ecologists, landscape architects, ethicists, and aestheticians may work fruitfully together in the effort to design ecologically sustainable landscapes that succeed culturally.

Ideally, we want landscapes that show which aesthetically valuable properties and which ecologically sound properties come together, and a human population that recognizes that a meaningful life demands this. We want educated people who do not destroy what they value as they seek it out—a population whose cultural practices do not lead to a repetition of the experience of Easter Islanders. We aim for a public that does not, as Nassauer puts it, mistake a well-kept prairie park for a weed patch. Hedgerows that maintain diversity can come to be perceived as creating beautiful contoured patterns. Colorful native flowers can be perceived and reflected upon as an indication of soil unpoisoned by harsh chemicals. An adequate canopy will signify the presence of songbirds. Too rapid runoff of rainwater will result in one's seeing concrete curbs as ugly rather than neat. Aesthetics, ethics, and sound ecology will come together, and when they do a healthy nature that includes meaningful human experiences will result.

It is often objected that insisting on a scientific basis for appreciation of nature "takes all the fun out of it." I doubt it; I have never myself experienced knowledge getting in the way of aesthetic experience. Ecological notions are no more necessarily separable from the aesthetic than are ethical ones. And if we want a healthy environment, it is time to insist that they all be integrated perceptually and conceptually and imaginatively.

THIRTEEN

Aesthetics and Ethics
in Communities

M ANY claims have been made about the power of the arts. As the title
of this chapter suggests, one of the things I believe aesthetic activity can do is contribute to conditions required for the sustainability of communities. But I also want
to alert the reader to some limits of making this and other claims about the power
of art. In an age of hyperbole, more measured avowals are called for. For this reason, I have chosen to begin by considering a speech made by Evan Mauer, the director of the Minneapolis Institute for the Arts, early in 1998. It was a clearly written, heart-felt articulation of many of the claims that are generally made for the
power of the arts. The occasion—a Minneapolis mayoral inauguration—made it
natural for the speaker to stress the role of the arts in community building, as well
as particularly useful for the purpose of this discussion.

Mauer began by citing the claims made by persons who supported the establishment of cultural and artistic institutions (civic libraries, museums, symphonies, etc.) in nineteenth-century America. The arts were then, as now, alleged
to elevate, humanize, educate, refine, uplift, ennoble—generally to make those who
come into contact with them better people and citizens. Mauer's claims, he acknowledged, fit solidly into this tradition. Here's what he asserted the arts do:

1. Through an expression of people's and peoples' most important values, art ties
   people to nature, history, and each other.
2. The arts embody and express religious beliefs, foundation myths, and civic ethics.
3. By embodying essential elements of humanity, the arts allow persons to understand themselves and others better ("better," one assumes, than we could do without the arts and the more we engage with the arts).
4. Arts can unite culturally diverse American cities.
5. The arts are the best way to achieve bonds of communication, understanding, and
   respect.
6. The arts can improve academic achievement.

At the end of his talk, Mauer claimed to have "shown that [the arts] can . . . be the
most effective means of bringing together our diverse population and of helping
our children become better students, better citizens, and better future achievers."[1]
I contend that he did not *show* anything, in the sense of providing the sort of proof
philosophers seek. Rather, he simply made a series of claims. This is, unfortunately,

true of most arts advocacy. Eliot Eisner, one of America's foremost art educators, discusses this tendency in his paper "Does Experience in the Arts Boost Academic Achievement?" He answers that very little in the way of solid research supports a positive response. It has not been definitively proved, for instance, that art courses increase test scores in math or reading, or even serve to keep some students from dropping out of high school. "I cannot help but wonder if we sometimes claim too much," he worries.[2] His review of the research done between 1986 and 1996 justifies his concern. "At this moment I can find no good evidence that [the transfer of achievement in arts classes to other disciplines] occurs if what we count as evidence is more than anecdotal reports that are often designed for purposes of advocacy."[3]

Eisner's concerns, which I share, are directly relevant to the view expressed in Mauer's sixth claim; I fear that these concerns apply to the other five as well. To begin with, many are overstated. Are the arts the best or most effective way of expressing values or uniting diverse societies? I have heard people (a former governor of Minnesota, for instance) give this role to sports. Indeed, it is extremely interesting to substitute 'baseball' for 'the arts' in Mauer's claims. (One will, of course, have to revise the claims for countries where other sports reign.) Baseball certainly expresses basic American values. It ties people to history, to each other, and, at least in places where it is still played outside, to nature. Obviously, spiritual values and civic ethics are expressed. The playing of the game is more important (or at least is supposed to be more important) than the success of any individual. "All people are created equal" applies (except, one might argue, for the designated hitter rule), but with all of the issues of justice that come with that principle. Tensions between equality of distribution and differential distribution of rewards based on differential merit are manifest. No one gets more than three strikes, but people with better hand-eye coordination score more runs and get more recognition. Perhaps baseball does not express our foundation myths (I leave it to the reader-fan to show how it might), but it certainly unites diverse communities. Few artists have done more than Jackie Robinson on this score. Baseball can also be credited, I think, with enhancing communication, understanding, and respect. It is certainly arguable that it has kept as many students from dropping out of high school as have art courses.

In fact, claims made for the arts can be made for a wide range of human pursuits, from cockfighting in Bali[4] to World War II to dealing with El Niño. Eisner correctly observes that what is needed is a theory that relates the arts with the effects that they are purported to have. What we need is an explanation of what it is about art that makes it possible for it to contribute to the sustainability of communities. Eisner calls for empirical research. This is, of course, needed. But a theoretical foundation is also required, and I hope that the ideas proposed in earlier chapters of this book begin to provide it.

This demands, of course, that I say what I mean by the terms 'art' and 'community'. I have offered a detailed account of my theory of art, but let me repeat key definitions here.

X is a work of art if and only if

- X is an artifact,
- X is treated in aesthetically relevant ways; that is, X is treated in such a way that someone who is fluent in a culture is led to direct attention to intrinsic properties of X considered worthy of that attention (perception and reflection) within that culture, and
- When someone has an aesthetic experience as a result of attending to X, he or she realizes that the cause of the experience is an intrinsic property or set of intrinsic properties of X considered worthy of attention within the culture.

By 'intrinsic', I refer to properties such that it is necessary to inspect directly an object or event to verify a claim that the object or event has that property. One must look at a painting to know if the colors are balanced, must listen to a sonata to know if it is unified, and so on.

'Community' has been defined in a plethora of ways, and writers have also offered theories that subdivide the notion—distinguish political from religious communities, market from domestic communities, healthy from sick communities, voluntary from involuntary communities, free from unfree communities. I do not want to add another theory of community per se. Rather, I want to focus on one aspect of some communities that contributes, I will argue, to their sustainability. This aspect, I will try to show, can be connected with my theory of the integration of the aesthetic and ethical in such a way that the explanation urged by Eisner is forthcoming. That is, I will offer an answer to the question, What is it about art that accounts for the role it plays in sustaining communities? (And bear in mind that this is a much more modest claim than is often made. I simply claim that art sometimes and by no means exclusively plays this role. Sports, wars, and natural disasters can as well.) Art's contribution is special; that is, the nature of art is such that when it plays a positive sustaining role in communities, it does so in its own unique ways.

My claim is that art makes a special kind of contribution to one necessary feature of sustainable communities: in a sustainable community, individual members are aware of other members and take some responsibility for their well-being.[5]

A great deal of philosophical blood has been shed on what constitutes human well-being, and I shall not add to what I have suggested about what constitutes meaningful lives in earlier chapters. I have some confidence that what I say will not contradict my readers' intuitions; if it does, then no additional discourse on well-being that I can provide here will be much help. The notion of taking some responsibility for others of whom one is aware also deserves more attention than I can provide here. Brief reflection on what happens when communities, big or small, more or less durable, come into being will have to suffice.

Erving Goffman's concept of a focused group has helped me consider what can turn a mere collection of individuals into a community, and how artistic activity turns a collection of people into a focused group. Goffman suggests that games provide a helpful case study in this regard. He gives a detailed analysis of the conditions operative in board games, for example, that turn the players into a group with a shared focus. Several things operative in board games also function in baseball and, more important, in art.[6] But more important than the specification of the particular rules in operation is Goffman's characterization of what happens when people do what is required to play a game and thus become a focused group. Involvement in joint activity results in each individual's becoming "an integral part of the situation, lodged in it and exposed to it, infusing himself into the encounter."[7] A consequence is that the activity is made stable or, as I would say, is sustained or at least sustainable. Goffman says that in focused groups a "euphoria function" keeps things going.[8] In games, this may require new recruits and subsequent reallocation of resources. It also requires that a certain level of participant interest be maintained, and it is essential that the participants remain "at ease." "To be at ease in a situation is to be . . . entranced by the meanings [the activities] generate and stabilize; to be ill at ease means that one is ungrasped by immediate reality and that one loses the grasp that others have of it."[9]

Does art have the effect of creating focused groups in this sense? I think the answer is clearly yes. Fans of Bach or the Spice Girls may as individuals derive pleasure from what they listen to in the privacy of their own rooms. But for most people, there is also a sense of connection to others who derive similar pleasure, and this in itself yields another special kind of pleasure. Paul Guyer thinks that at least early in his career Kant thought that judgments of beauty arise only in society. Robinson Crusoe, then, might have taken pleasure in the beauty of the flowers on his island, but

> In the absence of society these objects would not take on any value *in addition* to their natural beauty, such as that of occasioning communication either with or about the individual. . . . For while agreement with the responses of others is not necessary to explain one's own pleasure in a beautiful object, it well may be that the art of reflecting upon one's own pleasures and discriminating them, by conjectures about their origin, into pleasures in the agreeable, the good, and the beautiful is an art which has a point and can even be acquired only in a social setting."[10]

It is obvious that social pleasures can be felt only in society, and I claim that many, probably most aesthetic pleasures, at least for some people, are social pleasures. And some artworks and landscapes are more likely to provide for social pleasures over the long run than others. History has shown that Bach's fan clubs are more likely to be shaped by euphoria functions than those of pop groups, more likely, that is, to feel pleasure over a considerable length of time. Art certainly provides occasions for becoming entranced by meanings. And when individuals are left cold by artworks, it is impossible to be "at ease," to be grasped by realities that seem to enthrall others.

But how does artistic activity function to create focused groups of the sort that are or might become communities? Suppose we have a collection of individuals who are not jointly focused on anything. How might art turn them into a focused group and ultimately into a community? My characterization of community demands awareness of others and a sense of responsibility for their well-being. Two sorts of activity that are readily recognized as artistic can contribute to creating focused groups: creation and contemplation.

Creation, to put it very simply, is what art makers do. By 'contemplation', I mean to include the wide range of things audiences do: perceive, reflect, describe, evaluate, display, make purchase decisions, and the like. (All of these things, of course, once more cry out for further discussion, and again I will have to rely on readers' intuitions.) There may be some occasions of artistic creation in which the maker is not aware of and does not care about the audience. These are rare, I believe. However, since I am concerned about the role art *can* play in producing sustainable communities, it is sufficient to claim that sometimes artists are aware of and are concerned with and for potential contemplators. (I will say more later about the ways in which failure to be aware of a sufficiently broad audience and to care about it has been a divisive factor in contemporary society—a destroyer rather than a builder of communities.)

If a member of a collection of individuals creates something with an awareness of other members of the collection, a first step is taken in the direction of making it possible for the collection to focus as a group. If the creator also takes responsibility for the good of the group—concentrates on exposing what is made in a way that will infuse the experience of others and produce feelings of pleasure or generate solidarity (as Goffman puts it, generates "relatedness, psychic closeness, and mutual respect"[11])—another necessary condition of community is met. Not all artists do this; but many do. And many do so successfully. I am certain that Bach did it; I expect the Spice Girls do as well. Much everyday activity of human beings exhibits the same structure. On a beach with strangers, someone picks up a shell and alerts general attention by saying, "Wow, look at this! Isn't it beautiful?" In this simple act, we find a basic element that makes creation of a focused group possible, even likely.

Contemplation is also essential. Obviously individuals can all by themselves savor objects and events aesthetically—enjoy a shade of blue or consider the intrinsic properties of a lily of the field or the sound of a slit-gong (the long, hollow percussion instruments used by some peoples in New Guinea). But this has not typically been the extent of what I mean by 'contemplation'. Human beings by nature engage in descriptive and evaluative commentary. When they do, it is rarely just to hear themselves talk. Or, in cultures where art is not spoken of, individuals engage in collective actions that draw attention to objects and events whose intrinsic properties are valued. Again, this is not done simply for individual gratification. Such speech and action is done in an awareness of others and often in the belief that others will benefit. Fans of Bach, the Spice Girls, or of songs written for Efe ceremonies in Yoruban cultures describe and evaluate as well as enjoy their individual encounters.

To return to the example of folks on the beach, one imagines acquaintances and strangers responding to the speaker's call for attention to the beauty of the shell. Some come closer, ask to hold it for themselves, or inquire whether there are many others like it in the area. For however fleeting a time, a focused group exists. The focus will be maintained if, for instance, some contemplators decide to go shelling together or to establish a shell museum. Focus will have to be maintained even longer if what is undertaken is the building of an earthen mound, a pyramid, or a cathedral. But maintained and sustained, a focused group turns into a community.

Activities like shelling in groups or setting up formal or informal institutions for presenting or displaying suggest how focused groups differ from communities—a difference, I think, of degree and not of kind. Rituals or traditions direct and intensify awareness of other members of the group. When individuals consciously and conspicuously participate in these, they begin to take responsibility for the group's continued existence and well-being. They are concerned with what has often been called "the good of the commons."

Eliot Eisner says that effective justification for including the arts in education requires looking at the arts themselves and asking what "demands they make on those who would create, perceive, or understand them."[12] His own answer is complex.

- The arts produce a feeling for what it takes to transform one's ideas, images, and feelings into a specific medium and form.
- The arts refine awareness of aesthetic qualities both in art and in the world and life more generally.
- The arts teach connections that have been made between form and content across cultures and times.
- The arts promote imagination of possibilities, desire and tolerance for ambiguity, recognition and acceptance of multiple perspectives and resolutions.

I agree that the arts can do all of these, and that all enhance awareness of others and provide a fertile soil in which a shared sense of responsibility can flourish.

But my answer to Eisner's question about how the demands the arts put on us produce certain effects is grounded in my definitions of 'art' and 'aesthetic'. When one creates art of the sort that transforms focused groups into communities, one does it in the awareness of others and with the intention that they will respond when, and because, they attend to intrinsic properties of what has been created and to the fact that someone created it with that intention. Both creators and responders are also aware of and respond to the fact that the other members of the group are responding in (some) similar ways—or at least that their response results from attention to some of the same intrinsic properties. Members also engage in a variety of forms of contemplation—pointing, discussing, displaying, for example—in the belief that they will bring others to respond to certain intrinsic properties. Art can teach and refine skills required for awareness and contemplation. It provokes further acts of creation that, in turn, encourage more occasions for awareness and contemplation. By being embodied in the lives of communities and by embodying rituals and traditions, artworks can instill a sense of responsibility. People engage in creation and communal contemplation at least in part for the good of others and hence tend to act out of a sense of responsibility for the well-being of the group. Again, one sees how the aesthetic and the ethical come together.

Some art forms and artworks contribute more than others to sustaining communities. Judgments about which these are require broad and deep cross-cultural awareness and knowledge. Considerable progress has been made in recent years with respect to the diversity of cultures whose art is presented in schools, museums, concert halls, the media, and other public arenas. But many people fear that this has contributed to an entrenchment of subcultures that works against the creation of unified communities that can be sustained over the long haul. Even if subcultures respect one another (which, of course, we cannot assume), confronting and respecting do not automatically result in acceptance, let alone enjoyment. Looking at artifacts does not necessarily produce an ability to participate in the aesthetic pleasures of cultures other than one's own, for this requires seeing as the members of those other cultures see. As I argued in the opening chapter, aesthetic response is to a great degree socially constructed—the result of becoming fluent in the traditions of a culture. Can theories of art and beauty that recommend specific artistic practices contribute to the deepened understanding required for responding with sustained pleasure as well as respect? If so, how? And what theory or theories are most likely to contribute to the creation of sustainable communities? I am not so presumptuous as to pretend to know the complete answers. But thinking about the role of good art as well as the general role of art is certainly one condition for beginning to articulate an answer.

I believe that good art is more likely to contribute to sustaining communities than bad art. Good art, I have argued earlier, is art that repays sustained attention. Individuals return again and again to aesthetic objects and events that reward perceiving and reflecting upon intrinsic properties therein. As I recognized previously, sometimes individuals feel pleasure, and the activity stops there. This value should not be denied nor sniffed at. But art that sustains evokes more. When personal pleasure leads individuals to invite others to attend to those properties, communal practices and institutions that generate and regenerate attention develop. The more often and the longer that attention is paid, the more likely a focused group is to develop and continue to exist. A nonoppressive community is sustained only as long as the well-being of the commons is believed by members to be a mutual concern. As an individual, I will invite others to attend only to intrinsic properties that reward me and that I believe will reward them; that is, I try to contribute to the well-being of others of whom I am aware. (In chapter 14, I shall discuss in more detail the difference between inviting and forcing others to attend; forcing is not typically done out of a sense of obligation for the good of those forced.) Intrinsic properties that one values are valued-in-a-community. The more and the longer that a particular artwork inspires me to invite others to engage in similar perception and reflection, the more and the longer I and those others will tend to maintain our interrelationship. Goffman's "euphoria function" is satisfied. But this is precisely what constitutes sustainability. Group contemplation and discussion require that members enter into relationship with the objects and with each other. When this is combined with the ways in which artworks present the shared ideas, values, myths, metaphors, and feelings that characterize flourishing communities, sustainability is enhanced. The 'good' in the phrase 'good art' is a moral term, as well as an aesthetic term.

The claim made for art that it provides windows across cultures that invite deeper understanding of worldviews that differ from one's own is, of course, true.

But within single communities, it is not always the case that art objects and events present diverse views. The provision of multiple perspectives in a single work is culture-specific; even in the West, it is a relatively recent phenomenon. One simply cannot show that cultures are most sustainable when their arts challenge viewers to consider various viewpoints. This was not true, for example, of Christian art of medieval Europe; although the communities therein did not last forever, they were sustained over several centuries. The art of the Sepiks of New Guinea expresses only the ideas and emotions (fears and hopes) of the males who have dominated in what seems to many outsiders an almost appallingly sustained manner. Again, one must be very careful about making claims for the arts that are too strong. My own liberal insistence on the value of a marketplace of free artistic ideas is challenged by cultures such as the Sepiks', where art that oppresses many members undeniably permeates daily life and helps to hold the communities together.

The difficulty that many Westerners, especially women, have with admiring or even making sense of art of such different cultures as the Sepiks' indicates how careful one must be in making claims for art's power to illuminate, let alone unite, diverse communities. "Deep fluency" is required before one can arrive at the level of entry into a culture that is a condition of understanding and respect. Nonetheless, art does provide access and helps us to see the world through others' eyes. This comes about both by looking at others' art and by learning how others see our own art. In *No Mercy: A Journey to the Heart of the Congo*, Redmond O'Hanlon relates an experience in which his guide and companion, Dr. Marcellin, becomes insulted at O'Hanlon's amusement at African "superstitions." Marcellin angrily responds with a catalog of what he perceives as white men's superstitions: the fetishes (crosses) worn around many of their necks, the cannabalistic rites they euphemistically call "eucharist," and so on. "You white men—we don't even know how you breed. You had a god born without any sex! And then he never had a woman! And what about the god's mother—in those fetish statues you have everywhere—a woman who'd never had a man, with that idiot smile on her face and a baby in her arms? If that's not just plain silly, if that's not stupid, I don't know what is."[13] Seeing others' art and our art as others see it is an excellent way to remain open to the revisions demanded by sustainability in a changing world.[14]

I believe that in my own culture good art is more likely than bad art to develop the kinds of community-enhancing skills that Eisner and I claim good art requires. Something that challenges and rewards repeated attention is more likely to challenge one to exercise careful, nuanced attention. Inferior or sentimental art allows for laziness—or anaesthetized rather than heightened, aestheticized attention. Daniel Jacobson writes, "The ethical function of narrative art lies in its ability to get us to see things anew. . . . How much to hope for from art, and how much to fear it, will hang on one's diagnosis of our condition. Are we, as some believe, suffering from a surfeit of contrary ethical views? Or are we still often talking past each other, unable to imagine other ways of seeing than our own, and hence incapable of confronting them?"[15]

Isaiah Berlin has insightfully worried along similar lines. There is no guarantee that diverse communities will be able to achieve means for harmonizing different values and projects, he says.[16] Art *can* present diverse ideas in ways that engage discussion rather than threaten dissolution. Communities are more likely to sustain themselves if they achieve a delicate balance between the tolerance for new ideas that allows for revision necessary for continued existence and the chaos that may result from a Babel of competing voices. Great art often repays attention precisely because it embodies not simply multiple perspectives, but even contradictions. But one must recognize the possibility of great art that expresses and entrenches a single shared worldview.

Art can express a sense of shame as well as a sense of pride, often at the same time and with the same goal of regeneration. A public project in southwestern Pennsylvania exemplifies a community struggling to sustain and regenerate itself. Success demanded coming to grips with "a company-town mindset that waits for The Company to take the lead, [and where] residents can be history-proud, history-shamed, anxious about their future, yet incredibly passive."[17] Acid mine damage had created deadly streams and a starkly degenerated landscape. The single-minded industrial focus of the mid-twentieth-century community that produced these could not sustain itself into the final decades of that century. Historians, scientists, designers, and artists are working together to turn this graveyard into a park—into an aesthetic environment in which art plays a key role. It will "re-energize" the area and its inhabitants if it succeeds. What is clear as one reads about this and similar projects is that the aesthetic activity permeates a sense of awareness and shared responsibility for others.

What communities cannot stand, as Jean Bethke Elshtain has written, is cynicism, for this undercuts any possibility of regeneration.[18] Art that feeds cynicism (and there are many examples of this in contemporary technological societies) is not likely, therefore, to contribute to sustainability—unless it also encourages revisions of harmful institutions and practices. Nor, I think, can communities stand for long when art contributes to factionalization or to putting power in the hands of a few who may, like Machiavelli, be aware of others but concerned only for their own personal well-being or for the well-being of a chosen minority. Art can oppress as well as liberate. What counts as well-being for a group allows for—indeed, demands—diverse answers. But coupled with the notion of the commons, I believe (hope) it is less likely to be restricted to vested interests of a single class, race, gender, or religion.

Perhaps powerful forces in general can be beneficial only if they are capable of malevolence as well. Art can destroy as well as build. This empirical claim calls for more evidence, of course. The story will have to be complex. William McNeill warns against simplistic reductionism in a review article on Jared Diamond's *Guns, Germs and Steel: The Fate of Human Societies.* Diamond argues that since one cannot explain Europe's outpacing of other societies in technology in terms of intelligence, the main factors must have been environment and biogeography. McNeill considers this an oversimplification.

> I do not accept Diamond's dismissive appraisal of "cultural idiosyncrasies unrelated to environment." A more persuasive view might be to suppose that in the early phases of our history, when technical skills and organizational coordination were still unde-

veloped, human societies were indeed closely constrained by the local availability of food, as Diamond convincingly argues. But with the passage of time, as inventions multiplied and more effective modes of coordinating collective effort across space and time were adopted, the course of human history became increasingly autonomous simply because our capacities to reshape actual environments to suit our purposes became greater and greater. Cultural idiosyncrasies—systems of meaning constructed out of nothing more tangible than words and numerical symbols, and largely independent of any external reference whatever—came into their own. This is the ordinary domain of history. . . . Introspection surely tells us that conscious purposes and shared meanings govern much of human behavior; and a science of history that leaves this dimension out, as Diamond's does, is unlikely to explain satisfactorily the modern world or any other part of the human record.[19]

The question of the "superiority" of technology aside, McNeill is surely correct that purposes and meanings are factors that matter as much as environment and geography. A full understanding of the role of art in sustaining (as well as undermining) communities demands careful case studies of the ways in which artistic symbols and activities serve to establish and perpetuate forms of life. One must, as it were, put art into the proper context. Formalist theories that locate art's value exclusively in emotions generated by a work's intrinsic properties deprive art of its sustaining role, for such a role can be played only when art is clearly connected to the multifaceted activities of a community and when members of the community recognize that connection.

Murray Edelman provides a detailed analysis of one specific social function art has played in communities (to both good and bad ends), namely, politics. By supplying images that enable individuals to become part of a focused group (or as Edelman puts it in this context, "a politically conscious group"), "Works of art . . . construct and periodically reconstruct perceptions and beliefs that underlie the political actions in the news, even when their role is concealed, as is usually the case. They create diverse levels of reality and multiple realities. . . . At other times they construct beliefs in one true reality, as do both positivist and scientific writings and fundamentalist religious tracts."[20]

Art helps individuals to define themselves as insiders and to distinguish themselves from outsiders. Art can also be a tool in the hands of those in power who act to create shared perceptions, and often, as Marx warned, those perceptions constitute a false consciousness. We are all familiar with sentimental pictures of loving, well-fed, healthy families that are supposed to express universal American family values. But there are also many cases of artworks that more realistically reveal the dark underside of the human condition.

Current as well as past conditions, events, and anxieties make people susceptible to particular ways of seeing and understanding realities, including the outcomes of political processes. . . . It is artists who provide the ways of seeing, the categories, and the premises that yield modes of understanding everyday life. Twentieth-century art has been especially explicit in revealing the premises that have dominated contemporary thought. The wars, genocides, homelessness, and other conspicuous public events of the century have inspired a great deal of shock, fear, and outrage, which works of art have objectified and so made more readily available for expression in everyday activities and political statements.[21]

Myths and narratives "justify and rationalize the power, incomes, and perquisites of people who hold high positions."[22] But, I contend, they also expose them. Works of art both broaden and narrow perspectives. In getting members of a group to classify in terms of what is heroic, calamitous, or even funny, governments and political candidates serve their goal of getting constituencies to see things from a particular point of view. I am more interested here in considering how art generally contributes to sustainability. But Edelman's very interesting discussion of specific ways in which political parties and authorities use specific arts for specific purposes supports my more abstract assertions, I believe.

Individual communities have special needs; things, and hence art, that will work to sustain one community will not necessary work in others. Up to this point, I have tried to avoid the imperialism that comes with making universal judgments about what in general is sustaining about art. However, I want to conclude by saying more about what I think "we" need. I confess that issues of diversity and attempts to deal justly with them have often left me not quite knowing who "I" am, let alone who "we" are. I am white but female, economically well-off but overweight, an American but a Minnesotan, a Minnesotan but one whose first twenty-one years were spent in Illinois, heterosexual but postmenopausal, and so on. Thus, I will speak here just as someone who strives to be a member of the group Cass Sunstein has called "enlightened citizens of a free democracy."[23] Putting aside questions of degrees of enlightenment and of freedom (questions which certainly deserve serious attention[24]), one can ask, What does this "we" need from art in order to sustain ourselves?

Yuriko Saito provides one approach to answering this question. In discussing the questions of whether there are correct and incorrect interpretations of art, she argues that we have a moral obligation to try to experience works of art correctly, to attempt to do more than simply get as much aesthetic pleasure as possible from an object or event without regard to what the artist meant or what it meant when it was produced, and without regard to the category in which the work belongs. Doing otherwise, she insists, shows a selfish, self-centered, close-minded attitude, "an unwillingness to put aside our own agenda, whether it an ethnocentric or present-minded perspective or the pursuit for easy pleasure and entertainment."[25] One ought (ethically *and* aesthetically ought) to respect each work, give it a chance to open our eyes and minds. I agree with Saito, but hers is, admittedly, a very strong position. Whether one is ready to go as far as she does, one must admit that art can open eyes and minds, and to this extent it is highly recommended, perhaps required, to sustain a democratic society of enlightened citizens. This returns us, of course, to Eliot Eisner's point that the arts should be required in democratic societies' educational systems because of its propensity to create a tolerance and even enthusiasm for multiple perspectives. The arts can also play a related and significant role in a marketplace of free ideas.

In my own attempts to answer the question of what "we" need from art in "our" efforts to sustain communities and subcommunities, I rely heavily on ideas presented about a century ago by Leo Tolstoy. He defined art as the communication in a medium of feelings so sincerely felt and skillfully presented by the artist that members of the audience who experience the work come to feel the same way.[26] The upshot is that artists and audience members are united in a spiritual community or, as I would put it, are aware of and have a sense of responsibility for the well-being of the commons. The unabashedly moral character of this view is present in all of the concepts in the phrase "enlightened citizens of a free democracy."

Art, particularly good art, also develops the skills required for the enlightenment that we consider a necessary condition for sustainable free democracies. There is no guarantee, of course, that the existence of great art alone will make for a more sustainable community. Works must be reflected upon—for example, read, but read carefully, seen and heard, but seen and heard with attention and repetition. Two of the most frequently assigned fictional works in America's high schools are *To Kill a Mockingbird* and *The Color Purple*. This must be because teachers believe that they encourage and challenge students and because they are worthy of their attention. There is a difference between reading a book and *reading* a book. *Reading* is engaging in aesthetic activity of the sort that contributes to the development of skills necessary for becoming an enlightened citizen—critical analysis and moral imaginativeness, to name just two. But not just anything can be *read* in such a way. One can read but not *read* a Harlequin romance. These are books, but not books that demand much of the reader. Enlightened citizens of a free democracy need precisely the things that good art demands: powers of observation, organization, puzzle solving, imagination. To be a member of a focused group, one must be able to focus. To be a member of an enlightened focused group, one must be able to focus in enlightened and enlightening ways, as a mature moral agent. In short, one must know what is justifiable and how to express the ideas and attitudes that sustain awareness of and responsibility for the well-being of other free democrats. The arts generate and regenerate deliberative skills of the sort that I argued in chapter 11 they challenge and invite us to develop.

Both internal and external forces can work against sustainability. A community is sustainable when insiders' practices perpetuate those positive features that enhance awareness and responsibility for the good of the commons. But this requires knowledge of what is really good. A community that requires and inspires total celibacy, for instance, will not last long. Even apparently admirable practices may have a dark side. The flourishing society on Easter Island was brought to a level of squalid subsistence by the people's own obsessions. We admire the religious, aesthetic zeal these stones still exhibit today—but one asks oneself, with a self-conscious glance over one's shoulder at our own environmentally unfriendly practices, "How did they fail to see what they were doing?" In our own culture, many artists have, unfortunately, deliberately separated themselves from the majority of the population. They seem increasingly unaware of others and cannot or will not seriously heed obligations for the general good. Mass art is too often contemptuously taken as incompatible with good art.[27] Art that is used to drive wedges between groups within a community will not contribute to but will act against sustainability.

At the same time, communities cannot sustain themselves in the face of overwhelming external human forces. Powerful external forces must either ignore a community or treat it with sufficient respect if it is to survive. Richard Anderson, in a discussion of Aztec art and aesthetics, describes this culture's preoccupation with apocalypse and the elaborate ways in which their rituals and ceremonies aimed to forestall its inevitability in the hands of powerful gods. "There is some irony in the fact that the Aztec's world *was* soon destroyed—not by an earthquake sent by the gods, but by the conquering Spanish; the irony is heightened when one realizes that the essence of Aztec culture *did* survive this experience largely through art works such as architecture, the illustrated codices, stone sculpture, and so on."[28] Even if art cannot by itself sustain the ideas that keep cultures alive long enough to attain and maintain what we might call "the flourishing point," it does make a contribution. The very outsiders who act to destroy a community often borrow those artistic forms and practices that made them worth attacking. The Spanish borrowed from the Aztecs, who had borrowed from the Toltecs. The Romans copied Greek architecture, Europeans incorporated in their paintings the art forms of the Africans they subjugated, white American musicians imitate black American music, and so on.

Art advocates have high hopes for art's ability to encourage intercultural respect. There is much about art that justifies such hope. If communities cannot stand in the face of too much cynicism, neither can they stand in the face of too little hope. In his novel *The Discovery of Heaven*, Harry Mulisch expresses one kind of hope that art seems to generate.

> In a world full of war, famine, oppression, deceit, monotony, what—apart from the eternal innocence of animals—offers an image of hope? A mother with a newborn child in her arms? The child may end up as a murderer, or a murder victim, so that the hopeful image is a prefiguration of a pietà: a mother with a newly dead child on her lap. No, the image of hope is someone passing with a musical instrument in a case. It is not contributing to oppression, or to liberation either, but to something that continues below the surface: the boy on his bike, with a guitar in a mock-leather cover on his back; a girl with a dented violin case waiting for the tram.[29]

A child with a musical instrument is not the only cause of hope, of course; a child with a baseball glove or ballet slippers or a math book may be as well. I argued in chapter 12 that we must beware of sentimentally attributing too much innocence to animals; this goes for children as well. But surely Mulisch is correct in identifying implements for making art as paradigmatic sources for the creation of the focused groups that ideally engender awareness of and responsibility for the well-being of others. Such implements have, in short, the appearance of merit and the merit of appearance.

FOURTEEN

Aesthetics and Ethics in Education

QUESTIONS concerning aesthetic value become particularly daunting when one considers the extent to which the world daily grows not only more un-aesthetic—(ugly, graceless, even repulsive) but also more anaesthetic—(dulling, numbing, alienating). Cities are falling apart and being bombed, and what appears to stand most securely are temples to efficiency and economy that so distress the eye that we train ourselves to shut them out whenever possible. Our streams are visibly polluted, and our beaches, forests, landscapes, and roadways so mutilated by human and industrial misuse and refuse that pilgrimages undertaken for aesthetic inspiration increasingly depress rather than uplift. So we turn ourselves off by turning on our TVs and Walkmans, often with no intention of giving what we see or hear serious or sustained attention.

Thus, a primary question facing educators and other public servants must be this: how do we develop aesthetic values that will combat the unaesthetic, anaesthetic forces that confront us? And what strategies are there for identifying and instilling the requisite values in a culturally diverse society? How can one avoid the imperialism that marks the foisting of one's own community's way of looking and one's own sense of what is important on those who may not share the same focus and attitudes?

Implicit in this query is the more general question: how can one instill aesthetic and ethical values that will contribute to healthy citizens and communities? This way of putting the question might lend itself to the separatist view that I have been fighting in this book, for it makes it look as if ethical and aesthetic values are exclusive. Thus, I restate it this way: how do persons and communities shape education in such a way that it leads students (at all ages) without oppressing them to attend to intrinsic properties valued in "our" community and also introduces students to intrinsic properties valued by "other" communities, at least those communities that deserve respect. Furthermore, how can education contribute to creating communities that value intrinsic properties that do not endanger our own or others' communities?

I would like to use three "stories" to introduce my theory of education. The first two are personal and connected to my views about what constitutes the difference between good and bad (or not-so-good) art. The third comes from my own cultural tradition but leads, I think, to a more general view.

1. Most weeks for me, as for all of us, are hectic and stressful. By midday Friday, I am eager to get home, where, whenever possible, I relax by pouring myself a stiff drink of Scotch and watching TV. The perfect program for this, when it was still on, was *Dallas*. Nothing else has quite replaced it for me. Both activities—drinking and watching most TV—are fairly mindless, exactly the sort of thing that serves well at week's end. Obviously contrived plots and flat characters dull one's sense in much the same way that alcohol does. Both are welcome when one wants to escape.

2. One summer when my son was a camper at the National Music Camp at Interlochen, Michigan, I attended a rehearsal of the high school choir. The practice had been going on for some time, and the young people (juices flowing as they inevitably will at that age) had become a bit fidgety. The director, Melvin Larimer, tapped the stand and said, "People, we are singing Bach, and he deserves your respect and attention." I was impressed with the way that his remark brought the students back to the business at hand.

These stories suggest what I think is the difference between good art and bad art. Bad art is mindless and dulls the senses; good art demands, deserves, and repays sustained attention, no matter what the community or traditions. Consider the difference between 'aesthetic' and 'anaesthetic'; we do not typically use the latter term in our aesthetic discussions, but I think we should. It captures nicely the fact that bad art does the opposite of what good art does in terms of encouraging or stimulating attention.

3. The third story is the myth of Sisyphus. Readers will remember that in Greek mythology Sisyphus was doomed to spend eternity repeatedly pushing a heavy boulder up a long, steep hill, only to have it roll down again as soon as it and he reached the top. Probably because it provides so poignant an image of human life (a lot of us feel like Sisyphus on Monday mornings), several writers have attempted to answer the question, How might one give meaning to the life of Sisyphus? If we can answer this, perhaps the rest of us will have a chance for a better life, and a better chance to contribute to enriching the lives of others.

My own answer is derived from my theories of art, the aesthetic, and the role and nature of aesthetic criticism. But first I want to mention two philosophers who have reflected on the question of how one might turn Sisyphus's life into one with some meaning. The most famous is probably Albert Camus's reflection that this story, capturing as he thinks it does the human condition, suggests, "There is but one truly serious problem, and that is suicide."[1] The absurdity of human life, Camus worried, seems to dictate death. "A man is talking on the telephone behind a glass partition; you cannot hear him, but you see his incomprehensible dumb show: you wonder why he is alive. . . . Likewise the stranger who at certain seconds comes to meet us in a mirror, the familiar and yet alarming brother we encounter in our own photography is also the absurd."[2]

Camus's response, one that I find hard to accept, let alone live by, is that Sisyphus's life is meaningful when he heroically accepts his fate—is conscious of the fact that "his rock is his thing,"[3] and hence is superior to the rock and to his fate. "One always finds one's burden again. But Sisyphus teaches the higher fidelity that negates the gods and raises rocks. He too concludes that all is well. The universe henceforth without a master seems to him neither sterile nor futile. Each atom of that stone, each mineral flake of that night-filled mountain, in itself forms a world. The struggle itself toward the heights is enough to fill a man's heart. One must imagine Sisyphus happy."[4]

I, however, cannot imagine being made happy in this way. Alternatives, fortunately, exist. Richard Taylor suggests two. First, we might inject something into Sisyphus's veins that make him feel good. (This, of course, is like drinking Scotch.) If Sisyphus *feels* good, what difference will it make to him what he is doing? If the meaningful life is the happy life, where happiness is defined in terms of feeling pleasure rather in terms of living well, and if we have a happy-drug, then all lives can be meaningful. Taylor's second alternative is to give Sisyphus a purpose, to provide his rock pushing with a goal. Tell him that he is helping to build a temple or a road or increasing his upper body strength.

The injection view provides meaning from the inside, as it were; the goal view provides it from the outside. The trouble with both ways of solving the problem is that neither allows for a way to distinguish between lives in terms of different kinds or degrees of meaning. On the internal view, pushing a rock uphill, nursing the sick, playing the violin, and raping and pillaging all yield equally meaningful lives as long as the doers get the right injection. On the external view, as long as there is a goal—building temples or muscles, watching or writing *Dallas* or *Hamlet,* exterminating rats or Jews—again all lives must be equally meaningful.

Of course, most people do not want to be told that there is meaning to their lives in spite of the fact that they feel miserable. This "grin and bear it" view may prove correct—but it is hard to accept, especially in this day and age. But an adequate solution to the problem of putting meaning into our own lives and the lives of others (and, as the title of this chapter suggests, it is the lives of students with whom I am most concerned) must also provide a way of evaluating, even ranking, lives. In the absence of the ability to make some decisions about how to contribute to enriching lives, it is hard to see how educators would proceed effectively.[5] I believe that considering what distinguishes good from bad art, rich from impoverished aesthetic experiences, suggests a solution.

Combining my definitions of 'art' and 'aesthetic' and my observations about *Dallas* and the Interlochen choir rehearsal, we can derive the following points.

1. In discussions of art, extrinsic information often draws the viewer's attention to certain intrinsic properties of objects and events.
2. The properties to which attention is thus drawn are considered worthy of attention in a community's aesthetic traditions.
3. Objects and events whose intrinsic properties repay sustained perception and reflection are aesthetically valuable.

These points taken together provide a theory of criticism and suggest a way of putting meaning into Sisyphus's life and thus yield suggestions for thinking about how one might proceed with education. Art education is a particular concern of mine, but there are implications for general education since aesthetic experiences are, fortunately, not limited to art classrooms—nor, indeed, to classrooms per se at all. Instead of injecting him or giving him any old goal, we shall invite and teach him to take delight in intrinsic features of his world considered worthy of perception and reflection. Aes-ethical education can do at least two things that will make the life of Sisyphus (and all students) richer: it will invite him to attend to intrinsic features that repay attention and help him to identify those features—the view from the mountain, the shapes made as light falls on the rough surface of the rock, the harmonies created by the colors of the trees, path, and sky, the ideas and feelings communicated by the rhythms of stepping and breathing, the narratives he and others construct about their experiences. Thinking of criticism and education as inviting attention and pointing to what is worthy of attention has been described aptly by Susan Bernick; she calls criticism a "helping profession."[6] She compares it to therapy, in which a counselor attempts to bring clients to a point where they can adequately and successfully take control of their own lives. In the case of criticism, the best critics so enthrall us with their descriptions that they encourage us to continue the quest on our own.

Both invitation and identification are complex activities that deserve more analysis. Invitations are issued when one person (X) wants another (Y) to share in an activity that X believes will give delight to Y. (X would not *invite* Y to be tortured, for example.) This means that X takes on certain responsibilities. A responsible inviter cannot renege on invitations. He or she must consider the sort of person Y is, what she enjoys, what his capacities are, and so forth. Invitations can be casually or formally extended and can be issued for casual or formal affairs, and X will always make sure that Y knows which it is. A responsible inviter will do the things that may be necessary for Y to get delight. X will tell Y what to bring or wear, if that is relevant. X must consider what sort of food Y is likely to enjoy. A ten-year-old will probably not consider the offer of liver or brussels sprouts much of an invitation.

But X must do more than consider Y's pleasure. X must treat Y with respect. X must realize that Y is capable of enjoying more than just standard or "lowest common denominator" fare. Even a ten-year-old who comes from a hamburger tradition can broaden his or her horizons—can come to enjoy sharing a taco or pizza or sushi tradition. If Y is treated as a cretin or as a glutton whose only goal is to gorge, that is probably how Y will act. When people are not invited with respect, they do not typically give much respect in return. *Dallas*, unlike *Hamlet*, does not treat one as capable of very much. It is not surprising that it does not repay sustained perception and reflection. People who come to enjoy Shakespeare do not usually want to watch reruns of *Dallas*.

Responsible inviters will thus consider what Y does enjoy and is capable of enjoying. Teachers as inviters have a clear opportunity for doing this. Ten-year-olds are probably not ready to enjoy certain intrinsic features of certain objects—subtle adult relationships or the complex obligation of telling another's story, for instance. That does not mean that they are not capable of attending to a wide range of intrinsic properties—to the way a human hand has been captured in marble or

oil paint or to the ways that tension is built into battle scenes or into conflicts between friends. They are also quite capable of being introduced to other traditions.
They can easily see and delight in the differences between Egyptian and Greek
treatments of the human body, for instance. Even the youngest lovers of fiction can
understand why repeating the phrase "I think I can" is important to the Little
Engine's story. One's invitation to Sisyphus must take account of what he might
take pleasure in, where he is, and so forth. But one must not be too quick to say,
"He'll be too tired to enjoy anything very subtle or sophisticated." As a human being, he is capable of a great deal, and we should at least provide opportunities for
him to enrich his life in a variety of ways.

But how can we decide just what to point to, or what to serve, on the dinner
analogy? At least two things should be done: Sisyphus must be provided with a tradition, and he must be introduced to other traditions that he may benefit from
learning about and from. This brings us back to a question raised at the beginning
of this chapter: how, in a culturally diverse population, can one instill aesthetic values if one suspects that not everyone will respond in the same way to particular
properties? Perhaps an even more difficult question is whether one should. Again,
ethics and aesthetics come together.

Issues of multiculturalism are, of course, widely discussed today. Louis Gates Jr.
aptly titled one of his books *Loose Canons*, thus describing the current scene with
regard to what is considered worthy of teaching. From the other end of the political spectrum, Alan Bloom frets in *The Closing of the American Mind* that ours is a
nation that is becoming, in my terminology, traditionless. The list of writings on
similar themes lengthens daily. Some writers have provided lists of what we all
should know and read. This is a display of arrogance, perhaps, but nonetheless one
must start somewhere to help our Sisyphusian students. It simply is not enough to
tell them to "do their own thing." One strategy for deciding what to point to might
be to let Sisyphus in on the things that people in power hold dear. There probably
is no substitute for doing some of this if we want to make it possible for others to
share the power.

But one need not stop with finding out what the powerful say or prefer. As we
pass along critical abilities—the skills and knowledge and dispositions required for
attending to intrinsic properties—we teach people to take what is good and throw
out the rest. One does not have to accept everything that Plato or Kant or Jesus or
Muhammad said as gospel truth. One can choose for oneself to use some or reject
it all, after, of course, one has studied such thinkers. The same is true of Milton or
Mozart or Monet or Mao or Machiavelli or Marx. Informed choice is possible only
when one is informed. As teachers, we cannot avoid choosing what we think is best
based on our own experiences, which are, of course, grounded in, though not limited to, our own communities. We can also ask other communities to send us their
best and try to make it accessible to ourselves and to our students. When students
are taught aesthetic and critical principles, they are more apt to make informed
choices about what to use and what to reject and how to justify their decisions. They
even may teach teachers about "mistakes" in the canon!

Learning a tradition is not something that can be done overnight, obviously. A language like English, with all its complex and subtle connotations, is never fully mastered. And some people argue that we can never step out of our own shoes and see the world as others see it. Some deconstructionists argue that others are radically Other. We can never comprehend what another person means, they claim, for interpretation is always doomed to be misinterpretation. I think this is false, and the fact that children delight in tales from cultures quite distant from their own is one piece of evidence for the ways in which art, especially, provides inroads. I do agree that we must always be aware that there are limits to how much one does or can know about another's interests and intentions. Still, we can, with work, come to know something of the Chinese or African or medieval or Baroque worldviews. With *work*. One cannot stop with simple stories of children in Lapland or Liberia. More is required to discover the wealth of things about the contexts in which the products of far-off and even not so far-off places and periods were conceived and created.

The fact that there is so much to learn and teach can be paralyzing. We must begin somewhere and, like it or not, where we begin is in our own culture. It is only through an understanding of our own community's traditions, including, first and foremost, its language, that we can communicate or act socially and politically. Fluency in the traditions is a prerequisite of effective and responsible action. Before we can understand other cultures, we have to have some understanding of our own. One must be able to speak a language and work within one's own traditions fairly well before one can master the language and traditions of others. We have to be able to "translate" not just languages per se, but the practices and values of others. Problems of translation are enormous. We say, "They have a word for it" that takes us a paragraph to describe. Or we shrug and say, "They just don't have a word for it." Or we have the same words, but only familiarity with a subculture enables one to understand the differences the same words signal. ("Pretty good" in Minnesota, but not in California, is a term of high praise.) When differences are radical, one can never be certain that one has gotten a good translation. No matter how great the similarities, aesthetic understanding requires the ethical and other contextual nuances that shape valuing one set of intrinsic properties rather than another and that affect the ways people have of pointing to them. What we need are translators—people who have been trained to help us bridge differences. Rather than giving up on Shakespeare or Mozart, we have an obligation to invite others to join in the experiences of them that we believe will provide them pleasure. We also need to seek out persons from other cultures who will return our invitations and provide us with enriching fare.

I have throughout this book criticized formalist theories for an acontextual and anticontextual approach that has robbed the aesthetic of much of its connectedness to, and hence value in, the lives of individuals and communities. Within education, especially art education, formalism has often been combined with theories that put individual self-expression first. This has often had anticontextualist consequences: too much history, philosophy, politics, and the like is said to be dangerous, for it may get in the way of an individual's discovering and communicating his or her own identity, or it may interfere with doing one's own thing. It will not come as a surprise to the reader that I find such a position absurd. One cannot communicate in the absence of a language or express oneself in the absence of conventions that provide clues about what one is trying to convey. I have asserted that the fact that some fiction may be false does not mean that when it contains truths about the world these truths must be irrelevant. Similarly, the fact that some people use philosophy or history to oppress does not imply that either of these is intrinsically oppressive. The more one knows about one's own culture or the cultures of others, the more successful one is likely to be in communicating within those cultures.

In recent years, several art curricula that I would describe as "contextual" have been developed. The one with which I am most familiar is discipline-based art education, in which criticism, aesthetics, and history play key roles, alongside artistic production. Much more remains to be done by way of learning how to connect the arts with life issues and with the development of the skills, knowledge, and disposition required to create meaningful lives. Exclusive concentration on formalist analysis or self-expression fails to provide sufficient guidance, I believe, for the shaping of meaningful lives. We do not simply have problems with providing students with access to the wide range of diverse cultures required in an increasingly global society. Within national cultures, we confront a plethora of ethical and civic problems—violence, emptiness, and pollution, among others. Educators (and parents, religious authorities, politicians) have failed to do much in the way of solving these. Aesthetic educators share responsibility—a responsibility that I believe can best be met with and through an aes-ethical education. We have ample evidence that students lead lives that are not meaningful or, if meaningful, derive their core from a satisfaction that comes from nonsustainable practices—activities that are demeaning, defacing, and destructive. If the goal of education is to produce sustainable communities, we have to produce individuals who become full members of groups in which each is aware of and takes responsibility for the good of the commons.

This, of course, requires all of us to reflect on what constitutes a meaningful life; it also requires that we engage our students in such reflection. Art does stimulate, particularly when people with skills for inviting and pointing direct attention to aes-ethical properties, ask questions that enrich the experience, and "aestheticize" it. The best teachers do precisely this.

In part III, I argued that in situations where both ethical and aesthetic considerations (and all other kinds) can claim relevance, there are several possibilities.

1. One kind of consideration can be so overwhelming that the import of all other kinds is dwarfed, even blocked out.
2. Considerations of one sort easily give way to others, and vice versa.
3. Considerations of both sorts can (sometimes must) simultaneously color a single experience and/or judgment.

But there is another possibility—a much more complex one and one that is, in a sense, on a different level. The difference is brought out in the following questions.

The first concerns a particular choice bounded more or less by a specific time and place. The second is what I call a "meaning of life question."

1. Should Gauguin go to Tahiti or stay with his family?
2. Should I model my life after Gauguin or Goody Two-Shoes?

Meaning of life questions deal with matters that permeate one's life. They indicate human concerns with broad value issues. For example, in discussing landscape aesthetics, J. Baird Callicott asks the following:

> Would you rather eat store-bought or home-grown? Would you rather rise to roosters crowing and birds singing or to the alarm clock? Do you want to have woods for your children to play in or roller rinks? Would you rather provide your family with the chance to see a woodcock, prairie grouse, and muskrat or more Disneylands and movies? Would you like to look at the sky from your tractor seat and see an occasional hawk and heron or just powerlines and crop dusters?[7]

His own preferences obviously lean toward the rural, but not everyone will concur. Unlike a situation in which one is forced to choose whether to build a power line that will provide many people with cheap electricity but diminish the scenic value, where some will want the power line and others will demonstrate against its construction, the rural-urban decision affects all of one's life. So does a set of alternatives like these: which of the following would you rather be or include in your circle of friends?

1. A moderately good harpsichordist who is moderately moral
2. An above average harpsichordist who is a little immoral
3. A below average harpsichordist who is entirely moral
4. A wonderful harpsichordist who is entirely immoral

Individual answers will differ here, just as they do in decisions about whether to live in the country or the city. The point is that there is a real choice here—real questions whose answers are not immediately obvious. Making choices like these requires that we think not just about occasions of specific decisions but of overall networks or patterns of choices and the adherence to the principles or consequences that these decisions involve. Artworks provide possibilities for consideration and thus contribute to making the decisions that affect patterns, not just specific decisions. We see that generosity is possible or that moderation sometimes easily gives way to excess. Making choices like the ones provided in the list requires that we think not just about occasions of particular decisions but of overall networks or patterns of choices and the adherence to the principles or consequences that these decisions involve. The larger patterns will even determine many of the particular decisions. Thus, complete answers to specific questions ("Should we build the power line?" or "Should I leave my family?" or "Should she have used goldfish to produce this painting?") will often require answering more general questions first. These are questions that should be put to students in a context in which they can consider the type of person they want to be and the sort of merit aesthetic and ethical for which they want to aim.

Take the single-mindedness that individuals admire to a greater or lesser degree in Gauguin. In chapter 5, we saw that Michael Slote and Richard McCarty think it is the passion behind it that we admire. Slote thinks that even at the end of his life Gauguin will have felt that deserting his family was wrong, for this is part of what constitutes "admirable immorality." He writes, "If the fact of immorality is not always an overriding consideration for us and if we can think better of someone for acting *without attention* [emphasis mine] to right or wrong, is it so very surprising that we should sometimes see virtue in traits that actually run counter to morality?"[8]

I think Slote is wrong to believe that we admire someone who gives no attention to right or wrong; indeed, he himself insists that Gauguin felt remorse, and how can that be explained without attention to morality? I believe that somewhere in the pattern of his life, moral threads must appear, even if they are not strands that foreground dedication to family or lead to a particular decision. But, again, people of good faith will disagree. What is important is to put such possibilities before our students.

Bernard Williams thinks we admire Gauguin only because he has been successful. But is success required? Suppose Gauguin tries to be a good father and fails. Aren't such attempts admirable? Why should artistic success be more important than success at parenting? More to the point, suppose his teachers urged Gauguin to devote his life to painting, but he died at sea? Don't we occasionally admire such attempts, even if we think there is little chance of success? Don't we want our students to aim high, even if the odds are against them? Some people admire individuals who spend their lives making enormous shrines out of pop bottles, even when they think the creations are downright ugly. Where is the success here that might make us think such creators lead meaningful lives?

Norman Dahl believes that there must be a good chance for success—that otherwise the moral risk will not be worth taking, and hence not admirable.[9] I think there is something to this, but we must, at least, be clear about the type of success involved. Depending on the goal, various lives are successful. Fulfilling one's "appointed lot" may demand admiration, or one may be a successful role model in terms of dedication to a goal but not be successful as an artist. Even if Gauguin fails to get to Tahiti, we may admire his earlier artistic successes and admire the attempt to return to his islands because it exemplifies his overall pursuit of artistic goals.

At any rate, while success may intensify our admiration, what is crucial, I think, is not simply the outcome but an overall pattern of life. Here is an artist willing to do certain things (leave a family, sacrifice goldfish) that, combined with other actions, create one kind of meaningful life. Being single-minded is only one kind of meaningful life among many. We would not want everyone to be a Gauguin, any more than we want everyone to write only the sort of music that we personally value most. We appreciate variety. Mature people do not want a world of clones— which is why the best teachers do more than attempt to replicate themselves. We do not, I would guess, even want a world of Mother Teresas. Certainly, we do not want a world of Goody Two-Shoes, for it would be deadly dull. We want some style, some flair, some risk taking, and this is why Susan Wolf is correct in saying that a life can be "perfectly wonderful" without being "perfectly moral."

Moral conflicts are as serious as they are because they relate to the general question of what sort of person we want to be, not just to what is required of us at the moment. Students need help reflecting on this. What we admire in others' lives, even when they are breaking rules we hold dear, are what can be called "pattern" virtues or traits. We would not admire Gauguin if all he did was desert his family to paint—even if he felt remorse. He must make other sacrifices: go hungry, lose sleep, thwart convention generally, give up some personal pleasures, forgo material benefits, and exert effort. The texture of a life, as well as individual actions or traits, is a subject for assessment.

These pattern virtues are connected to considerations not just about morality or aesthetics (or religion or politics or economics, etc.) but about the meaning of life generally, and the meaningful life is one in which all of these considerations will play a role, sometimes primary, sometimes secondary or tertiary. Recognition of these virtues requires taking a broad view of human lives and experiences. Several moral philosophers have argued that there is a deep connection between the ethically meaningful life and the rational life. David Wiggins, for example, argues that whatever is ethically valuable is rationally assertible.[10] Norman Dahl argues that one kind of meaningful life exhibits moral behavior, where moral behavior is understood in part as rational behavior—behavior that results from desires or motives that follow correct reasoning.[11] He grants that other kinds of meaningful lives are possible. I have advocated a life that displays merit aesthetic and ethical, for I believe it is not rational to overlook either source of value. Failure to consider either moral or aesthetic features in any case results in an impoverished life.

Dahl insists, "There are certain desires or motives that a person will come to have if she exercises reason correctly."[12] Reasoning or reflecting properly—that is, considering all relevant properties—will entail recognizing limits on both the moral and the aesthetic. There may well be reasons to desert one's family. A little flair, an occasional kicking up of those shoes for which she was so grateful, might have made Goody's life richer. I am inclined to think that there are limits on what one should do with human beings and even goldfish, in spite of the fact that the aesthetic ends are dramatic.

What should Gauguin have done? Feeling the full punch of his dilemma requires that we and our students understand that both great painters and great parents lead meaningful lives. Neither the moral nor the aesthetic always overrides the other. But we would not admire Gauguin if he had mindlessly ignored his artistic talents or his duties as parent and citizen. Lives are admirable only if *all* relevant considerations are given due attention, and decisions about particular actions to be performed reflect this.

The value judgments involved in assessing pattern virtues—deciding whether a life is meaningful—are, I have suggested, on a different level from those involved in assessing particular actions. The former demand an understanding of the holistic nature of human life of exactly the sort that art provides. There is no basis for claiming in advance that on any particular occasion one kind of consideration will take precedence over all others. In discussing this point with me, the classicist Elizabeth Belfiore has said that her immediate reaction to the goldfish painting example was such disgust that she was certain that her viewing would change on learning that a painting so was produced. However, her knowledge that the pyramids were built by slaves or that the Parthenon was built with tribute money does not diminish her appreciation of these constructions. Yet again, when she learned that some Mayan art people were engaged in various forms of torture and self-torture, her enjoyment was reduced. Her responses, she fears, are "inconsistent." I do not think it is as much a matter of inconsistency as it is of not knowing or being able to predict in advance what kinds of considerations may take first place. There are no principles here of the sort required for inconsistency to even make much sense. Like the debate over whether we should make use of the data obtained by Nazi doctors in concentration camps, people will come down on different sides. We respect their opinions, however, only if we believe they have given the matter serious attention. The skills and dispositions required to determine merit aesthetic and ethical make those opinions worth considering and worth respecting.

From the meaning-of-life level, the status of moral and aesthetic considerations seems equal; that is, one may not always override the other. Each will be bounded by the other. Aesthetic considerations will be limited by actions that are genuinely evil; moral considerations will be limited by artistic passion, or by a fear of being just plain boring. Often the very attempt to distinguish one kind of consideration from the other will fail.

Learning theory is still in its infancy. We do not know the best ways of learning how to read our own languages, let alone the best ways of learning others. The situation is even bleaker when we consider how badly we seem to be doing with the task of creating meaningful lives—lives that display merit aesthetic and ethical— for our students. We ask cultures to send us their best. But what is *best*? Again, an answer to this, or at least an answer to what is "aesthetically better," can be found in the three points stated previously.

> A is a better work of art than B if and only if sustained attention to A yields more rewards than sustained attention to B.

Choice of what to point out to Sisyphus is based on what we think deserves and repays sustained attention. If I had a chance, I would be more likely to show Sisyphus a Vermeer than a Rockwell, give him Coleman Hawkins rather than Elvis Presley to listen to. Some television (even some Scotch) repays sustained attention and contributes to ethical as well as aesthetic reflections on life issues and patterns. There will undoubtedly be times when Sisyphus wants to watch *Dallas* and drink beer, and that's all right. But we must not conclude from the fact that he once asks for these that they are all he will ever enjoy. To do so is to fail to offer him opportunities that he may find helpful and to fail to treat him with the respect that all human beings deserve.

There is only one way to decide when or if something is valuable: give it sustained attention and see if that perception and reflection is repaid. It is also essential to remember (and this brings us back to the requirement of responsible inviting) that we may be wrong. Not everything that delights us will repay the sustained attention of everyone else. Sisyphus may not like landscapes or be interested in figured bass composition for the harpsichord. Given the problems he faces, he may be more worried about perseverance than he is about selfishness. Our obligation to tell his story, if fulfilled, will guide us in making these decisions. He will have some suggestions about things that will enrich our lives, things that only someone from his tradition and with his experiences is likely to have noticed and to have reflected upon sufficiently.

We may need to make difficult choices between traditions as well as between works to point to within traditions. Not all traditions are equally good, equally deserving of attention and respect. For one thing, not all traditions give respect to human beings generally. Traditions directing attention to intrinsic properties considered worthy of perception and reflection are not, as we have seen, morally neutral. Some traditions are elitist, limiting, oppressive, or restrictive of creativity; some are simply boring. If the goal is to provide for a life that repays sustained attention to intrinsic properties, it is also to challenge, liberate, empower—to draw people into ethical deliberation of the sort that the arts provide so beautifully. Art will contribute to a meaningful life when it is not considered a frill—an activity at the periphery of a community's forms of life—but as an integral component of it. By insisting that context and criticism be parts of education, art will naturally take a place at the core. Art education, like all education, should instill and develop what in the eighteenth century were called the "five wits." These were common wit, imagination, fantasy, estimation, and memory. When art education does this, and is recognized as doing this, it will automatically be regarded as worthwhile. Information concerning history of production and judgments about what is worthy of attention put artworks where they belong—at the center of human experiences and value. It will, in short, direct attention to merit aesthetic and ethical.

Notes

Chapter One

1. Marcia Muelder Eaton, *Art and Nonart: Reflections on an Orange Crate and a Moose Call* (Cranbury, N.J.: Fairleigh Dickinson University Press, 1983); "A Sustainable Definition of Art," in *Theories of Art Today*, ed. Noell Carroll (Madison: University of Wisconsin Press, 2000).

2. Of course, this might be expressed in a language other than English.

3. Whether it extends to other species is a hotly contested debate that I shall not get into here. I tend to think that when elephants or chimpanzees "paint," they are doing little more than relieving zoo boredom, but my argument does not turn on aesthetic responses being unique to humans.

4. What follows is based largely on a paper published earlier, "The Social Construction of Aesthetic Response," *British Journal of Aesthetics*, Vol. 35, No. 2, April 1995, pp. 95–107.

5. Errol Bedford, "Emotions and Statements about Them," in *The Social Construction of Emotions*, ed. Rom Harre (Oxford: Basil Blackwell, 1986), p. 30.

6. These are the components identified by Linda Woods in "Loneliness," in Harre, p. 195.

7. James R. Averill, "The Acquisition of Emotions in Adulthood," in Harre, p. 100.

8. Charles Dickens, *David Copperfield* (first published in 1850; New York: Bantam Books, 1988, pp. 52 and 58.

9. Ronald de Sousa, *The Rationality of Emotion* (Cambridge: Massachusetts Institute of Technology Press, 1990), p. 182.

10. Rom Harre and Robert Findlay-Jones, "Emotion Talk across Time," in Harre, pp. 220–23.

11. Paul Heelas, "Emotion Talk across Cultures," in Harre, pp. 234ff.

12. Richard Eldridge, *On Moral Personhood: Philosophy, Literature, and Self-Understanding* (Chicago: University of Chicago Press, 1989), p. 10.

13. An early article in the debate is Colin Radford, "How Can We Be Moved by the Fate of Anna Karenina?" *Proceedings of the Aristotelian Society*, Suppl. Vol. 49, 1975, pp. 67–93.

14. This is true not only of aesthetic experience, I think, but of other experiences. 'Intrinsic' should be understood epistemologically not only in aesthetics but also elsewhere. However, I shall argue only for its epistemological nature with respect to an understanding of the aesthetic.

15. David Hume, "Toward a Standard of Taste," 1757, in *Essays Moral, Political, and Literary*, ed. T. H. Greene and T. H. Grosse (London: 1875).

16. Roger Scruton, "Analytic Philosophy and the Meaning of Music," in *Analytic Aesthetics*, ed. Richard Shusterman (Oxford: Basil Blackwell, 1989), p. 93.

17. Eduardo Crespo, "A Regional Variation: Emotion in Spain," in Harre, pp. 213–14.

18. For a discussion of makoto, see Paul Reasoner, "Japanese Poetry: Objectivity in Aesthetics and the Aesthetic" (Ph.D. diss., University of Minnesota, 1987).

19. Paul Guyer, "Pleasure and Society in Kant's Theory of Taste," in *Essays in Kant's Aesthetics*, ed. Ted Cohen and Paul Guyer (Chicago: University of Chicago Press, 1982), p. 51.

20. Ibid., p. 52.

21. Claire Arman-Jones, "The Thesis of Constructionism," in Harre, p. 43.

22. Barrie Falk, "The Communicability of Feeling," in *Pleasure, Preference, and Value*, ed. Eva Schaper (Cambridge: Cambridge University Press), pp. 65 and 66.

23. Ibid. p. 72.

24. Ibid. p. 74.

25. Ibid. p. 8off.

26. Arman-Jones, "The Thesis of Constructionism., p. 57.

27. Ellen Dissanayake, *What Is Art for?* (Seattle: University of Washington Press, 1988), p. 167.

Chapter Two

1. What follows is based on a previously published paper, "Where's the Spear? The Nature of Aesthetic Relevance," British Journal of Aesthetics, Vol. 32, No. 1, January, 1992, pp. 1–12.

2. H. D. F. Kitto, *Poesis: Structure and Thought* (Berkeley: University of California Press, 1966), pp. 14–15.

3. Richard Wollheim, *Painting as an Art* (Princeton, N.J.: Princeton University Press, 1987), p. 89.

4. Ibid. p. 91.

5. Peter Kivy, *Music Alone: Philosophical Reflections on the Purely Musical Experience* (Ithaca, N.Y.: Cornell University Press, 1990), p. 91.

6. Hans-Georg Gadamer, "On the Contribution of Poetry to the Search for Truth," in *The Relevance of Beauty and Other Essays* (Cambridge: Cambridge University Press, 1986), pp. 105–15.

7. I, of course, would not make this distinction, since I think that simple verses are also art.

8. Charles Hope, "Storm over the Storm," *New York Review of Books*, Vol. 14, February 1991, p. 26.

9. Marcia Muelder Eaton, "Teaching through Puzzles in the Arts, in *National Society for the Study of Education Yearbook: The Arts, Education, and Aesthetic Knowing*, ed. Ralph A. Smith and Bennett Reimer (Chicago: National Society for the Study of Education, 1991), pp. 151–168.

10. The particular example Rodriquez mentioned in private conversation was *The Big Family No. 2*, by Zhang Xiaogang.

11. Arthur Danto, "The Last Work of Art: Artworks and Real Things," in *Aesthetics: A Critical Anthology*, ed. George Dickie and R. J. Sclafani (New York: St. Martin's Press, 1977), p. 561.

12. For more on this, see Eaton, *Art and Nonart*, chapter 5.

13. For a discussion of this view, see Anthony Savile, *The Test of Time* (Oxford: Clarendon Press, 1982).

14. Barbara Herrnstein-Smith, *Contingencies of Value: Alternative Perspectives* (Cambridge: Harvard University Press, 1988), pp. 51–52.

15. *Vogue Knitting*, Fall 1990, p. 46.

16. Rainer Maria Rilke, *Requiem; and Other Poems*, trans. and ed. J. B. Leishman (London: Hogarth Press, 1949).

17. Gadamer, *The Relevance of Beauty*, p. 34.

18. Hans-Georg Gadamer, "The Festive Character of Theater," *The Relevance of Beauty and Other Essays*, p. 58.

19. Marcel Proust, "Chardin," in *Contra Sainte Beuve, suive de Nouveau Melange* (Paris, 1954), quoted in Wollheim, *Painting as an Art*, p. 98.

Chapter Three

1. This chapter is based on two earlier papers, "The Intrinsic, Non-Supervenient Nature of Aesthetic Properties," *Journal of Aesthetics and Art Criticism*, Vol. 52, No. 4, 1994 and "Intention, Supervenience, and Aesthetic Realism," *British Journal of Aesthetics*, Vol. 38, No. 3, 1998.

2. This debate has been waged primarily in the "Discussion" section of *The Journal of Aesthetics and Art Criticism*: Robert Wicks, "Supervenience and Aesthetic Judgment," Vol. 46, pp. 509–11; Nick Zangwill; "Long Live Supervenience," Vol. 50, pp. 391–422; Robert Wicks, "Supervenience and the 'Science of the Beautiful,'" Vol. 50, pp. 322–24; Nick Zangwill, "Supervenience Unthwarted: Rejoinder to Wicks," Vol. 52, pp. 466–69.

3. Robert Wicks, "Supervenience and the 'Science of the Beautiful,'" p. 323.

4. Zangwill, "Supervenience Unthwarted: Rejoinder to Wicks," p. 466.

5. Ibid., p. 468.

6. Some readers might not be ready to accept a central presupposition of all of these questions, namely, that there *are* aesthetic properties and/or that aesthetic attributions can be objectively verified or justified. Unless one is an aesthetic realist (more will be said about what this entails later) of some sort, if one thinks that aesthetic properties do not exist and that aesthetic judgments are unjustifiable, then all five problems evaporate. But I am writing for those with realist leanings.

7. Nick Zangwill, "The Beautiful, the Dainty, and the Dumpy," *British Journal of Aesthetics*, Vol. 35, No. 4, October 1995, pp. 317–29. I think adding this distinction when one is already saddled with the difficulties of the supervenient-nonsupervenient controversy only makes things messier, so I shall ignore it in what follows.

8. G. E.Moore, "The Concept of Intrinsic Value," in *Philosophical Studies* (London: Routledge & Kegan Paul, 1922), p. 261.

9. R. M. Hare, *The Logic of Morals* (Oxford: Clarendon Press, 1952), p. 145.

10. R. M. Hare, "Supervenience," *Proceedings of the Aristotelian Society*, Suppl., Vol. 63, 1984, p. 1.

11. Simon Blackburn, "Moral Realism," in *Morality and Moral Reasoning*, ed. John Casey (London: Methuen, 1971), p. 105.

12. Hare, *The Logic of Morals*, p. 3.

13. Jaegwon Kim, "Supervenience and Nomological Incommensurables," *American Philosophical Quarterly*, Vol. 15, 1978, p. 150.

14. Ibid., p. 151.

15. See Geoffrey Hellman and Frank Thompson, "Physicalism: Ontology, Determinism, and Reduction," *Journal of Philosophy*, Vol. 72, 1975, 551–64; and "Physical Materialism," *Nous*, Vol. 11, 1977, 309–45.

16. James C. Klagge, "An Alleged Difficulty concerning Moral Properties," *Mind*, Vol. 93, 1984, p. 370.

17. Ibid., p. 376.

18. I have always been puzzled by the fact that many theorists assume that color statements are not aesthetic statements. I find it quite normal for people to report preferences for and appreciation of certain colors. "I like that shade of green that permeates the world the first few weeks of spring," seems perfectly aesthetic to me. So does, "It's the red that is so dramatic." Perhaps Pettit and others would deny that they are, strictly speaking, *descriptions*. In any case, if this is to avoid being question-begging, it needs elaboration. I shall say more about this later when I discuss the difficulty of distinguishing aesthetic from non-aesthetic properties.

19. Philip Pettit, "The Possibility of Aesthetic Realism," in *Pleasure, Preference, and Value: Studies in Philosophical Aesthetics*, ed. Eva Schaper (Cambridge: Cambridge University Press, 1983), p. 18.

20. Ibid., p. 18.

21. Ibid., pp 23–26.

22. Jerrold Levinson, "Aesthetic Supervenience," *The Southern Journal of Philosophy*, Vol. 22, Suppl., 1984, p. 93.

23. John Bender, "Supervenience and the Justification of Aesthetic Judgments," *The Journal of Aesthetics and Art Criticism*, Vol. 46, 1987, p. 31.

24. Ibid., p. 31.

25. Ibid.

26. Ibid.

27. Ibid.

28. Robert Wicks, "Supervenience and Aesthetic Judgment," p. 509.

29. Zangwill, "Long Live Supervenience," p. 321.

30. John McDowell, "Values and Secondary Qualities," in *Essays on Moral Realism*, ed. Geoffrey Sayre-McCord (Ithaca, N.Y.: Cornell University Press, 1988), pp. 172–73.

31. John McDowell, "Aesthetic Value, Objectivity, and the Fabric of the World," in *Pleasure, Preference, and Value: Studies in Philosophical Aesthetics*, ed. Eva Schaper (Cambridge: Cambridge University Press, 1983), p. 8. See also P. M. S. Hacker, "Are Secondary Qualities Relative?" *Mind*, Vol. 95, 1986, pp. 180–97.

32. Simon Blackburn, "Supervenience Revisited," in *Essays on Moral Realism*, ed. Geoffrey Sayre-McCord (Ithaca, N.Y.: Cornell University Press, 1988), p. 60.

33. Ibid., p. 60.

34. Ibid., p. 64.

35. Pettit, "The Possibility of Aesthetic Realism," p. 19.

36. Monroe Beardsley, "The Descriptivist Account of Aesthetic Attributions," *Revue Internationale de Philosophie*, Vol. 28, 1974, p. 337.

37. Victoria Ball, "The Aesthetics of Color," *The Journal of Aesthetics and Art Criticism*, Vol. 23, 1964–65, pp. 441–52.

38. Goran Hermeren, *The Nature of Aesthetic Qualities* (Lund: Lund University Press, 1988), pp. 15ff.

39. Quote in William Fleming, *Art and Ideas* (New York: Holt, Rinehart, and Winston, 1974), p. 119.

40. I use 'loud' here in the sense of sound, not in its metaphorical sense of being gaudy. Tanya Rodriquez has suggested to me that there may well be a metaphorical connection, in which case hurting the ears may still be part of the meaning of the term when it refers to hurting one's eyes.

41. Norman Chase Gillespie, "Subvenient Identities and Supervenient Differences," *The Southern Journal of Philosophy*, Vol. 22, 1984, p. 113.

42. I am indebted to Michael Hancher for this example.

43. For a wonderful analysis of this, see Jon Wenstrom, "Modernist Irony" (Ph.D. diss., University of Minnesota, 1991). An example of self-protective irony provided by Wenstrom is the following. Two graduate students are discussing the Ph.D. preliminary oral exam in their department. One, who has just failed the first sitting, complains that the exams are not a real test of one's abilities. The hearer, who has passed and in fact believes they are a good test but does not want to alienate the first, says, "Oh no, these exams are the surest way ever invented to test one's deepest merit." The overstatement makes it appear that the speaker believes what he is saying is false, when in fact he believes at least a less exaggerated version of it. The speaker "protects" himself by using what is taken to be irony by the hearer. Wenstrom believes that such use of irony is common in modern poetry. Frost, he argues, often uses it when he wants to "back off" from what are probably his genuine romantic tendencies.

Chapter Four

1. Immanuel Kant, Third Critique, 1790.

2. Casken made this comment to me when we were both visiting scholars at the Rockefeller Center in Bellagio, Italy.

3. Martha Nussbaum, *Love's Knowledge* (Oxford: Oxford University Press, 1990), p. 154.

4. We did see in chapter 3 that there are some aestheticians for whom metaphysical questions are paramount, e.g., Nick Zangwill.

5. R. M. Hare, "Ontology in Ethics," in *Morality and Objectivity* (London: Routledge & Kegan Paul, 1985), p. 48.

6. Roger Scruton, "Analytic Philosophy and the Meaning of Music," in *Analytic Aesthetics*, ed. Richard Shusterman (Oxford: Basil Blackwell, 1989), p. 87.

7. In making this point, I have been influenced by Catherine Lord, "Intentionality and Realization in Aesthetic Experience," in *Aesthetic Quality and Aesthetic Experience*, ed. Michael Mitias (Wurzbrug: K&N, 1988), pp. 65–71. She may not recognize her ideas in my version!

8. Ludwig Wittgenstein, *Philosophical Investigations*, trans. G. E. M. Anscombe (Oxford: Basil Blackwell, 1958), p. 212.

9. Charles Altieri, "Style as the Man," in Shusterman, *Anallytic Aesthetics*, p. 75.

10. Goodman argued that representation cannot be captured in a nondense symbol system. See *Languages of Art* (Indianapolis: Bobbs, Merrill, 1969). I think he should take up embroidery.

11. John Bender, "Realism, Supervenience, and Irresolvable Aesthetic Disputes," *Journal of Aesthetics and Art Criticism*, Vol. 54, No. 4, Fall 1996, p. 379.

12. Ibid., p. 378.

13. For an excellent discussion of this, see David Brink, *Moral Realism and the Foundations of Ethics* (Cambridge: Cambridge University Press, 1989).

14. Bender, "Realism, Supervenience, and Irresolvable Aesthetic Disputes," p. 373.

15. For more recent work on intentions, see Noel Carroll, "Art, Intentions, and Conversations"; Gary Iseminger, "Actual Intentionalism and Hypothetical Intentionalism"; and Jerrold Levinson, "Intention and Interpretation: A Last Look," all in *Intention and Interpretation*, ed. Gary Iseminger (Philadelphia: Temple University Press, 1992); and Brian Rosebury, "Irrecoverable Intentions and Literary Interpretation," *British Journal of Aesthetics*, Vol. 37, No. 1, January 1997, pp. 15–30.

Part II

1. Richard Posner, "Against Ethical Criticism," *Philosophy and Literature*, Vol. 21, No. 1, April 1997, p. 1.

2. Ibid., p. 24.

Chapter Five

1. This chapter is based on an earlier published paper, "Integrating Moral and Aesthetic Value," *Philosophical Studies*, Vol. 67, 1992, pp. 219–40.

2. Plato in Republic 3, esp. 400–1, says that music imitates character and has a profound ethical effect. He extends this idea to the other arts. However, his view, particularly since the Renaissance, is not common. I am grateful to Elizabeth Belfiore for this example. Norman Dahl has also pointed out to me that for the Greeks 'virtue' would have encompassed both ethics and aesthetics.

3. Philippa Foot, "Are Moral Considerations Overriding?" in *Virtues and Vices and Other Essays in Moral Philosophy* (Oxford: Basil Blackwell, 1978), pp. 181–88.

4. Michael Slote, "Admirable Immorality," in *Goods and Virtues* (Oxford: Clarendon Press, 1983), pp. 77–107.

5. Ibid., p. 77.

6. Bernard Williams, "Moral Luck," in *Philosophical Papers: 1973–1980* (Cambridge: Cambridge University Press, 1981), pp. 20–39.

7. Ibid., p. 23.

8. Slote gives other examples of what he thinks constitute admirable immorality: a father who refuses to turn his son in to the police even though he knows that morality demands that he should do so and a political decision to bomb or torture in order to bring an enemy to its knees. I am not convinced by either of these examples. Parental love, for instance, can be a case of a paradigmatically morally admired trait within some moral systems. One can certainly imagine cultures in which such love would be "socially constructed" (see chapter 1) as a primary good. Foot talks about a gap between what we are told or taught and what we learn to do, and her point may be relevant here. In a "man's world," motherly love may be denigrated. By "man's world," I intend to suggest two things. First, feminist philosophers have pointed out that rule-oriented moral systems do not define the moral systems of many women. In a woman's world, it might be considered evil to turn one's child in to the authorities. Second, in the Gauguin example, it is interesting to consider how the case might change if a woman artist were to decide to desert her children and pursue a career in a far-off, exotic locale. However, it is Slote's aesthetic example that concerns me in this paper.

9. Slote, "Admirable Immorality," p. 91.

10. Owen Flanagan, "Admirable Immorality and Admirable Imperfection," *Journal of Philosophy*, Vol. 83, No. 1, 1986, pp. 41–60.

11. Ibid., p. 48.

12. Susan Wolf, "Moral Saints," *Journal of Philosophy*, Vol. 79, No. 8, August 1982, pp. 419–39.

13. Flanagan, "Admirable Immorality and Admirable Imperfection," p. 53.

14. Ibid., p.55.

15. Ibid., p. 60.

16. Marcia Baron, "On Admirable Immorality," *Ethics*, Vol. 96, No. 3, April 1986, pp. 557–66.

17. Richard McCarty, "Admirable Immorality and the Overridingness Thesis," draft.

18. Richard McCarty, "Are There Contra-Moral Virtues?" draft.

19. Two of the most influential members of the formalist school are Clive Bell and Roger Fry. See Bell's *Art* (London: Chatto & Windus, 1914) and Fry's *Vision and Design* (London: Chatto & Windus, 1920).

20. Peter Lamarque and Stein Haugom Olsen, *Truth, Fiction, and Literature: A Philosophical Perspective* (Oxford: Clarendon Press, 1994), p. 5.

21. Ibid., p. 123.

22. Ibid., p. 41.

23. Ibid., p. 45–46.

24. Ibid., p. 265.

25. Peter Lamarque, "Tragedy and Moral Value," in *Art and Its Messages*, ed. Stephen Davies (University Park: Pennsylvania State University, 1997), p. 59.

26. Ibid., pp. 63–64.

27. Lamarque and Olsen, *Truth, Fiction, and Literature*, p. 327.

28. Ibid., pp.144–45.

29. Ibid., p. 328.

30. Malcolm Budd, *Values of Art; Pictures, Poetry, and Music* (London: Penguin Books, 1995), p. 10.

31. Jerrold Levinson, "Messages in Art," in Davies, *Art and Its Messages*, p. 80.

32. Ibid., p. 82.

33. Lamarque and Olsen, *Truth, Fiction, and Literature*, p. 455.

34. Ronald W. Hepburn, "Art, Truth, and the Education of Subjectivity," *Journal of the Philosophy of Education,"* Vol. 24, No. 2, 1990, p. 187.

Chapter Six

1. This chapter is based on an earlier published paper, "Serious Problems, Serious Values: Are There Aesthetic Dilemmas?" in *Ethics and the Arts*, ed. David Fenner (New York: Garland Press, 1996), pp. 279–92.

2. Stuart Hampshire, "Logic and Appreciation," in *Aesthetics and Language*, ed. William Elton (Oxford: Basil Blackwell, 1967), pp. 162–63.

3. Many philosophers distinguish between conflicts of belief and conflicts of desire, and many assert that moral conflicts are of the latter sort. I do not want to prejudge the issue of whether moral (or aesthetic) dilemmas belong exclusively to the desire, not to the belief, category. But there is a useful distinction to be made—and, possibly, applied. Bernard Williams claims that when beliefs conflict, they either conflict obviously (i.e., are such that they clearly cannot both be true: 'It is raining' and 'It is not raining') or are by themselves consistent but would not be consistent in combination with some third belief. 'The woman is tall' and 'The woman is the boss' do not conflict, per se. But they do conflict if it turns out that 'the woman' refers to the boss, and 'The boss is short' is true. Desires, on the other hand, according to Williams, conflict when some contingent fact makes it impossible for two desires to both be satisfied. I want a drink and I want to be warm, and the drinks are out in the cold. See Bernard Williams, "Ethical Consistency," in *Essays on Moral Realism*, ed. Geoffrey Sayre-McCord (Ithaca, N.Y.: Cornell University Press, 1988), pp. 42–43. A moral conflict, he thinks, is simply "a conflict between two moral judgments that a man is disposed to make relevant in deciding what to do" (p. 45). For example, one believes one ought to do something in light of some features of a situation and ought to refrain from doing that thing in light of some other features of the same situation. Moral conflicts, he says, are more like conflicts of desire than conflicts of belief, for the discovery that two beliefs cannot be true weakens belief

(in either one or both propositions), whereas the discovery that two desires cannot both be satisfied does not serve to weaken either or both desires. I am inclined to agree with Williams, but exactly how beliefs and desires contribute to moral choices will not be crucial to my discussion.

4. I shall, for simplicity's sake, discuss dilemmas in terms of only two options; clearly, in some situations there may be more than two.

5. For this type of characterization, see Walter Sinnot-Armstrong, *Moral Dilemmas* (Oxford: Basil Blackwell, 1988), p. 29.

6. Some philosophers believe that the contradiction can be avoided by rejecting this move. See Ruth Barcan Marcus, "Moral Dilemmas and Consistency," *Journal of Philosophy*, Vol. 77, March 1980, p. 134.

7. William Styron, *Sophie's Choice* (New York: Random House, 1979).

8. Martha Nussbaum, *Love's Knowledge* (Oxford: Oxford University Press, 1992), pp. 131–32.

9. While I was a resident scholar at the Rockefeller Study Center in Bellagio, Italy, March 6-April 8, 1992, I had the opportunity to talk about these issues with the artists John Casken, Joseph Heller, and Anita Desai, who were also visiting the center. All were extremely patient and helpful. I am most grateful to the Rockefeller Foundation for their support.

10. Norman Bowie, private conversation.

11. Marcia Muelder Eaton, "James's Turn of the Speech-Act," *British Journal of Aesthetics*, Vol. 23, No. 4, Autumn 1983, pp. 33–45.

12. George Dickie, *Evaluating Art* (Philadelphia: Temple University Press, 1988).

13. In conversation.

14. "Masterpiece Is Damaged at the Louvre," *Minneapolis Star Tribune*, 11 July 1992, p. 10A.

15. I offer a fuller discussion of this in my book *Aesthetics and the Good Life* (Cranbury, N.J.: Associated University Presses, 1983).

Chapter Seven

1. Much of what follows is based on an earlier published paper, "Aesthetics: The Mother of Ethics?" *Journal of Aesthetics and Art Criticism*," Vol. 55, No. 4, Fall 1997, pp. 355–364.

2. Joseph Brodsky, "Uncommon Visage," *Poets and Writers Magazine*, March-April, 1988, p. 17.

3. "Une dependance de l'esthetique," *Chroniques de l'ermitage, Oeuvres Completes,* Vol. 4 (Paris: NRF, 1933), p. 387.

4. Mary Devereaux, "Censorship," in *Ethics and the Arts: An Anthology*, ed. David Fenner (New York: Garland Press, 1995), p. 48.

5. Noel Carroll, "Moderate Moralism" *The British Journal of Aesthetics*, Vol. 36, 1996, pp. 223–38.

6. Mark Packer, "The Aesthetic Dimension of Ethics and Law: Some Reflections on Harmless Offense," *American Philosophical Quarterly*, Vol. 33, 1996, p. 57.

7. Julia Driver, "Caesar's Wife: On the Moral Significance of Appearing Good," *Journal of Philosophy*, Vol. 89, No. 7, July 1992, p. 343.

8. Alan Goldman, *Aesthetic Value* (Boulder, Colo.: Westview Press, 1995), p. 149.

9. Brodsky, "Uncommon Visage," p. 21.

10. Wayne Booth, *The Company We Keep: An Ethics of Fiction* (Berkeley: University of California Press, 1988).

11. Elizabeth M. Wildinson and L. A. Willoughby, "Introduction" to Friedrich Schiller's *On the Aesthetic Education of Man* (first published 1794; Oxford: Clarendon Press, 1967), p. xxiii.

12. Schiller, in Ibid., p. 6.14

13. Charles Peirce, *Writings*, p. 8.255.

14. Ibid., p. 5.130

15. Ibid., p. 1.358

16. Michel Foucault, " An Aesthetic of Existence," Interview with Allesandro Fontano, *Panorama,* July 1984; reprinted in *Politics, Philosophy, Culture: Interviews and Other Writings,* Lawrence D. Kritzman, ed. (New York: Routledge, 1988), p. 49.

17. Ibid. p. 49.

18. Charles Altieri, *Canons and Consequences* (Evanston, Ill.: Northwestern University Press, 1990), pp. 227 and 228.

19. Ibid., p. 238.

20. Ibid., p. 238.

21. Sharon Welch, "An Ethics of Solidarity and Differences," in *Postmodernism, Feminism, and Cultural Politics,* ed. Henry Girous (New York: State University of New York Press, 1991), pp. 94ff.

22. Hilary Putnam, "Literature, Science, and Reflection," in *Meaning and the Moral Sciences* (Boston: Routledge & Kegan Paul, 1978), pp. 87–90; David Wiggins, "Truth, Invention, and the Meaning of Life," *Proceedings of the British Academy,* Vol. 62, 1976, pp. 331–78.

23. Sabina Lovibond, *Realism and Imagination in Ethics* (Minneapolis: University of Minnesota Press, 1983).

24. Mark Johnson, *Moral Imagination* (Chicago: University of Chicago Press, 1993), p. 31.

25. Ibid., p. 182.

26. Ibid., p. 208.

27. Ibid., pp. 210ff.

28. R. W. Hepburn, "Vision and Choice in Morality," Part 1 of a symposium in *Proceedings of the Aristotelian Society,* Suppl. Vol. 30, 1956, p. 15.

29. Iris Murdoch, "Vision and Choice in Morality." Part II of a symposium in *Proceedings of the Aristotelian Society,* Suppl. Vol. 30, 1956, p. 40.

30. Ibid., p. 39.

31. Cora Diamond, "Having a Rough Story about What Moral Philosophy Is," in *The Realist Spirit: Wittgenstein, Philosophy, and the Mind* (Cambridge, Mass.: MIT Press, 1991), pp. 374–75.

32. Ibid., p. 379.

33. Brodsky, "Uncommon Visage," p. 17.

34. Joseph Brodsky, "English Lessons from Stephen Spender," *New Yorker,* 8 January 1996, p. 59.

35. Brodsky, "Uncommon Visages," p. 17.

36. Ibid.

37. Ibid., p. 20.

38. Brodsky, "English Lessons," pp. 62 and 59.

39. Martha Nussbaum, *The Fragility of Goodness: Luck and Ethics in Greek Tragedy and Philosophy* (Cambridge: Cambridge University Press, 1986), p. 15.

40. Stuart Hampshire, "Logic and Appreciation," in *Aesthetics and Language,* ed. William Elton (Oxford: Basil Blackwell, 1967), p. 162.

41. Goldman, *Aesthetic Value*, p. 145.

42. Marcia Cavell, "Taste and Moral Sense," in *Ethics and the Arts*, ed. David Fenner (New York: Garland Press, 1996), p. 275.

43. Ibid., p. 293.

44. Ibid., p. 295.

45. R. M. Hare, *Freedom and Reason* (New York: Oxford University Press, 1965), p. 150. I am grateful to Peter Kivy for this reference.

Part III

1. This point is related to one that Thomas Nagel has made concerning the variety of sources of human value in "The Fragmentation of Value," in *Moral Dilemmas*, ed. Christopher Gowans (New York: Oxford University Press, 1987), pp. 269–82. He has argued that in addition to adherence to principles of rights and to considerations of consequences, primary sources of value include creativity and autonomy. The complexity of human nature and experience (and I would add the diversity of cultural goals and practices) preclude any built-in guarantee or a priori knowledge concerning the overridingness of any single source of value. Nagel thinks that this accounts for the existence of genuine moral dilemmas (and I shall argue in chapter 6 that the existence of genuine aesthetic dilemmas shows that aesthetic values can be as serious as moral values). I believe it also accounts for the fact that moral considerations do not always wipe out aesthetic enjoyment, and aesthetic responses do not preclude moral reflection.

2. Richard Wollheim, *Painting as an Art* (Princeton, N.J.: Princeton University Press, 1987), p. 46.

3. Foot, "Are Moral Considerations Overriding?" p. 183.

Chapter Eight

1. Much of what follows is based on an earlier published paper, "Anthony Powell and the Aesthetic Life," *Philosophy and Literature*, Vol. 9, No. 2, Fall 1985, pp. 166–83.

2. Frederick Karl, *A Reader's Guide to the Contemporary English Novel*, rev. ed. (New York: Octagon Books, 1972), p. 313.

3. I shall in my citations abbreviate these titles as follows: *QU, BM, AW, LM. CCR, KO, VB, SA, MP, BFR, TK, HSH.* I shall refer to the set of twelve as *Dance*. All page references are to the four-volume paperback edition of the novels (New York: Popular Library, 1976).

4. "A Who's Who of 'The Music of Time,'" *Time and Tide*, Vol. 41, 2 July 1960, pp. 764–65, and 9 July 1960, pp. 808–9.

5. Hilary Spurling, *Invitation to the Dance: A Guide to Anthony Powell's* Dance to the Music of Time (Boston: Little, Brown, 1977).

6. Marvin Mudrick, review of *Dance, Hudson Review*, Vol. 17, 1964, p. 119.

7. Anthony West, review of *Dance, New Yorker*, Vol. 38, 16 February 1963, p. 163.

8. Mudrick, review of *Dance*, p. 119.

9. Ibid.

10. John David Russell, *Anthony Powell, A Quintet, Sextet, and War* (Bloomington: Indiana University Press, 1970), p. 22.

11. Anthony Powell, *Afternoon Men* (Boston: Little, Brown, & Company, 1952), p. 48.

12. Ibid. p. 119.

13. Anthony Powell, *From a View to Death* (Boston: Little, Brown, 1968), p. 168.

14. Anthony Powell, *To Keep the Ball Rolling: The Memoirs of Anthony Powell, Volume II, Messengers of Day* (London: William Heinemann, 1976), p. 36.

15. Anthony Powell, *To Keep the Ball Rolling: The Memoirs of Anthony Powell, Volume I, Infants of the Spring* (London: William Heinemann, 1976), p. 28.

16. Ibid., p. 133.

17. Kingsley Amis, "Afternoon World," *Spectator*, 13 May 1955, p. 619.

18. Robert K. Morris, *The Novels of Anthony Powell* (Pittsburgh: University of Pittsburgh Press, 1968), p. 9.

19. Karl, *A Reader's Guide*, p. 243.

Chapter Nine

1. This chapter is based on a paper published earlier, "Laughing at the Death of Little Nell: Sentimental Art and Sentimental People," *American Philosophical Quarterly*, Vol. 26, No. 4, 1990, pp. 269–82.

2. Allen B. Sprague, "The date of sentimental and derivatives," *Proceedings of the Modern Language Association*, Vol. 48, 1933, pp. 303–7.

3. The connection between 'sentimental' and 'sentiment' is very interesting, for while 'sentimental' was taking on negative connotations, 'sentiment' remained neutral. In the eighteenth century, the latter was, of course, the ground of several moral theories, and indeed "sentimentalism" is still sometimes used to refer neutrally to such theories. David Hume used 'sentiment' to mean just 'feeling'; Thomas Reid used it to refer to a combination of feelings and judgments—thus combining the two Latin roots. For more on this, see J. L. Mackie, *Hume's Moral Theory* (London: Routledge & Kegan Paul, 1980); and Louis I. Bredvold, *The Natural History of Sensibility* (Detroit: Wayne State University Press, 1962). Virtue was connected with positive feelings or sentiment, vice with negative; positive sentiments were tied to beauty, and negative sentiments to ugliness. There are also important connections between 'sentimental' and 'sensibility' or the French 'sensibilite'. In France, according to Anita Brookner, *sensibilite* was largely a literary movement characterized by descriptions of characters' emotional experiences in ways meant to instruct morally. Deep feeling was considered a sure sign of virtue. In one novel, a mother decides which of two suitors should have her daughter's hand by taking them both to the theater. The one who cries throughout wins. See Anita Brookner, *Greuze: The Rise and Fall of an Eighteenth Century Phenomenon* (Greenwich, Conn.: New York Graphics, 1972). As feelings came to be equated with virtue and acting as if one felt deeply substituted for acting in accordance with moral principles, sentimentality opened itself to negative criticism.

4. Quoted in Sprague, "The date of sentimental and derivatives," p. 306.

5. Oscar Wilde, Letter to Lord Alfred Douglas, 1887, in *The Letters of Oscar Wilde*, Ed. Rupert Hart-Davis (London: Rupert Hart-Davis, 1962), p. 501.

6. Kermit Roosevelt, *A Sentimental Safari* (New York: Knopf, 1963).

7. "Theatre in the Round's *'84 Charing Cross Rd.* Lacks a Sentimental Tug," *Minneapolis Star Tribune*, 13 January 1988, p. 9Ew.

8. James C. Thomson Jr., Peter W. Stanley, and John Curtis Perry, *Sentimental Imperialists: The American Experience in East Asia* (New York: Harper & Row, 1981), p. xi.

9. "For the Love of Helga," *New York Times*, 6 February 1987, p. 26Y.

10. Quoted in Douglas C. McGill, "'Helga' Show Renews Debate on Andrew Wyeth," *New York Times*, 3 February 1987, p. K6.

11. See, for example, Herbert Ross Brown, *The Sentimental Novel in America, 1789–1860* (Durham, N.C.: Duke University Press, 1940); and E. Douglas Branch, *The Sentimental Years, 1836–1860* (New York. D. Appleton-Century Company, 1934). The contribution made by sentimentality to humanitarianism is the subject of Johannes Henrik Harder's *Observations on Some Tendencies of Sentiment and Ethics Chiefly in Minor Poetry and Essay in the Eighteenth Century until the Execution of Dr. W. Dodd in 1777* (Amsterdam: Drukkerij M. J. Portieljie, 1933). One of his observations is that melancholy is connected to humanitarianism through an interest in pain and suffering. Love of solitude, contemplation of nature, saintliness, sympathy—all features which such authors as Robert Burton and John Milton associated with melancholy—are equally associated with charity. Only when it is "false" does melancholy lead to sentimentality and not to charitable action, according to Harder.

12. Mrs. Arthur Long, F.R.S.L. (Marjorie Bowen), "A Sentimental Journey in the Indies," in *Essays by Divers Hands (Transactions of the Royal Society of Literature in the United Kingdom)*, Vol. 14, ed. by the Right Honl. Earl of Lytton (London: Oxford University Press, 1935), p. 116.

13. Ibid., p. 20.

14. For other examples of the use or explanation of 'sentimental', see Harry Austin Defarrari, *The Sentimental Moor in Spanish Literature before 1600* (Philadelphia: University of Pennsylvania Press, 1927); Michael Bell, *The Sentiment of Reality* (London: George Allen and Unwin, 1983); Geoffrey Atkinson, *The Sentimental Revolution* (Seattle: University of Washington Press, 1966); and W. F. Galloway, "The Sentimentalism of Goldsmith," *Proceedings of the Modern Language Association*, Vol. 48, 1933, pp. 1167–80.

15. Since hypocrisy and shallowness are characteristics of both insincerity and sentimentality, it may be thought that the latter is simply one form of insincerity. There are, however, important differences—indicated , for example, by the strangeness of the phrase "genuinely insincere" but not "genuinely sentimental." For discussions of sincerity, see Stuart Hampshire, "Sincerity and Singlemindedness," in his *Freedom of Mind* (Oxford: Oxford University Press, 1972), pp. 245ff.; and A. D. M. Walker, "The Ideals of Sincerity," *Mind*, Vol. 87, 1978, pp. 481–97.

16. I. A. Richards, *Practical Criticism* (New York: Harcourt, Brace, and World, 1929), pp. 242–43.

17. Ibid., p. 254.

18. Michael Tanner, "Sentimentality," *Proceedings of the Aristotelian Society*, Vol. 77, 1976–77, pp. 127–47.

19. Ibid., p. 133.

20. Ibid., pp. 136–39.

21. Ibid., p. 140.

22. Mary Midgley, "Brutality and Sentimentality," *Philosophy*, Vol. 54, 1979, p.385.

23. Mark Jefferson, "What Is Wrong with Sentimentality?" *Mind*, Vol. 92, 1983, pp. 519–29.

24. Ibid., p. 524.

25. This example was provided in private conversations.

26. Anthony Savile, *The Test of Time* (Oxford: Clarendon Press, 1982), pp. 236–50.

27. For more on this, see Malcolm Budd, "Belief and Sincerity in Poetry," in *Pleasure, Preference, and Value*, ed. Eva Schaper (Cambridge: Cambridge University Press, 1983), pp. 143–44.

28. Geoffrey Atkinson, *The Sentimental Revolution*, p. 169.

29. James Serpell, *In the Company of Animals: A Study in Human-Animal Relationships* (Oxford: Basil Blackwell, 1987).

30. Mark Jefferson, "What Is Wrong with Sentimentality?" pp. 526–28.

31. Mrs. Arthur Long (Marjorie Bowen), "A Sentimental Journey in the Indies," p. 114.

32. V. S. Naipaul, *A Bend in the River* (first published 1979; New York: Vintage Books, 1989), p. 129.

33. In this context, I think that the judgmentalist-nonjudgmentalist debate concerning the nature of emotion is relevant. Judgmentalists argue that emotion always has a belief component: pride involves the judgment that one is praiseworthy, fear the belief that an object is dangerous, and so on. See, for example, Donald Davidson, "Hume's Cognitive Theory of Pride," *Journal of Philosophy*, Vol. 73, 1976, pp. 744–57. Nonjudgmentalists argue that at least sometimes emotions are aroused without the normally associated belief being present. Patricia Greenspan gives as an example a person who, having been attacked by a dog in the past, feels a tremendous fear when old, toothless Fido enters the room. She knows Fido is not dangerous to her or to others, is willing to let her young children play with him, etc. "Emotions and Evaluations," *Pacific Philosophical Quarterly*, Vol. 62, 1981, pp. 158–69. Sentimental feelings are sometimes like this, I think. Feeling choked up, nostalgic, touched, etc., may not imply the belief that pets always get home safely, that the past was consistently blissful, or that children are always kind. Unpernicious sentimentality may be like the urge to flee the room when good, old, toothless Fido enters—more or less an involuntary reaction (and one that embarrasses us occasionally). Pernicious sentimentality, on the other hand, seems to always involve false belief or the deception of others or oneself.

34. Charles Dickens, *The Old Curiosity Shop*, ed. Angus Easson (Hammondsworth, England: Penguin Books, 1987), p. 440.

35. Ibid., pp. 652 and 654.

36. Ibid., p. 655.

37. Ibid., p. 620.

38. Joe Mitchell Chapple, ed., *Heart Throb* (New York: National Magazine, 1904).

39. Ellen Goodman, "Drama Critics and Voter Cynics," *Minneapolis Star-Tribune*, 30 September 1988, p. 16A.

40. Norman Dahl, "Morality and the Meaning of Life: Some First Thoughts," *Canadian Journal of Philosophy*, Vol. 17, 1987, pp. 1–22.

41. Gustave Flaubert, *Sentimental Education*, trans. Robert Baldrich (Hammondsworth, England: Penguin Classics, 1964), p. 286. For a discussion of Flaubert's depiction of sentimentality, see Peter Cortland, *Sentiment in Flaubert's Education Sentimentale* (Muncie, Ind.: Ball State University Press, 1966); *The Sentimental Adventure* (The Hague: Mouton, 1967).

42. Bruce Lebus, private conversations and student paper.

Chapter Ten

1. Colin McGinn, *Ethics, Evil, and Fiction* (Oxford: Clarendon Press, 1997) pp. 1–2, 175–77.

2. Berys Gaut, "The Ethical Criticism of Art," in *Aesthetics and Ethics: Essays at the Intersection,* ed. Jerrold Levinson (Cambridge: Cambridge Univerity Press, 1998), p. 182.

3. Richard Miller, "Three Versions of Objectivity: Aesthetic, Moral, and Scientific," in Levinson, *Aesthetics and Ethics*, p. 26.

4. Ibid., p. 32.

5. Peter Railton, "Aesthetic Value, Moral Value, and the Ambitions of Naturalism," in Levinson, *Aesthetics and Ethics*, p. 60.

6. Ibid., p. 63.

7. Ibid., p. 67.

8. Stephen Davies, "Introduction," in *Art and Its Messages* (University Park: Pennsylvania State University Press, 1997), p. 11.

9. Jenefer Robinson, "L'Education Sentimentale," in Davies, *Art and Its Messages*, p. 48.

10. T. J. Diffey, "What Can We Learn From Art?" in Davies, *Art and Its Messages*, p. 29.

11. Peter Lamarque, "Tragedy and Moral Value," in Davies, *Art and Its Messages*, p. 59.

12. Karen Hanson, "How Bad Can Good Art Be?" in Levinson, *Aesthetics and Ethics*, p. 215.

13. Berys Gaut, "The Ethical Criticism of Art," in Levinson, *Aesthetics and Ethics*, p. 194.

14. Ibid., p. 195.

15. Eva Dadlez, *What's Hecuba to Him? Fictional Events and Actual Emotions* (University Park: Pennsylvania State University Press, 1997), pp. 103–8.

16. Hanson, "How Bad Can Good Art Be?" p. 221.

17. Northrup Frye, *The Educated Imagination* (Bloomington: Indiana University Press, 1964), p. 64.

18. Noel Carroll, "Art, Narrative, and Moral Understanding," in Levinson, *Aesthetics and Ethics*, p. 126.

19. Ibid., p. 136.

20. Ibid., p. 138.

21. Ibid., p. 142.

22. Eileen John, "Reading Fiction and Conceptual Knowledge: Philosophical Thought in Literary Context," *Journal of Aesthetics and Art Criticism*, Vol. 56, No. 4, Fall 1998, p. 332.

23. Peter Kivy, *Philosophies of Art: An Essay in Differences* (Cambridge: Cambridge University Press, 1997), p. 179ff.

24. Mary Devereaux, "Beauty and Evil: The Case of Leni Reifenstahl's *Triumph of the Will*," in Levinson, *Aesthetics and Ethics*, pp. 227–50.

25. Rob van Gerwen, "Artistic Excellence as Moral Category," as yet unpublished.

26. Devereaux, "Beauty and Evil ," p. 246.

27. James C. Anderson and Jeffrey T. Dean, "Moderate Autonomis," *British Journal of Aesthetics*, Vol. 38, No. 2, April 1998, p. 165.

28. Ibid., p. 164.

29. Kivy, *Philosophies of Art*.

30. Charles Frazier, *Cold Mountain* (New York: Atlantic Monthly Press, 1997), p. 14.

31. Watty Piper, *The Little Engine That Could* (first published 1930; Uhrichsville, Ohio: Barbour Publishing, 1997).

32. Leo Tolstoy, *What Is Art?* 1898.

33. Oscar Wilde, *The Selfish Giant* (first published 1890; New York: Scholastic, 1984,) no page numbers provided.

34. Jenefer Robinson, "L'Education Sentimentale," pp. 42ff.

35. Richard Eldridge, *Moral Personhood* (Chicago: The University of Chicago Press, 1989), p. 33.

36. For a detailed analysis of this technique, see Marcia Muelder Eaton, "James' Turn of the Speech-Act," *British Journal of Aesthetics*, Vol. 25, No. 4, Autumn 1985, pp. 166–83.

37. Martha Nussbaum, *The Fragility of Goodness: Luck and Ethics in Greek Tragedy and Philosophy* (Cambridge: Cambridge University Press, 1986), p. 45.

38. Henry James, *The Sacred Fount* (first published 1901; New York: Grove Press, 1953), p. 111.

39. Eileen John, "Reading Fiction and Conceptual Knowledge," p. 345.

40. Iris Murdoch, *The Philosopher's Pupil* (London: Penguin Books, 1983), p. 53.

41. Hugo A. Meynell, *The Nature of Aesthetic Value* (Albany: State University of New York Press, 1986), p. 40.

42. Anthony Powell, *A Question of Upbringing* (first published 1951;New York: Popular Library, 1976), p. 2.

43. An excellent description of Picasso's use of distorted figures and other intrinsic properties is provided by Anthony Blunt, *Picasso's 'Guernica'* (London: Oxford University Press, 1969).

44. E. F. Granell, *Picasso's Guernica: The End of a Spanish Era* (Ann Arbor, Mich.: UMI Research Press, 1967), p. 8.

45. Valerie A. Briginshaw, "Analysis of Variation in Choreography and Performance: Swan Lake Act II Pas de Deux," in *Dance Analysis: Theory and Practice,* ed. Janet Adshead (London: Dance Books, 1988), p. 132.

46. Christine M. Lomas, "Art and the Community: Breaking the Aesthetic of Disempowerment," in *Dance, Power, and Difference: Critical and Feminist Perspectives on Dance Education,* ed. Sherry S. Shapiro (Champaign, Ill.: Human Kinetics Publishers, 1998), pp. 149–70.

47. Malcolm Budd, *Values of Art: Pictures, Poetry, and Music* (London: Penguin Books, 1995), pp. 167ff.

48. Graham McFee, "Art and Life," unpublished paper read at conference on aesthetics and ethics, University of Utrecht, December 1998.

49. Iris Murdoch, *The Sovereignty of Good* (London: Routledge & Kegan Paul, 1970), p. 65.

50. Richard Eldridge, *On Moral Personhood* (Chicago: The University of Chicago Press, 1989), p. 165.

51. Eva Dadlez, *What's Hecuba to Him?* p. 144.

52. John Berger, *Ways of Seeing* (London: Penguin Books, 1972).

Chapter Eleven

1. Richard Posner, "Against Ethical Criticism," *Philosophy and Literature,* Vol. 21. No. 1, April 1997, p. 7.

2. For example, see Stephen Toulmin, *An Examination of the Place of Reason in Ethics* (Cambridge: Cambridge University Press, 1950); and R. M. Hare, *The Language of Morals* (Oxford: Clarendon Press, 1952).

3. Richard Eldridge, *On Moral Personhood: Philosophy, Literature, Criticism, and Self-Understanding* (Chicago: University of Chicago Press, 1989), p. 4.

4. Ibid., p. 67.

5. Peter Lamarque and Stein Olsen, *Truth, Fiction, and Literature,* pp. 390–91.

6. Kendall Walton, "Appreciating Fictions: Suspending Disbelief or Pretending Belief," *Depositio,* Vol. 5, No. 13–14, pp. 1–18. I am not accusing Walton himself of being a separatist, only of providing some ammunition to those who are.

7. Susan Feagin, "Paintings and Their Places," in *Art and Its Messages,* ed. Stephen Davies (University Park: Pennsylvania State University Press, 1997), p. 23.

8. Ibid., p. 24.

9. Noel Carroll, "Art, Narrative, and Moral Understanding," in *Aesthetics and Ethics: Essays at the Intersection,* ed. Jerrold Levinson (Camridge: Cambridge University Press, 1998), p. 131.

10. A controversy related to the make-believe debate concerns the roles of sympathy and empathy in our encounters with fiction. I have participated in this discussion and obviously

think it interesting and important. I think both sympathy and empathy are sometimes involved in aesthetic experiences and may even be necessary for their to be a moral response. However, I shall not add to the discussion of empathy in this volume. See Susan Feagin, *Reading with Feeling* (Ithaca: Cornell University Press, 1996), p. 83f.

11. E. M. Dadlez, *What's Hecuba to Him?* pp. 49–50.

12. Ibid., pp. 157–58.

13. Joseph Brodsky, "English Lessons from Stephen Spender," *New Yorker*, 1 January 1996, p. 59.

14. Martha Nussbaum, *The Fragility of Goodness*, p. 69.

15. Ibid., p. 364.

16. V. S. Naipaul, *The Bend in the River*, p. 47.

17. Posner, "Against Ethical Criticism," p. 11.

18. Iris Murdoch, *The Message to the Planet* (New York: Penguin Books, 1991), pp. 222–24.

19. Ronald W. Hepburn, "Art, Truth, and the Education of Subjectivity," *Journal of the Philosophy of Education*, Vol. 24, No. 2, 1990, p. 189.

20. Gregory Currie, "Realism of Character and the Value of Fiction," in Levinson, *Aesthetics and Ethics*, p. 163.

21. Richard Eldridge, *On Moral Personhood*, p. 16.

22. Ibid., p. 151.

23. Hepburn, "Art, Truth, and the Education of Subjectivity," p. 190.

24. Dadlez, *What's Hecuba to Him?* p. 195.

25. Nussbaum, *The Fragility of Goodness*, p. 5.

26. I believe that both good art and bad art figure in our lives. It is sad when the only art that people engage with is not very challenging—does not demand sustained attention. The stories from which individuals glean moral principles or models for life or ethical deliberation are often not very admirable. But that soap operas as well as literary masterpieces figure in our making sense of the world seems to me obvious. There are people who don't seem very concerned with making sense of human behavior: mathematics or carpentry consumes them and gives meaning to their lives. I tend to think that lack of interest in other people is a moral failure, but I shall not attempt to prove that here!

27. Ibid., p. 54.

28. Rob van Gerwen, *Art and Experience* (Utrecht: University of Utrecht, Department of Philosophy, 1996), pp. 140, 182.

29. The terms 'imagination', 'sensation', 'perception'. etc., are, of course, used very differently by different authors, and one must be careful not to be confused. As I use 'perceive', it is restricted to sensation; my term 'attention', which involves both sensation and reflection, is a bit closer to van Gerwen's 'perception'. However, he believes that perception is immediate; I believe that attention may be mediated.

30. Peter Brooks, *Reading for Plot* (New York: Vintage Books, 1984), p. 3. This passage is quoted in Richard Eldridge, *On Moral Personhood*, p. 11.

31. Nussbaum, *The Fragility of Goodness*, p. 28.

32. Oliver Sacks, "Neurology and the Soul," *New York Review of Books*, 22 November 1990, p. 46.

33. "All," of course, may be too strong. I am talking about normal, relatively reasonable, relatively mature people. Sacks's examples prove that some mentally ill people have the urge to narrative. There may be others, psychopaths or autistics, for example, who do not.

34. Ford Madox Ford, *The Good Soldier* (first published 1915; London: Penguin Books, 1988), p. 13.

35. Connie Palmen, *The Laws*, trans.Richard Huijing (New York: George Braziller, 1993), p. 22.

36. Michel Foucault, "An Aesthetic of Existence," interview with Allesandro Fontano, *Panorama*, 1984; reprinted in *Politics, Philosophy, Culture: Interviews and Other Writings*, Allesandro Fontano, ed. (New York: Routledge, 1988), p. 49.

37. Mark Bernstein, "Well-Being," *American Philosophical Quarterly*, Vol. 35, No. 1, 1998, pp. 39–40.

38. Ibid., p. 45.

39. Connie Palmen, *The Laws*, p. 22.

40. Sarah Conly, "Objectivity of Morals and Subjectivity of Agents," *American Philosophical Quarterly*, Vol. 22, No. 4, October 1985, p. 281.

41. David Novitz, *The Boundaries of Art* (Philadelphia: Temple University Press, 1992).

42. Ibid., p. 281.

43. Ibid., p. 282.

44. Ted Cohen, "On Consistency in One's Personal Aesthetics," in Levinson, *Aesthetics and Ethics*, p. 113.

45. Eldridge, *On Moral Personhood*, p. 25.

46. Ibid. p. 20.

47. Nussbaum, *The Fragility of Goodness*, p. 68.

48. Quoted in Hugo A. Meynell, *The Nature of Aesthetic Value* (Albany: State University of New York Press, 1986), p. 26.

49. Nussbaum, *The Fragility of Goodness*, p. 389.

50. There may be some qualitative differences in gossip between men and between women, but probably no quantitative differences. See Campbell Leaper and Heithre Holliday, "Gossip in Same-Gender and Cross-Gender Friends' Conversations," *Personal Relationships*, Vol. 2, 1995, pp. 237–46.

51. Norbert Elias and John L. Scotson, *The Established and the Outsiders* (London: Frank Cass, 1965); "News from Behind My Hand: Gossips in Organizations," *Organization Studies*, Vol. 14, No. 1, 1993, pp. 23–36.

52. Melainie Tebbutt, *Women's Talk, A Social History of 'Gossip' in Working-class Neighbourhoods, 1880–1960)*, (Aldershot, England: Scolar Press, 1995).

53. Jorg R. Bergmann, *Discreet Indiscretions, The Social Organization of Gossip* (New York: Aldine de Gruyter, 1987), pp. 26–33.

54. Gregory Currie, "The Moral Psychology of Fiction," in Davies, *Art and Its Messages*, p. 51.

55. Anthony Powell, *At Lady Molly's* (New York: Popular Library, 1976), p. 66.

56. Ibid., p. 53.

57. William Maxwell, *So Long, See You Tomorrow* (New York: Vintage Books, 1996).

58. Ibid., p. 28.

59. Ibid., p. 31.

60. Ibid., p. 43.

61. Ibid., p. 49.

62. Ibid., p. 51.

63. Ibid., pp. 55–56.

64. Ibid., p. 134.

65. Ibid., p. 135.

Chapter Twelve

1. Much of this chapter is based on earlier published papers, "The Beauty That Requires Health," a chapter in *Placing Nature: Culture and Landscape Ecology*, ed. Joan Nassauer (Washington, D.C.: Island Press, 1997, and reprinted by permission of Island Press.); "Fact and Fiction in the Appreciation of Nature," *Journal of Aesthetics and Art Criticism*, Vol. 56, No. 2, Spring 1998, pp. 149–55.

2. Kenneth Clark, *Landscapes into Art* (London: John Murray, 1949), p. 3.

3. Immanuel Kant, *Critique of Judgment*, see chap. 4, n. 1. Unfortunately Kant's position is not with problems; he seems to contradict himself here, for elsewhere in this *Critique* he insists that pleasure taken in nature is separate from morality. For a discussion of this, see Malcolm Budd, "Kant on Aesthetic Appreciation, Part II," *British Journal of Aesthetics*, Vol. 38, No. 2, April 1998, pp. 117–26.

4. C. H. Nilon, "Urban Wildlife Management in 2020," in *2020 Vision: Meeting the Fish and Wildlife Conservation Challenge for the 21st Century*, ed. T. J. Peterle, Proceedings of a symposium held at the fifty-third Midwest Fish and Wildlife Conference, Des Moines, Iowa, 3 December 1991, p. 61.

5. Aldo Leopold, "The Land Ethic," in *Sand County Almanac* (London: Oxford University Press, 1996), p. 61.

6. For a discussion of this position, see Stan Godlovitch, "Valuing Nature," *British Journal of Aesthetics*, Vol. 38, No. 2, 1998, pp. 180–97.

7. Allen Carlson, "Appreciation and the Natural Environment," *Journal of Aesthetics and Art Criticism*, Vol. 37, No. 3, Spring 1979, pp. 267–76. I have a minor quibble with Carlson's view that nature is "unproduced." If scientists and designers are right about the extent of human dominance in the global landscape, then nature is becoming less and less unproduced. Certainly many environments typically described as "natural" are highly designed and managed. Indeed, many ecologists and landscape architects have recently drawn attention to the extent to which people are made to think or feel as if they are "out in nature" when, in fact, they are in highly artificial, even deceptive landscapes. A related confusion comes from widespread attitudes that exclude human beings from nature. Too often the very individuals who urge a renewed sense of human beings' connectedness with other organisms also talk as if people are enemies of nature. Some theorists have stopped using the term. Where I want to make it clear that I am including the role of humans in landscapes or ecosystems, I shall refer to more or less "pristine" landscapes. This difference aside, I believe that Carlson's question, Do we appreciate nature in the way we appreciate art? is an extremely important one, as is the answer that he gives.

8. J. T. Lyle, *Regenerative Design for Sustainable Development* (New York: Wiley, 1994), p. 99.

9. Carlson, "Appreciation and the Natural Environment," p. 273.

10. Allen Carlson, "Nature, Aesthetic Judgment, and Objectivity," *Journal of Aesthetics and Art Criticism*, Vol. 40, No. 1, Fall 1981, p. 24. Carlson and Arnold Berleant have engaged in a debate about the nature of aesthetics and the extent to which objects with the special status of artworks regarded in a special way are the central focus of aesthetic experience. Berleant has called for an "aesthetics of engagement," in which one's whole being is relevant. In this passage of Carlson's I think the debate between him and Berleant fades, insofar as it is nature rather than art that they are interested in. An exchange between these two theories is found in *Journal of Aesthetics and Art Criticism*, Vol. 52, Spring 1994, pp. 237–41.

11. Quoted in R. T. T. Forman, "Ecologically Sustainable Landscapes: The Role of Spatial Configuration," in *Changing Landscapes: An Ecological Perspective*, ed. I. S. Zonneveld and

R.. T. T. Forman (New York: Springer-Verlag, 1990), p. 262. Some theorists worry about sustainable development, a term that many consider an oxymoron. Stability, richness, productivity, and diversity of species are all relevant, but some of these factors pay a more central role in some theories of sustainability than in others. See, for example, J. T. Lyle, *Design for Human Ecosystems: Landscape, Land Use, and Natural Resources* (New York: Van Nostrand Reinhold, 1985).

12. For a discussion of this, see Clive Pointing, *A Green History of the World* (New York: St. Martin's Press, 1991).

13. Kenneth Clark, *Looking at Pictures* (London: John Murray, 1960), p. 16.

14. R. W. Hepburn, "Trivial and Serious in Aesthetic Appreciation of Nature, in *Landscapes: Natural Beauty and the Arts*, ed. S. Keman and I. Gaskill (Cambridge: Cambridge University Press, 1993), p. 68.

15. Emily Brady, "Imagination and the Aesthetic Experience," *Journal of Aesthetics and Art Criticism*, Vol. 56, No. 2, Spring 1998, p. 139.

16. R. W. Hepburn, "Landscape and the Metaphysical Imagination," *Environmental Values*, Vol. 5, 1996, p. 191.

17. Ibid., p. 143.

18. Ibid., p. 144.

19. Ibid., p. 145.

20. Ibid., p. 146.

21. Felix Salten, *Bambi*, trans. Whittaker Chambers (New York: Simon and Schuster, 1928), p. 16.

22. For a more extensive discussion of the role *Bambi* has played in shaping views toward nature, see Ralph H. Lutts, "The Trouble with *Bambi*," *Forest and Conservation History*, Vol. 4, October 1992, pp. 160–71.

23. Philip Terry, "The Sublime, the Beautiful, and the Swamp: Getting the Humanities into Environmental Studies," unpublished paper; American Culture Studies Program, Bowling Green University.

24. Richard T. Forman, *Land Mosaics: The Ecology of Landscapes and Regions* (Cambridge: Cambridge University Press, 1995), p. 10.

25. Noel Carroll, "On Being Moved by Nature: Between Religion and Natural History," in *Arguing about Art*, ed. A. Neill and A. Ridley (New York: McGraw-Hill, 1995), p. 140.

26. Stan Godlovitch, "Icebreakers: Environmentalism and Natural Aesthetics," *Journal of Applied Philosophy*, Vol. 11, 1994, pp. 15–30. Carlson has responded to Carroll and Godlovitch in "Nature, Aesthetic Appreciation, and Knowledge," *Journal of Aesthetics and Art Criticism*, Vol. 53, No. 4, Fall 1995, pp. 393–400.

27. R. F. Noss and B. Csuti, "Habitat Formation," in *Principles of Conservation Biology*, ed. G. K. Meffe and C. R. Carrol (Sunderland, Mass.: Sinauer, 1993).

28. For more on this, see Joan Nassauer, "Cultural Sustainability: Aligning Aesthetics and Ecology," in *Placing Nature: Culture and Landscape Ecology*, ed. Joan Nassauer (Washington, D.C.: Island Press, 1997, pp. 65–84.

29. Joan Nassauer, "The Appearance of Ecological Systems as a Matter of Policy," *Landscape Ecology*, Vol. 6, No. 4, 1992, p. 248.

30. In proposing this, I am also indebted to Kendall Walton's important work, "Categories of Art," *Philosophical Review*, Vol. 79, 1970, pp. 334–67; and to Arnold Berleant's *The Aesthetics of the Environment* (Philadelphia: Temple University Press, 1992).

31. W. S. Alverson, W. Kuhlmann, and D. M. Waller, *Wild Forests* (Washington, D.C.: Island Press, 1994), p. 75. Fascinating "perceivable facts" have been uncovered by attending to less visible holistic connections between fragmentation, edge increase, corridor inter-

ruption, and so on. For example, red-headed woodpeckers seem not to be sensitive to forest area, whereas pileated woodpeckers are never found breeding in forests of less than a hundred hectares. And it is not only spatial scale that demands attention. One must also attend to temporal scale. What will a particular seashore look like in a hundred or a thousand years if certain practices are carried out now? Is it true, as Clive Ponting says (*A Green History of the World*, p. 23), that an uncultivated patch in many parts of England would revert to oak and ash forest in 150 years? For an interesting discussion of geological effects on the landscape and on human history, see H. R. Muelder and D. M. Delo, *Years of This Land* (New York: Appleton-Century, 1943); and E. Cushing, *Quarternary Landscapes* (Minneapolis: University of Minnesota Press, 1991).

32. Lyle, *Design for Human Ecosystems*, p. 77.

33. Here it is obvious how indebted I am to Kendall Walton's "Categories of Art." He argues that one must know the appropriate category of a work, for example, epic or sonnet, to fully and correctly experience it. Although his theory of the category determinedness of experiences of artworks explicitly addresses artworks as wholes, what he says can easily be extended to parts, for there will subcategories that related to parts of epics or parts of symphonies and that thus distinguish one type of epic or symphony from another. Carlson discusses categories in nature that are analogous to Walton's categories of art in "Nature, Aesthetic Judgment, and Objectivity." In what follows, I attempt to give a fuller account of this possibility.

34. P. C. Hellmund, "A Model for Ecological Greenway Design," in *Ecology of Greenways*, ed. D. S. Smith and P. C. Hellmund (Minneapolis: University of Minnesota Press, 1993), p. 123.

35. J. B. Jackson, *A Sense of Place, A Sense of Time* (New Haven: Yale University Press, 1994), p. 102.

36. Ibid., p. 195.

37. Ibid., p. 62.

38. R. F. Noss and A. Y. Cooperrider, *Saving Nature's Legacy* (Washington, D.C.: Island Press, 1994), p. 14.

39. Ibid., p. 22.

40. Quoted in Ibid., p. 22.

41. John McPhee, *Encounters of the Archdruid* (New York: Farrar, Straus, & Giroux, 1971), p.29.

42. John Lyle, *Design for Human Ecosystems*, p. 76.

43. Hepburn, "Trivial and Serious in Aesthetic Appreciation of Nature," p. 65.

44. Martin Warnke, *The Political Landscape* (Cambridge: Harvard University Press, 1995).

45. Curt Meine, "Inherit the Grid," in Nassauer, *Placing Nature*, pp. 45–64.

46. See Judith A. Martin and Sam Bass Warner Jr., "Urban Conservation: Sociable, Green, and Affordable," in Nassauer, *Placing Nature*, pp. 109–22.

47. For a discussion of these preferences, see T. R. Herzoz, "A Cognitive Analysis of Preference for Urban Nature," *Journal of Environmental Psychology*, Vol. 9, 1989, pp. 27–43; and Rachel Kaplan, "The Role of Nature in the Urban Context," in *Behavior and the Natural Environment*, ed. I. Altman and J. F. Wohlwill (New York: Plenum, 1983).

48. Joan Nassauer, "Messy Ecosystems, Orderly Frames," *Landscape Journal*, Vol. 14, 1995, pp. 161–70.

49. Chin is not the only artist who has engaged in such experiments. In 1983, for example, Joseph Beuys planned the "Spufeld Altenwalder Project" for Hamburg. Trees and shrubs were planted that would help to bind toxic substances in the soil and groundwater. Other

artists such as Alan Sonfist have created earthworks that similarly challenged existing categories.

50. The catalog for an exhibit of Hull's work, "Visions of America: Landscapes as Metaphors in the Late Twentieth Century," shown at the Denver Art Museum and the Columbus Museum of Art, provides an excellent sample of contemporary landscape artworks and discussions of them by prominent critics (New York: Abrams, 1994).

51. Mara Miller, *The Garden as Art* (Albany: State University of New York Press, 1993), p. 15.

52. Ibid., p.54.

53. Rutherford H. Platt, "From Commons to Commons: Evolving Concepts of Open Space in North American Cities," in *The Ecological City: Preserving and Restoring Urban Biodiversity*, ed. R. H. Platt, R. A. Rowntree, and P. C. Muick (Amherst: University of Massachusetts Press, 1994).

54. Martin and Warner, "Urban Conservation."

55. Joan Nassauer, "Aesthetic Objectives for Agricultural Policy," *Journal of Soil and Water Conservation*, Vol. 44, No. 4, 1989; and "Landscape Care: Perceptions of Local People in Landscape Ecology and Sustainable Development," in *Landscape and Land Use Planning*, Vol. 8 (Washington, D.C.: American Society of Landscape Architects, 1988).

56. See, for example, J. R. Stilgoe, *Common Landscapes of America, 1589–1845* (New Haven: Yale University Press, 1982); and M. H. Segall, "Visual Art: Some Prospects in Cross-Cultural Psychology," in *Beyond Aesthetics*, ed. D. R. Brotherwell (London: Thames & Hudson, 1976).

57. Nassauer, "Cultural Sustainabilty: Aligning Aesthetics and Ecology."

58. See, for example, J. F. Wohlwill and G. Harris, "Response to Congruity or Contrast for Man-made Features in Natural Recreation Settings," *Leisure Sciences*, Vol. 3, 1994, pp. 349–65.

59. For a discussion of recent developments in ways in which landscape architects are trying to take due account of aesthetic values, see Paul H. Gobster, "An Ecological Aesthetic for Forest Landscape Management," *Landscape Journal*, Vol. 18, No. 1, Spring 1999, pp. 54–64.

60. Joan Nassauer, "The Appearance of Ecological Systems as a Matter of Policy."

Chapter Thirteen

1. Evan Mauer, "Keynote Speech at Inauguration of Mayor Sharon Sayles-Belton," January 2, 1998. Typescript available from Minneapolis Institute of Arts, Minneapolis, p. 6.

2. Eliot Eisner, "Does Experience in the Arts Boost Academic Achievement?" paper delivered at conference on arts in the workplace, sponsored by Getty Education Institute, Los Angeles, 1997, typescript, p. 1.

3. Ibid., p. 8.

4. For an analysis of the aesthetic and other social aspects of this, see Clifford Goertz, "Deep Play: Notes of the Balinese Cockfight," in *The Interpretation of Cultures* (New York: Basic Books, 1973), pp. 412–53. I am grateful to Ronald Moore for this example.

5. I have been tremendously influenced here by the work of Robert Terry. See his *Authentic Leadership* (San Francisco: Jossey-Bass Publishers, 1993).

6. Erving Goffman, *Encounters: Two Studies in the Sociology of Interaction* (Indianapolis: Bobbs Merrill, 1962). In board games, rules of relevance dictate which features of the situation matter. In chess, for example, the material out of which the pieces are made is irrelevant; initial placement of tokens on the board is relevant. Rules of realized resources tell us

what is real. For example, the queen in chess is not a real queen outside the boundaries of the game; within the game only "she" can move in certain ways. Transformation rules allocate resources. In chess, usually each player gets the same number of pieces, but if the group decides that handicapping will create a better game, then one player may receive or take fewer pieces. Obviously, in terms of these particular rules, the board game model does not apply directly to art. Something like rules of relevance are at work (the colors of a painting matter; its temperature does not), as are rules of realized resources (in one sense, a painting may *really* be Queen Elizabeth I, in another sense, obviously not). Transformation rules, at least interpreted as resource allocation, are not applicable. (There may be activities within the general rubric of artistic activity—say, museum going—in which this is relevant.)

7. Ibid., p. 38.

8. Ibid., p. 44.

9. Ibid., p. 44.

10. Paul Guyer, "Pleasure and Society in Kant's Theory of Taste," in *Essays in Kant's Aesthetics*, ed. Ted Cohen and Paul Guyer (Chicago: University of Chicago Press, 1982), pp. 51 and 52.

11. Ibid., p. 40.

12. Eisner, "Does Experience in the Arts Boost Academic Achievement?" p. 15.

13. Redmond O'Hanlon, *No Mercy: A Journey to the Heart of the Congo* (New York: Alfred A. Knopf, 1997), p. 336. I am grateful to Laurie Hall Muelder for this example.

14. For discussions of ways in which the artists John T. Scott and Kosen Ohtsubo have interpreted the necessity for using traditions from the past to meet present and future needs of a community, see Marcia Muelder Eaton, *What about Beauty?* (Minneapolis: University of Minnesota Press, 1998).

15. Daniel Jacobson, "Sir Philip Sidney's Dilemma," *Journal of Aesthetics and Art Criticism,* Vol. 54, No. 4, Fall 1996, p. 335.

16. Isaiah Berlin, "The Romantic Revolution," in *The Sense of Reality, Studies in Ideas and Their History,* ed. Henry Hardy (New York: Farrar, Straus and Giroux, 1996), pp. 168–93.

17. T. Allan Comp, "A Place of Regeneration," *Forecast,* Spring-Summer, 1997, pp. 15–18.

18. Jean Bethke Elshtain, "Communities and Community: Critique and Retrieval" in *Diversity and Community: A Critical Reader,* ed. Philip Alperson (New York and Oxford: Blackwell Publishers, 2001).

19. William McNeill, review of Jared Diamond's *Guns, Germs and Steel: The Fate of Human Societies, New York Review of Books,* 15 May 1997, pp. 49–50.

20. Murray Edelman, *From Art to Politics: How Artistic Creations Shape Political Conceptions* (Chicago: University of Chicago Press, 1994), p. 9.

21. Ibid., p. 40.

22. Ibid., p. 102.

23. Cass Sunstein, "A New Deal for Free Speech," talk delivered at the Understanding Communities conference at the University of Louisville, 27 May 1998.

24. For a discussion of these issues, see *Diversity and Community: A Critical Reader,* ed. Philip Alperson (New York and Oxford: Blackwell Publishers, 2001).

25. Yuriko Saito, "The Aesthetics of Unscenic Nature," *Journal of Aesthetics and Art Criticism,* Vol. 56, No. 1, 1998, p. 103.

26. Leo Tolstoy, *What Is Art?* 1896.

27. For an excellent discussion of mass art and the generally bad rap it has gotten from philosophers, see Noel Carroll, *A Philosophy of Mass Art* (Oxford: Oxford University Press, 1998). With Carroll, I believe that there is nothing incompatible about having mass art that is also good art.

28. Richard Anderson, *Calliope's Sisters: A Comparative Study of Philosophies of Art* (Englewood Cliffs, N.J.: Prentice Hall, 1990), p. 152.

29. Harry Mulisch, *The Discovery of Heaven*, trans. Paul Vincent (New York: Penguin Books, 1996), p. 56.

Chapter Fourteen

1. Albert Camus, *The Myth of Sisyphus and Other Essays*, trans. Justin O'Brien (New York: Alfred Knopf, 1955), p. 5.

2. Ibid., p. 15.

3. Ibid., p. 123.

4. Ibid., p. 123.

5. For more on this, see David Wiggins, "Truth, Invention, and the Meaning of Life," *Proceedings of the British Academy*, Vol. 62, No. 4, 1976, pp. 331–78.

6. Susan Bernick, unpublished manuscript.

7. J. Baird Callicott, "Leopold's Land Aesthetic," *Journal of Soil and Water Conservation*, Vol. 38, No. 4, 1983, p. 332.

8. Michael Slote, "Admirable Immorality," p. 107.

9. Dahl has argued this point with me in private conversation.

10. David Wiggins, "Truth, Invention, and The Meaning of Life," p. 344.

11. Norman Dahl, "Morality and the Meaning of Life," *Canadian Journal of Philosophy*, Vol. 17, No. 1, March 1987, pp. 1–22.

12. Ibid., p. 13.

Index